PUBLIC

FOR

SUCCESS

PUBLIC SPEAKING
FOR
SUCCESS

DALE CARNEGIE

An imprint of Manjul Books

First published in India by Anthem,
an imprint of:

Manjul Books Pvt. Ltd.
10, Nishat Colony, Bhopal - 462 003 INDIA
Phone : 91-755-4240340, Fax : 91-755-2736919
E-mail : manjulbooks@manjulindia.com
Website : www.manjulindia.com

First published - 2006

Copyright 2004© by JMW Group, Inc.

Cover & book design by Manjul Creative Team

ISBN - 81 - 89631 - 04 - 7

Printed & bound in India by
Thomson Press (India) Ltd. Faridabad, INDIA

All rights reserved. No part of this publication may be reproduced,
stored in or introduced into a retrieval system, or transmitted, in any
form, or by any means (electronic, mechanical, photocopying,
recording or otherwise) without the prior written permission of the
publisher. Any person who does any unauthorized act in relation to
this publication may be liable to criminal prosecution and civil claims
for damages.

TABLE OF CONTENTS

INTRODUCTION TO UPDATED EDITION

Is there the faintest shadow of a reason why you should not be able to think as well in a perpendicular position before an audience as you can sitting down? Is there any reason why should you pay host to butterflies in your stomach and become a victim of the "trembles" when you get up and address an audience? Surely, you realize that this condition can be remedied, that training and practice will wear away your audience fright and give you self-confidence.

Dale Carnegie

When people are asked what their greatest fear is, the most frequent response is dying and the second most frequent is speaking in public.

True, many people, who are intelligent, articulate and at ease in expressing their ideas on a one-to-one basis with others, become tongue-tied and terrified when faced with even a small audience. Business people have been stymied in their careers because they fear speaking up at a staff meeting; men and women with important ideas keep them to themselves rather than express them at a community, church or school conference. But this is a fear that can easily be overcome.

Dale Carnegie was a pioneer in teaching people how to overcome the fear of speaking in front of others. His courses in public speaking have been attended by hundreds of thousands of people throughout the world. Early in his career, he was urged to write a book outlining the principles that made his courses so successful.

In this book you will learn the essential elements of preparing and delivering a speech. You will learn how to develop the information needed, the art of capturing your audience in the first few minutes of your talk, how to add examples, anecdotes, statistics and analogies that make your talk meaningful to the audience, how to persuade your listeners to accept your message, how to use your body language to enhance your talk. You will also learn when and how to use humor and how to wind up your talk to assure that your points have been made and will be remembered and acted upon.

In addition, you will be given pointers on how to remember what you plan to say without memorizing it and how to develop your own platform presence and personality. Included are exercises to improve your diction and grammar, and dozens of examples of how many famous and not so famous orators made their talks outstanding.

As this book was written in the 1920s, many of the public figures noted or quoted in the book, were well-known at the time, but may not be familiar to today's readers. However, the principles that they applied are as valuable now as they were then, and you can gain as much from them as the original readers of this book. In addition, more current examples have been added.

This book provides the blueprint for becoming a successful speaker, but it is only a blueprint. It's up to you to implement what you read here by using every opportunity to get up and speak to groups on your job, at the next community meeting you attend, or by volunteering to give a talk on a subject in which you have particular interest at a meeting of a business or professional organization or at a church group or community association to which you belong. By applying the techniques you learn in this book, when facing an audience, large or small, you will be at ease, self-confident and will project your ideas in a rational and exciting manner. You will find it a satisfactory and rewarding experience.

PREFACE TO ORIGINAL EDITION

This is not a course in old-fashioned, Fourth of July, spread-eagle oratory. It is an intensive and thoroughly tested course to help the business and professional man in his speaking, both in public and in private.

The course has not been written to order. It has grown and developed out of many years of successful teaching work in Y.M.C.A. classes. It has been used in Association schools since 1912. It is workable. It is intensely practical.

The course has aided thousands of business and professional men to become creditable speakers many of whom were formerly unable to say half a dozen sentences effectively when facing an audience.

In addition to this, and far more important, this course has developed men. It has increased their faith and vision, and shown them how to use their latent forces to the fullest possible extent. It has made leaders out of many who were previously only mute followers.

It has helped many in a financial way. Increased self-confidence and the ability to influence others are often reflected in one's earning capacity.

The founder of the course and author of the text, Mr. Dale Carnegie, spent years teaching and developing this course in the Y.M.C.A. Schools of New York, Brooklyn, Trenton, Philadelphia, Wilmington and Baltimore. He has also conducted classes for business men in the Advertising Club and Rotary Club of New York, in the Manufacturers' Club and Penn Athletic Club of Philadelphia, in the Chamber of Commerce of Brooklyn and in the Federal Reserve Bank of New York. Mr. Carnegie has probably taught more people to speak in public than any other living man.

This book is designed for the fourth edition of this course, which has been entirely rewritten from beginning to end, and represents the accumulated experience of the author in more than fifteen years of teaching this subject in Europe and America.

iii

Mr. Carnegie has also had considerable experience in teaching public speaking to the members of the banking fraternity. Among the various organizations he has served as public speaking instructor, are the Federal Reserve Bank of New York, New York Chapter and Washington Chapter of the American Institute of Banking.

Dale Carnegie
1888-1955

Dale Carnegie was a pioneer in what is now referred to as the human potential movement. His teachings and writings have helped people all over the world become self-confident, personable and influential individuals.

In 1912, Carnegie offered his first course in public speaking at a Y.M.C.A. in New York City. As in most public speaking courses given at that time, Carnegie started the class with a theoretical lecture, but quickly noticed that the class members looked bored and restless. Something had to be done.

Dale stopped his lecture and calmly pointed to a man in the back row and asked him to get up and give an impromptu talk about his background. When the student finished, he asked another student to speak about himself and so on until everybody in the class had given a brief talk. With the encouragement of their classmates and guidance from Carnegie, each of them overcame their fright and gave satisfactory talks. "Without knowing what I was doing," Carnegie later reported, "I stumbled on the best method of conquering fear."

His course became so popular that he was asked to give it in other cities. As the years went by, he kept improving the content of the course. He learned that the students were most interested in improving their interpersonal relations. This resulted in the emphasis of the course being shifted from public speaking to getting along better with others. The talks became the means to an end rather than the end itself.

In addition to what he learned from his students, Carnegie engaged in extensive research on the approach to life of successful men and women. He incorporated this into his classes. This led to the writing of his most famous book *How To Win Friends and Influence People*.

This book became an instant best seller and since its publication in 1936 (and its revised edition in 1981), over 20 million copies have been sold. It has been translated into 36 languages. In 2002, *How to Win Friends and Influence People* was named the #1 Business Book of the 20th Century. His book, *How To Stop Worrying and Start Living*, written in 1948, has also sold millions of copies and has been translated into 27 languages.

Dale Carnegie courses are given in most countries, and have influenced the lives of men and women at all levels of society from the workers in factories and offices, to the owners and managers of businesses, to the leaders of governments.

Dale Carnegie died on November 1, 1955. An obituary in a Washington newspaper summed up his contribution to society: "Dale Carnegie solved none of the profound mysteries of the universe. But, perhaps, more than anyone of his generation, he helped human beings learn how to get along together; which seems sometimes to be the greatest need of all."

Chapter 1

DEVELOPING COURAGE AND SELF-CONFIDENCE

"Courage is the chief attribute to manliness."

-Daniel Webster

"It is never safe to look into the future with eyes of fear."

- E. H. Harriman

"Never take counsel of your fears."

- Stonewall Jackson

"If you persuade yourself that you can do a certain thing, provided this thing be possible, you will do it, however difficult it may be. If, on the contrary, you imagine that you cannot do the simplest thing in the world, it is impossible for you to do it, and molehills become for you unscalable mountains."

- Emile Coue

"Courage is grace under pressure."

- Ernest Hemingway

"The ability to speak effectively is an acquirement rather than a gift."

-William Jennings Bryan

"To secure personal advancement, it is much more profitable to be eloquent, than to be wise and grave in council."

- London Daily Telegraph

Chapter 1

DEVELOPING COURAGE AND SELF-CONFIDENCE

When people who enroll in public speaking courses are asked what they hope to obtain from it, the vast majority surprisingly give the same response. "When I am called upon to stand up and speak," person after person comments, "I become so self-conscious, so frightened, that I can't think clearly, can't concentrate, can't remember what I had intended to say. I want to gain self-confidence, poise and the ability to think on my feet. I want to get my thoughts together in logical order and I want to be able to say my say clearly and convincingly before a business, church or community group or any audience."

To cite a concrete case: Years ago, a gentleman called Mr. D.W. Ghent, joined my public speaking course in Philadelphia. Shortly after the opening session, he invited me to lunch with him in the Manufacturers' Club. He was a man of middle age and had always led an active life, was head of his own manufacturing establishment, a leader in church work and civic activities. While we were having lunch that day, he leaned across the table and said, "I have been asked many times to talk before various gatherings, but I have never been able to do so. I get so fussed, my mind becomes an utter blank. So, I have sidestepped it all my life. But I am chairman now of a board of college trustees. I must preside at their meetings. I simply have to do some talking. . . Do you think it will be possible for me to learn to speak at this late date in my life?"

"Do I think, Mr. Ghent?" I replied. "It is *not* a question of my *thinking*. I *know you can* and I *know you will* only practice and follow the directions and instructions."

He wanted to believe that, but it seemed too rosy, too optimistic. "I am afraid you are just being kind," he answered, "that you are merely trying to encourage me."

After he had completed his training, we lost touch with each other for a while. Some years later we met and lunched together again at the Manufacturers' Club. We sat in the same corner and occupied the same table that we had had on the first occasion. Reminding him of our former conversation, I asked him if I had been too sanguine then. He took a little red-backed notebook out of his pocket and showed me a list of talks and dates for which he was booked. "And the ability to make these," he confessed, "the pleasure I get in doing it, the additional service I can render to the community, these are among the most gratifying things in my life. Not only have I given countless public speeches, but just recently I was chosen from all the community leaders in this city to give the introduction when Lloyd George, then the Prime Minister of Great Britain, addressed a mass meeting in Philadelphia." And this was the man who had sat at that same table less than three years before and solemnly asked me if I thought he would ever be able to talk in public!

Was the rapidity with which he forged ahead in his speaking ability unusual? Not at all. There have been hundreds of similar cases. For example, to quote one more specific instance, a Brooklyn physician, whom we will call Dr. Curtis, spent the winter in Florida near the training grounds of the Giants. Being an enthusiastic baseball fan, he often went to see them practice. In time, he became quite friendly with the team, and was invited to attend a banquet given in their honor.

After the coffee and nuts were served, several prominent guests were called upon to "say a few words." Suddenly, with the abruptness and unexpectedness of an explosion, he heard the toastmaster remark: "We have a physician with us tonight; and I am going to ask Dr. Curtis to talk on a baseball player's health."

Was he prepared? Of course. He had had the best preparation in the world. He had been studying hygiene and practicing medicine for almost a third of a century. He could have sat in his chair and talked about this subject all night to the man seated on his right or left. But to get up and say the same things to even a small audience, that was another matter. That was a paralyzing matter. His heart doubled its pace and skipped beats at the very contemplation of it. He had never made a public speech in his life and every thought that he had had now took wings.

What was he to do? The audience was applauding. Every one

was looking at him. He shook his head. But that served only to heighten the applause, to increase the demand. The cries of "Dr. Curtis! Speech! Speech!" grew louder and more insistent.

He was in positive misery. He knew that if he got up he would fail, that he would be unable to utter half a dozen sentences. So he arose, and, without saying a word, turned his back on his friends and walked silently out of the room, a deeply embarrassed and humiliated man.

Small wonder that one of the first things he did after getting back to Brooklyn was to enroll in my course in Public Speaking For Success. He didn't propose to face that embarrassing situation and be stricken dumb a second time.

He was the kind of student that delights an instructor. He was dead earnest. He wanted to be able to talk; and there was no half-heartedness about his desires. He prepared his talks thoroughly, he practiced them with a will; and he never missed a single session of the course.

He did precisely what such a student always does; he progressed at a rate that surprised him, that surpassed his fondest hopes. After the first few sessions, his nervousness subsided, his confidence mounted higher and higher. In two months, he had become the star speaker of the group. He was soon accepting invitations to speak elsewhere; he now loved the feel and exhilaration of it, the distinction and the additional friends it brought him.

A member of the New York City Republican Campaign Committee, hearing one of his public addresses, invited Dr. Curtis to stump the city for his party. How surprised that politician would have been had he realized that, only a year before, the speaker had gotten up and left a public banquet hall in shame and confusion because he was tongue-tied with audience fear!

The gaining of self-confidence and courage, and the ability to think calmly and clearly while talking to a group, is not one-tenth as difficult, as most people imagine It is not a gift bestowed by Providence on only a few rarely endowed individuals. It is like the ability to play golf. Anyone can develop one's own latent capacity if there is sufficient desire to do so.

Is there the faintest shadow of a reason why you should not be able to think as well in a perpendicular position before an audience as you can when sitting down? Surely, you know there is not. In fact, you ought to think better when facing a group. Their presence ought to stir you and lift you. A great many speakers will tell you that the presence of an audience is a stimulus, an inspiration, that drives their brains to function more clearly, more keenly. At such times, thoughts, facts, ideas, that they did not know they possessed, drift smoking by, as Henry Ward Beecher said; and they have but to reach out and lay their hands hot upon them. That ought to be your experience. It probably will be if you practice and persevere.

However, you may be absolutely sure; training and practice will wear away your audience fright and give you self-confidence and an abiding courage.

Do not imagine that your case is unusually difficult. Even those, who afterwards became the most eloquent representatives of their generation, were at the outset of their careers, afflicted by this blinding fear and self-consciousness.

William Jennings Bryan, considered the greatest orator of his generation, admitted that, in his first attempts, his knees fairly smote together.

Mark Twain, the first time he stood up to lecture, felt as if his mouth were filled with cotton and his pulse were speeding for some prize cup.

General U.S. Grant took Vicksburg and led to victory one of the greatest armies the world had ever seen up to that time; yet, when he attempted to speak in public, he admitted he trembled with fear.

Jean Jaures, the most powerful political speaker that France produced during his generation, sat for a year, tongue-tied in the Chamber of Deputies, before he could summon up the courage to make his initial speech.

"The first time I attempted to make a public talk," confessed Lloyd George, "I tell you I was in a state of misery. It is no figure of speech, but literally true, that my tongue clove to the roof of my mouth; and at first, I could hardly get out a word."

John Bright, the illustrious Englishman, who, during the civil war, defended in England the cause of union and emancipation, made his maiden speech before a group of country folk gathered in a school building. He was so frightened on the way to the place, so fearful that he would fail, that he implored his companion to start

6

applause to bolster him up, whenever he showed signs of giving way to his nervousness.

Charles Stewart Parnell, the great Irish leader, at the outset of his speaking career, was so nervous, according to the testimony of his brother, that he frequently clenched his fists until his nails sank into his flesh and his palms bled.

Benjamin Disraeli, who later became prime minister of Great Britain, admitted that, he would rather have led a cavalry charge, than to have faced the House of Commons for the first time. His opening speech there was a ghastly failure.

In fact, so many of the famous speakers of England have made poor showings at first, that there is now a feeling in Parliament, that it is rather an inauspicious omen for a young man's initial talk to be a decided success. So take heart.

After watching the careers and aiding somewhat in the development of so many speakers, the author is always glad when a student has, at the outset, a certain amount of flutter and nervous agitation.

There is a certain responsibility in making a talk. Even if it is to only two dozen people, there is a certain strain, a certain shock, a certain excitement. The speaker ought to be keyed up like a thoroughbred, straining at the bit. The immortal Cicero said two thousand years ago, that all public speaking of real merit was characterized by nervousness.

Speakers often experience this same feeling even when they are talking over the radio. "Microphone fright," it is called. When Charlie Chaplin went "on the air," he had his speech all written out. Surely he was used to audiences. He toured this country in vaudeville; and before that he was on the legitimate stage in England. Yet, when he went into the radio studio and faced the microphone, he had a feeling in the stomach not unlike the sensation one gets when he crosses the Atlantic during a stormy February.

James Kirkwood, a famous motion picture actor and director, had a similar experience. He used to be a star on the speaking stage; but, when he came out of the studio after addressing the invisible audience, he was mopping perspiration from his brow. "An opening night on Broadway," he confessed, "is nothing in comparison to that."

7

Some people, no matter how often they speak, always experience this self-consciousness just before they commence, but in a few seconds after they have gotten on their feet, it disappears.

Even Lincoln felt shy for the few opening moments. "At first he was very awkward," relates his law partner, Herndon, "and it seemed a real labor to adjust himself to his surroundings. He struggled for a time under a feeling of apparent diffidence and sensitiveness, and these only added to his awkwardness. I have often seen and sympathized with Mr. Lincoln during these moments. When he began speaking, his voice was shrill, piping and unpleasant. His manner, his attitude, his dark yellow face wrinkled and dry, his oddity of pose, his diffident movements; everything seemed to be against him, but only for a short time." In a few moments he gained composure and warmth and earnestness, and his real speech began.

Your experience may be similar to his.

In order to get the most out of this training, and to get it with rapidity and dispatch, four things are essential.

FIRST: Start With A Strong And Persistent Desire

This is of far more importance than you probably realize. If your instructor could look into your mind and heart now and ascertain the depth of your desires, he or she could foretell, almost with certainty, the swiftness of the progress you will make. If your desire is pale and flabby, your achievements will also take on that hue and consistency. But, if you go after this subject with persistence and with the energy of a bulldog after a cat, nothing underneath the Milky Way will defeat you.

Therefore, arouse your enthusiasm for this study. Enumerate its benefits. Think of what additional self-confidence and the ability to talk more convincingly, will mean to you. Think of what it may mean and what it may mean in dollars and cents. Think of what it may mean to you socially; of the friends it will bring, of the increase of your personal influence, of the leadership it will give you. And it will give you leadership, more rapidly, than almost any other activity you can think of or imagine.

Philip D. Armour, founder of the meat packing company that bears his name, after he had amassed millions said, "I would rather have been a great speaker than a great capitalist."

It is an attainment that almost every person of education longs for. After Andrew Carnegie's death, there was found, among his papers, a plan for his life drawn up when he was thirty-three years of age. He then felt, that in two more years, he could so arrange his business as to have an annual income of fifty thousand; so he proposed to retire at thirty- five, go to Oxford and get a thorough education, and "pay special attention to speaking in public."

Think of the glow of satisfaction and pleasure that will accrue from the exercise of this new power. The author has traveled around, over no small part of this terrestrial ball and has had many and varied experiences; but for downright and lasting inward satisfaction, he knows of few things that will compare to standing before an audience and making the audience think your thoughts after you. It will give you a sense of strength, a feeling of power. It will appeal to your pride of personal accomplishment. It will set you off and raise you above your associates. There is magic in it and a never to be forgotten thrill. "Two minutes before I begin," a speaker confessed, "I would rather be whipped than start; but two minutes before I finish, I would rather be shot than stop."

In every course of study, some people grow faint-hearted and fall by the wayside; so you should keep thinking of, what reading this book will mean to you, until your desire is white hot. You should start this learning experience with an enthusiasm that will carry you through every chapter, triumphant to the end. Tell your friends that you have decided to improve your speaking technique by reading this book. Set aside one specific time for the reading of these lessons In short, make it as easy as possible to go ahead. Make it as difficult as possible to retreat.

When Julius Caesar sailed over the channel from Gaul and landed with his legions on what is now England, what did he do to insure the success of his arms? A very clever thing: he halted his soldiers on the chalk cliffs of Dover; and, looking down over the waves two hundred feet below, they saw red tongues of fire consume every ship in which they had crossed. In the enemy's country, with the last link with the Continent gone, the last means of retreating burned, there was but one thing left for them to do: to advance, to conquer. That is precisely what they did. Such was the spirit of the immortal Caesar. Why not make it yours, too, in this war to exterminate your foolish fear of audiences.

SECOND: Know Thoroughly What You Are Going To Talk About

Unless you have thought out and planned your talk and know what you are going to say, you can't feel very comfortable when you face your auditors. You are like the blind leading the blind. Under such circumstances, you ought to be self-conscious, ought to feel repentant, ought to be ashamed of your negligence.

"I was elected to the New York State Legislature in the fall of 1881," Theodore Roosevelt records in his Autobiography, "and found myself the youngest man in that body. Like all young men and inexperienced members, I had considerable difficulty in teaching myself to speak. I profited much by the advice of a hard-headed old countryman, who was unconsciously paraphrasing the Duke of Wellington, who was himself doubtless paraphrasing somebody else. The advice ran, 'Don't speak until you are sure you have something to say, and know just what it is; then say it, and sit down.' "

This "hard-headed old countryman" ought to have told Roosevelt of another aid in overcoming nervousness. He ought to have added, "It will help you to throw off your embarrassment, if you can find something to do before an audience. If you can exhibit something, write a word on the blackboard or point out a spot on the map or move a table or throw open a window or shift some books and papers. Any physical action with a purpose behind it, may help you to feel more at home."

True, it is not always easy to find an excuse for doing such things; but there is the suggestion. Use it if you can; but use it the first few times only. A baby does not cling to chairs, after it once learns to walk.

THIRD : Act Confident

William James, the great American psychologist, wrote as follows:

"Action seems to follow feeling, but really action and feeling go together; and by regulating the action, which is under the more direct control of the will, we can indirectly regulate the feeling, which is not."

"Thus, the sovereign voluntary path to cheerfulness, if our spontaneous cheerfulness be lost, is to sit up cheerfully and to act and speak, as if cheerfulness were already there. If such conduct does not make you feel cheerful, nothing else on that occasion can.

"So, to feel brave, act as if we were brave, use all of our will to that end, and a courage fit will very likely replace the fit of fear."

Apply William James' advice. To develop courage when you are facing an audience, act as if you already had it. Of course, unless you are prepared, all the acting in the world will avail, but little. But granted that, you know what you are going to talk about, step out briskly and take a deep breath. In fact, breathe deeply for thirty seconds, before you ever face your audience. The increased supply of oxygen will buoy you up and give you courage. When a youth of the Peuhl tribe in Central Africa attains manhood and wishes to take a wife, he is compelled to undergo the ceremony of flagellation. The women of the tribe assemble, singing and clapping their hands to the rhythm of tom-toms. The candidate strides forth, stripped naked to the waist. Suddenly a man armed with a cruel whip, sets upon the lad, beating his bare skin, lashing him, flogging him like a fiend. Welts appear; often the skin is cut, blood flows; scars are made that last a lifetime. During this scourging, a venerable judge of the tribe crouches at the feet of the victim to see if he moves or exhibits the slightest evidence of pain. To pass the test successfully, the tortured aspirant must not only endure the ordeal; but, as he endures it, he must sing a paean of praise.

In every age, in every clime, courage has always been admired; so, no matter how your heart may be pounding inside, stride forth bravely, stop, stand still like the scourged youth of Central Africa, and, like him, act as if you loved it.

Draw yourself up to your full height and look your audience straight in the eyes, and begin to talk as confidently as if every one of them owed you money. Imagine that they do. Imagine that they have assembled there to beg you for an extension of credit. The psychological effect on you will be beneficial.

Do not nervously button and unbutton your coat, fiddle with your jewelry and fumble with your hands. If you must make nervous movements, place your hands behind your back and twist your fingers there where no one can see the performance or wiggle your toes.

As a general rule, it is bad for a speaker to hide behind furniture; but it may give you a little courage the first few times to stand behind a table or chair and to grip them tightly or hold a coin firmly in the palm of your hand.

How did Theodore Roosevelt develop his characteristic courage and self-reliance? Was he endowed by nature with a venturesome and daring spirit? Not at all. "Having been a rather sickly and awkward boy," he confesses in his *Autobiography*, "I was, as a young man, at first both nervous and distrustful of my own prowess. I had to train myself painfully and laboriously not merely as regards my body but as regards my soul and spirit."

Fortunately, he has told us how he achieved the transformation. "When a boy," he writes, "I read a passage in a book by Frederick Marryat, the author of many sea tales, which always impressed me. In this passage, the captain of some small British war vessel is explaining to the hero, how to acquire the quality of fearlessness. He says that, at the outset, almost every man is frightened when he goes into action, but that the course to follow is for the man to keep such a grip on himself that he can act just as if he were not frightened. After this is kept up long enough, it changes from pretense to reality, and the man does in fact become fearless by sheer dint of practicing fearlessness when he does not feel it. (I am using my own language, not Marryat's.)

"This was the theory upon which I went. There were all kinds of things of which I was afraid at first, ranging from grizzly bears to 'mean' horses and gunfighters; but by acting as if I was not afraid, I gradually ceased to be afraid. Most men can have the same experience, if they choose."

You can have that very experience in giving talks, if you wish. "In war," said Marshal Foch, the commander of the allied forces in the first world war, "the best defensive is an offensive." So take the offensive against your fears. Go out to meet them, battle them, conquer them by sheer boldness at every opportunity.

Have a message, and then think of yourself as a messenger instructed to deliver it. We pay slight attention to the messenger. It is the message that we want. The message; that is the thing. Keep your mind on it. Keep your heart in it. Know it like the back of your hand. Believe it feelingly. Then talk as if you were determined to say it. Do that, and the chances are ten to one, that you will soon be master of the occasion and master of yourself.

FOURTH: Practice! Practice! Practice!

The last point we have to make here is, emphatically, the most important. Even though you forget everything you have read so far, do remember this: the first way, the last way, the never failing way to develop self-confidence in speaking is to speak. Really, the whole matter finally simmers down to but one essential; practice, practice, practice. That is the sine qua non of it all, "the without which not."

"Any beginner," warned Roosevelt, "is apt to have 'buck fever.'" 'Buck fever' means a state of intense nervous excitement, which may be entirely divorced from timidity. It may affect speakers the first time they have to speak to a large audience, just as it may affect them the first time they see a wild animal or go into battle. What the speaker needs is not courage, but nerve control, cool headedness. *This can be achieved only by actual practice. Only by custom and repeated exercise of self-mastery, nerves can thoroughly be brought under control. This is largely a matter of habit; in the sense of repeated effort and repeated exercise of will power, the speaker will grow stronger and stronger with each exercise of it."*

So, persevere. Don't put off reading the chapters you schedule to read because the other duties of the week have rendered it difficult to find the time. You want to get rid of your audience fear? Let us see what causes it.

"Fear is begotten of ignorance and uncertainty," says James Robinson in *The Mind in the Making.* To put it another way, it is the result of a lack of confidence.

And what causes that? It is the result of not knowing what you can really do. And not knowing what you can do is caused by a lack of experience. When you get a record of successful experience behind you, your fears will vanish; they will melt like night mists under the glare of a July sun.

One thing is certain, the accepted way to learn to swim is to plunge into the water. You have been reading this book long enough. Let us toss it aside now and get busy with the real work in hand.

Choose your subject, preferably one on which you have some knowledge and construct a three-minute talk. Practice the talk by yourself a number of times. Then give it, if possible, to the group for whom it is intended or before your class, putting into the effort all your force and power.

IN A NUTSHELL

1.   Most of the students who have taken my public speaking course have indicated that the prime reason they enrolled in the course was that they wanted to conquer their nervousness, to be able to think on their feet, and to speak with self-confidence and ease before a group of any size.

2.   The ability to do this is not difficult to acquire. It is not a gift bestowed by Providence on only a few rarely endowed individuals. It is like the ability to play golf. Anyone can develop his or her own latent capacity, if there is sufficient desire to do so.

3.   Many experienced speakers can think better and talk better when facing a group than they can in conversation with an individual. The presence of the larger number proves to be a stimulus, an inspiration. If you faithfully follow this course, the time may come when that will be your experience too and you will look forward with positive pleasure to making an address.

4.   Do not imagine that your case is unusual. Many people who afterwards became famous speakers were, at the outset of their careers, beset with self-consciousness and almost paralyzed with audience fright.

5.   No matter how often you speak, you may always experience this self-consciousness just before you begin; but, in a few seconds after you have gotten on your feet, it will vanish completely.

6.   In order to get the most out of this book and to get it with rapidity and dispatch, do these five things:

a.   Start this book with a strong and persistent desire. Enumerate the benefits this training will bring you. Arouse your enthusiasm for it. Think what it can mean to you financially, socially and in terms of increased influence, making new friends and developing leadership. Remember that upon the depth of your desire will depend the swiftness of your progress.

b.   Make an effort to present talks when and wherever possible. Talk up at business conferences, church committees, parent-teachers associations, community groups or political meetings.

c.   Prepare. You can't feel confident unless you know what you are going to say.

d.   Act confident. "To feel brave," advises William James, "act as if we were brave, use all of our will to that end and a courage fit will very likely replace the fit of fear." Theodore Roosevelt confessed that he conquered his fear of grizzly bears, mean horses and gunfighters by that method. You can conquer your fear of audiences by taking advantage of this psychological fact.

e. Practice. This is the most important point of all. Fear is the result of lack of confidence; and a lack of confidence is the result of not knowing what you can do; and that is caused by a lack of experience. So get a record of successful experience behind you, and your fear will vanish,

SPEECH BUILDING
WORDS OFTEN MISPRONOUNCED

One of the really serious things in life for him who would be educated in this country is the learning of English pronunciation. Do you accent the following words on their last syllables? if not, you should do so. (proper pronunciation in [ ] when spelling differs from pronunciation)

aDEPT	griMACE [griMIS]
ADDict (noun)	addICT (verb)
adDRESS	magaZINE
aDULT	preTENSE
deTOUR	reCOURSE
disCOURSE	reSOURCE
doMAIN	roBUST
ENcore	rouTINE
freQUENT (verb)	FREquent (adj)

ERRORS IN ENGLISH
Shall and Will

Many speakers do not use *shall* and *will* with correctness and discrimination. Remember that *shall* and *will* always convey either something that will come to pass naturally or something that the speaker is determined to bring to pass by the power of his own effort. If you mean to state that a thing will come to pass in the natural order of events, use shall when referring to yourself; and will, when referring to all other subjects.

To express determination on your part to bring things about, you simply reverse this rule. You use *will* when speaking of yourself and *shall* when speaking of all other subjects. To illustrate:

15

The following sentences simply prophesy that the persons referred to will come home tomorrow. They are statements of simple futurity.

I *shall* come home tomorrow.

We *shall* come home tomorrow.

You *will* come home tomorrow.

They *will* come home tomorrow.

The next ones also imply futurity, and not promises or determination:

We *shall* be glad to send a representative.

I *shall* be glad to call at your office.

The fault *will* not be ours.

The following sentences mean that "I am determined to come home tomorrow regardless of what happens"; that "we are determined to come home tomorrow in spite of circumstances"; that "I wish that you and they will come home tomorrow." The third and fourth sentences may even mean that "I request or command you to do so regardless of your desires."

I *will* come home tomorrow.

We *will* come home tomorrow.

You *shall* come home tomorrow.

They *shall* come home tomorrow.

In asking questions, always use shall in connection with I and we.

Shall I file the letters lying on my desk?

Shall we come home tomorrow?

In questions where you and they are used in connection with shall and will, use shall in the question when shall is expected in the answer, and will in the question if will is expected in the answer. Examples are as follows:

Shall you be glad when you finish?

(Ans.) I *shall*.

Will you work hard?

(Ans.) I *will*.

Shall they pass?

(Ans.) They *shall* not.

Shall they have the goods?

(Ans.) They *shall*.

Leave and Let

To *leave* means to depart from some one or some thing;
to *let* means to permit. Examples:

Leave the room at once.

Let me do it.

CORRECT USAGE OF WORDS

AMONG - BETWEEN. *Between* should be used when referring to
only two people or things; *among* should be used when referring to
more than two. "There is a keen rivalry *between* our two salesmen."
"There is a decided spirit of friendliness *among* all our employees."

AS - THAT. Do not use *as* in this manner: "I do not know *as* I want
to do that." Say "I do not know *that* I want to do that."

AMASS - ACCUMULATE. He spent his entire life *amassing* his
wealth." This use is wrong. *Accumulate* expresses a gradual, *amass* a
rapid, gathering.

ANTICIPATE - EXPECT. *Anticipate* means more than merely *expect*;
it suggests forecasting, taking measures to meet. If you *expect* a storm
you may *anticipate* it by taking your raincoat.

VOICE EXERCISE - CORRECT BREATHING

"In the perfection of a beautiful voice," said Madame Melba, "correct
breathing is the greatest technical essential." Consequently, the
mastering of correct breathing must be our first step in voice
improvement. Breath is the very foundation of voice; it is the raw
material out of which our words are fashioned.

The right use of the breath will give one full, deep, round tones;
attractive tones, not thin, harsh sounds; tones that will please; tones
that will carry.

If correct breathing is so important as all this, we must find out
at once what it is and how to practice it.

The famous Italian masters of singing have always taught that it is diaphragmatic breathing. And what is that? Something strange and new and arduous? Not at all. It shouldn't be. You did it perfectly as a baby. You practice it now during a part of every twenty-four hours. When you lie on the flat of your back tonight in bed, you will breathe freely, naturally, correctly; you will use diaphragmatic breathing. For some strange reason, it is difficult to breathe any other way, except correctly, when you are lying in that position.

Your problem, therefore, is simply this: To use the same breathing methods when you are standing up as you employ when you are on the flat of your back. That does not sound so difficult, does it?

Your first exercise then is this: Lie on the flat of your back and breathe deeply. Note that the main activity of the process centers in the middle of the body. When you breathe deeply in this position, you do not raise your shoulders.

This is what is happening: your spongy, porous lungs are being filled and extended with air like a toy balloon. The balloon must expand but how, where? It is encased at the top and on the sides by a bony box made by the ribs, spine and breast bone. To be sure the ribs will give somewhat, but the easiest way for the lungs to expand is by pushing downwards, upon a soft muscle, that forms the floor of the chest and the roof of the abdomen. This muscle, the diaphragm, divides your body into two distinct compartments. The upper part, the chest, contains your heart and lungs; the lower part, the abdomen, houses the stomach, liver, intestines and other vital organs. This huge muscle is arched like a roof, like a dome.

Suppose you were to take one of the paper plates or dishes that one purchases, at the ten cent store, for picnics. Turn it upside down and press on the arched surface; and what happens? It flattens and spreads and pushes out on all sides as it flattens. That is precisely what your diaphragm does when the lungs, filling with air, press down against the top of its arch.

Lie down on the flat of your back now, take a deep breath, put your fingers right below the breast bone. Don't you feel the diaphragm flattening and pushing out? Now put your hands at your sides along the lower extremities of your ribs. Breathe deeply. Don't you feel the balloon-like lungs pushing out the floating ribs?

Practice this diaphragmatic breathing for five minutes, the last thing each night in bed, and for five minutes, the first thing in the morning. At night, it will tend to soothe and quiet your nerves and make you drowsy. In the morning, it will brighten and freshen you. If this is done faithfully, it will not only improve your voice, but it will add years to your life. Opera singers and vocal teachers are noted for their longevity. The famous Manuel Garcia lived to be 101; and he attributed his long life very largely to this daily exercise of deep breathing.

Chapter 2

SELF-CONFIDENCE THROUGH PREPARATION

"The best way for you to gain confidence is to prepare so well on something that you really want to say, that there can be little chance to fail."

-Public Speaking For Success Today, Loci Wood-Thorpe

" 'To trust to the inspiration of the moment.' That is the fatal phrase upon which many promising careers have been wrecked. The surest road to inspiration is preparation. I have seen many men of courage and capacity fail for lack of industry. Mastery in speech can only be reached by mastery in one's subject."

-Lloyd George

"Before a speaker faces his audience, he should write a letter to a friend and say, 'I am to make an address on a subject and I want to make these points.' He should then enumerate the things he is going to speak about in their correct order. If he finds that he has nothing to say in his letter, he had better write to the committee that invited him and say that the probable death of his grandmother will possibly prevent his being present on the occasion."

-Dr. Edward Everett Hale

"Men give me some credit for genius. All the genius I have ties in this. When I have a subject in hand, I study it profoundly. Day and night, it is before me. I explore it in all its bearings. My mind becomes pervaded with it. Then the efforts that I make are what people are pleased to call the fruits of genius. It is the fruit of labor and thought."

-Alexander Hamilton

manner and tone revealed it unmistakably. How could he expect the audience to be any more impressed than he himself was? He kept referring to the article saying the author said so and so. There was a surfeit of Forbes' Magazine in it; but regrettably little of Mr. Jackson.

So the writer addressed him somewhat in this fashion, "Mr. Jackson, we are not interested in this shadowy personality who wrote that article. He is not here. We can't see him. But we are interested in you and your ideas. Tell us what you think, personally, not what somebody else said. Put more of Mr. Jackson in this. Why not take this same subject for next week? Why not read this article again and ask yourself whether you agree with the author or not? If you do, think out his suggestions and illustrate them with observations from your own experience. If you don't agree with him, say so and tell us why. Let this article be merely the starting point from which you launch your own speech."

Mr. Jackson accepted the suggestion, reread the article and concluded that he did not agree with the author at all. He did not sit down in the subway and try to prepare this next speech to order. He let it grow. It was a child of his own brain; and it developed and expanded and took on stature, just as his physical children had done. And like his daughters, this other child grew day and night when he was least conscious of it. One thought was suggested to him while reading some item in the newspaper; another illustration swam into his mind, unexpectedly, when he was discussing the subject with a friend. The thing deepened and heightened, lengthened and thickened as he thought over it during the odd moments of the week.

The next time Mr. Jackson spoke on this subject, he had something that was his or that he dug out of his own mine, currency coined in his own mint. And he spoke all the better because he was disagreeing with the author of the article. There is no spur to rouse one like a little opposition.

What an incredible contrast between these two speeches by the same man in the same fortnight on the same subject! What a colossal difference the right kind of preparation makes!

Let us cite another illustration of how to do it and how not to do it. A woman, whom we shall call Mrs. Flynn, was a student in my course in Washington, D.C. One afternoon she devoted her talk to eulogizing the capital city of the nation. She had hastily and superficially gleaned facts from a booster booklet issued by the Washington Tourist Bureau and they sounded like it dry, disconnected, undigested. She had not thought over the subject adequately. It had not elicited her enthusiasm. She did not feel what she was saying deeply enough to make it worth while expressing. The whole affair was flat and flavorless and unprofitable.

A SPEECH THAT COULD NOT FAIL

A fortnight later something happened that touched Mrs. Flynn to the core. A thief stole her Cadillac out of a public garage. She rushed to the police and offered rewards, but it was all in vain. The police admitted that it was well nigh impossible for them to cope with the crime situation; yet, only a week previously, they had found time to walk about the street, chalk in hand, and fine Mrs. Flynn because she had parked her car fifteen minutes overtime. These "chalk cops," who were so busy annoying respectable citizens that they could not catch criminals, aroused her ire. She was indignant. She had something now to say, not something that had been read in a book issued by the Tourist Bureau, but something that was leaping hot out of her own life and experience. Here was something that was part and parcel of the real world; something that had aroused her feelings and convictions. In her speech eulogizing the city of Washington, she had laboriously pulled out sentence by sentence; but now she had but to stand on her feet and open her mouth; and her condemnation of the police welled up and boiled forth like Vesuvius in action. A speech like that is almost foolproof. It can hardly fail. It was experience plus reflection.

WHAT PREPARATION REALLY IS

Does the preparation of a speech mean the getting together of some faultless phrases written down or memorized? No. Does it mean the assembling of a few casual thoughts that really convey very little to you personally? Not at all. It means the assembling of *your* thoughts, *your* ideas, *your* convictions, *your* urges. And you have such thoughts, such urges. You have them every day of your waking life. They even swarm through your dreams. Your whole existence has been filled with feelings and experiences. These things are lying deep in your subconscious mind as thick as pebbles on the seashore. Preparation means thinking, brooding, recalling, selecting the ones that appeal to you most, polishing them, working them into a pattern, a mosaic of your own. That doesn't sound like such a difficult program, does it? It isn't. Just requires a little concentration and thinking to a purpose.

I asked several well-known speakers what the secret of their success was. One of them, Dwight L. Moody, one of the great evangelic preachers of his time, responded: "I have no secret. When I choose a subject, I write the name of it on the outside of a large envelope. I have many such envelopes. If, when I am reading, I meet a good thing on any subject I am to speak on, I slip it into the right envelope and let it lie there. I always carry a notebook, and if I hear anything that will throw light on that subject, I put it down and slip it into the envelope. Perhaps I let it lie there for a year or more. When I want a new sermon, I take everything that has been accumulating. Between what I find there and the results of my own study, I have material enough. Then, all the time I am going over my sermons, taking out a little here, adding a little there. In that way they never get old."

THE SAGE ADVICE OF DEAN BROWN OF YALE

When the Yale Divinity School celebrated the one hundredth anniversary of its founding, the Dean, Dr. Charles Reynold Brown, delivered a series of lectures on the Art of Preaching. Dr. Brown has been preparing addresses himself weekly for a third of a century and also training others to prepare and deliver; so he was in a position to dispense some sage advice on the subject, advice that will hold good regardless of whether the speaker is a man of the cloth preparing a discourse on the ninety-first Psalm or a shoe manufacturer preparing a speech on Labor Unions. So I am taking the liberty of quoting Dr. Brown here:

"Brood over your text and your topic. Brood over them until they become mellow and responsive. You will hatch out of them a whole flock of promising ideas as you cause the tiny germs of life there, contained to expand and develop... ."

"It will be, all the better, if this process can go on for a long time and not be postponed until Saturday forenoon, when you are actually making your final preparation for next Sunday. If a minister can hold a certain truth in his mind for a month, for six months perhaps, for a year it may be, before he preaches on it, he will find new ideas perpetually sprouting out of it, until it shows an abundant growth. He may meditate on it as he walks the streets or as he spends some hours on a train, when his eyes are too tired to read.

"He may indeed brood upon it in the night-time. It is better for the minister not to take his church or his sermon to bed with him habitually, a pulpit is a splendid thing to preach from, but it is not a good bed-fellow. Yet, for all that, I have sometimes gotten out of bed in the middle of the night to put down the thoughts which came to me, for fear I might forget them before morning... ."

"When you are actually engaged in assembling the material for a particular sermon, write down everything that comes to you, bearing upon that text and topic. Write down what you saw in the text when you first chose it. Write down all the associated ideas which now occur to you... ."

"Put all these ideas of yours down in writing, just a few words, enough to fix the idea and keep your mind reaching for more all the time, as if it were never to see another book as long as it lived. This is the way to train the mind in productiveness. You will, by this method, keep your own mental processes fresh, original, creative... ."

"Put down all of those ideas which you have brought to the birth yourself, unaided. They are more precious for your mental unfolding than rubies and diamonds and much fine gold. Put them down, preferably on scraps of paper, backs of old letters, fragments of envelopes, waste paper, anything which comes to your hand. This is much better every way than to use nice, long, clean sheets of fullscape. It is not a mere matter of economy, you will find it easier to arrange and organize these loose bits when you come to set your material in order... ."

"Keep on putting down all the ideas which come to your mind, thinking hard all the while. You need not hurry this process. It is one of the most important mental transactions in which you will be privileged to engage. It is this method which causes the mind to grow in real productive power... ."

"You will find that the sermons you enjoy preaching the most and the ones which actually accomplish the most good in the lives of your people will be those sermons which you take most largely out of your own interiors. They are bone of your bone, flesh of your flesh, the children of your own mental labor, the output of your own creative energy. The sermons which are garbled and compiled will always have a kind of secondhand, warmed over flavor about them. The sermons which live and move and enter into the temple, walking and leaping and praising God, the sermons which enter into the hearts of men, causing them to mount up with wings like eagles and to walk in the way of duty and not faint these real sermons, are the ones which are actually born from the vital energies of the man who utters them."

HOW LINCOLN PREPARED HIS SPEECHES

How did Lincoln prepare his speeches? Fortunately, we know the facts; and, as you read here of his method, you will observe that Dean Brown, in his lecture, commended several of the procedures that Lincoln had employed three-quarters of a century previously. One of Lincoln's most famous addresses was that in which he declared with prophetic vision: "A house divided against itself cannot stand. I believe this government cannot endure, permanently, half slave and half free." This speech was thought out as he went about his usual work, as he ate his meals, as he walked the street, as he sat in his barn milking his cow, as he made his daily trip to the butcher shop and grocery, an old gray shawl over his shoulders, his market basket over his arm, his little son at his side, chattering and questioning, growing peeved and jerking at the long bony fingers in a vain effort to make his father talk to him. But Lincoln stalked on, absorbed in his own reflections, thinking of his speech, apparently unconscious of the boy's existence.

From time to time during this brooding and hatching process, he jotted down notes, fragments, sentences here and there on stray envelopes, scraps of paper, bits torn from paper sacks, anything that was near. These he stowed away in the top of his hat and carried them there until he was ready to sit down and arrange them in order, and to write and revise the whole thing, and to shape it up for delivery and publication.

In the joint debates of 1858, Senator Stephen Douglas delivered the same speech wherever he went; but Lincoln kept studying and contemplating and reflecting until he found it easier, he said, to make a new speech each day than to repeat an old one. The subject was forever widening and enlarging in his mind.

A short time before he moved into the White House, he took a copy of the Constitution and three speeches; and with only these for reference, he locked himself in a dingy, dusty back room over a store in Springfield; and there, away from all intrusion and interruption, he wrote out his inaugural address.

How did Lincoln prepare his Gettysburg address? Unfortunately, false reports have been circulated about it. The true story, however, is fascinating. Let us have it:

When the commission in charge of the Gettysburg cemetery decided to arrange for a formal dedication, they invited Edward Everett to deliver the speech. He had been a Boston minister, President of Harvard, governor of Massachusetts, United States senator, minister to England, secretary of state and was generally considered to be America's most capable speaker. The date first set for the dedication ceremonies was October 23, 1863. Mr. Everett very wisely declared that it would be impossible for him to prepare adequately on such short notice. So the dedication was postponed until November 19, nearly a month, to give him time to prepare. The last three days of that period he spent in Gettysburg, going over the battlefield, familiarizing himself with all that had taken place there. That period of brooding and thinking was most excellent preparation. It made the battle real to him.

Invitations to be present were dispatched to all the members of Congress, to the President and his cabinet. Most of these declined; the committee was surprised when Lincoln agreed to come. Should they ask him to speak? They had not intended to do so. Objections were raised. He would not have time to prepare. Besides, even if he did have time, had he the ability? True, he could handle himself well in a debate on slavery or in a Cooper Union address; but no one had ever heard him deliver a dedicatory address. This was a grave and solemn occasion. They ought not to take any chances. Should they ask him to speak? They wondered, wondered.... But they would have wondered a thousand times more, had they been able to look into the future and to see that this man, whose ability they were questioning, was to deliver on that occasion, what is very generally accepted now as one of the most enduring addresses ever delivered by the lips of mortal man.

Finally, a fortnight before the event, they sent Lincoln, a belated invitation, to make "a few appropriate remarks." Yes, that is the way they worded it: "a few appropriate remarks." Think of writing that to the President of the United States!

Lincoln immediately set about preparing. He wrote to Edward Everett, secured a copy of the address that classic scholar was to deliver; and, a day or two later, going to a photographer's gallery to pose for his photograph, Lincoln took Everett's manuscript with him and read it during the spare time that he had at the studio. He thought over his talk for days, thought over it while walking back and forth between the White House and the war office, thought over it while stretched out on a leather couch in the war office waiting for the late telegraphic reports. He wrote a rough draft of it on a piece of fullscape paper and carried it about in the top of his tall silk hat. Ceaselessly, he was brooding over it; ceaselessly, it was taking shape. The Sunday before it was delivered, he said to Noah Brooks, a Washington journalist, "It is not exactly written. It is not finished anyway. I have written it over two or three times and I shall have to give it another lick before I am satisfied."

He arrived in Gettysburg the night before the dedication. The little town was filled to overflowing. Its usual population of thirteen hundred had suddenly swelled to fifteen thousand. The sidewalks became clogged, impassable; men and women took to the dirt streets. Half a dozen bands were playing; crowds were singing "John Brown's Body." People gathered before the home of Mr. Wills, where Lincoln was being entertained. They serenaded him; they demanded a speech. Lincoln responded with a few words that conveyed with more clearness than tact, perhaps, that he was unwilling to speak until the morrow. The facts are that he was spending the latter part of that evening giving his speech "another lick." He even went to an adjoining house where Secretary Seward was staying and read the speech aloud to him for his criticism. After breakfast the next morning, he continued "to give it another lick," working on it until a rap came at the door informing him that it was time for him to take his place in the procession. "Colonel Carr, who rode just behind the President, stated that when the procession started, the President sat erect on his horse and looked the part of the commander-in-chief of

31

the army; but, as the procession moved on, his body leaned forward, his arms hung limp and his head was bowed. He seemed absorbed in thought."

We can only guess that even then he was going over his little speech of ten immortal sentences, giving it "another lick."

Some of Lincoln's speeches, in which he had only a superficial interest, were unquestioned failures; but he was possessed of extraordinary power when he spoke of slavery and the union. Why? Because he thought ceaselessly on these problems and felt deeply. A companion who shared a room with him one night in an Illinois tavern awoke next morning at daylight to find Lincoln sitting up in bed, staring at the wall; and his first words were: "This government cannot endure permanently, half slave and half free."

How did Christ prepare His addresses? He withdrew from the crowd. He thought. He brooded. He pondered. He went out alone into the wilderness and meditated and fasted for forty days and forty nights. "From that time on," records Saint Matthew, "Jesus began to preach." Shortly after that, He delivered one of the world's most celebrated speeches: the Sermon on the Mount.

"That is all very interesting," you may protest; "but I have no desire to become an immortal orator. I merely want to make a few simple talks on my job or at my club or at a town meeting occasionally."

True, and we realize your wants fully. This book was written for the specific purpose of helping you and other people like you to do just that. But, unpretending as the talks of yours may prove to be, you can profit by and utilize in some measure, the methods of the famous speakers of the past.

HOW TO PREPARE YOUR TALK

Readers of this book may be enrolled in one of the many public speaking courses that use this book as an integral part of their programs. Students are asked to make speeches several times during the course. What topics ought you to speak on? Anything that interests you. If possible, choose your own topics; you will be more fortunate still if your topic chooses you. However, you will often have topics suggested for you by your instructor.

Don't make the almost universal mistake of trying to cover too much ground in a brief talk. Just take one or two angles of a subject and attempt to cover them adequately. You will be fortunate if you can do that in the short speeches that are necessitated by the time schedule of most courses.

Determine your subject a week in advance, so that you will have time to think it over in odd moments. Think over it for seven days; dream over it for seven nights. Think of it the last thing when you retire. Think of it the next morning while you are eating breakfast, while you are bathing, while you are riding down town, while you are waiting for elevators, for lunch, for appointments. Discuss it with your friends. Make it a topic of conversation.

Ask yourself all possible questions concerning it. If, for example, you are to speak on divorce, ask yourself what causes divorce, what are the effects economically, socially. Should we have uniform divorce laws? Why? Or should we have any divorce laws? Should divorce be made more difficult ? Easier?

Suppose you were going to talk on why you enrolled in a public speaking course. You ought then to ask yourself such questions as these: What are my troubles ? What do I hope to get out of this instruction? Have I ever made a public talk? If so, when? Where? What happened? Why do I think this training is valuable? Do I know people who are forging ahead in their jobs and in other aspects of their lives largely because of their self-confidence, their presence, their ability to talk convincingly? Do I know others who will probably never achieve a gratifying measure of success because they lack these positive assets ? Be specific. Tell the stories of these people without mentioning their names.

If you stand up and think clearly and keep going for two or three minutes, that is all that will be expected of you during your first few talks. A topic, such as why you enrolled for the course, is very easy; that is obvious. If you will spend a little time selecting and arranging your material on that topic, you will be almost sure to remember it, for you will be speaking of your own observations, your own desires, your own experiences.

On the other hand, let us suppose that you have decided to speak on your business or profession. How shall you set about preparing such a talk? You already have a wealth of material on that subject. Your problem, then, will be to select and arrange it. Do not attempt to tell us all about it in three minutes. It can't be done. The attempt will be too sketchy, too fragmentary. Take one and only one phase of your topic; expand and enlarge that. For example, why not tell us how you came to be in your particular business or profession? Was it a result of accident or choice? Relate your early struggles, your defeats, your hopes, your triumphs. Give us the kind of human interest narrative that one finds, for instance, in the *Readers Digest*. The truthful, inside story of almost any man's life, if told modestly and without offending egotism, is most entertaining. It is almost sure-fire speech material. Or take another angle of your business: what are its troubles? What advice would you give to a young person entering it?

Or tell us about the people with whom you come in contact - the honest and dishonest ones. Tell us of your problems with your employees or co-workers, your problems with your customers. What has your business taught you about the most interesting topic in the world: human nature? If you speak about the technical side of your business, about things, your talk may very easily prove uninteresting to others. But people, personalities - one can hardly go wrong with that kind of material.

Above all else, don't make your talk an abstract preachment. That will bore us. Make your talk a regular layer cake of illustrations and general statements. Think of concrete cases you have observed, and of the fundamental truths, which you believe, those specific instances illustrate. You will also discover that these concrete cases are far easier to remember than abstractions; are far easier to talk about. They will also aid and brighten your delivery.

Here is the way a very interesting writer does it. This is an excerpt from an article by B.A. Forbes on the necessity of executives delegating responsibilities to their associates. Note the illustrations, the gossip about people.

"Many of our present-day gigantic enterprises were at one time one-man affairs. But most of them have outgrown this status. The reason is that, while every great organization is the lengthened shadow of one man, business and industry are now conducted on such a colossal scale that of necessity even the ablest giant must gather about him, brainy associates to help in handling all the reins.

"F.W. Woolworth, founder of the five and ten cent stores that bear his name, once told me that his was essentially a one-man business for years. Then he ruined his health; and it was while he lay week after week in the hospital that he awakened to the fact that if his business was to expand as he hoped, he would have to share the managerial responsibilities."

"Bethlehem Steel for a number of years was distinctly of the one-man type. Charles M. Schwab was the whole works. By and by Eugene G. Grace grew in stature and developed into an abler steel man than Schwab, according to the repeated declarations of the latter. Today Bethlehem Steel is no longer simply Schwab."

"Eastman Kodak in its earlier stages consisted mainly of George Eastman, but he was wise enough to create an efficient organization long ago. All the greatest Chicago packing houses underwent a similar experience during the time of their founders. Standard Oil, contrary to the popular notion, never was a one man organization after it grew to large dimensions."

"J.P. Morgan, although a towering giant, was an ardent believer in choosing the most capable partners and sharing the burdens with them."

"There are still ambitious business leaders who would like to run their business on the one-man principle, but willy-nilly, they are forced by the very magnitude of modem operations to delegate responsibilities to others."

Some people, in speaking of their businesses, commit the unforgivable error of talking only of the features that interest them. Shouldn't the speaker try to ascertain what will entertain not himself but his hearers? Shouldn't he try to appeal to their selfish interests? If, for example, he sells fire insurance, shouldn't he tell them how to prevent fires on their own property? If she is a banker, shouldn't she give them advice on finance or investments? While preparing, study your audience. Think of their wants, their wishes. That is sometimes half the battle.

In preparing some topics, it is very advisable that if time permits, do some reading to discover what others have thought, what others have said on the same subject. But don't read until you have first thought yourself dry. That is very important. Then go to the public library and lay your needs before the librarian. If you are not in the habit of doing research work, you will probably be surprised at the aids librarians can put at your disposal; perhaps a special volume on your very topic, outlines and briefs for debate, giving the principal arguments on both sides of the public questions of the day; the Reader's Guide to Periodical Literature listing the magazine articles that have appeared on various topics since the beginning of the century; the Century Book of Facts, the World Almanac, the Encyclopedias and dozens of reference books. They are tools in your workshop. Use them. In recent years, we have the advantage of using the Internet as a major source for obtaining information about virtually any subject.

THE SECRET OF RESERVE POWER

Luther Burbank, probably the greatest botanist of all time, said, shortly before his death: "I have often produced a million plant specimens to find but one or two superlatively good ones and have then destroyed all the inferior specimens." A speech ought to be prepared somewhat in that lavish and discriminating spirit. Assemble a hundred thoughts and discard ninety.

Collect more material, more information, than there is any possibility of employing. Get it for the additional confidence, it will give you, for the sureness of touch. Get it for the effect, it will have on your mind and heart and whole manner of speaking. This is a basic, important factor of preparation; yet speakers, both in public and private, constantly ignore it.

"I have drilled hundreds of sales representatives and customer service personnel," a noted sales executive commented, "and the principal weakness which I have discovered in most of them has been their failure to realize the importance of knowing everything possible about their products and getting such knowledge before they start to sell."

"Many salespeople have come to my office and after getting a description of the article and a line of sales talk have been eager to get right out and try to sell. Many of these men and women have not lasted a week and a large number have not lasted forty-eight hours. In educating and drilling salespeople, in the sale of a food specialty, I have endeavored to make food experts of them. I have compelled them to study food charts issued by the U.S.

Department of Agriculture, which show in food the amount of water, the amount of protein, the amount of carbohydrates, the amount of fat and other ingredients. I have had them study the elements that make up the products that they are to sell. I have had them go to school for several days and then pass examinations. I have had them sell the product to other salespeople. I have offered prizes for the best sales talks."

"I have often found salespeople who get impatient at the preliminary time required for the study of their articles. They have said, 'I will never have time to tell all of this to retail grocers. They're too busy. If I talk protein and carbohydrates, they won't listen and, if they do listen, they won't know what I am talking about.' My reply has been, 'You don't get all of this knowledge for the benefit of your customer, but for the benefit of yourself. If you know your product from A to Z, you will have a feeling about it that is difficult to describe. You will be so positively charged, so fortified, so strengthened in your own mental attitude that you will be both irresistible and unconquerable.' "

Ida M. Tarbell, the well known historian of the Standard Oil Company, told the writer that years ago, when she was in Paris, Mr. S.S. McClure, the founder of McClure's Magazine, cabled her to write a short article about the Atlantic Cable. She went to London, interviewed the European manager of the principal cable company and obtained sufficient data for her assignment. But she did not stop there. She wanted a reserve supply of facts; so she studied all manner of cables on display in the British Museum; she read books on the history of the cable and even went to manufacturing concerns on the edge of London and saw cables in the process of construction.

Why did she collect ten times as much information as she could possibly use? She did it because she felt it would give her reserve power; because she realized that the things she knew and did not express would lend force and color to the little she did express.

One professional orator, who has spoken to approximately thirty million people, confided to me that if he did not, on the way home, kick himself for the good things he had left out of his talk, he felt that the performance must have been a failure. Why? Because he knew from long experience that the talks of distinct merit are those in which there abounds a reserve of material, a plethora, a profusion of it; far more than the speaker has time to use.

"What!", you object. "How can I can find time for all this? I have a job, a family and a whole slew of commitments. I can't be running to museums and libraries and reading books and sitting up in bed at daylight mumbling my speeches."

I've heard these excuses over and over again so it is taken into consideration. I suggest to my students that they talk on matters on which they have already done considerable thinking. Sometimes they will not be asked to plan any kind of a speech in advance; but will be given an easy topic for impromptu speaking after they face their audience. This will afford you most useful practice in thinking on one's feet; the sort of thing that you may be forced to do in most discussions.

Dr. Franklin C. Ashby, a twenty-first century disciple of Dale Carnegie, adds these suggestions :

• Learn as much as you can about the subject of your talk.

• Gather all the possible information about the topic. Jot down ideas, key words or phrases.

• Use all research sources available to you to saturate yourself with information.

• Check the internet and read professional, technical or specialized publications to learn about the latest developments in the area you will discuss.

• Identify the major points you wish to make. Highlight them in your notes.

• Organize facts to support those points.

• Prepare notes and graphics, where pertinent, to ensure all points are covered effectively.

• Be aware of objections and disagreements with your ideas and be prepared to discuss and rebut them.

Follow the suggestions given in this chapter. They will give you the ease and freedom you are seeking and also the ability to prepare talks effectively.

If you procrastinate until you have leisure to prepare and plan your talk, the leisure will probably never be found. However, it is easy to do the habitual, the accustomed thing, isn't it? So why not set aside one specific evening a week, from eight to ten o'clock, to be devoted to nothing but this task? That is the sure way, the systematic way. Why not try it?

IN A NUTSHELL

1.   When speakers have a real message in their head and heart, an inner urge to speak, they are almost sure to do themselves credit. A well-prepared speech is already nine-tenths delivered.

2.   What is preparation? The setting down of some mechanical sentences on paper? The memorizing of phrases? Not at all. Real preparation consists in digging something out of yourself, in assembling and arranging your own thoughts, in cherishing and nurturing your own convictions.

3.   Do not sit down and try to manufacture a speech in thirty minutes. A speech can't be cooked to order like a steak. A speech must grow. Select your topic well in advance of the speaking date, think over it during odd moments, brood over it, sleep over it, dream over it. Discuss it with friends. Make it a topic of conversation. Ask yourself all possible questions concerning it. Put down on pieces of paper all thoughts and illustrations that come to you and keep reaching out for more. Ideas, suggestions, illustrations will come drifting to you at sundry times, when you are bathing, when you are driving down town, when you are cooking dinner. It has been the method of almost all successful speakers.

4.   After you have done a bit of independent thinking, go to the library and do some reading on your topic, if time permits. The librarian can render you great assistance. Use the Internet. There is a plethora of information available on line.

5.   Collect far more material than you intend to use. Imitate Luther Burbank. He often produced a million plant specimens to find one or two superlatively good ones. Assemble a hundred thoughts, discard ninety.

6.   The way to develop reserve power is to know far more than you can use, to have a full reservoir of information. In preparing a speech, use the methods discussed earlier in this chapter.

SPEECH BUILDING
WORDS OFTEN MISPRONOUNCED

Your most inexcusable sin is the mispronunciation of a word in common, everyday use. Always accent the second syllables of the following words :

acCLImate	inEXplicable
alTERnately	inQUIry
conDOLence	irREVocable
exPOnent	lyCEum
fiNANCE (noun and verb) *	muSEum
inCOMparable	muNICipal
inCOGnito	SeATtle

*The first syllable of *finance*, both verb and noun, may be pronounced *fin* (*i* as in *it*), or *fi* (*i* as in *ice*) ; but remember that the accent must go on the last syllable. This word is commonly mispronounced.

Can you pronounce correctly the italicized words in the following sentences? If in doubt, see Chapter 1.

1. In his *address,* the *expert* agriculturist made no *pretense* whatever to having done any original *research.*

2. Do *adults* read the *romances* appearing in the *magazines*?

3. He *protested* that we would not *detour.*

4. He said in a *robust* voice that he would *contest* the decision as a matter of *routine.*

ERRORS IN ENGLISH

Review. For the purposes of review, a paragraph or so will head this section of each chapter. A number of mistakes previously discussed will be given. Finding them will be an interesting game and, at the same time, will increase your ability to detect errors and to profit by them.

There are four errors in the following paragraph:

I am determined that I shall go, even though it shall cause the heavens to fall and will bring unhappiness to all concerned. So leave me do it, whatever can come.

New Study Material. The English language is burdened with a number of verbs that cause trouble. A thorough understanding of their definitions and of their principal parts will soon cause you to use them correctly.

Let us consider three different sets of verbs in this category. They are *lay* and *lie*; *set* and *sit*; *raise* and *rise*.

Lay-Lie

To *lay* means to put an object somewhere. So, you may say:

I am *laying* the stamps here.

He *lays* the book on the table.

I have *laid* the matter before the board of directors.

He *laid* the foundation for an immense fortune.

To *lie* means to recline. Examples of use are as follows:

I am *lying* down.

I *lie* down.

He *lay* on his bed yesterday.

They have *lain* down on the whole proposition.

In addition, there is another use of *lie* in the sense of prevarication. The principal parts are *lie, lied, lying, lied*. No examples are necessary to show the usage of these verbs.

Set-Sit

To *set* means to put something somewhere or to make some one to sit. Of course, the latter usage is merely a corollary of the first. Examples are as follows:

I *set* it here as I want to use it.

I am *setting* the medicine on the table.

I *set* my watch by standard time last night.

I had *set* the trap before he came.

I *set* the baby on the bed.

To *sit* means to rest, as upon a chair with the body bent at the hips or to rest upon the haunches. It also means to take or occupy a seat. Examples are:

I *sit* to take my meals.

I am *sitting* down now.

I *sat* in the ante-room.

I have *sat* and waited for hours.

Sit here.

Raise-Rise

To *raise* means to move upward, to cause to rise, to exalt. Examples are:

I *raised* the flag.

I am *raising* the floor.

He *raised* his price.

He has *raised* a new question.

To *rise* means to ascend, as a hill; to become erect; to emerge; to revolt; etc. Examples are:

I *rise* to a point of order.

I am *rising* to ask a question.

The river *rose* last night.

The price has *risen*.

CORRECT USAGE OF WORDS

ANTIPATHY - DISLIKE. *Antipathy* is instinctive; *dislike* is often acquired. You have an *antipathy* for cats; you may *dislike* your landlord.

AUTHENTIC - GENUINE. *Authentic* suggests possessing authority and being true to the facts; *genuine* means, not counterfeit. If a Tahiti Islander wrote a book on ice hockey and signed his name to it, the treatise would be *genuine* but probably not *authentic*.

BEHAVIOR - CONDUCT. *Behavior* refers to our mode of acting in the presence of others; it generally refers to a specific instance. *Conduct* refers to the general tone of our actions in the more serious aspects of life.

BOUND - DETERMINE. We are *bound* to do things by outside influences. We *determine* to do a thing by our own decisions. You may be *bound* by law to send your child to school and *determined* to send him or her to college.

VOICE EXERCISE - CORRECT BREATHING

The famous singer, Jean De Reszke, advised, "carry the neck high." Let us stand up now and obey his admonition, not by raising the shoulders, but by lifting the chest to its proper position. Stand with your weight on the balls of your feet. Put your hand on the top of your head. Without lifting your heels from the floor, try now to shove your hand off your hair. Try to do it, not with your arm muscles, but by standing as tall as possible. There. That is it. Fine! You are now standing straight, abdomen in, neck and chest high, the back of your neck stretched back. Have you raised your shoulders? If so, relax, drop them. You want to carry your chest high, not your shoulders. Without lowering the chest, exhale. Hold it high as the last bit of breath escapes.

Now you are ready to breathe correctly. Close your eyes. Inhale deeply, slowly, easily through the nose. Try to feel the same sensation that you felt when you were practicing diaphragmatic breathing in bed, as we suggested in Chapter 1. Feel the bottom of your lungs expanding, expanding, expanding, pushing out the lower ribs to the side; feel the sensation under your arms; feel it at the back; feel the diaphragm being pushed down and flattening like an inverted paper dish under pressure from above; feel the diaphragm expanding as you place your fingers over the soft spot, "the doll squeak," children call it, just underneath the breast bone. Exhale slowly.

Now, once more. Inhale through your nose. Let me caution you again: do not raise your shoulders and do not try to enlarge your lungs at the top.

With your neck high, breathe in again, feeling the expansion in the middle of your body.

Enrico Caruso, the famous Italian opera star, practiced deep breathing ever day of his life. Consequently he developed a diaphragm of extraordinary power. When students came to him, as they often did, seeking advice about this all important matter of correct breathing; he usually said to them: "Press your fist with all your strength against my relaxed diaphragm." Then with a quick, sharp intake of breath, the famous tenor forced his diaphragm down and his body out with such force as to fling off the pressure of the fist.

However, the mere knowledge of correct breathing that you are gathering now will avail you naught unless you apply it.

So practice it daily as you walk along the street. Practice it when you have an odd moment in the office. After you have been concentrating on some task for an hour, throw open the window and fill your lungs with air. This won't be time lost. It will be time saved, vigor reinforced, health strengthened. This practice cannot be indulged in too often. It will, if faithfully followed, become a habit. You will wonder then that you ever breathed in any other fashion. To breathe from the top of the lungs is only half breathing. And "he who only half- breathes," says a passage from the Sanskrit, "only half lives."

Chapter 3

HOW FAMOUS SPEAKERS
PREPARED THEIR ADDRESSES

"There's a vast difference between having a carload of miscellaneous facts sloshing around loose in your head and getting all mixed up in transit; and carrying the same assortment properly boxed and crated for convenient handling and immediate delivery."

-Lorimer: Letters from a Self-Made Merchant to
His Son at College

"The power to grasp the essential features of problems is the great differentiation between the educated and the non-educated man. Undoubtedly the greatest advantage to be gained from a college education is the acquisition of a disciplined mind."

-John Grier Hibben, President of Princeton University

"What is it that first strikes us, and strikes us at once, in a man of education and which, among educated men, so instantly distinguishes the man of superior mind? . . . The true cause of the impression made upon us is that his mind is methodical."

-Samuel Tayllor Coleridge

"I never give 'em hell, I just tell the truth and they think it's hell"

-Harry S. Truman

HOW FAMOUS SPEAKERS
PREPARED THEIR ADDRESSES

I was present once at a luncheon of the New York Rotary Club when the principal speaker was a prominent government official. The high position that he occupied gave him prestige, and we were looking forward with pleasure to hearing him. He had promised to tell us about the activities of his own department; and it was one in which almost every person in the room was interested.

He knew his subject thoroughly, knew far more about it than he could possibly use; but he had not planned his speech. He had not selected his material. He had not arranged it in orderly fashion. Nevertheless, with a courage born of inexperience, he plunged heedlessly, blindly into his speech. He did not know where he was going, but he was on his way.

His mind was, in short, a mere hodgepodge; and so was the mental feast he served us. He brought on the ice-cream first, and then placed the soup before us. Fish and nuts came next. And, on top of that, there was something that seemed to be a mixture of soup and ice-cream and good red herring. I have never, anywhere or at any time, seen a speaker more utterly confused.

He had been trying to talk impromptu; but, in desperation now, he drew a bundle of notes out of his pocket, confessing that his secretary had compiled them for him; and no one questioned the veracity of his assertion. The notes themselves evidently had no more order than a flat car full of scrap iron. He fumbled through them nervously, glancing from one page to another, trying to orient himself, trying to find a way out of the wilderness; and he attempted to talk as he did so. It was impossible. He apologized and, calling for water, took a drink with a trembling hand, uttered a few more scattering sentences, repeated himself, dug into his notes again. Minute by minute, he grew more helpless, more lost, more bewildered, more embarrassed. Nervous perspiration stood out on his forehead and his handkerchief shook as he wiped it away. We in the audience sat watching the fiasco, our sympathies stirred, our feelings harrowed. We suffered positive and vicarious embarrassment. But with more doggedness than discretion, the speaker continued, floundering, studying his notes, apologizing and drinking. Every one, except him, felt that the spectacle was rapidly approaching total disaster; and it was a relief to us all when he sat down and ceased his death struggles. It was one of the most uncomfortable audiences I have ever been in; and he was the most ashamed and humiliated speaker I have ever seen. He had begun without knowing what he was going to say and he had finished without knowing what he had uttered.

No sane person would start to build a house without some sort of plan; but why will one begin to deliver a speech without the vaguest kind of outline or program?

A speech is a voyage with a purpose and it must be charted. If you start nowhere, you will generally get there.

I wish that I could paint this saying of Napoleon's in flaming letters of red, a foot high over every doorway on the globe where students of public speaking foregather: "The art of war is a science in which nothing succeeds which has not been calculated and thought out."

That is just as true of speaking as of shooting. But do speakers realize it; or, if they do, do they always act on it? They do not. Most emphatically they do not. Many a talk has just a trifle more plan and arrangement than a bowl of Irish stew.

What is the best and most effective arrangement for a given set of ideas? To answer this takes careful study. It is always a new problem, an eternal question that every speaker must ask and seek the answer again and again. No infallible rules can be given; but we can, at any rate, illustrate briefly here with a concrete case, just what we mean by orderly arrangements.

HOW A PRIZE-WINNING SPEECH WAS CONSTRUCTED

Here is a speech that was delivered by a student of my course before the Thirteenth Annual Convention of the National Association of Real Estate Boards. It won first prize in competition with twenty-seven other speeches on various cities. This speech is well constructed, full of facts, stated clearly, vividly, interestingly. It has spirit. It marches. It will merit reading and study.

Mr. Chairman and Friends:

Back 144 years ago, this great nation, the United States of America, was born in my City of Philadelphia, and so it is quite natural that a city having such an historical record should have that strong American spirit that has not only made it the greatest industrial center in this country, but also one of the largest and most beautiful cities in the whole world.

Philadelphia has a population close to two millions of people; and our city has an area that is equal to the combined size of Milwaukee and Boston, Paris and Berlin and out of our 130 square miles of territory we have given up nearly 8,000 acres of our best land for beautiful parks, squares and boulevards, so that our people would have the proper places for recreation and pleasure, and the right kind of an environment that belongs to every decent American. Philadelphia, friends, is not only a large, clean and beautiful city, but it is also known everywhere as the great workshop of the world, and the reason it is called the workshop of the world is because we have a vast army of over 400,000 people employed in 9,200 industrial establishments that turn out one hundred thousand dollars' worth of useful commodities, every ten minutes of the working day, and, according to a well-known statistician, there is no city in this country that equals Philadelphia in the production of woolen goods, leather goods, knit goods, textiles, felt hats, hardware, tools, storage batteries, steel ships and a great many other things. We build a railroad locomotive every two hours day and night, and more than one-half the people in this great country ride in street cars made in the City of Philadelphia. We manufacture a thousand cigars every minute, and last year, in our 115 hosiery mills, we made two pairs of stockings for every man, woman and child in this country. We make more carpets and rugs than all of Great Britain and Ireland combined, and, in fact, our total commercial and industrial business is so stupendous that our bank clearings last year, amounting to thirty-seven billions of dollars, would have paid for every Liberty Bond in the entire country.

But, friends, while we are very proud of our wonderful industrial program; and while we are also very proud of being one of the largest medical, art and educational centers in this country; yet, we feel a still greater pride in the fact that we have more individual homes in the City of Philadelphia than there are in any other city in the whole world. In Philadelphia, we have 397,000 separate homes, and if these homes were placed on twenty-five-foot lots, side by side, in one single row, that row would reach all the way from Philadelphia, clear through to this Convention Hall, at Kansas City, and then on to Denver, a distance of 1,881 miles.

But, what I want to call your special attention to, is the significance of the fact, that tens of thousands of these homes are owned and occupied by the working people of our city, and when a man owns the ground upon which he stands and the roof over his head, he is fully committed to the American way of life.

Philadelphia is not a fertile soil for socialism or anarchy, because our homes, our educational institutions and our gigantic industry have been produced by that true American spirit that was born in our city and is a heritage from our forefathers. Philadelphia is the mother city of this great country; and the very fountain head of American liberty. It is the city where the first American flag was made; it is the city where the first Congress of the United States met; it is the city where the Declaration of Independence was signed; it is the city where that best loved relic in America, the Liberty Bell, has inspired tens of thousands of our men, women and children, so that we believe, we have a sacred mission, which is not to worship the golden calf, but to spread the American spirit and to keep the fires of freedom burning, so that with God's permission, the Government of Washington, Lincoln and Theodore Roosevelt may be an inspiration to all humanity.

Let us analyze that speech. Let us see how it is constructed, how it gets its effects. In the first place, it has a beginning and an ending. That is a rare virtue, my dear reader, more rare than you may be inclined to think. It starts somewhere. It goes there straight as wild geese on the wing. It doesn't dawdle. It loses no time.

It has freshness, individuality. The speaker opens by saying something about his city that the other speakers could not possibly say about theirs. He points out that his city is the birthplace of the entire nation.

He states that it is one of the largest and most beautiful cities in the world. But that claim is general, trite; standing by itself, it would not impress anyone very much. The speaker knew that; so he helped his audience visualize the magnitude of Philadelphia by stating it "has an area equal to the combined size of Milwaukee, Boston, Paris and Berlin." That is definite, concrete. It is interesting. It is surprising. It makes a mark. It drives home the idea better than a whole page of statistics would have done.

Next he declares that Philadelphia is "known everywhere as the great workshop of the world." Sounds exaggerated, doesn't it? Like propaganda. Had he proceeded immediately to the next point, no one would have been convinced. But he doesn't. He pauses to enumerate the products in which Philadelphia leads the world: "woolen goods, leather goods, knit goods, textiles, felt hats, hardware, tools, storage batteries, steel ships."

Doesn't sound so much like propaganda now, does it?

Philadelphia "builds a railroad locomotive every two hours day and night, and more than one-half the people in this great country ride in street cars made in the city of Philadelphia."

"Well, I never knew that," we muse. "Perhaps I rode down town yesterday in one of those street cars. I'll look tomorrow and see where my town buys its cars."

"A thousand cigars every minute, two pairs of stockings for every man, woman and child in this country."

We are still more impressed... . Maybe my favorite cigar is made in Philadelphia... and these socks I have on... .

What does the speaker do next? Jump back to the subject of the size of Philadelphia that he covered first and give us some fact that he forgot then? No, not at all. He sticks to a point until he finishes it, has done with it, and need never to return to it again. For that we are duly grateful, Mr. Speaker. For what is more confusing and muddling than to have a speaker darting from one thing to another and back again, as erratic as a bat, in the twilight? Yet many a speaker does just that. Instead of covering his points in order -1, 2, 3, 4, 5, he covers them as a football captain calls out signals -27, 34, 19, 2. No, he is worse than that. He covers them like this -27, 34, 277, 19, 2, 34, 19.

But this speaker, however, steams straight ahead on schedule time, never idling, never turning back, swerving neither to the right nor left; like one of those locomotives he has been talking about.

But, he makes now the weakest point of his entire speech: Philadelphia, he declares, is "one of the largest medical, art and educational centers in this country." He merely announces that; then speeds on to something else; only twelve words to animate that fact, to make it vivid, to engrave it on the memory. Only twelve words lost, submerged, in a sentence containing a total of sixty-five. It doesn't work. Of course not. The human mind does not operate like a string of steel traps. He devotes so little time to this point, is so general, so vague, seems so unimpressed himself that the effect on the hearer is almost nil. What should he have done? He realized that he could establish this point with the selfsame technique that he just employed to establish the fact that Philadelphia is the workshop of the world. He knew that. He also knew that he would have a stop watch held on him during the contest, that he would have five minutes, not a second more; so he had to slur over this point or slight others.

There are "more individual homes in the city of Philadelphia than there are in any other city in the world." How does he make this phase of his topic impressive and convincing? First, he gives the number: 397,000. Second, he visualizes the number: "If these homes were placed on twenty-five foot lots, side by side, in one single row, that row would reach all the way from Philadelphia, clear through this Convention Hall at Kansas City, and then on to Denver, a distance of 1,881 miles."

His audience probably forgot the number he gave before he had finished the sentence. But forget that picture? That would have been well-nigh impossible.

So much for cold material facts. But they are not the stuff out of which eloquence is fashioned. This speaker aspired to build up to a climax, to touch the heart, to stir the feelings. So now on the home stretch, he deals with emotional material. He tells what the ownership of those homes means to the spirit of the city. He eulogizes Philadelphia as "the very fountain head of American liberty." Liberty! A magic word, a word full of feeling, a sentiment for which millions have laid down their lives. That phrase in itself is good, but it is a thousand times better when he backs it up with concrete references to historic events and documents, dear, sacred, to the hearts of his hearers... . "It is the city where the first American Flag was made; it is the city where the first Congress of the United States met; it is the city where the Declaration of Independence was signed... Liberty Bell... a sacred mission... to spread the American spirit... to keep the fires of freedom burning, so that with God's permission, the Government of Washington, Lincoln and Theodore Roosevelt may be an inspiration to all humanity." That is a real climax!

So much for the composition of this talk. But admirable as it is from the standpoint of construction, this speech could have come to grief, could easily have been brought to naught, had it been expressed in a calm manner devoid of all spirit and vitality. But the speaker delivered it as he composed it; with a feeling and enthusiasm born of the deepest sincerity. Small wonder that it won first prize.

THE WAY DOCTOR CONWELL PLANNED HIS SPEECHES

There are not, as I have already said, any infallible rules that will solve the question of the best arrangement. There are no designs or schemes or charts that will fit all or even a majority of speeches; yet here are a few speech plans that will prove usable in some instances. Dr. Russell H. Conwell, the author of the famous "Acres of Diamonds", which you can read in the Appendix, once informed me that he had built many of his innumerable speeches on this outline:

1. State your facts.
2. Argue from them.
3. Appeal for action.

Many students of my course have found this plan very helpful and stimulating.

1. Show something that is wrong.
2. Show how to remedy it.
3. Ask for cooperation.

Or, to put it in another way:

1. Here is a situation that ought to be remedied.
2. We ought to do so and so about the matter.
3. You ought to help for these reasons.

Chapter XV of this book , entitled How To Get Action, outlines still another speech plan. Briefly it is this:

1. Secure interested attention.
2. Win confidence.
3. State your facts; educate people regarding the merits of your proposition.
4. Appeal to the motives that make men act.

If interested, turn now to Chapter XV and study this plan in detail.

SENATOR BEVERIDGE'S METHOD OF BUILDING A TALK

Hon. Albert J. Beveridge has written a very short and very practical book entitled "The Art of Public Speaking." "The speaker must be master of his subject," says this noted political campaigner. "That means that all the facts must be collected, arranged, studied, digested, not only data on one side, but material on the other side and on every side, all of it. And be sure that they are facts, not mere assumptions or unproved assertions. Take nothing for granted."

"Therefore, check up and verify every item. This means painstaking research, to be sure, but what of it? Are you not proposing to inform, instruct, and advise your fellow citizens? Are you not setting yourself up as an authority?

"Having assembled and marshalled the facts of any problem, *think out for yourself the solution those facts compel.* Thus, your speech will have originality and personal force, it will be vital and compelling. There will be you in it. Then write out your ideas as clearly and logically as you can."

In other words, present the facts on both sides and then present the conclusion that those facts make clear and definite.

WOODROW WILSON FITS THE BONES TOGETHER

"I begin," said Woodrow Wilson when asked to explain his methods, "with a list of the topics I want to cover, *arranging them in my mind in their natural relations.* That is, I fit the bones of the thing together; then I write it out in shorthand. I have always been accustomed to writing in shorthand, finding it a great saver of time. This done, I copy it on my own typewriter, changing phrases, correcting sentences and adding material as I go along."

Theodore Roosevelt prepared his talks in the characteristic

Rooseveltian manner: he dug up all the facts, reviewed them, appraised them, determined their findings, arrived at his conclusions, arrived with a feeling of certainty that was unshakable.

Then, with a pad of notes before him, he started dictating and he dictated his speech very rapidly, so that it would have rush and spontaneity and the spirit of life. Then he went over this typewritten copy, revised it, inserted, deleted, filled it with pencil marks and then dictated it all over again. "I never won anything," said he, "without hard labor and the exercise of my best judgment and careful planning and working long in advance."

Often, he called in critics to listen to him as he dictated or read his speech to them. He refused to debate with them the wisdom of what he had said. His mind was already made up on that point and made up irrevocably. He wanted to be told, not what to say, but how to say it. Again and again he went over his typewritten copies, cutting, correcting, improving. That was the speech that the newspapers printed. Of course, he did not memorize it. He spoke extemporaneously. So the talk he actually delivered, often differed somewhat, from the published and polished one. But the task of dictating and revising was excellent preparation. It made him familiar with his material, with the order of his points. It gave him a smoothness and sureness and polish that he could hardly have obtained in any other fashion.

Sir Oliver Lodge, a late 19th century-early 20th century physicist and philosopher, told me that dictating his talks; dictating them rapidly and with substance, dictating them just as if he were actually talking to an audience; he had discovered to be an excellent means of preparation and practice.

Many of the students of public speaking courses have found it illuminating to dictate their talks to the dictaphone or tape recorder, and then to listen to themselves. Illuminating? Yes, and sometimes disillusioning and chastening also, I fear. It is a most wholesome exercise. I recommend it.

This practice of actually writing out what you are going to say, will force you to think. It will clarify your ideas. It will hook them in your memory. It will reduce your mental wandering to a minimum. It will improve your diction.

Ronald Reagan, earned his reputation as a great communicator by his ability to present his ideas effectively and with enthusiasm. He had the added advantage over speakers of earlier generations in that, he not only could dictate his talks into a tape recorder and then listen to them, but could videotape them and observe his demeanor and body language before presenting the talk in public.

BENJAMIN FRANKLIN'S CLASSIC TALE

Benjamin Franklin tells in his *Autobiography* how he improved his diction, how he developed readiness in using words and how he taught himself method in arranging his thoughts. This story of his life is a literary classic, and, unlike most classics, it is easy to read and thoroughly enjoyable. It is almost a model of plain, straightforward English. This is a book that every person interested in self-improvement will enjoy and benefit from reading it. I think you will like the selection I refer to; here it is:

"About this time I met with an odd volume of the Spectator. It was the third. I had never before seen any of them. I bought it, read it over and over and was much delighted with it. I thought the writing excellent and wished, if possible, to imitate it. With this view, I took some of the papers and making short hints of the sentiment in each sentence, laid them by a few days; and then, without looking at the book, tried to complete the papers again by expressing each hinted sentiment at length and as fully as it had been expressed before, in any suitable words that should come to band. Then I compared my Spectator with the original, discovered some of my faults and corrected them. But I found a stock of words, and a readiness in recollecting and using them, which I thought I should have acquired before that time, if I had gone on making verses; since the continual occasion for words of the same import, but of different length, to suit the measure, or of different sounds for the rhyme, would have laid me under a constant necessity of searching for variety, and also have tended to fix that variety in my mind, and make me master of it. Therefore, I took some of the tales and turned them back again. I also sometimes jumbled my collections of hints into confusion; and after some weeks endeavored to reduce them into the best order, before I began to form the full sentences and complete the paper. This was to teach me method in the arrangement of thoughts. By comparing my work afterwards with the original, I discovered many faults and amended them; but I sometimes had the pleasure of fancying that, in certain particulars of small import, I had been lucky enough to improve the method of the language, and this encouraged me to think I might possibly in time come to be a tolerable English writer, of which I was extremely ambitious."

PLAY SOLITAIRE WITH YOUR NOTES

You were advised in the last chapter to make notes. Having got your various ideas and illustrations down on scraps of paper, play solitaire with them, toss them into series of related piles. These main piles ought to represent, approximately, the main points of your talk. Subdivide them into smaller lots. Throw out the chaff until there is nothing but number one wheat left; and even some of the wheat will probably have to be put aside and not used. You ought never to cease this process of revision until the speech has been made; even then you are very likely to think of points and improvements and refinements that ought to have been made.

Good speakers usually find when they finished that there have been four versions of the speech: the one that they prepared, the one that they delivered, the one that the newspapers said was delivered and the one that they wished on the way home, that they had delivered.

"SHALL I USE NOTES WHILE SPEAKING ?"

Although he was an excellent impromptu speaker, Lincoln, after he reached the White House, never made any address, not even an informal talk to his cabinet, until he had carefully put it all down in writing beforehand. Of course, he was obliged to read his inaugural addresses. The exact phraseology of historical state papers of that character is too important to be left to extemporizing. But, back in Illinois, Lincoln never used even notes in his speaking. "They always tend to tire and confuse the listener," he said.

And who of us would contradict him? Don't notes destroy about fifty percent of your interest in a talk? Don't they prevent, or at least render difficult, a very precious contact and intimacy that ought to exist between the speaker and the audience? Don't they create an air of artificiality? Don't they restrain an audience from feeling that the speaker has the confidence and reserve power that he ought to have?

Make notes, I repeat, during the preparation, elaborate ones, profuse ones. You may wish to refer to them when you are practicing your talk alone. You may possibly feel more comfortable if you have them stored away in your pocket when you are facing an audience; but, like the hammer and saw and axe in a Pullman coach, they should be emergency tools, only for use in the case of a smash-up, a total wreck and threatening death and disaster.

If you must use notes, make them extremely brief and write them in large letters on an ample sheet of paper. Then arrive early at the place where you are to speak and hide your notes behind some books on a table. Glance at them when you must, but endeavor to screen your weakness from the audience. John Bright used to secrete his notes in his big hat lying on the table before him.

However, in spite of all that has been said, there may be times when it is the part of wisdom to use notes. For example; some people, during their first few talks, are so nervous and self-conscious that they are utterly unable to remember their prepared speeches. The result? They shoot off at a tangent; they forget the material they had so carefully rehearsed; they drift off the high road and flounder about in a morass. Why should not such people hold a few very condensed notes in their hands during their maiden efforts? A child clutches the furniture when it is first attempting to walk; but it does not continue it very long.

DO NOT MEMORIZE VERBATIM

Don't read, and don't attempt to memorize your talk, word for word. That consumes time and courts disaster. Yet, in spite of this warning, some of the people reading these lines will try it; if they do, when they stand up to speak, they will be thinking of what? Of their messages? No, they will be attempting to recall their exact phraseology. They will be thinking backwards, not forwards, reversing the usual processes of the human mind. The whole exhibition will be stiff and cold and colorless and inhuman. Do not, I beg of you, waste hours and energy in such futility.

When you prepare for a meeting on a serious situation, do you sit down and memorize verbatim, what you are going to say? Do you? Of course not. You reflect until you get your main ideas clearly in mind. You may make a few notes and consult some records. You say to yourself, "I shall bring out this point and that. I am going to say that a certain thing ought to be done for these reasons." Then, you enumerate the reasons to yourself and illustrate them with concrete cases. Isn't that the way you prepare for the meeting? Why not use the same common sense method in preparing a talk?

GRANT AT APPOMATTOX

When Lee asked Grant to write down the terms of surrender, the leader of the Union forces turned to General Parker, asking for writing material. "When I put my pen to paper," Grant records in his Memoirs, "I did not know the first word I should make use of in writing the terms. I only knew what was in my mind and I wished to express it clearly, so there could be no mistaking it."

General Grant, you did not need to know the first word. You had ideas. You had convictions. You had something that you very much wanted to say and to say clearly. The result was that your habitual phraseology came tumbling out without conscious effort. The same holds good for everybody. Two thousand years ago, Horace wrote:

"Seek not for words, seek only fact and thought,

And crowding in will come the words unsought."

After you have your ideas firmly in mind, then rehearse your talk from beginning to end. Do it silently, mentally, as you walk the street, as you wait for cars and elevators. Get off in a room by yourself and go over it aloud, gesturing, saying it with life and energy. Canon Knox Little, of Canterbury, used to say a preacher never got the real message out of a sermon until he had preached it half a dozen times. Can you hope then, to get the real message out of your talk unless you have at least rehearsed it that many times ? As you practice, imagine there is a real audience before you. Imagine it so strongly that when there is one, it will seem like an old experience.

WHY THE FARMERS THOUGHT LINCOLN "AWFULLY LAZY"

If you practice your talks in this fashion, you will be faithfully following the examples of many famous speakers. Lloyd George, when he was a member of a debating society in his hometown in Wales, often strolled along the country lanes, talking and gesturing to the trees and fence Posts.

Lincoln, in his younger days, often walked, a round trip of thirty or forty miles to hear a famous speaker. He came home from these scenes so stirred, so determined to be a speaker, that he gathered the other hired workers about him in the fields and mounting a stump, he made speeches and told them stories. His employers grew angry, declaring that this "country orator was awfully lazy," that his jokes and his oratory were ruining the rest of the workers.

Herbert Asquith, who later became Britain's prime minister, gained his first facility by becoming an active worker in the Union Debating Society in Oxford. Later, he organized one of his own. Woodrow Wilson learned to speak in a debating society. So did most successful lawyers, politicians and public speakers.

Study the careers of famous speakers and you will find one fact that is true of them all: *they practiced*. THEY PRACTICED. And those who make the most rapid progress are those who practice most.

Chauncey M. Depew led a fairly active life as a railroad president and a United States Senator. Yet, during it all, he made speeches almost every night. "I did not let them interfere with my business," he said. "They were all prepared after I had arrived home from my office, late in the afternoon."

We all have three hours a day that we can do with as we please. That was all Darwin had to work with as he had poor health. Three hours out of twenty-four, wisely used, made him famous.

Theodore Roosevelt, when he was in the White House, often had an entire forenoon given over to a series of five minute interviews. Yet, he kept a book by his side to utilize even the few spare seconds that came between his engagements.

If you are very busy and pushed for time, read Arnold Bennett's *How To Live On Twenty-Four Hours A Day*. Buy an inexpensive paperback copy and keep it with you to read while waiting on line, riding in train or cab, or sitting in some doctor's waiting room. It will show you how to save time, how to get more out of the day.

You must have relaxation and a change from your regular work. We expect people in this course to meet together, an additional night, each week for rehearsal. If you cannot do that, play the game of extemporaneous speaking in your own home with your own family.

One way to gain speaking experience is to seek places where people are encouraged to speak. One of the participants in my course woke up one Sunday morning and shook his wife awake and asked, "Is there any place in New York where I can make a speech today?" She reminded him that anyone could speak at a Quaker meeting if the spirit moved him or her. Somewhere in Brooklyn, he located a Quaker meeting house and was so moved by the spirit that he spoke for twenty minutes.

In most cities in the United States, and in some cities throughout the world, there are Toastmasters' Clubs, informal groups that meet on a regular basis, usually over dinner, where members give brief talks on subjects of interest to them, Men and women from all walks of life join together to share ideas and gain the experience of giving public talks. Look for a Toastmasters' Club in your area, join it and get up there and talk, talk, talk.

HOW DOUGLAS FAIRBANKS AND MARY PICKFORD ENTERTAIN THEMSELVES

There were no greater movie stars in the 1920s and 30s than Douglas Fairbanks, Mary Pickford and Charlie Chaplin, yet, with all their wealth and fame, they were able to find no greater entertainment, no more enjoyable way of spending their evenings, than by practicing extemporaneous speaking.

Here is their story as Douglas Fairbanks told it in the American Magazine:

"One evening we were fooling and I pretended to introduce Charlie Chaplin at a dinner. He had to rise and make a speech to fit the introduction. And out of that developed a game that we have been playing almost every night for two years. We three (Mary Pickford, Fairbanks and Chaplin) each write a subject on a slip of paper and fold the slips and shake them up. Each of us draws. No matter what the word is, each of us has to rise and talk for sixty seconds on that word. We never use the same word again. That's what keeps the stunt new. And we use all kinds of words. I remember one evening when two of the words were 'Faith' and 'Lampshades.' 'Lampshades' fell to me and I had one of the hardest times I ever had talking for sixty seconds on 'Lampshades.' Just try if you think it is easy. You start out bravely 'Lampshades have two uses. They modify and soften the glare of light and they are decorative.' Then you are through unless you know a lot more about lampshades than I do. I got through somehow. But the point is how all three of us have sharpened up since we began that game. We know a lot more about a variety of miscellaneous subjects. But, far better than that, we are learning to assemble our knowledge and thoughts on any topic at a moment's notice and to give it out briefly. We are learning to think on our feet. I say 'we arc learning' because we are still at this game. We haven't tired of it in almost two years which means that it is still making us grow."

IN A NUTSHELL

1. "The art of war," said Napoleon, "is a science in which nothing succeeds which has not been calculated and thought out." That is as true of speaking as of shooting. A talk is a voyage. It must be charted. The speaker, who starts no where, usually gets there.

2. No infallible, ironclad rules can be given for the arrangement of ideas and the construction of all talks. Each address presents its own particular problems.

3. The speaker should cover a point thoroughly when it is presented and then not refer to it again. As an illustration, see the prize-winning address on Philadelphia. There should be no darting from one thing to another and then back again as aimlessly as a bat in the twilight.

4. The Russell H. Conwell built many of his talks on this plan:

a. State your facts.

b. Argue from them.

c. Appeal for action.

5. You will probably find this plan very helpful:

a. Show something that is wrong.

b. Show how to remedy it.

c. Appeal for action.

6. Here is an excellent speech plan (for further details see Chapter XV):

a. Secure interested attention.

b. Win confidence.

c. State your facts.

d. Appeal to the motives that make men act.

7. All the facts on both sides of your subject, must be collected, arranged, studied, digested. Prove them; be sure they are facts; then think out for yourself, the solution those facts compel.

8. Before speaking, Lincoln thought out his conclusions with mathematical exactness. When he was forty years of age, and after he had been a member of Congress, he studied Euclid so that he could detect sophistry and demonstrate his conclusions.

9. When Theodore Roosevelt was preparing a speech, he dug up all the facts, appraised them, then dictated his speech very rapidly, corrected the typewritten copy and finally dictated it all over again.

10. If possible, dictate your talk to a tape recorder and listen to it. Even better, videotape yourself and review not only how you speak, but how you look when you make the talk.

11. Do not read your talk. An audience can hardly be brought to endure listening to a read speech,

12. After you have thought out and arranged your talk, then practice it silently as you walk along the street. Also get off somewhere by yourself and go over it from beginning to end, using gestures, letting yourself go. Imagine that you are addressing a real audience. The more of this you do, the more comfortable you will feel when the time comes for you to make your talk.

SPEECH BUILDING

WORDS OFTEN MISPRONOUNCED

"Correct pronunciation and enunciation are the infallible hallmarks of education and association with well-bred people."

-The Gentle Art of Good Talking, by Beatrice Knollys

Do you always accent the following words on their first syllables? This is required for good English.

ADmirable	DESpicable	ORdeal
ADvent	EXquisite	ORdinarily
ADverse	FORmidable	PACifist
AFfluence	GONdola	PREamble
Alias (AIL-ee as)	HARass	PREFerable

CARton	HOSpitable	PRImarily
CHAStisement	IMpotent	RESpite
COMbat	INdustry	REVocable
COMbatant	INterested	TEMporarily
COMparable	INteresting	TRAVerse
CONcrete (noun and adjective)		THEater
CONtrary	JUStifiable	VEhement
CONversant	LAMentable	VOLuntarily
DECade	MAINtenance	
DEFicit	MISchievous	

Can you pronounce correctly the italicized words in these sentences? If in doubt, will you please refer to the exercises in pronunciation at the end of Chapters I and II.

1. An *inquiry* was instituted to determine why the *adult* was traveling *incognito*.
2. Each of the *municipal* employees made a *pretense* of having a *robust* pain in his *abdomen*.
3. The *adult* told in his *address* how the *museum* is *financed*.
4. After he becomes *acclimated*, he will be more *robust physically* and more *adept* at his duties.
5. The order for his *discharge* was *irrevocable*.
6. He *financed* the entire *domain*.
7. She went to the *lyceum* in a *gondola* of *incomparable* beauty of lines.

ERRORS IN ENGLISH

"There is no more revealing symbol of education than one's style of speech. It will be recognized by discerning men more quickly than a Roman nose or a cauliflower ear."

-Harry Collins Spillman

Review. There are five errors in the following paragraph. Find them, please.

The letters had laid on his desk for several days without answer because he was accustomed to set there and do nothing. He had rose to the position of superintendent and did not know how to set either himself or his staff to work. As the sun sat in the west, he was still setting there.

New Study Material. Some of the most commonly misused verbs are given in the examples below. Run over these carefully. You will find that a short drill every now and then with the first set of examples will teach you to overcome any irregularities, which you may have had. The second set contains the ordinary wrong uses. Observe these mistakes enough so that you will see your errors, but do not impress the errors on your memory. It is one of the best rules of modern pedagogy that one learns far more rapidly and more efficiently by impressing the right than by observing the wrong.

Right

He *became* wealthy.

They *began* to complain.

I *bade* him to come. (invited)

We were *bidden* to the party.

I *bid* $5.00. (offer)

$5.00 was *bid*.

The wind *blew* hard all day.

The wind has *blown* hard.

I *brought* my purse.

The purse was *brought*.

They *broke* down on the road.

They have *broken* down.

The pipes *have burst*.

He *came* home.

He *has come* home.

She *dived* off the bridge.

She *had dived* off the bridge.

He *did* the best he could.

He *has done* the best he could.

He *drank* heavily for years.

He *has drunk* heavily for years.

Wrong

He *become* wealthy.

They *begun* to complain.

I *bid* him to come.

We were *bid* to the party.

The wind *blowed* hard all day.

The wind *has blowed* hard.

I *brung* my purse.

The purse was *brung*.

They *break* down on the road.

They *have broke* down.

The pipes have *busted*.

He *come* home.

He *has came* home.

She *dove* off the bridge.

She *had dove* off the bridge.

He *done* the best he could.

He *has did* the best he could.

He *drunk* heavily for years.

He *has drank* heavily for years.

CORRECT USAGE OF WORDS

People are *fortunate* when they gets things by good luck. If they accomplish what they set out to do, they are *successful*. If they gain the things that most people desire, they are said to be *prosperous*. Lincoln was *fortunate* in having a strong, rugged constitution. When he tried to run a grocery store, he was neither *successful* nor *prosperous*. *Flourishing* is derived from a Latin word meaning to bloom and flower.

Thriving literally means to grasp for one's self, and carries with it a sense of thriftiness.

Try is a very general and comprehensive term. One may *try* almost anything without much concern about the success of the trial. We generally *attempt* only those things that we very much want to do. An *endeavor* is a continuous attempt. One should *endeavor* to increase each day his knowledge of words. *Aim* is more general and less specific than attempt. Almost every one vaguely aims to do many things which he really never *attempts* or *endeavors* to do. *Strive* implies hard, earnest effort or a struggle; as, "He had to strive against all kinds of difficulties." To *struggle* is to use much effort.

VOICE EXERCISE - RELAXATION

"Probably more voices are ruined by strain," said the famous opera singer, Madame Schumann-Heink, "than through any other cause. The singer must relax all the time. This does not mean flabbiness. It does not mean that the singer should collapse before singing. Relaxation, in the singer's sense, is a delicious condition of buoyancy, of lightness, of freedom, of ease and an entire lack of tightening in any part. When I relax, I feel as though every atom in my body were floating in space. There is not one single little nerve on tension."

Madame Schumann-Heink is referring to singing; but, of course, the same facts apply to speaking. Strain ruins voices, she says; yet what is more common in this hurried age than strain and nervous tension? These things show in the voice as plainly as they show in the face. Relaxation! That should be our watch word. Relaxation! That should be our shibboleth. Relaxation is the secret of good voice.

How are we to set about cultivating it? First, learn to relax the whole body. Your entire physical being acts as a sounding board for your voice. The least imperfection in the sounding board of a piano, even a screw loose in the case, will affect the tone and as your voice is affected by every part of your body, tension here and there will impair its perfect functioning.

How can you relax? It is simple. Just relax, that is all. It is not a question of doing anything. It is a question of not doing. It is not effort that is wanted; it is the lack of it. Hold your arm out straight from your shoulder and in front of you. Relax it now. When it fell, did it swing back and forth a few times like a pendulum? If it did not swing at all, you did not relax it; you pulled it down. Try it once more. How was that?

Each night when you go to bed, lie on the flat of your back and practice the deep diaphragmatic breathing that we discussed in the first two chapters. But before you begin your deep breathing, relax. Relax your whole body. Relax thoroughly. Feel as inert as a bag of wool. Try to imagine that all the energy that is in your arms, your legs, your neck is flowing into the center of the body. You ought to be so relaxed that your jaw will fall open. Let your arms and legs and body feel heavy on the bed, so heavy and lifeless that it seems as if you would never have the strength to lift them again. Feel lazy. Now, breathe deeply, slowly) naturally, thinking nothing but ease and relaxation.

True, thoughts of the worries, the problems, the anxieties of the day just past and the day to come, may swarm through your brain like an army of mosquitoes to pester and annoy you, to keep you taut. If they do, smoke out such thoughts as you would smoke out the mosquitoes. Smoke them out with such soothing declarations as these: "I'm at ease. I'm thoroughly relaxed. I feel as though I hadn't the strength to lift my arm. I'm thoroughly relaxed."

That thought and the rhythm of your deep breathing ought to induce drowsiness very quickly; and you will drift away into a deep. How refreshing, how soothing, how sustaining such a sleep will be.

When you have developed the delightful feeling of this kind of relaxation, try to induct more of it into your daily life. And when you speak, try to feel as Madame Schumann-Heink does when she sings, "I feel as though every atom in my body were floating in space." When you can do that and breathe correctly and control your breath, you are on the high road to good voice production.

Chapter 4

THE IMPROVEMENT OF MEMORY

"No matter what walk of life one is in, a well developed memory is sure to prove of incalculable value."

-Saturday Evening Post

"When I intend to speak on anything that seems to me important, I consider what it is that I wish to impress upon my audience. I do not write my facts or my arguments, but make notes on two or three or four slips of note paper, giving the line of argument and the facts as they occur to my mind and I leave the words to come at call while I am speaking. There are occasionally short passages, which for accuracy, I may write down; as sometimes, also almost invariably the concluding words or sentences, may be written."

-John Bright

"The one who thinks over his experiences most and weaves them into a systematic relationship with each other will be the one with the best memory."

-William James

"If there is any one thing that I have learned which is more important than anything else and which I practice every day under any and all circumstances; it is concentration on the particular job I have in hand."

-Eugene Grace, former president of the Bethlehem Steel Co.

"The secret of a good memory is attention, and attention to a subject depends upon our interest in it. We rarely forget that which has made a deep impression on our minds."

-Tyron Edwards

"He who is not very strong in memory should not meddle with lying."

-Michel de Montaigue

WHY LINCOLN READ ALOUD

Lincoln, in his youth, attended a country school where the floor was made out of split logs, greased pages, torn from the copybooks and pasted over the windows, served instead of glass to let in the light. Only one copy of the textbook existed and the teacher read from it aloud. The pupils repeated the lesson after him, all of them talking at once. It made a constant uproar and the neighbors called it the "blab school."

At the "blab school," Lincoln formed a habit that clung to him all his life. He forever after, read aloud everything he wished to remember. Each morning, as soon as he reached his law office in Springfield, he spread himself out on the couch, hooked one long, ungainly leg over a neighboring chair and read the newspaper audibly. "He annoyed me," said his partner, "almost beyond endurance. I once asked him why he read in this fashion. This was his explanation: 'When I read aloud, two senses catch the idea, first, I see what I read; second, I hear it and therefore I can remember it better.'

His memory was extraordinarily retentive. "My mind," he said, "is like a piece of steel, very hard to scratch anything on it, but almost impossible, after you get it there, to rub it out."

Appealing to two of the senses was the method he used to do the scratching. Go and do likewise.

The ideal thing would be not only to see and hear the thing to be remembered, but to touch it, and smell it, and taste it.

But, above all else, see it. We are visual minded. Eye impressions stick. We can often remember a face, even though we cannot recall that person's name. The nerves that lead from the eye to the brain are twenty times as large as those leading from the ear to the brain. The Chinese have a proverb that says "one time seeing is worth a thousand times hearing."

Write down the name, the telephone number, the speech outline you want to remember. Look at it. Close your eyes. Visualize it in flaming letters of fire.

HOW MARK TWAIN LEARNED TO SPEAK
WITHOUT NOTES

The discovery of how to use his visual memory enabled Mark Twain to discard the notes that had hampered his speeches for years. Here is his story as he told it in *Harper's Magazine*:

"Dates are hard to remember because they consist of figures. Figures are monotonously unstriking in appearance and they don't take hold, they form no pictures and so they give the eye no chance to take hold. Pictures can make dates stick. They can make nearly anything stick, particularly if you make the picture yourself. Indeed, that is the great point, make the picture yourself. I know about this from experience. Thirty years ago, I was delivering a memorized lecture every night; and every night I had to help myself with a page of notes to keep from getting myself mixed. The notes consisted of beginnings of sentences and were eleven in number; and they ran something like this:

In that region the weather

At that time it was a custom

But in California one never heard

"Eleven of them. They initialed the brief of the lecture and protected me against skipping. But they all looked about alike on the page; they formed no picture; I had them by heart, but I could never with certainty, remember the order of their succession; therefore, I always had to keep those notes by me and look at them every little while. Once I mislaid them; you will not be able to imagine the terrors of that evening. I now saw that I must invent some other protection. So I got ten of the initial letters by heart in their proper order-1, A, B, and so on; and I went on the platform the next night with these marked in ink on my ten finger nails. But it didn't answer. I kept track of the fingers for awhile; then I lost it and after that I was never quite sure which finger I had used last. I couldn't lick off a letter after using it, for while that would have made success certain, it would also have provoked too much curiosity. There was curiosity enough without that. To the audience I seemed more interested in my fingernails than I was in my subject; one or two persons asked afterward what was the matter with my hands.

"It was then that the idea of pictures occurred to me! Then my troubles passed away. In two minutes I made six pictures with my pen and they did the work of the eleven catch sentences and did it perfectly. I threw the pictures away as soon as they were made, for I was sure I could shut my eyes and see them any time. That was a quarter of a century ago; the lecture vanished out of my head more

If you wish to try the test, spend fifteen minutes memorizing these picture numbers. If you prefer, make pictures of your own. For ten, think of *wren* or fountain *pen* or hen or anything that sounds like ten. Suppose that the tenth object recalled to you a windmill. See the hen sitting on the windmill or see it pumping ink to fill the fountain pen. Then, when you are asked what was the tenth object called, do not think of ten at all; but merely ask yourself where was the hen sitting. You may not think it will work, but try it. You can soon astound people with what they will consider to be an extraordinary capacity for remembering. You will find it entertaining if nothing else.

MEMORIZING A BOOK AS LONG AS
THE NEW TESTAMENT

One of the largest universities in the world is the El Hazar at Cairo. It is a Moslem institution with twenty-one thousand students. The entrance examination requires every applicant to repeat the Koran from memory. The Koran is about as long as the New Testament; and three days are required to recite it!

In China, students, have to memorize some of their religious and classical books.

How are these Arab and Chinese students, many of them men of mediocre ability, able to perform these apparently prodigious feats of memory?

By *repetition*, the second "natural law of remembering."

You can memorize an almost endless amount of material if you will repeat it often enough. Go over the knowledge you want to remember. Use it. Apply it. Employ the new word in your conversation. Call the stranger by name if you want to remember it. Talk over in conversation, the points you want to make in your public address. The knowledge that is used tends to stick.

THE KIND OF REPETITION THAT COUNTS

But the mere blind, mechanical going over a thing by rote is not enough. Intelligent repetition, repetition done in accordance with certain well-established traits of the mind, that is what we must have. For example, one professor gave his students a long list of nonsense syllables to memorize, such as "deyux," "qoli," and so on. He found that these students memorized as many of these syllables by thirty-eight repetitions, distributed over a period of three days, as they did by sixty-eight repetitions done at a single sitting. Other psychological tests have repeatedly shown similar results.

That is a very significant discovery about the working of our memories. It means that we know now that people, who sit down and repeat a thing over and over until it is finally fastented in their memory, are using twice as much time and energy, as is necessary to achieve the same results, when the repeating process is done at judicious intervals.

This peculiarity of the mind, if we can call it such, can be explained by two factors:

First, during the intervals between repetitions, our subconscious minds are busy making the associations more secure. As William James sagely remarked: "We learn to swim during the winter and to skate during the summer." Second, the mind, coming to the task at intervals, is not fatigued by the strain of an unbroken application. Sir Richard Burton, the translator of the "Arabian Nights," spoke twenty-seven languages like a native; yet he confessed that he never studied or practiced any language for more than fifteen minutes at a time, "for, after that, the brain lost its freshness."

Surely, now, in the face of these facts; no one, with any degree of common sense, will delay the preparation of a talk until the night before it is to be given because that person's memory will, of necessity, be working at only one-half its possible efficiency.

Here is a very helpful discovery about the way in which we forget. Psychological experiments have repeatedly shown that of the new material we have learned, we forget more during the first eight hours than during the next thirty days. An amazing ratio! So, immediately before you make a speech, look over your data, think over your facts, refresh your memory.

Lincoln knew the value of such a practice, and employed it. The scholarly Edward Everett preceded him on the program of speechmaking at Gettysburg. When he saw that Everett was approaching the close of his long, formal oration, Lincoln "grew visibly nervous, as he always did when another man was speaking and he was to follow." Hastily adjusting his spectacles, he took his manuscript from his pocket and read it silently to himself to refresh his memory.

WILLIAM JAMES EXPLAINS THE SECRET OF A GOOD MEMORY

So much for the first two laws of remembering. The third one, *association*, however, is the indispensable element in recalling. In fact, it is the explanation of memory itself. "Our mind is," as William James has sagely observed, "essentially an associating machine. Suppose I am silent for a moment and then say in commanding accents: 'Remember! Recollect!' Does your faculty of memory obey the order and reproduce any definite image from your past? Certainly not. It stands staring into vacancy and asking, 'What kind of a thing do you wish me to remember?' It needs, in short, a cue. But, if I say, remember the date of your birth or remember what you had for breakfast or remember the succession of notes in the musical scale; then your faculty of memory immediately produces the required result: the *cue* determines its vast set of potentialities towards a particular point. And if you now look to see how this happens, you immediately perceive that the *cue* is something contiguously associated with the thing recalled. The words, 'date of my birth,' have an ingrained association with a particular number, month and year; the words, 'breakfast this morning,' cut off all other lines of recall except those which lead to coffee and bacon and eggs; the words, 'musical scale,' are inveterate mental neighbors of do, re, mi, fa, sol, la, etc. The laws of association govern, in fact, all the trains of our thinking that are not interrupted by sensations breaking on us from without. Whatever appears in the mind must be *introduced*; and, when introduced, it is as the associate of something already there. This is as true of what you are recollecting as it is of everything else you think of. An educated memory depends upon an organized system of associations; and its goodness depends on two of their peculiarities: first, on the persistency of the associations and second, on their number. The 'secret of a good memory' is thus the secret of forming diverse and multiple associations with every fact we care to retain. But this forming of associations with a fact. What is it but thinking about the fact as much as possible? Briefly, then, of two people with the same outward experiences, *the one who thinks over experiences most*, and weaves them into the most systematic relations with each other, will be the one with the best memory."

HOW TO LINK YOUR FACTS TOGETHER

Very good, but how are we to set about weaving our facts into systematic relations with each other? The answer is: by finding their meaning, by thinking them over. For example, if you will ask and answer these questions about any new fact, that process will help to weave it into a systematic relation with other facts.

a.   Why is this so?

b.   How is this so?

c.   When is it so?

d.   Where is it so?

e.   Who said it is so?

If it is a stranger's name, for example, and it is a common one, we can perhaps tie it to some friend who bears the same name. On the other hand, if it is unusual, we can take occasion to say so. This often leads the stranger to talk about his or her name. For example: while writing this chapter, I was introduced to a Mrs. Soter. I requested her to spell the name and remarked upon its unusualness. "Yes," she replied, "it is very uncommon. It is a Greek word meaning 'the Savior'." Then she told me about her husband's people who had come from Athens and of the high positions they had held in the government there. I have found it quite easy to get people to talk about their names, and it always helps me to remember them.

Observe the stranger's appearance sharply. Note the color of his or her eyes and hair; and look closely at facial features. Note dress style. Listen to the manner of talking. Get a clear, keen, vivid impression of that person's looks and personality; and associate these with his or her name. The next time these sharp impressions return to your mind, they will help bring the name with them.

Haven't you had the experience, when meeting someone for the second or third time, to discover that although you could remember that person's business or profession you could not recall the name? The reason is this: a person's business is something definite and concrete. It has a meaning. It will adhere like a band-aid, while a

There is, however, a method of tying your points together that is easy, rapid, and all but foolproof. I refer to the use of a nonsense sentence.

To illustrate: suppose you wish to discuss a veritable jumble of ideas, unassociated and hence hard to remember, such as; for example, *cow, cigar, Napoleon, house, religion*. Let us see if we cannot weld those ideas like the links of a chain by means of this absurd sentence: "The cow smoked a cigar and hooked Napoleon, and the house burned down with religion."

Now, will you please cover the above sentence with your hand while you answer these questions? What is the third point in that talk; the fifth; fourth; second; first?

Does the method work? It does! And the readers of this book are urged to use it.

Any group of ideas can be linked together in some such fashion and the more ridiculous the sentence used for the linking; the easier it will be to recall.

WHAT TO DO IN CASE OF A COMPLETE BREAKDOWN

Let us suppose that, in spite of all the preparation and precaution, a speaker, in the middle of the talk, suddenly finds his or her mind a blank, suddenly is staring at the audience completely balked, unable to go on - a terrifying situation. The speaker's pride rebels at sitting down in confusion and defeat. One may feel that the next point or some point will come to mind in the next ten, fifteen seconds but even fifteen seconds of frantic silence before an audience would be little less than disastrous. What is to be done? When a certain U.S. Senator found himself in this situation he asked his audience if he were speaking loudly enough, if he could be heard distinctly in the back of the room. He knew that he was. He was not seeking information. He was seeking time. And in that momentary pause, he grasped his thought and proceeded.

But perhaps the best lifesaver in such a mental hurricane is this: use the last word, or phrase, or idea in your last sentence for the beginning of a new sentence. Let us see how it works in practice. Let us imagine that a speaker, talking on Business Success, finds himself in a blind mental alley after having said: "The average employee does not get ahead because he takes so little real interest in his work, displays so little initiative."

"*Initiative.*" Start a sentence with "*initiative.*" You will probably have no idea of what you are going to say or how you are going to end the sentence, but nevertheless, begin. Even a poor showing is more to be desired than utter defeat.

"Initiative means originality, doing a thing on your own, without eternally waiting to be told."

That is not a scintillating observation. It won't make speech history. But isn't it better than an agonizing silence? Our last phrase was what? "waiting to be told." All right, let us start a new sentence with that idea.

"The constant telling and guiding and driving of employees who refuse to do any original thinking is one of the most exasperating things imaginable."

Well, we got through that one. Let us plunge again. This time we must say something about imagination.

"Imagination, that is what is needed. Vision. 'Where there is no vision,' Solomon said, 'the people perish.' "

We did two that time without a hitch. Let us take heart and continue.

"The number of employees who perish each year in the battle of business is really lamentable. I say lamentable, because with just a little more loyalty, a little more ambition, a little more enthusiasm, these same men and women might have lifted themselves over the line of demarcation between success and failure. Yet the failure in business never admits that this is the case."

And so on... . While the speaker is saying these platitudes off the top of his mind, he should, at the same time, be thinking hard of the next point in his planned speech, of the thing he had originally intended to say.

This endless chain method of talking will, if continued very long, trap the speaker into discussing plum pudding or the price of canary birds. However, it is a splendid first aid to the injured mind broken down temporarily through forgetfulness; and, as such, it has been the means of resuscitating many a gasping and dying speech.

WE CANNOT IMPROVE OUR MEMORIES FOR ALL CLASSES OF THINGS

I have pointed out in this chapter, how we may improve our *methods* of getting vivid impressions, of repeating and of tying our facts together. But memory is, so essentially, a matter of association that "there can be," as William James pointed out, "no improvement of the general or elementary faculty of memory; there can only be improvement of our memory for special systems of associated things."

By memorizing, for instance, a quotation a day from Shakespeare, we may improve our memory for literary quotations to a surprising degree. Each additional quotation will find many friends in the mind to tie to. But the memorizing of everything from Hamlet to Romeo, will not necessarily aid one, in retaining facts about the stock market or the best way to roast a turkey.

Let us repeat: if we apply and use the principles discussed in this chapter, we will improve our *manner* and *efficiency* for memorizing anything; but, if we do not apply these principles, then the memorizing of ten million facts about baseball will not help us in the slightest in memorizing facts about the stock market. Such unrelated data cannot be tied together. "Our mind is essentially an associating machine."

IN A NUTSHELL

1.   The average person does not use above ten percent of the actual inherited capacity for memory. Ninety percent is wasted by violating the natural laws of remembering.

2.   These natural laws of remembering are three: impression, repetition, association.

3.   Get a deep, vivid impression of the thing you wish to remember. To do that you must-

    a.   Concentrate. That was the secret of Roosevelt's memory.

    b.   Observe closely. Get an accurate impression. A camera won't take pictures in a fog; neither will your mind retain foggy impressions.

c.   Get your impressions through as many of the senses as possible. Lincoln read aloud whatever he wished to remember so that he would get both a visual and an auditory impression.

d.   Above all else, be sure to get eye impressions. They stick. The nerves leading from the eye to the brain are twenty times as large as those leading from the ear to the brain. Mark Twain could not remember the outline of his speech when he used notes; but when he threw away his notes and used pictures to recall his various headings, all his troubles vanished.

4.   The second law of memory is repetition. Thousands of Moslem students memorize the Koran, a book about as long as the New Testament, and they do it very largely through the power of repetition. We can memorize anything, within reason, if we repeat it often enough. But bear these facts in mind as you repeat-

a.   Do not sit down and repeat a thing over and over until you have it engraved on your memory. Go over it once or twice, then drop it; come back later and go over it again. Repeating at intervals, in that manner, will enable you to memorize a thing in about one-half the time required to do it at one sitting.

b.   After we memorize a thing, we forget as much during the first eight hours, as we do during the next thirty days; so go over your notes just a few minutes before you rise to make your talk.

5.   The third law of memory is association. The only way anything can possibly be remembered, at all, is by associating it with some other fact. "Whatever appears in the mind," says William James, "must be introduced; and, when introduced, it is as the associate of something already there. The one who thinks over his experiences most, and weaves them into the most systematic relation with each other, will be the one with the best memory."

6.   When you wish to associate one fact with others already in the mind, think over the new fact from all angles. Ask about it, such questions as these: "Why is this so? How is this so? When is it so? Where is it so? Who said it is so?"

7.   To remember a stranger's name, ask questions about it- how is it spelled, etc.? Observe his or her looks sharply. Try to connect the name with the face. Find out his or her business, profession or occupation and try to invent some nonsense phrase that will connect the name with that activity.

8.   To remember dates, associate them with prominent dates already in the mind. For example, the three hundredth anniversary of Shakespeare's birth occurred during the Civil War.

9.   To remember the points of your address, arrange them in such logical

order that one leads naturally to the next. In addition, one can make a nonsense sentence out of the main points, for example, "The cow smoked a cigar and hooked Napoleon and the house burned down with religion."

10.   If, in spite of all precautions, you suddenly forget what you intended to say, you may be able to save yourself from complete defeat by using the last words of your last sentence as the first words in a new one. This can be continued until you are able to think of your next point.

SPEECH BUILDING

WORDS OFTEN MISPRONOUNCED

How many of the following words do you hear mispronounced almost daily? One may say AD-dress for ad-DRESS, and A-dult for A-DULT, and find his errors undetected by many educated people; but who can forgive such sloven, such gross faults as "praps" and "presidunt" and "progrum"? They are as offensive to the cultivated ear as soiled linen to the eye. For them and their ilk, there can be no excuse, no forgiveness, no explanation except sheer intellectual lethargy and frowziness. Their use condemns one as lacking in culture, as deficient in mental self-respect. Yet I have heard an occasional radio announcer speak of the "program." Have you?

Do not say:

except	for	accept
agin	"	again
ailmunt	"	ailment
ambassadur	"	ambassador
unuther	"	another
becuz	"	because
barrul	"	barrel
cramberry	"	cranberry
crejulus	"	credulous
ejication	"	education
fillum	"	film
forchin	"	fortune
frum	"	from

87

few-ul	for	fuel
genl'mun	"	gentlemen
guv'ment	"	government
indivijual	"	individual
kep'	"	kept
lemme	"	let me
levul	"	level
literachoor	"	literature
marvul	"	marvel
meludy	"	melody
modust	"	modest
nearust	"	nearest
novus	"	novice
parsnup	"	parsnip
praps	"	perhaps
perul	"	peril
pitcher	"	picture
po-um	"	poem
portrut	"	portrait
perdicament	"	predicament
presidunt	"	president
progrum	"	program
reco'nize	"	recognize
sassy	"	saucy
savij	"	savage
slep	"	slept
spirut	"	spirit
stiddy	"	steady
supprised	"	surprised
swep	"	swept
turnup	"	turnip
victum	"	victim
wuz	"	was

for memorizing lines and not have the *ability* to act well.

CAN - MAY. *Can* denotes power and ability. Do not confuse *can* with *may* which refers to permission. "*Can* I use your knife?", literally means have I the power to use it. The chances are that I have, unless I am paralyzed. If I wish to ask for permission, I should say, "*May* I use your knife."

VOICE EXERCISE - RELAXING THE THROAT

Strain and tension, we learned in the last chapter, impair the voice and render it disagreeable. Where does this tension usually get in its deadly work? In what part of the body?

There can be no question about that. It raises its head like a viper and licks out its fiery tongue almost always in the same place: the throat. The nervous gripping of the muscles there causes roughness of the voice, fatigue, hoarseness and even sore throat. There is the so-called "teacher's sore throat," the well-known "minister's sore throat," and the "speaker's sore throat." A person can converse in business all day, month after month, without suffering from a sore throat. Why, then, should that affliction be contracted when he or she attempts to do considerable public speaking? The answer can be given in one word: tension. The organs of speech are not being properly used. Nervousness unconsciously contracts the muscles of the throat. By taking deep breaths, the chest rises and the muscular effort continues to hold it high. The strain of these chest muscles tightens the throat. He, by trying to be emphatic and to be heard, the speaker tries to force the words out. The result ? Breathy tones, harsh tones, unpleasant tones, tones that will not carry.

The right way to deal with this is to relax the throat entirely. It ought to be merely the chimney up which the column of air passes from your lungs.

" The old Italian singing masters used to boast. "L'Italiano -non ha gola"- "The Italian singer has no throat." None of the great singers, Caruso, Melba, Patti, Mary Garden, none of them sang as if he or she had a throat. That is the way a speaker should speak. All the muscles above the collarbone should be relaxed. In reality, all the muscles from the waist up should be relaxed.

How are you going to be sure of this highly desired, relaxed and open throat? Here is a very simple way to do it, one that you cannot easily forget. Suppose that someone has asked you, "Do the Italian singers have a throat?" You are going to reply with a "no." Close your eyes. Think of a yawn. Feel yourself starting to make one. It begins, you know, with a deep breath; in fact, it is the need for more breath that causes the yawn. As you take the breath, and the moment before the yawn breaks, your throat is open and relaxed. Now, instead of yawning, speak. Think no, say "no." Didn't that tone sound well to your ears? Why? Because the conditions for it were right.

We have learned some fundamental lessons now in tone production: deep diaphragmatic breathing, a relaxed body, an open throat.

Practice this exercise twenty times a day. Start to yawn. Feel the lower part of your lungs filling with air, pushing against the lower ribs, the back, flattening and pressing down that arched muscle called the diaphragm. Now, instead of yawning, speak. Speak a musical sentence like this: *Lovely Lolita drifting along in the moonlight over the murmuring lagoon.*

As you speak, feel that you are drinking in the words, not back into your throat, but up into the open chambers of your head. Feel the same openness in the head chambers that you feel when drinking in a deep breath through the nose.

Lastly, after taking in the deep breath, relax the chest entirely. Feel it pivoted on, riding on, the cushion of air inside. Your relaxed breast ought to ride on the breath just as your tires and your car ride on the air in the blown up inner tubes. If you do not relax your chest in this manner, the muscular effort that you use in holding it high will tighten your throat. On the other hand, do not construe this to mean that you are to have a caved in chest as you are breathing. No. Hold the chest, not the shoulders, high during inspiration and then let the weight of it ride on the air pressure in the middle of your body.

Chapter 5

KEEPING THE AUDIENCE AWAKE

"The man or woman of enthusiastic trend always exercises a magnetic influence over those with whom he or she comes in contact."

-H. Addington Bruce

"Be intensely in earnest. Enthusiasm invites enthusiasm."

-Russell H. Conwell

"I like the person who bubbles over with enthusiasm. Better be a geyser than a mud puddle."

-John G. Shedd, President of Marshall Field and Co.

"He did it with all his heart and prospered."

-Second Chronicles

"Merit begets confidence, confidence begets enthusiasm, enthusiasm conquers the world."

-Walter H. Cattingham, President of Sherwin Williams Co.

"Enthusiasm is the mother of effort; and without it nothing great was ever accomplished."

-Ralph Waldo Emerson

"Be too large to worry, too noble for anger, too strong for fear and too happy to permit the presence of trouble. Think well of yourself and proclaim this fact to the world; not in loud words but in great deeds."

-Optimists' creed

"Achievement is the knowledge that you have studied and worked hard and done the best that is in you. Success is being praised by others, and that's nice too, but not as important or satisfying. Always aim for achievement and forget about success."

-Helen Hayes

Chapter 5

KEEPING THE AUDIENCE AWAKE

S herman Rogers and I once addressed the same meeting of the St. Louis Chamber of Commerce. I spoke first and, had I had a good excuse, I would have left immediately afterwards, for he was billed as "the lumber-jack orator." I frankly expected to be bored for I class the usual so-called "oratory" with wax flowers. This day, however, I was delightfully surprised; Mr. Rogers made easily, one of the best talks I have ever heard.

And who is Sherman Rogers? A genuine lumber-jack, who has spent most of his life in the big woods of the West. He knows nothing and cares less than nothing about the rules for public speaking that have been set down so elaborately in learned books on eloquence. His talk did not have polish; but it had punch. It lacked finesse; but it had fire. He made grammatical errors and did half a dozen things that are not according to Hoyle; but it is not faults that kill a talk; it is lack of virtues.

His speech was a huge, raw piece of palpitating experience, torn right out of his own life as a laborer and a boss of laborers. It didn't smack of books. It was a live thing. It fairly crouched and sprang at you. Everything that he said leaped flaming hot from his heart. The effect on the audience was electrical.

The secret of his success? The secret of every phenomenal success: "Every great movement in the annals of history," said Emerson, "is the triumph of enthusiasm."

It is derived, that magic name, from two Greek words: *en*, meaning in; and *theos*, meaning God. Enthusiasm is literally *God* in us. The enthusiastic person, is one, who speaks as if he or she were possessed by God.

There was a time, when I put considerable reliance in the *rules* of public speaking; but with the passing of the years I have come to put more and more faith in the *spirit* of speaking.

"Eloquence," said William Jennings. Bryan,"may be defined as the speech of one who knows what he is talking about; and means what he says, it is thought on fire. Knowledge is of little use to the speaker without earnestness. Persuasive speech is from heart to heart, not from mind to mind. It is difficult for a speaker to deceive the audience as to their own feelings. Over two thousand years ago, one of the Latin poets expressed this thought when he said: 'If you would draw tears from others' eyes, yourself the signs of grief must show.' "

"If I wish to compose or write or pray or preach well," said Martin Luther, "I must be angry. Then all the blood in my veins is stirred and my understanding is sharpened."

Perhaps we don't have to be exactly angry, you and I, but we must be aroused and sincere and intensely in earnest. Even a horse is affected by spirited talk. A famous animal trainer said that he had known an angry word to raise the pulse of a horse, ten beats per minute. Surely, an audience is as sensitive as a horse. This is a most important fact to remember: every time we speak we determine the attitude of our hearers. We hold them in the hollow of our hands. If we are lackadaisical, they will be lackadaisical. If we are reserved, they will be reserved. If we are only mildly concerned, they will be only mildly concerned. But if we are deadly in earnest about what we say, and if we say it with feeling and spontaneity and force and contagious conviction, they cannot keep from catching our spirit to a degree.

Much as we would like to think we are moved by reason; the whole world is, in fact, moved by emotion. The speaker who tries to be very serious or very witty may easily fail, but the speaker who appeals to you with real convictions never fails. No matter whether the greatest subject to the speaker is a personal concern or a national issue, he or she must be really deeply convinced that it has meaning for you, in order for the speech to excite you. It won't matter how his or her convictions are clothed, but only with what sincerity and emotional power, they are launched at you.

Given heat and earnestness and enthusiasm, a speaker's influence expands like steam. He can have five hundred faults; but he can hardly fail. The great pianist, Arthur Rubinstein, it is said, played myriads of false notes; but nobody cared, for he could get the poetry of Chopin into souls that had never seen anything in a sunset before, except a big red disk sinking behind a barn on the horizon.

History records that before Pericles, the mighty Athenian leader, spoke, he prayed to the gods that not a single unworthy word might escape his lips. He had his heart in his messages; and they went straight to the heart of a nation.

Willa Cather, one of America's most distinguished woman novelists, said, "Every artist's secret" and every public speaker ought to be an artist, "is passion. It is an open secret and perfectly safe. Like heroism, it is inimitable in cheap materials."

Passion.... Feeling.... Spirit.... Emotional sincerity; get these qualities in your talk and your auditors will condone; yes, will hardly be conscious of minor shortcomings. History bears this out: Lincoln spoke in an unpleasantly high tone. Demosthenes stammered. Some prominent and successful speakers had weak voices, stammered or stuttered or swallowed their words, yet they had an earnestness that triumphed over all these defects; an emotional urge that blasted all handicaps to nothingness.

HAVE SOMETHING THAT YOU VERY MUCH WANT TO SAY

The essence of a good speech is that the speaker really has something that he really wants to say.

This was illustrated some years ago in a public speaking competition at Columbia University. There were half a dozen undergraduates; all of them elaborately trained, all of them anxious to acquit themselves well. But, with only a single exception, what they were striving for was to win the medal. They had little or no desire to persuade. They had chosen their topics because these topics permitted oratorical development. They had no deep personal interest in the arguments they were making. And their successive speeches were merely exercises in the art of delivery. The exception was a Zulu Prince. He had selected as his theme, 'The Contribution of Africa to Modern Civilization.' He put intense feeling into every word he uttered. His speech was no mere exercise; it was a living thing, born of conviction and enthusiasm. He spoke as the representative of his people, of his continent; he had something to say that he wanted to say; and he said it with sympathetic sincerity.

Although, he was possibly no more accomplished in the art than two or three of his competitors, he was awarded the medal. What the judges recognized was that his address had the true fire of the orator. In comparison with his fervid appeal, the other speeches were only exercises in elocution.

Right here is where many speakers fail. Their expression is motivated by no conviction; no desire, no impetus is stirring in their talks.

"Ah, very good," you say, "but how am I to develop this earnestness and spirit and enthusiasm that you praise so highly?" This much is sure: you will never develop it by talking from the surface. Any discerning listener can detect whether you are talking from skin-deep impressions or whether your expression is welling up from deep within you. So shake yourself out of your inertia. Put your heart in your work. Dig. Seek for the hidden resources that lie buried away inside you. Get the facts and the causes behind the facts. Concentrate. Dwell on them, brood over them until they matter to you. In the last analysis, you see it is all conditioned back upon thorough preparation and the right kind of preparation. Heart preparation is as essential as head preparation. To illustrate:

I trained a number of people in the New York City Chapter of the American Institute of Banking to speak during a thrift campaign. One of the women, in particular, lacked force. She was talking merely because she wanted to speak, not because she was fired with zeal for thrift. The first step in training that woman was to warm her mind and heart. I told her to go off by herself and to think over the subject until she became enthusiastic about it. I asked her to remember that the Probate Court Records in New York show that more than 85% of the people leave nothing at all at death; that only a very small percentage have assets of any significance. She was to keep constantly in mind that she was not asking people to do her a favour or something that they could not afford to do. She was to say to herself, "I am preparing these people to have meat and bread and clothes and comfort in their old age, and to leave their families protected." She must remember she was going out to perform a great social service.

She thought over these facts, burned them into her mind and got a realizing sense of their importance. She aroused her own interest, stirred her own enthusiasm and came to feel that her mission was almost holy. Then, when she went out to talk, there was a ring to her words that carried conviction.

THE SECRET OF A TRIUMPH

"I must live," cried a young man to Voltaire; and the philosopher replied. "I do not perceive the necessity."

That, in many instances, will be the attitude of the world towards what you have to say: it won't perceive the necessity of its being said. But you, if you would succeed, must *feel* the necessity, if there is one. The thing ought to grip you. It ought, for the time being, seem to you like the most important thing on *terra firma*.

Dwight L. Moody, the noted evangelist, became so stirred in the preparation of his sermon on *Grace*, so wrought up in his search for truth, that he seized his hat, left his study, strode out into the street and accosted the first man he met with the abrupt inquiry: "Do you know what *Grace* is?" Is it any wonder that a man, fired with such emotional earnestness and intensity, exerted a magic power over audiences?

A short time ago, a member of a course I was conducting in Paris, spoke evening after evening, in a colorless fashion. He was something of a student and he had his facts all right, piles of them. But he had not welded them together with the heat of his own interest. He lacked spirit. He didn't talk as if what he had to say was very vital, so naturally, the audience paid little heed. They took his speech at his own appraisement. Time and again, stopping him, I endeavored to drill force into him, to wake him up; but I often felt as if I were trying to coax steam out of a cold radiator. Finally, I did succeed in persuading him that his method of preparation was at fault. I convinced him that he ought to establish some kind of telegraphic communication between his head and his heart. I told him that he must give us not only the facts, but that he ought to reveal his attitude towards those facts.

The next week he appeared with ideas about which he felt strongly enough to make the expression of them worthwhile. At last, he was passionately concerned about something. He had a message that he truly loved. He was willing to sweat blood for it, and his talk won long and hearty applause. It was an abrupt triumph. He had generated a little heartfelt earnestness. That is a fundamental part of preparation. As we learned in Chapter 2, the preparation of a speech, a real speech, does not consist in merely getting some mechanical words down on paper, nor of memorizing phrases. Neither does it consist in lifting a few thoughts second hand from some book or newspaper article. No, no. But it does consist in digging away down deep into your own mind and heart and life, and bringing forth some convictions and enthusiasms that are essentially yours. Yours! YOURS! Dig. Dig. Dig. It is there. Never doubt it. Mines of it, quantities of it, of whose existence you have never even dreamed. Do you, yourself, realize the strength of your own potentialities? I doubt it. William James said that most people do not develop more than ten percent of their possible mental powers. Worse than an eight-cylinder machine with only one cylinder sparking! Yes, the great thing in a speech is not the cold phraseology, but the spirit, the convictions behind that phraseology. Always remember that you are the most important factor in your talk. Hear these golden words from Emerson! They contain a world of wisdom: *"Use what language you will, you can never say anything but what you are."* That is one of the most significant statements I ever heard about the art of self-expression; and, for the sake of emphasis, I am going to repeat it: *"Use what language you will, you can never say anything but what you are."*

A LINCOLN SPEECH THAT WON A LAWSUIT

Lincoln may never have read that, but one thing is certain: he knew the truth of it. One day the widow of a Revolutionary War soldier, an old woman bent with age, hobbled into his office, telling him of a pension agent who had taken from her the exorbitant fee of two hundred dollars, for collecting a sum of twice that amount, that was due with her. Lincoln was indignant and he brought suit immediately.

How did he prepare for this case? He prepared by reading a biography of Washington and a history of the Revolutionary War, by quickening his enthusiasm, by kindling his feelings and emotions. When he spoke, he recounted the oppressions that had stirred the patriots to turn and fight for liberty. He pictured the untold hardships they had gone through, the suffering they had endured at Valley Forge, hungry, barefooted and with bleeding feet creeping over the ice and snow. Then, in wrath, he turned to the rascal who had fleeced a widow of one of those heroes out of half her pension. His eyes flashed as he poured out his bitterest denunciation, "skinning" the defendant, as he declared he would do.

"Time rolls by," he said in conclusion. "The heroes of '76 have passed away and are encamped on the other shore. The soldier has gone to rest and now, crippled, blinded, and broken, his widow comes to you and to me, gentlemen of the jury, to right her wrongs. She was not always thus. She was once a beautiful young woman. Her step was as elastic, her face as fair and her voice as sweet as any that rang in the mountains of old Virginia. But now she is poor and defenseless. Out here on the prairies of Illinois, many hundreds of miles away from the scenes of her childhood, she appeals to us who enjoy the privileges achieved for us by the patriots of the Revolution, for our sympathetic aid and manly protection. All I ask is, shall we befriend her?"

As he finished, some of the jury were in tears, and they returned a verdict for every cent the old woman asked. Lincoln became her surety for costs, paid her hotel bill and her fare home and charged her nothing for his legal services. A few days later, Lincoln's partner picked up a little scrap of paper in the office, read Lincoln's outline for his speech and burst into laughter:

"No contract. Not professional services. Unreasonable charge. Money retained by Def't not given to Pl'ff. Revolutionary war. Describe Valley Forge privations. Pl'ff's husband. Soldier leaving for army. Skin Def't. Close."

I hope that I have made plain that the first requisite in generating your warmth and enthusiasm is to prepare until you have a real message you want to get across. The next step is-

"ACT IN EARNEST"

As we noted in Chapter 1, William James has pointed out "action and feeling go together; and, by regulating the action which is under the most direct control of the will, we can indirectly regulate the feeling which is not."

So, to feel earnest and enthusiastic, stand up and *act* in earnest and be enthusiastic. Stop leaning against the table. Stand tall. Stand still. Don't rock back and forth. Don't bob up and down. Don't shift your weight from one foot to the other and back again like a tired horse. In short, don't make a lot of nervous movements that will proclaim your lack of ease and self-possession to the housetops. Control yourself physically. It will convey a sense of poise and power. Stand up and stand out like a strong competitor in a race. I repeat: fill your lungs with oxygen. Fill them to the full. Look straight at your audience. Look at them, as if you had something urgent to say and as if you knew it was urgent. Look at them with the confidence and courage of a teacher viewing her pupils, for you are a teacher and they are there to hear you and to be taught. So speak out confidently and with energy. "Lift up your voice," said the Prophet Isaiah, "lift it up. Be not afraid."

And use emphatic gestures. Never mind, just now, whether they are beautiful or graceful. Think only of making them forceful and spontaneous. Make them now, not for the sense they will convey to others, but for what they will do for you. And they will do wonders. Even if you are speaking to a radio audience, gesture, gesture. Your gestures won't, of course, be visible to the unseen hearers, but the result of your gestures will be audible to them. They will give increased aliveness and energy to your tones and to your whole manner.

How often have I stopped a lifeless speaker in the midst of a talk and drilled and compelled the speaker to use emphatic gestures, which did not at the time feel appropriate. But the physical action of the forced gestures, finally awakened and stimulated the speaker and the gestures became spontaneous. Even the speaker's face brightened and was reflected in a more earnest, more emphatic bearing and attitude. *Acting in earnest makes one feel in earnest.* "Assume a virtue," Shakespeare advised, "if you have it not."

Above all else, open your mouth and speak out. The average man, who attempts to speak in public, cannot be heard even thirty feet away.

When addressing a small group, such as a committee in your church, or community group or a group of colleagues at your job, you will probably not have a public address system to amplify your voice. But even in a small group it's important to speak up. People at the other end of the room may not hear your voice clearly and distinctly. Use conversational tones; but enlarge them. Intensify them. We can read fine print, a foot from the eye; but it takes bold headlines to be seen across a hall.

When addressing a larger group, you will probably use a microphone. Unfortunately, many people do not know how to make the most of this tool. They stand too far away or too close, Adjust the microphone so it is at the level of your mouth. This is particularly important, when the previous speaker is much taller or shorter than you. Reset it before you start talking. Ideally you should stand between six inches and twelve inches away from the microphone. Speak in your natural voice. It's not necessary to shout into the mike.

Sometimes its necessary to turn away from the microphone when demonstrating or pointing to an exhibit or chalk board. Try to avoid this by stating your point first. Remember that although you hear yourself, your voice may not carry out to the back or even the center of the room when you are even a step away from that mike.

If you know you will be moving around as part of your presentation, arrange to use a portable microphone. You've all seen singers walking around holding a mike close to their mouths while they sing. Some speakers do much the same. Doing this keeps their voices out to the audience, but it also hides their faces and can be distracting. Rather than holding a portable mike, it's far better to use a wireless lavaliere microphone, which can be clipped on your clothes or worn as a pendant. These wireless devices allow you to walk anywhere in the room and still be connected to the P.A. system.

THE FIRST THING TO DO WHEN THE AUDIENCE GOES TO SLEEP

A country preacher once asked Henry Ward Beecher how to keep an audience awake on a hot Sunday afternoon, and Beecher told him to have an usher take a sharp stick and prod the preacher.

I like that. It is superb. It is glorified common sense. It would do more for the average speaker than nine-tenths of all the erudite tomes that have ever been written on the art of eloquence.

One of the surest ways to get students to limber up and abandon and really let themselves go, would be to knock them down before they started. It would put fire and spirit and aliveness into the speech. Actors know the value of shaking themselves awake before they make their stage entrance. Houdini did it by leaping about the back stage, striking the air vigorously with his fists, sparring with an imaginary antagonist. Another actor sometimes deliberately planned to work himself into a perfect rage over any pretext, perhaps it was because some stage hand was breathing too audible, any excuse that would serve to give him the heightened energy, the surging of spirit that he courted. I have seen actors standing in the wings, waiting for their cues and beating their breasts savagely. I have sent students, just before they spoke, into an adjoining room to pummel their bodies until their blood leaped and their faces and eyes glowed with life. I frequently force students to preface their practice talks in my course, repeating the A.B.C.'s with violent gestures and all the vigor and anger that can possibly be commanded. Isn't it highly desirable to go before your hearers like a thoroughbred, straining at the bit?

Immediately before you speak, get, if possible, a thorough rest. The ideal thing is to undress and go to bed for a few hours. If possible, follow that with a cold plunge and a vigorous rubdown. Better still, far better, take a swim.

Geri Pell, who travels the country giving talks on financial management, often must fly to a city, arriving less than an hour before addressing her audience. She makes a point of putting a sleeping mask and earplugs in her travel bag and to use them on the plane so she can get an undisturbed nap during the flight.

The most successful speakers are people of great vitality and recuperative force, people who have pre-eminently the explosive power, by which they can thrust their materials out. They are catapults and all go down before them.

"WEASEL WORDS" AND ONIONS

Put energy behind what you say, and say it positively. But don't be too positive. Only an ignoramus is positive about everything; but only a weakling prefaces every remark with *it seems to me, or perhaps, or in my opinion.*

The almost universal trouble with beginning speakers is not that they are too positive, but that they vitiate their talks with these timid phrases. I remember listening to a tourist describe a motor trip through Connecticut. "On the left side of the road," he said, "there *seemed* to be a field of onions." Now, there is no *seeming* about onions. They either are or are not. And it does not require extraordinary powers to recognize an onion field when one sees it.

Yet this shows to what absurd lengths a speaker will sometimes go.

Teddy Roosevelt called such expressions "weasel words", for a weasel sucks the heart out of an egg and leaves nothing but the empty shell. That is what these phrases do to your talk.

Shrinking, apologetic tones and eggshell phrases will riot confidence and conviction. Imagine business houses using such slogans as these: "It seems to us the Dell is the computer you will eventually buy." "In our opinion, the Prudential has the strength of Gibraltar." "We think you'll use our flour eventually; why not now?"

Propagandists have shown us that if one repeats the same thing with vigor over and over again, whether or not it be true, people will believe them. The Nazi leaders constantly reiterated that the Germans were a superior people, that even non-Germans began to believe it.

But do not, as I have said, be too positive on all occasions. There are times, there are places, there are subjects, there are audiences, where too much positiveness will hinder rather than help. In general, the higher the level of intelligence of one's hearers, the less successful mere forceful assertions will be. Thinking people want to be led not driven. They want to have the facts presented and to draw their own conclusions. They like to be asked questions not to have a ceaseless stream of direct statements poured at them.

LOVE YOUR AUDIENCE

A few years ago, I had to employ and train a number of public lecturers in England. After painful and costly trials, three of them had to be dismissed and one had to be sent back three thousand miles to America. Their main trouble was that they were not genuinely interested in serving their audiences. They were chiefly concerned, not about others, but about themselves and their pay envelopes. Everyone could feel it. They were cold to their audiences; and their audiences, in return, were cold to them. I have made a special study of Lincoln as a public speaker. He is, undoubtedly, the most loved man America has ever produced; and unquestionably, he has delivered some of America's best speeches. Although he was a genius in some ways, I am inclined to believe that his power with audiences was due, in no small measure, to his sympathy and honesty and goodness.

He loved people. "His heart," said his wife, "is as large as his arms are long." "The secret of my success," said Madam Schumann-Heink, the famous prima donna, "is absolute devotion to the audience. I love my audiences. They are all my friends. I feel a bond with them, the moment I step before them." So that is the secret of her worldwide triumph. Let us try to cultivate the same spirit.

KNOW YOUR AUDIENCE
Even the most skilled orator may fail to communicate effectively if the audience doesn't understand the message. Whether your listeners are just people you know well or a large diversified audience, choose words that are easily understood by them. If the people you are addressing come from a technical background, you can use technical terminology. Your listeners will clearly and readily understand those special terms. But if you present technical material to an audience unfamiliar with it, skip the technical language and "translate" it into words they can understand and use examples that they can relate to.

IN A NUTSHELL

1.   Every time you speak, you determine the attitude of your hearers towards what you say. If you are lackadaisical, they will be lackadaisical. If you are only mildly concerned, they will be only mildly concerned. If you are enthusiastic, they will be sure to catch something of your spirit. Enthusiasm is one of the bigger, if not the biggest, factors in delivery.

2.   The speaker who tries to be very serious or very witty, may easily fail, but the speaker who appeals to you with real conviction never fails. If the speaker is really deeply convinced of the value of the message, the speech will go like a flame.

3.   In spite of the tremendous importance of this quality of contagious conviction and enthusiasm, most people lack it.

4.   The essence of a good speech is that the speaker really has something which he or she really wants to say.

5.   Think over your facts, burn their real importance into your mind. Try your own enthusiasm before you attempt to convince others.

6.   Establish a telegraphic communication between your head and heart. We want you not only to give us the facts but also to reveal your attitude towards those facts.

7.   "Use what language you will, you can never say anything but what you are." The big thing in a speech is not the words spoken but the spirit of the person behind the words.

8.   To develop earnestness, to feel enthusiastic, act enthusiastic. Stand tall, look straight at your audience. Use emphatic gestures.

9.   Above all else, open your mouth and speak so you can be heard. Many speakers cannot be heard thirty feet away. Learn to use the microphone as your major tool in reaching large audiences.

10.   When a country minister asked Henry Ward Beecher what to do when an audience went to sleep on a hot Sunday afternoon, Beecher replied, "Have an usher get a sharp stick and prod the preacher." This is one of the best bits of advice ever given on the art of public speaking.

11.   Don't weaken your speech with "weasel" words, such as" it seems to me," "in my humble opinion."

12.   Love your audience.

13.   Tailor the words you use to the level of understanding your audience possesses.

SPEECH BUILDING

WORDS OFTEN MISPRONOUNCED

"In spoken language, pronunciation is the most striking element, and thus it happens that it is, more than any other one thing, the most obvious test of general culture." -From the preface to "18,000 Words Often Mispronounced,' by W.H.P. Phyfe.

Do you sound the *I's* capitalized in the following, as the *I* in ice? Do it.

bIography	dIlate
clIentele	trIbunal
dIgest (noun)	vIand (not veand)

Do you sound the *I's* and the *Y's* capitalized in the following like the *I* in it? This is the correct sound.

admIrable	genuIne

antI	hemI-
antIdote	hYpocrisy
civilIzation	indIgestion
conspIracy	Italian
cowardIce	Italic
dIgestion	lubrIcate
dIploma	mischIevous (chiv-us, not che-vus)
dIplomacy	nitro-glycerIne
dIvorce	semI-
fInancial	sInce (not sens)
fragile	

The *I* in *mercantile* should be sounded, not as the *e* in *eel*, but as either *i* in *it* or *i* in *ice*.

The *E's* capitalized in the following should be sounded as *e* in *eel*.

abstEmious	pEnalize
amEnable	pEriod
cafEteria (e not a)	pEriodic
crEdence	sacrilEgious
hystEria	sEnile

Do not say "crik" for "creek"; "klik" for clique" (klek) ; "slik" for "sleek"; nor "soot" for "suite" (Swet).

The *E's* capitalized in the following should be sounded as *e* in *ebb*.

| dEaf | eugEnics |
| ephEmeral | tEpid |

ERRORS IN ENGLISH

"The language of the individual is one of the qualities by which he is judged."

-Management of Men, E.L. Munson

Review. There are seven mistakes in the first paragraph of the following selection. The second paragraph contains six, and the third has seven. You will note that all the errors contained in these paragraphs have been considered in the book so far.

He continued his story. "'I will be drownded,' thinks I, 'but I shall do the best I can and leave the rest to God.' I laid down on a log but it wouldn't leave me ride it. I set up as the end rais'ed and run straight upon the top of a rock."

"I shrunk from being hit by some piece of timber and et my heart from fear as I seen men sunk in the whirlpools. I would have went under surely or would have been hung by something catching around my neck, if I had stayed with the log."

"But I looked around and seen the bank near at hand with a clear passage to it. I sprung from my perch and swum for all I knowed. When I reached shore, I sung out and rung the alarm bell. Then I hopped a horse and run him bard to reach you people in time."

New Study Material. Like sometimes means similar to, as "His hat is *like* mine." Occasionally, *like* means in the *same manner* as. As an example of this latter use, "He laughs like me." Be very sure that you never use like to introduce a subject with a verb. You will find below two examples where it is used improperly. Observe them.

Right	**Wrong**
It looks as if it might rain.	It looks like it might rain.
Talk as I do.	Talk like I do.

As-as is used in positive statements; *so-as* is used in negative statements.

Right: She is *as well as* may be expected.

Right: It is not *so good as* it was last time.

Wrong: It is not *as good as* it was last time.

RULE: *Either* and *neither* should be used only when referring to two things; when designating one of three or more, use *any one* or *none*.

Right: He had all three of his saddle horses in the show ring, but *none* of them got a ribbon.

Wrong: He had all three of his saddle horses in the show ring, but *neither* of them got a ribbon.

Right: He had two sons in the school but *neither* of them got honors.

Wrong: He had two sons in the school but *none* of them got honors.

Right: *Either* war or peace must be decided upon.

Wrong: *Either* of three things must be passed upon by the commission.

RULE: *You*, even though it refers to one person only, is never followed by *was*.

Right: You *were* the only man there.

Wrong: You *was* the only man there.

RULE: Do not use *except* to join two clauses or sentences.

For example:

Right: You will not get the order *unless* you cut your price.

Wrong: You will not get the order *except* you cut your price.

RULE: The expression, *had ought*, is always incorrect. Examples are:

Right: He *ought* to have taken the offer.

Wrong: He *had ought* to have taken the offer.

CORRECT USAGE OF WORDS

CARE - CAUTION. *Care* suggests watchful attention; *caution* is a stronger word and implies that strict observation must be exercised to avoid harm.

A department store marks a package of dishes, "Handle with *care*." We exercise *caution* in crossing a condemned bridge, or *caution* may keep us from attempting it. *Watchfulness* looks for a possible danger, *wariness* for a probable one. You must be *watchful* when driving a machine in city traffic; you must be *wary* in fording a swollen river. *Concern* implies a serious but more mild interest than is denoted by *anxiety*. One may be *concerned* about the outcome of an election, one feels *anxious* and distressed about a mother hurt in an accident. *Solicitude* is a stronger word than *concern*; but suggests less mental disturbance than *anxiety*. *Solicitude* often implies tender care; we speak of a parent's *solicitude* for a child.

GOT - SECURE - RECEIVE. The correct meaning of *got* is to *secure* through your own desire and effort. In these sentences, for example, *got* is used incorrectly: "What has that got to do with it?" "Have you got time to listen?" "We have got to hurry." In each of these sentences the word *got* should be dropped. It is not needed. It is incorrect. Say: "Have you time to listen?" It is alright to say: "I have got his prices," if I have secured them. "I got the position I applied for," is correct for it implies action on my part. But we violate the laws of good usage when we say, "We got your letter this morning," unless, of course, we made a special trip or effort to get it. If the postman brought it, we received it.

VOICE EXERCISE - BREATH CONTROL

"If I were to teach a young girl right at this moment," declared Madame Julia Claussen, a well-known concert singer, during the course of an interview, "I would simply ask her to take a deep breath, and note the expansion at the waist just above the diaphragm. Then I would ask her to say as many words as possible upon that breath, at the same time having the muscles adjacent to the diaphragm to support the breath; that is, to sustain it and not collapse or try to push it up. The trick is to get the most tone, not with the most breath, but with the least breath and especially the very least possible strain at the throat which must be kept in a floating, gossamer-like condition all the time. For me the most difficult vowel is "ah." The throat then is most open and the breath stream most difficult to control properly. Therefore, I make it a habit to begin my practice with *oo, oh, ah, ay, ee* in succession."

Very good, Madame Julia Claussen. We are not young girls, and neither are we interested in singing; but we are going to accept your suggestions and use them to improve our speaking voices.

First, let us take a deep breath, as she suggests. Start to yawn as you drink it in, deep, now, deep; feel your porous lungs expanding like a toy balloon; feel them pushing out the lower ribs at both sides and in the back. Feel them shoving down and flattening out that arched muscle called the diaphragm. Give your principal attention to the diaphragm. It is a soft muscle. It needs strengthening.

Now, before the yawn breaks, with your throat open, begin to sing "ah." Sing it for as long a time as your supply of breath will permit. How long will that be? That depends upon how good your breath control is. The natural tendency will be for your deep breath to rush out suddenly like air from a punctured balloon. Why? Because the lungs are elastic, they are expanded now and they want to contract. The floating ribs have been pushed outward by the extending lungs; and they are tending now to press the air out of the lungs. The

111

diaphragm, too, unless you control it, will quickly resume its arched position, pushing the breath out of the inflated porous lungs.

However, if you permit the air to escape with a rush, your tones will be breathy. They will not be clear. They will not be pleasant. They will not have carrying power. How, then, are we to control this escape of carrying power? "It is impossible," said Caruso, "to sing artistically without a thorough mastery of breath control." It is also impossible to have the ideal speaking voice without it.

How, then, are we to set about controlling the escape of the breath? Unless we are careful, our first tendency may be to control it by tightening the throat. Than that, what could be more ill advised? In the words of Madame Julia Claussen, the throat "must be kept in a floating, gossamer-like condition all the time."

The throat should have nothing to do with the escape of the breath. The throat isn't pressing against our expanded lungs. So we should direct our control to the things that are, the diaphragm and the ribs. Control them. Let them press easily, gently, as you sing "ah." See how long a time you can hold that tone firm, without wavering.

Now let us try the other notes that Madame Julia Claussen suggests: "*oo, oh, ah, ay, ee.*"

Chapter 6

ESSENTIAL ELEMENTS IN SUCCESSFUL SPEAKING

"I never allow myself to become discouraged under any circumstances. The three great essentials to achieve anything worthwhile are: first, hard work; second, stick to itiveness, third, common sense."

-Thomas A. Edison

"Much good work is lost for the lack of a little more."

-E.M. Harriman

"Never despair, but, if you do, work on in despair."

- Edmund Burke

"Patience is the best remedy for every trouble."

-Plautus, 225 B.C.

"Let patience have her perfect work."

-Dr. Russell H. Conwell

"They can conquer who believe they can. He has not learned the first lesson of life who does not every day surmount a fear."

-Emerson

"Victory is will."

-Napoleon

"When once a decision is reached and execution is the order of the day, dismiss absolutely all responsibility and care about the outcome."

- William James

"Approach each new problem not with a view of finding what you hope will be there, but to get the truth, the realities that must be grappled with. You may not like what you find. In that case you are entitled to try to change it. But do not deceive yourself as to what you do find to be the facts of the situation."

-Bernard M. Baruch

"You've got to say to yourself: 'I think that if I keep working at this and want it badly enough, I can have it,' It's called perseverance,"

-Lee J. Iacocca

Chapter 6

ESSENTIAL ELEMENTS IN SUCCESSFUL SPEAKING

I f you can dream and not make dreams your master;
   If you can think and not make thoughts your aim;
If you can meet with triumph and disaster;
And treat those two imposters just the same,

"If you can force your heart, and nerve, and sinew
To serve your turn long after they are gone;
And so hold on when there is nothing in you
Except the will which says to them, 'Hold on,'

"If you can fill the unforgiving minute
With sixty seconds' worth of distance run,
Yours is the earth and everything that's in it,
And, what is more, you'll be a man, my son."

This famous poem by Rudyard Kipling has been an inspiration to its readers for more than a century, Inventors posted it on their walls, explorers read and re-read it before going on their quests. If we all followed Kipling's injunction and persevere in our efforts, we would achieve much in our lives. Yet from the time I first became engaged in educational work, I was astounded to learn how large a percentage of students who enrolled in night schools of all sorts grew weary and fainted by the wayside before their goals were attained. The number is both lamentable and amazing. It is a sad commentary on human nature.

This is the sixth chapter of this book and I know from experience that some of the people who are reading these lines are already

PUBLIC SPEAKING FOR SUCCESS

growing disheartened because they have not, in the five previous chapters, conquered their fear of audiences and gained self-confidence. What a pity, for "how poor are they that have not patience. What wound did ever heal but by degrees?"

THE NECESSITY OF PERSISTENCE

When we start to learn any new thing, like French, or golf, or public speaking, we never advance steadily. We do not improve gradually. We do it by sudden jerks, by abrupt starts. Then we remain stationary a time or we may even slip back and lose some of the ground we have previously gained. These periods of stagnation or retrogression are well known by all psychologists; and they have been named "plateaus in the curve of learning." Students of public speaking will sometimes be stalled for weeks on one of these plateaus. Work as hard as they may, they cannot get off it. The weak ones give up in despair. Those with grit persist, and they find that suddenly, overnight, without their knowing how or why it has happened, they have made great progress. They have lifted from the plateau like an airplane. Abruptly they have gotten the knack of the thing. Abruptly they have acquired naturalness and force and confidence in their speaking.

You may always, as we have noted elsewhere in these pages, experience some fleeting fear, some shock, some nervous anxiety, the first few moments you face an audience. Eminent speakers, famous actors and even the greatest of the musicians have felt it in spite of their innumerable public appearances. Their experience will be yours. If you will but persevere, you will soon eradicate everything but this initial fear; and that will be initial fear and nothing more. After the first few sentences, you will have control of yourself. You will be speaking with positive pleasure.

KEEPING EVERLASTINGLY AT IT

One time a young man who aspired to study law, wrote to Lincoln for advice; and Lincoln replied: "If you are resolutely determined to make a lawyer of yourself, the thing is more than half done already. Always bear in mind that your own resolution to succeed is more important than any other one thing."

Lincoln knew. He had gone through it all. He had never, in his entire life, had more than a total of one year's schooling. And books? Lincoln once said he had walked and borrowed every book within fifty miles of his home. A log fire was usually kept going all night in the cabin. Sometimes he read by the light of that fire. There were cracks between the logs, and Lincoln often kept a book sticking in a crack. As soon as it was light enough to read in the morning, he rolled over on his bed of leaves, rubbed his eyes, pulled out the book and began devouring it.

He walked twenty and thirty miles to hear a speaker and, returning home, he practiced his talks everywhere in the fields, in the woods, before the crowds gathered at Jones' grocery at Gentryville. He joined literary and debating societies in New Salem and Springfield and practiced speaking on the topics of the day.

A sense of inferiority always troubled him. In the presence of women, he was shy and dumb. When he courted Mary Todd, he used to sit in the parlor, bashful and silent, unable to find words, listening while she did the talking. Yet that was the man who, by practice and home study, made himself into the speaker who debated with the accomplished orator, Senator Douglas. That was the man who, at Gettysburg, and again in his second inaugural address, rose to heights of eloquence that have rarely been attained in all the annals of mankind.

Small wonder that, in view of his own terrific handicaps and pitiful struggle, he wrote, "If you are resolutely determined to make a lawyer out of yourself, the thing is more than half done already."

There is an excellent picture of Lincoln in the President's office in the White House. "Often when I had some matter to decide," said Theodore Roosevelt, "something involved and difficult to dispose of, something where there were conflicting rights and interests, I would look up at Lincoln, try to imagine him in my place, try to figure out what he would do in the same circumstances. It may sound odd to you, but, frankly, it seemed to, make my troubles easier of solution."

Why not try Roosevelt's plan? Why not, if you are discouraged and feeling like giving up the fight to make a speaker of yourself, why not pull out of your pocket one of the five dollar bills that bear a likeness of Lincoln, and ask yourself what he would do under the circumstances. You know what he would do. You know what he did do. After Stephen A. Douglas had beaten him in the race for the U.S. Senate, he admonished his followers not to "give up after one nor one hundred defeats."

THE CERTAINTY OF REWARD

How I wish I could get you to prop this book open on your breakfast table every morning for a week until you had memorized these words from William James, the famous Harvard psychologist:

"Let no youth have any anxiety about the upshot of his education, whatever the line of it may be. If he keeps faithfully busy each hour of the working day, he may safely leave the final result to itself. He can, with perfect certainty, count on waking up some fine morning to find himself one of the competent ones of his generation, in whatever pursuit he may have singled out."

And now, with the renowned Professor James to fall back upon, I shall go so far as to say that if you pursue this lessons learned in this book faithfully and with enthusiasm, and keep right on practicing intelligently, you may confidently hope to wake up one fine morning and find yourself one of the competent speakers of your city or community.

Regardless of how fantastic that may sound to you now, *it is true as a general principle*. Exceptions, of course, there are. A person with an inferior mentality and personality, and with nothing to talk about, is not going to develop into a local Daniel Webster; but, within reason, the assertion is correct.

Let me illustrate by a concrete example:

Governor Stokes of New Jersey attended the closing banquet of a public speaking class at Trenton, N.J. He remarked that the talks that he had heard the students make that evening were as good as the speeches that he had heard in the House of Representatives and Senate at Washington. Those Trenton speeches were made by men and women who had been tongue-tied with audience-fear, a few months previously. They were not incipient Ciceros; they were typical of people one finds in any American city. Yet they woke up one fine morning to find themselves among the competent speakers of their city.

The entire question of your success as a speaker hinges upon only two things; your native ability and the depth and strength of your desires.

"In almost any subject," said William James, "your passion for the subject will save you. If you only care enough for a result, you will most certainly attain it. If you wish to be rich, you will be rich; if you wish to be learned, you will be learned; if you wish to be good, you will be good. Only you must, then, really wish these things and wish them with exclusiveness and not wish at the same time, a hundred other incompatible things just as strongly."

And he might have added, with equal truth, "If you want to be a confident public speaker, you will be a confident public speaker. But you must really wish it."

I have known and carefully watched literally thousands of people trying to gain self-confidence and the ability to talk in public. Those that succeeded were, in only a few instances, people of unusual brilliancy. For the most part, they were the ordinary run of men and women that you will find in your own home town. But they kept on. Some students sometimes got discouraged or were too deeply immersed in some other aspects of their lives so they did not get very far; but the ordinary individual with grit and singleness of purpose, at the end of the course, was at the top.

That is only human and natural. Don't you see the same thing occurring all the time in commerce and the professions? John D. Rockefeller once said that the first essential for success in business was patience. It is likewise one of the first essentials for success in giving effective talks.

Marshal Foch, the Commander in Chief of Allied Forces in the first World War, declared that he had only one virtue: never despairing.

When the French had retreated to the Marne in 1914, General Joffre instructed the generals under him in charge of two million men to stop retreating and begin an offensive. This new battle, one of the most decisive in the world's history, had raged for two days when General Foch, in command of Joffre's center, sent him one of the most impressive messages in military records: "My center gives way. My right recedes. The situation is excellent. I shall attack."

That attack saved Paris.

So, my dear speaker, when the fight seems hardest and most

hopeless, when your center gives way and your right recedes, "the situation is excellent." Attack! Attack! Attack, and you will save the best part of your personality, your courage and faith.

CLIMBING THE "WILDER KAISER"

I enjoy climbing mountains. On one of my mountain climbing expeditions, I started out to scale a peak in the Austrian Alps called the Wilder Kaiser. Baedecker said that the ascent was difficult and a guide was essential for amateur climbers. We, a friend and I, had none and we were certainly amateurs; so a third party asked us if we thought we were going to succeed. "Of course," we replied.

"What makes you think so?" He inquired.

"Others have done it without guides," I said, "so I know it is within reason, and *I never undertake anything thinking defeat.*"

As an Alpinist, I am the merest, bungling novice; but that is the proper psychology for anything from essaying public speaking to an assault on Mount Everest.

Think success as you apply what you read this book. See yourself in your imagination talking in public with perfect self-control.

It is easily in your power to do this. Believe that you will succeed. Believe it firmly and you will then do what is necessary to bring success about.

Admiral Dupont, commander of a fleet during the Civil War, gave half a dozen excellent reasons why he had not taken his gunboats into Charleston harbor. Admiral Farragut listened intently to the recital. "But there was another reason that you have not mentioned," he replied.

"What is that?" questioned Admiral Dupont.

The answer came: "You did not believe you could do it."

The most valuable thing that most members acquire from a course or book in public speaking is an increased confidence in themselves, an additional faith in their ability to achieve. And than that, what is more important for one's success in almost any undertaking?

THE WILL TO WIN

Here is a bit of sage advice from Elbert Hubbard that I cannot refrain from quoting. If all of us would only apply and live the wisdom contained in it, we would be happier, more prosperous:

"Whenever you go out of doors, draw the chin in, carry the crown of the head high and fill the lungs to the utmost; drink in the sunshine; greet your friends with a smile and put soul into every handclasp. Do not fear being misunderstood and do not waste a minute thinking about your enemies. Try to fix firmly in your mind what you would like to do, and then, without veering off direction, you will move straight to the goal. Keep your mind on the great and splendid things you would like to do, and then, as the days go gliding by, you will find yourself unconsciously seizing upon the opportunities that are required for the fulfillment of your desire, just as the coral insect takes from the running tide the elements it needs. Picture in your mind the able, earnest, useful person you desire to be, and the thought you hold is hourly transforming you into that particular individual. Thought is supreme. Preserve a right mental attitude; the attitude of courage, frankness and good cheer. To think rightly is to create. All things come through desire and every sincere prayer is answered. We become like that, on which our hearts are fixed. Carry your chin in and the crown of your head high. We are gods in the chrysalis."

Napoleon, Wellington, Lee, Grant, Foch, MacArthur, Eisenhower all great military leaders have recognized that an army's will to win and its confidence in its ability to win, do more than any other one thing to determine its success.

"Ninety thousand conquered men," said Marshall Foch, "retire before ninety thousand conquering men only, because they have had enough, because they no longer believe in victory, because they are demoralized at the end of their moral resistance."

In other words, the ninety thousand retiring men are not really whipped physically; but they are conquered because they are whipped mentally, because they have lost their courage and confidence. There is no hope for an army like that. There is no hope for a person like that.

When the ranking chaplain of the U.S. Navy was asked what qualities were essential for the success of a navy chaplain, he replied with four G's: "Grace, gumption, grit and guts."

Those are also the requisites for success in speaking. Take them as your motto. Take this Robert Service poem as your battle song:

"When you're lost in the wild, and you're scared as a child,
And death looks you bang in the eye.
And you're sore as a boil; it's according to Hoyle
To cock your revolver and . . . die.
But the code of a man, says: 'Fight all you can,'
And self-dissolution is barred. In hunger and woe,
oh, it's easy to blow . . .
It's the hell-served-for-breakfast that's hard.

"You're sick of the game! 'Well, now, that's a shame.'
You're young and you're brave and you're bright.
'You've had a raw deal!' I know-but don't squeal.
Buck up, do your damnedest, and fight.
It's the plugging away that will win you the day,
So don't be a piker, old pard!
Just draw on your grit; it's so easy to quit:
It's the keeping-your-chin-up that's hard.

"It's easy to cry that you're beaten-and die.
It's easy to crawfish and crawl;
But to fight and to fight when hope's out of sight,
Why, that's the best game of them all!
And though you come out of each grueling bout
All broken and beaten and scarred,
Just have one more try-it's dead easy to die,
It's the keeping-on-living that's hard.

IN A NUTSHELL

1.   We never learn anything; be it golf, French, or public speaking; by
means of gradual improvement. We advance by sudden jerks and abrupt starts.

Then we may remain stationary for a few weeks, or even lose some of the proficiency we have gained. Psychologists call these periods of stagnation "plateaus in the curve of learning." We may strive hard for a long time and not be able to get off one of these "plateaus" and onto an upward ascent again. Some men, not realizing this curious fact about the way we progress, get discouraged on these plateaus and abandon all effort. That is extremely regrettable, for if they were to persist, if they were to keep on practicing, they would suddenly find that they had lifted like an airplane and made tremendous progress again overnight.

2.   You may never be able to speak, without some nervous anxiety, just before you begin. Most great speakers experience some initial nervousness. But, if you will persevere, you will soon eradicate everything but this initial fear; and, after you have spoken for a few seconds, that too will disappear.

3.   William James has pointed out that one need have no anxiety about the upshot of his education, that if he keeps faithfully busy, "he can, with perfect certainty, count on waking up some fine morning to find himself one of the competent ones of his generation, in whatever pursuit he may have singled out." This psychological truth that the famous sage of Harvard has enunciated, applies to you and your efforts in learning to speak. There can be no question about that. The people who have succeeded in learning to speak in public have not been, as a general rule, people of extraordinary ability. But they were endowed with persistence and dogged determination. They kept on. They arrived.

4.   Think success in your public speaking work. You will then do the things necessary to bring success about.

5.   If you get discouraged, try Theodore Roosevelt's plan of looking at Lincoln's picture and asking yourself what he would have done under similar circumstances.

6.   The ranking chaplain of the U.S. Navy said that the qualities essential for the success of a chaplain in the service could be enumerated with four words commencing with G. What are they?

SPEECH BUILDING
WORDS OFTEN MISPRONOUNCED
Many persons have the careless habit of dropping the g in words ending in *ing*. To correct this tendency the following passage from Robert Southey's "The Cataract of Lodore" should be read aloud daily with distinctness and precision until the student's own ears become sensitive to his sins of omission.

The cataract strong,
Then plunges along,
Striking and raging
As if a war waging
Its caverns and rocks among;
Rising and leaping,
Sinking and creeping,
Swelling and sweeping,
Showering and springing,
Flying and flinging,
Writhing and wringing,
Eddying and whisking,
Spouting and frisking,
Turning and twisting,
Around and around
With endless rebound:
Smiting and fighting,
A sight to delight in;
Confounding, astounding,
Dizzying and deafening the ear with its sound.

Collecting, projecting,
Receding and speeding,
And shocking and rocking,
And darting and parting,
And threading and spreading,
And whizzing and hissing,
And dropping and skipping,
And hitting and splitting,
And shining and twining,
And rattling and battling,
And shaking and quaking,

And pouring and roaring,
And waving and raving,
And tossing and crossing,
And flowing and going,
And running and stunning,
And foaming and roaming,
And dinning and spinning,
And dropping and hopping,
And working and jerking,
And guggling and struggling,
And heaving and cleaving,
And moaning and groaning,
And glittering and frittering,
And gathering and feathering,
And whitening and brightening,
And quivering and shivering,
And hurrying and scurrying,
And thundering and floundering;
Dividing and gliding and sliding,
And falling and brawling and sprawling,
And driving and riving and striving,
And sprinkling and twinkling and wrinkling,
And sounding and bounding and rounding,
And bubbling and troubling and doubling,
And grumbling and rumbling and tumbling,
And clattering and battering and shattering;
Retreating and beating and meeting and sheeting

Delaying and straying and playing and spraying,
Advancing and prancing and glancing and dancing,
Recoiling, turmoiling and toiling and boiling,
And gleaming and streaming and steaming and beaming,

And rushing and flushing and brushing and gushing,
And flapping and rapping and clapping and slapping,
And curling and whirling and purling and twirling,
And thumping and plumping and bumping and jumping,
And dashing and flashing and splashing and clashing;
And so never ending, but always descending,
Sounds and motions forever and ever are blending,
All at once and all o'er, with a mighty uproar,
And this way the water comes down at Lodore.

ERRORS IN ENGLISH

Review. There are five errors in the following paragraph:

As you was the only man there, you had ought to have offered to help. Neither of the three ladies could do it like you could. They did not know you as intimately as we do and may think you boorish.

New Study Material.

RULE: A singular subject demands a singular verb.

Right: The statement *doesn't* make sense

Wrong: The statement *don't* make sense.

Right: The landlord, as near as I can find out, *doesn't* intend to make any repairs.

Wrong: The landlord, as near as I can find out, *don't* intend to make any repairs."

Right: A sack of potatoes *was* in the pantry.

Wrong: A sack of potatoes *were* in the pantry.

RULE: *Neither* and *either*, as pronouns, always require a singular verb. For example:

Right: *Neither* of the offers was accepted.

Wrong: *Neither* of the offers were accepted.

Right: *Either* of the houses is suitable.

Wrong: *Either* of the houses are suitable.

RULE: If a first personal pronoun is used with some other word or words in a compound subject, it should stand second in a succession of *R* sounds that is wanted; it is a *trill*. Did you ever see the rattles on a rattlesnake vibrating rapidly in anger just before he strikes? If so, you will have some idea of the way the tip of your tongue ought to trill against the roof of your mouth just back of your front teeth. Haven't you heard a woodpecker on a rotten limb in early spring? The trill you make ought to be as rapid as his staccato. This trilling is something like the roll of a kettle drum.

Start to say burr; when you come to the R sound, break into a trill. *Brrrrrrrrrrrrr* Try the same exercise with *cur* and *slur*.

Now start to yawn, breathing deeply, feeling the activity in the middle of the body. Before you break into the yawn, start to trill the sound of R. Trill it as long as your breath will permit. Use the methods of breath control described in Chapter V.

Trilling the *R* is an important exercise; but do not imagine that doing it and the other voice exercises in class once a week for sixty seconds and ignoring them the rest of the time, will produce the desired results. The key to voice improvement is practice, practice, practice. These exercises, however, do not need to consume any of the time usually devoted to other things; you can do them mornings in your bathtub.

Read the following poem aloud often. Feel the tip of the tongue touching quickly, decisively, against the back of the teeth. Feel the tip of it, striking off the emphatic ideas with a neat, elastic touch.

SONG OF THE BROOK
By Alfred Lord Tennyson

I come from haunts of coot and hern,
I make a sudden sally,
And sparkle out among the fern,
To bicker down a valley.

By thirty hills I hurry down,
Or slip between the ridges,
By twenty thorps, a little town,
And half a hundred bridges.

Till at last by Philip's farm I flow
To join the brimming river,
For men may come and men may go,
But I go on forever.

I chatter over stony ways,
In little sharps and trebles,
I bubble into eddying bays,
I babble on the pebbles.

With many a curve my banks I fret
By many a field and fallow,
And many a fairy foreland set
With willow-weed and mallow.

I chatter, chatter, as I flow
To join the brimming river,
For men may come and men may go,
But I go on forever.

I wind about, and in and out,
With here a blossom sailing,
And here and there a lusty trout,
And here and there a grayling,

And here and there a foamy flake
Upon me, as I travel
With many a silvery water-break
Above the golden gravel,

And draw them all along, and flow
To join the brimming river,

For men may come and men may go,
But I go on forever.

I steal by lawns and grassy plots,
I slide by hazel covers;
I move the sweet forget-me-nots
That grow for happy lovers.
I slip, I slide, I gloom, I glance,
Among my skimming swallows;
I make the netted sunbeam dance
Against my sandy shallows.

I murmur under moon and stars
In brambly wildernesses;
I linger by my shingly bars,
I loiter round my cresses;

And out again I curve and flow
To join the brimming river,
For men may come and men may go,
But I go on forever.

After you have read this poem through once, in the manner we have just indicated, read it a second time, employing the voice exercises given in Chapter V. Breathe from the diaphragm. Prepare to yawn. Speak. Think of drinking in the sound up into the head chambers not into the throat. Control your diaphragm. Keep the air from rushing out. See if you can read the entire poem distinctly with four breaths.

Chapter 7

THE SECRET OF GOOD DELIVERY

"Know the fact, hug the fact. For the essential thing is heat and heat comes from sincerity."

-Ralph Waldo Emerson

"It is necessary to have something, more than knowledge of the subject. You must have earnestness in its presentation. You must feel that you have something to say that people ought to hear."

-William Jennings Bryan

"Do one thing at a time and do that one thing as if your life depended upon it."

-Motto of Eugene Grace, President Bethlehem Steel Company

"He is a benefactor to mankind who contracts the great rules of life into short sentences that they may be easily impressed on the memory; and so recur habitually to the mind."

-Samuel Johnson

"The ability to express and idea is as important as the idea itself."

-Bernard Baruch

even looking at them, staring sometimes over their heads, sometimes at her notes, sometimes at the floor. She called off her words into the primeval void with a far-away look in her eyes and a far-away ring in her voice.

That kind of a performance isn't delivering a talk at all. It is a soliloquy. It has no sense of communication. And that is the first essential of good talking: *a sense of communication*. The audience must feel that there is a message being delivered straight from the mind and heart of the speakers to their minds and their hearts. The kind of a talk I have just described might just as well have been spoken out in the sandy, waterless wastes of the Gobi desert. In fact, it sounded as if it were being delivered in some such spot rather than to a group of living human beings.

This matter of delivering a talk is, at the same time, a very simple and a very intricate process. It is also a very much misunderstood and abused one.

THE SECRET OF GOOD DELIVERY

An enormous amount of nonsense and twaddle has been written about delivery. It has been shrouded in rules and rites and made mysterious. Go to a library or book shop, and look for volumes on "oratory," Most are utterly useless.

Old fashioned oratory, in which the speaker engaged in verbal fireworks, like an actor in a Shakespearean play, will not be accepted by the sophisticated audiences today. A modern audience, regardless of whether it is fifteen people at a business conference or a thousand people in an arena or millions viewing it on their TV screens, wants the speakers to talk, just as directly, as they would in a chat and in the same general manner that they would employ in speaking to one of them in conversation.

In the same *manner*, but with considerably more force. In order to appear natural, speakers have to use much more energy in talking to forty people than they do in talking to one; just as a statue on top of a building has to be of heroic size in order to make it appear of lifelike proportions to an observer on the ground.

Speak to the members of your community association just as you would to John or Jane Smith. What is a meeting of the community association, after all, but a mere collection of John and Jane Smiths?

Won't the same methods that are successful with those people individually, be successful with them collectively?

I have just described the delivery of a certain novelist. In the same ballroom in which she had spoken, I had the pleasure, a few nights later of hearing Sir Oliver Lodge. His subject was "Atoms and Worlds." He had devoted to it more than half a century of thought and study and experiment and investigation. He had something that was essentially a part of his heart and mind and life, something that he wanted very much to say. He forgot; and I, for one, thanked God that he did forget; that he was trying to make a speech. That was the least of his worries. He was concerned only with telling the audience about atoms, telling us accurately and lucidly and feelingly. He was earnestly trying to get us to see what he saw and to feel what he felt.

And what was the result? He delivered a remarkable talk. It had both charm and power. It made a deep impression. He was a speaker of unusual ability. Yet I am sure he didn't regard himself in that light. I am sure that few people who heard him, ever thought of him as a public speaker at all.

If you speak in public so that people hearing you will suspect that you have had training in public speaking, you will not be a credit to your instructor. To be truly effective, you must speak with such intensified and exalted naturalness, that your auditors will never dream that you have been trained. A good window does not call attention to itself. It merely lets in the light. Good speakers are like that. They are so natural that their hearers never notice their manner of speaking; they are conscious only of the message.

HENRY FORD'S ADVICE

"All Ford cars are exactly alike," said their maker, "but no two people are just alike. Every new life is a new thing under the sun; there has never been anything just like it before and never will be again. Each of us ought to get that idea about ourself; we should look for the single spark of individuality that makes us different from other folks, and develop that fully. Society and schools may try to iron it out of us; their tendency is to put us all in the same mold, but I say don't let that spark be lost; it's your only real claim to importance."

All that is doubly true of public speaking. There is no other human being in the world like you. Hundreds of millions of people have two eyes and a nose and a mouth; but none of them look precisely like you; and none of them have exactly your traits and methods and cast of mind. Few of them will talk and express themselves just as you do, when you are speaking naturally. In other words, you have individuality. As a speaker, it is your most precious possession. Cling to it. Cherish it. Develop it. It is the spark that will put force and sincerity into your speaking. "It is your only real claim to importance."

The most famous debates ever held in America took place in 1858 in the prairie towns of Illinois between Senator Stephen A. Douglas and Abraham Lincoln. Lincoln was tall and awkward. Douglas was short and graceful. These men were, as unlike in their characters and mentality and personalities and dispositions, as they were in their physiques.

Douglas was the cultured man of the world. Lincoln was the rail-splitter who went to the front door in his bare feet to receive company. Douglas' gestures were graceful. Lincoln's were ungainly. Douglas was utterly destitute of humor. Lincoln was one of the greatest storytellers who ever lived. Douglas seldom used a simile. Lincoln constantly argued by analogy and illustration. Douglas was haughty and overbearing. Lincoln was humble and forgiving. Douglas thought in quick flashes. Lincoln's mental processes were much slower. Douglas spoke with the impetuous rush of a whirlwind. Lincoln was quieter and deeper and more deliberate.

Both of these men, unlike as they were, were able speakers because they had the courage and good sense to be themselves. If either had tried to imitate the other, he would have failed miserably. But each one, by using to the utmost his own peculiar talents, made himself individual and powerful. *Go thou and do likewise.*

That is an easy direction to give. But is it an easy one to follow? Most emphatically it is not. As Marshal Foch said of the art of war: "It is simple enough in its conception, but unfortunately, complicated in its execution."

It takes practice to be natural before an audience. Actors know that. When you were a little child, four years old, you probably could, had you but tried, have mounted a platform and "recited"

139

naturally to an audience. But when you are twenty-four, or forty-four, what will happen if you mount a platform and start to speak? Will you retain that unconscious naturalness that you possessed at four? You may, but it is dollars to doughnuts that you will become stiff and stilted and mechanical and draw back into your shelf like a snapping turtle.

The problem of teaching or of training people in delivery is not one of super-imposing additional characteristics; it is largely one of removing impediments, of freeing them, of getting them to speak with the same naturalness that they would display if some one were to knock them down.

Hundreds of times, I have stopped speakers in the midst of their talks and implored them to "talk like a human being." Hundreds of nights, I have come home mentally fatigued and nervously exhausted from trying to drill and force my students to talk naturally. No, believe me, it is not so easy as it sounds.

And the only way under high heaven by which you can get the knack of this enlarged naturalness is by practice. And, as you practice, if you find yourself talking in a stilted manner, pause and say sharply to yourself mentally: "Here! What is wrong? Wake up. Be human." Then pick out someone in the audience, someone in the back, the dullest looking person you can find and talk to that individual. Forget there is anyone else present at all. *Converse*! Imagine you are answering a question from that person. If he or she were to stand up and talk to you, and you were to respond, that process would immediately and inevitably make your talking more conversational, more natural, more direct. So, imagine, that is precisely what is taking place.

You may go so far as actually to ask questions and answer them. For example, in the midst of your talk, you may say, "and you ask what proof have I for this assertion? I have adequate proof and here it is..." Then proceed to answer the imaginary question. That sort of thing can be done very naturally. It will break up the monotony of one's delivery; it will make it direct and pleasant and conversational.

Sincerity and enthusiasm and high earnestness will help you, too. When people are under the influence of their feelings, their real self comes to the surface. The bars are down. The heat of emotions has burned all barriers away. They act spontaneously, talk spontaneously and act naturally.

So, in the end, even this matter of delivery comes back to the thing, which has already been emphasized repeatedly in these pages: namely, put your heart in your talks.

When Christopher Reeve, who portrayed Superman in the movies, became paralyzed in an accident, he became a spokesperson for people who were similarly challenged. When Congress was considering an appropriation to finance research for dealing with such ailments, Reeve appeared before the Senate Finance Committee. From his wheel chair, even though his paralysis had made his formerly sonorous voice sound weak and sometimes difficult to understand, his message came through powerfully because it came from deep within him. His heart was in his words.

"His heart was in his words." That is the secret. Yet I know that advice like this is not popular. It seems vague. It sounds indefinite. The average student wants foolproof rules. Something definite. Something one can put one's hands on. Rules as precise as the directions for operating a computer.

That is what I would like to give my students. It would be easy for them. It would be easy for me. Some speakers and professors have promulgated such rules, but there is only one little thing wrong with them: *they don't work.* They take all the naturalness and spontaneity and life and juice out of what is said. I know. In my younger days I wasted a great deal of energy trying them. They won't appear in these pages. They just don't work.

DO YOU DO THESE THINGS WHEN YOU TALK IN PUBLIC?

We are going to discuss here some of the features of natural speaking in order to make them more clear, more vivid. I have hesitated about doing it, for someone is almost sure to say, "Ah, I see, just force myself to do these things and I'll be all right." No, you won't. Force yourself to do them and you will be all wooden and all mechanical.

You used most of these principles yesterday in your conversation, used them as unconsciously as you digested your dinner last night. That is the way to use them. It is the only way. And it will come, as far as public speaking is concerned, as we have already said, only by practice.

FIRST: STRESS IMPORTANT WORDS, SUBORDINATE UNIMPORTANT ONES

In conversation, we hit one syllable in a word, and hit it hard, and hurry over the others; e.g., MassaCHUsetts, afFLICtion, atTRACtiveness, enVIRonment. We do almost the same thing with a sentence. We overemphasize one or two important words and virtually swallow the rest of the sentence. This is not a strange or unusual process I am describing. Listen. You can hear it going on about you all the time. You yourself did it a hundred, maybe a thousand, times yesterday. You will doubtless do it a hundred times tomorrow.

Here is an example. Read the following quotation from Napoleon, striking the words in capital letters hard. Run over the others quickly. What is the effect?

"I have SUCCEEDED in whatever I have undertaken, because I have WILLED it. I have NEVER HESITATED which has given me an ADVANTAGE over the rest of mankind."

This is not the only way to read these lines. Another speaker would do it differently perhaps. There are no ironclad rules for emphasis.

Read these selections aloud in an earnest manner, trying to make the ideas clear and convincing. Don't you find yourself stressing the big, important words and hurrying over the others?

"If you think you are beaten, you are.

If you think you dare not, you don't.

If you'd like to win, but think you can't,

It's almost a cinch you won't.

Life's battles don't always go

To the stronger or faster man;

But soon or late the man who wins

Is the one who, thinks he can."

-Anon

Now read this paraphrase of a quotation from Theodore Roosevelt:

"Perhaps there is no more important component of character than steadfast resolution. The child who is going to make a great person,

or is going to count in any way in afterlife, must resolve   not merely
to overcome a thousand obstacles, but to win in spite of a thousand
repulses and defeats."

-Theodore Roosevelt

Now read aloud this famous poem, *Invictus*, by William Henley.

Out of the night that covers me
Black as the pit from pole to pole
I thank whatever gods may be
For my unconquerable soul.
In the fell clutch of circumstance
I have not winced nor cried aloud
Under the bludgeonings of chance
My head is bloody, but unbow'd.

Beyond this place of wrath and tears
Looms but the horror of the shade,
And yet the menace of the years
Finds and shall find me unafraid.
It matters not how strait the gate.
How charged with punishments the scroll,
I am the master of my fate:
I am the captain of my soul

SECOND : CHANGE YOUR PITCH

The pitch of our voices in conversation flows up and down the
scale from high to low and back again, never resting, but always
shifting like the face of the sea. Why? No one knows and no one
cares. The effect is pleasing and it is the way of nature. We never
had to learn to do this: it came to us as children, unsought and
unaware, but let us stand up and face an audience, and the chances
are our voices will become as dull and flat and monotonous as the
alkali deserts of Nevada.

When you find yourself talking in a monotonous pitch, and
usually it will be a high one, just pause for a second and say to

yourself: "I am speaking like a stone statue. *Talk* to these people. Be human. Be natural."

Will that kind of a lecture to yourself help you any? A little, perhaps. The pause itself will help you. You have to work out your own salvation by practice.

You can make any phrase or word that you choose stand out like a green bay tree in the front yard by either suddenly lowering or raising your pitch on it. It is the secret ingredient that all great speakers use to excite their audiences.

In the following quotations, try saying the italicized words in a much lower pitch than you use for the rest of the sentence. What is the effect?

"I have but one merit, that of never *despairing*."

-Marshal Foch

"The great aim of education is not knowledge, *but action*."

-Herbert Spencer

"The only thing we have to fear is *fear itself*."

-Franklin D. Roosevelt

"Ask not what your country can do for you, but what *you can* do for your country."

-John F. Kennedy

THIRD : VARY YOUR RATE OF SPEAKING

When a little child talks, or when we talk in ordinary conversation, we *constantly change our rate of speaking*. It is pleasing. It is natural. It is unconscious. It is emphatic. It is, in fact, one of the very best of all possible ways to make an idea stand out prominently.

Walter B. Stevens, in his biography of Abraham Lincoln, tells us that this was one of Lincoln's favorite methods of driving a point home:

"He would, speak several words with great rapidity, come to the word or phrase he wished to emphasize, and let his voice linger and bear hard on that, and then he would rush to the end of his sentence like lightning. He would devote as much time to the word or two he wished to emphasize as he did to half a dozen less important words following it."

Such a method invariably arrests attention. To illustrate: I have often quoted in a public talk, the following statement by James Cardinal Gibbons, Archbishop of Baltimore, Maryland in the early years of the twentieth century, I wanted to emphasize the idea of courage; so I lingered on these italicized words, drew them out and spoke as if I, myself, were impressed with them; and I was. Will you please read the selection aloud, trying the same method and note the results.

"A short time before his death, Cardinal Gibbons said, 'I have lived eighty-six years. I have watched men climb up to success, hundreds of them, and of all the elements that are important for success, the most important is faith. No great thing comes to any man unless he has courage.' "

Try this: say "thirty million dollars" quickly and with an air of triviality so that it sounds like a very small sum. Now, say "thirty thousand dollars"; say it slowly; say it feelingly; say it as if you were tremendously impressed with the hugeness of the amount. Haven't you now made the thirty thousand sound larger than the thirty million?

FOURTH : PAUSE BEFORE AND AFTER IMPORTANT IDEAS

Lincoln often paused in his speaking. When he had come to a big idea that he wished to impress deeply on the minds of his hearers, he bent forward, looked directly into their eyes for a moment and said nothing at all. This sudden silence had the same effect as a sudden noise: it attracted notice. It made everyone attentive, alert, awake to what was coming next. For example, when his famous debates with Douglas were drawing to a close, when all the indications pointed to his defeat, he became depressed, his old habitual melancholy stealing over him at times and imparting to his words a touching pathos. In one of his concluding speeches, he suddenly *"stopped and stood silent for a moment,* looking around upon the throng of half-indifferent, half- friendly faces before him, with those deep sunken weary eyes that always seemed full of unshed tears. Folding his hands, as if they too were tired of the helpless fight, he said, in his peculiar monotone: 'My friends, it makes little difference, very little difference, whether Judge Douglas or myself is elected to the United States Senate; but the great issue which we have submitted to you today is far, above and beyond, any personal interests or the political fortunes of any man. And my friends,' here he paused again, and the audience were intent on every word, 'that issue will live and breathe and burn when the poor, feeble, stammering tongues of Judge Douglas and myself are silent in the grave.' "

"These simple words," relates one of his biographers, "and the manner in which they were spoken, touched every heart to the core."

Lincoln also paused after the phrase he wanted to emphasize. He added to their force by keeping silent while the meaning sank in and affected its mission. By your silence," said Rudyard Kipling, "ye shall speak." Nowhere is silence more golden than when it is judiciously used in talking. It is a powerful tool, too important to be ignored, yet the beginning speaker usually neglects it.

Read the following quotations aloud and with force and meaning. Observe where you naturally pause.

"The great American desert is not located in Idaho, New Mexico or Arizona. It is located under the hat of the average person. The great American desert is a mental desert rather than a physical desert."

-J. S. Knox

"There is no panacea for human ills; the nearest approach to it is publicity."

-Professor Foxwell

"There are two people I must please, God and Garfield. I must live with Garfield here, with God hereafter."

-James A. Garfield

"Its not doing the things we like, but liking the things we have to do that makes life happy"

-Johann Wolfgang von Goethe

"One ought never to turn one's back on a threatened danger and try to run away from it. If you do that, you will double the danger. Bur if you meet it promptly and without flinching, you will reduce the danger in half. Never run away from anything. Never!"

-Winston Churchill

Speakers may follow the directions I have set down in this lesson and still have a hundred faults. They may talk in public just as they do in conversation and consequently, they may speak with an unpleasant voice and make grammatical errors and be awkward and offensive and do a score of unpleasant things. Your natural method of every day talking may need a vast number of improvements. Perfect your natural method of talking in conversation and then carry that method to the platform.

IN A NUTSHELL

1. There is something besides the mere words in a talk that counts. It is the flavor with which they are delivered. "It is not so much what you say as how you say it."

2. Many speakers ignore their hearers, stare over, their heads or at the floor. They seem to be delivering a soliloquy. There is no sense of communication, no give and take between the audience and the speaker. That kind of an attitude would kill a conversation; it also kills a speech.

3. Good delivery is conversational tone and directness enlarged. Talk to members of your community group just as you would to John or Jane Smith. What is the community group, after all, but a collection of John and Jane Smiths?

4. Everyone has the ability to deliver a talk. Use the same naturalness you use in normal conversation when you speak in public. To develop it, you must practice. Don't imitate others. If you speak spontaneously you will speak differently from anyone else in the world. Put your own individuality, your own characteristic manner into your delivery.

5. Talk to your hearers just as if you expected them to stand up in a moment and talk back to you. If they were to rise and ask you questions, your delivery would almost be sure to improve emphatically and at once. So imagine that someone has asked you a question, and that you are repeating it. Say aloud, "You ask how do I know this? I'll tell you." . . . That sort of thing will seem perfectly natural; it will break up the formality of your phraseology; it will warm and humanize your manner of talking.

6. Put your heart into your talking. Real emotional sincerity will help more than any formal rules or protocols..

7.   Here are four things that all of us do unconsciously in earnest conversation. But do you do them when you are talking in public? Most people do not.

a.   Do you stress the important words in a sentence and subordinate the unimportant ones? Do you give almost every word including the, and, but, approximately the same amount of attention, or do you speak a sentence in much the same way that you say MassaCHUsetts?

b.   Does the pitch of your voice flow up and down the scale from high to low and back again?

c.   Do you vary your rate of speaking, running rapidly over the unimportant words, spending more time on the ones you wish to make stand out ?

d.   Do you pause before and after your important ideas ?

SPEECH BUILDING
WORDS OFTEN MISPRONOUNCED

In order to deserve a place among the best speakers, it is not enough that you should have what is commonly termed a good education and good sense; you must have paid particular attention to the subject of pronunciation, unless you have been surrounded during the whole period of your education with none but correct speakers, which is seldom or never the case, at least in this country

Do you sound the capitalized *O's* in the following, as *o* in *go?* You should.

HOnOlulu	ZOology
Orient	ZOological

Do you ever hear anyone say *putatuh* and *tubaccuh?* Do you always sound the *O's* in such words as

mosquito	swallow	Toronto
piano	tomato	widow
pillow	Toledo	window

Do you sound the capitalized *O's* in the following as *o* in *odd?* You should.

catalOg	dOlorous	prOduce (noun)
cOllect	dOmicile	stOlid
cOlloquial	horrid	

The *O's* capitalized in the following should be sounded not as *oo* in *book*, but as the *oo* in ooze.

brOOm	hOOp	rOOm
cOOp	nOOn	rOOt
fOOd	pOOr	sOOn
hOOf	rOOf	spOOn

The *cou* in *coupon* is pronounced *coo*, the *oo* sounded as in *ooze*. Do not say *cuepon*.

Can you pronounce, with sureness and ease, the italicized words in the following? The correct pronunciation of these words has been given in the preceding chapters.

He played an *Italian melody* of *incomparable beauty* with *admirable* and *exquisite* tenderness. *Ordinarily* the old *Lyceum theater* would have been *swept* with applause, and the *President* would have demanded an *encore*. But, this time, *lamentable* to record, some of the *adults* in the audience, troubled with *indigestion* were suffering from *genuine* pains in the *abdomen*; others were *deaf*; and there was a *clique*, *interested primarily* in *eugenics*, who declared it was *sacrilegious* to play on Sunday and *contrary* to the ideals of *civilization*. They were not *amenable* to reason; they were bereft of every *fragile* shred of *hospitable diplomacy*; so, in a fit of *hysteria*, they burst into the *Italian's suite* at the hotel, *harassed* the artist, hurled *turnips* and *cranberries* and *nitroglycerine* at him and *protested* that he must be *penalized* for playing on Sunday. It was a *lamentable* display of *cowardice* and *hypocrisy*, for their *genuine* grievance was not with the day but with the *financial* arrangements *irrevocably* made by their *finance* committee.

ERRORS IN ENGLISH

Review. There are three errors in the following paragraph:

Neither of the cars were the type he wanted. As he often said, "It don't need to be a Rolls-Royce, but either of these automobiles are too cheap for a man like me."

New Study Material. This is to be a lesson on the number of pronouns used with certain ordinary words.

RULE: *Each, one, anyone, anybody, everyone, and everybody* are

149

singular, and singular pronouns must be used in referring to them. For example:

Right: He never let *anyone* feel that he had made a mistake.

Right: He never let *anyone* feel that one had made a mistake.

Wrong: He never let *anyone* feel that they had made a mistake.

Right: *Everybody* said he or she had a good time.

Wrong: *Everybody* said they had a good time.

Right: *Anybody* else would at least have said good-bye when *he* or she went away.

Wrong: *Anybody* else would at least have said good-bye when *they* went away.

Right: *Everyone* ought to mind *his* or her own business.

Wrong: *Everyone* ought to mind *their* own business.

Right: *Each* of us is free to follow *his* or her own impulses.

Wrong: *Each* of us is free to follow *our* own impulses.

Right: Sometimes *one*, just feels as if *one* had to rest awhile.

Wrong: Sometimes *one* just feels as if *they* had to rest awhile.

RULE: If you are talking about several subjects connected by and, and these subjects are preceded by *each*, *every*, or *no*, you must use the singular pronoun.

Right: Each movement and each gesture has *its* meaning.

Wrong: Each movement and each gesture has *their* meaning.

RULE: If you have the pronoun one as a subject, you may use *one's* or *his* or her in connection with it, as, "*One* should do *one's* (or his or her) best before an audience.

CORRECT USAGE OF WORDS

Egoism is an excessive love of oneself, selfishness. It is the very opposite of altruism. *Self-conceit* is a flattering opinion of one's own abilities. *Egotism* shows self-conceit by words and acts. It reveals *egoism*. One may be *self-conceited* and have the good taste to hide it; *egotistical* people parade their importance. *Pride* is high and sometimes excessive self-respect. It may be justified, or it may be unreasonable, conceit. A *proud* person may or may not reveal his or her pride. *Vanity* is a show of pride. The *vain* person longs to be noticed, and admired, and appraised. *Vanity* literally means empty. It is often applied to *pride* in such shallow things as dress and personal appearance.

Imprudent literally means not seen before; hence not taking results into account. *Rash* originally meant quick, and has now come to mean overhasty. A *rash* person does things on a momentary impulse, without deliberation. *Foolhardy* literally means a brave fool. The *adventurous* person gets a pleasure out of incurring risks. The adventurous person would rather join a startup business than to take a job with an established firm. *Precipitate*, like the word *precipice*, is derived from two Latin words and literally means head before or headlong. A *precipitate* action is like plunging headlong over a cliff. Other words with somewhat similar meanings are: *Hasty, foolish, ill-advised, unwise, indiscreet, heedless, thoughtless, incautious, injudicious, impulsive, hazardous, venture-some.*

VOICE EXERCISE - BRIGHT AND ATTRACTIVE TONES

Here are three exercises which, if faithfully followed, will help to brighten your voice, to make it more attractive.

1. Develop nasal resonance. Take a deep breath, and note the free, open, expansive sensation in your nose as the air is rushing in. Repeat the following syllables. Pitch them in the nose. Dwell on the *ng* sounds at the end of each word, for two or three seconds. Let them ring in the nasal cavities like the sound of a bell.

Singing	....	Wringing	....
Bringing	....	Clinging	....
Flinging	....	Winging	....
Hanging	....	Banging	....
Longing	....	Wronging	....

2. For some strange reason, practicing the falsetto voice develops a bright quality in our ordinary speaking tones. Do you know what we mean by the falsetto? I think you can get it by following these directions: Whether you are a man or a woman, pitch your voice in the highest tones of which you are capable, almost a shriek. It is a funny tone. It will soon tire you. Don't practice it after you begin to feet a strain. Try this verse in a falsetto voice:

151

"A song, oh, a song for the merry May!

The cows in the meadow, the lambs at play,

A chorus of birds in the maple tree,

And a world in blossom for you and me."

The poet Longfellow advised the famous Shakespearian actress, Mary Anderson, to read aloud each day some joyous, lyric poetry to develop voice charm. The happiness tones, the tones of cheerfulness and sunshine, are always welcome, always attractive. If you read aloud hopeful, glad poems, and read them with feeling, you will soon develop in yourself and in your tones, the emotions you are imitating. There can be no doubt whatever about the psychological rightness of that statement.

3. One of the guiding principles followed by leading opera singers has always been that there must be, "the joy of singing." in every performanceWhen giving a talk, your hearers ought to feel that you are experiencing the joy of talking.

Read the following poem aloud several times. Try to feel what the author felt when he wrote it. Try to make his spirit your own. Let it ring and sing through your tones. Turn to this poem often and read it. Better still, memorize it, and dispense with the book:

"It isn't raining rain to me,

It's raining daffodils;

In every dimpled drop I see

Wild flowers on distant hills.

"The clouds of gray engulf the day

 And overwhelm the town;

It isn't raining rain to me,

It's raining roses down.

"It isn't raining rain to me,

But fields of clover bloom,

Where every buccaneering bee

May find a bed and room.

"A health unto the happy,
A fig for him who frets;
It isn't raining rain to me,
It's raining violets."

-Robert Loveman

❏❏❏

Chapter 8

PLATFORM PRESENCE AND PERSONALITY

"Action is eloquence and the eyes of the ignorant are more learned than their ears."

-Shakespeare

"Too little gesture is as unnatural as too much. It is strange that the happy medium is so rarely observed, considering that every child is an illustration of its proper use and that we may see examples of it in almost every man that talks to his neighbor on the street."

-Matthews, Oratory and Orators

"There is often as much eloquence in the tone of the voice, in the eyes, and in the air of a speaker as in the choice of words."

-La Rochefoucauld

"When you speak, forget action entirely. Concentrate your attention on what you have to say and why you want to say it. Put all the fire and spirit of your being into the expression of your thought. Be enthusiastic, sincere, deadly earnest. Some action is bound to result. Your restraints will be broken down if you make the inner thought, urge strong enough. Your body will respond with some kind of expressive action. In all your actual speaking, think only of what you want to say. Do not plan your gestures in advance. Let the natural urge determine the action."

-George Rowland Collins, Platform Speaking

"How truly language must be regarded as a hindrance to thought, though the necessary instrument of it, we shall clearly perceive on remembering the comparative force with which simple ideas are communicated by signs. To say 'Leave the room' is less expressive than to point to the door. Placing the finger on the lips is more forcible than whispering 'Do not speak.' A beck of the hand is better than 'Come here.' No phrase can convey the idea of surprise so vividly as opening the eyes and raising the eyebrows. A shrug of the shoulders would lose much by translation into words."

-Herbert Spencer

"Did you know that listeners get at least 65 percent of a message through body language? Experts say that body language could reinforce or cancel what your words say. Great communicators like Ronald Reagan, paid special attention to their gestures, facial expressions and body movements when they spoke."

-Arthur R. Pell

Chapter 8

PLATFORM PRESENCE AND PERSONALITY

P ersonality, with the exception of preparation, is probably the most important factor in public address. In eloquent speaking, it is manner that wins, not words. Rather, it is manner plus ideas. But personality is a vague and elusive thing, defying analysis like the perfume of the violet. It is the totality of the person; physical, spiritual and mental. It incorporates that person's traits, predilections, tendencies, temperament, cast of mind, vigor, experience, training; and indeed, every aspect of that person's life. It is as complex as Einstein's theory of relativity, almost as little understood.

Personality is very largely the result of genetics. It is largely determined before birth. True, the environment in which one is brought up has something to do with it. But, all in all, it is an extremely difficult factor to alter or improve. Yet we can, by taking thought, strengthen it to some extent and make it more forceful, more attractive. At any rate, we can strive to get the utmost possible out of this strange thing that nature has given us. The subject is of vast importance to every one of us. The possibilities for improvement, limited as they are, are still large enough to warrant a discussion and investigation.

If you wish to make the most of your individuality, go before your audience rested. A tired person is neither magnetic nor attractive. Don't make the all too common error of putting off your preparation and your planning until the very last moment, and then working a furious pace, trying to make up for lost time. If you do, you are bound to store up bodily poisons and brain fatigues that will prove terrific drags, holding you down, sapping your vitality, weakening both your brain and your nerves.

If at all possible, when you have a speaking engagement, try to get some rest and relaxation for a few hours before the scheduled time. Rest, that is what you need, physical and mental and nervous.

When you have to make an important talk, beware of your hunger. Eat sparingly. Many after dinner speakers, forego the dinner; have a light snack or eat nothing until after they make their presentations.

I never realized the effect eating too much had on making a talk until after I became a professional speaker myself and tried to deliver a two-hour talk each evening after having consumed a hearty meal. Experience taught me that I couldn't enjoy a beefsteak and French fried potatoes and salad and vegetables and a dessert; and then stand up an hour afterwards and do either myself or my subject or my body justice. The blood that ought to have been in my brain was down in my stomach wrestling with that steak and potatoes. Paderewski was right. He said when he ate what he wanted to eat before a concert, the animal in him got uppermost, that it even got into his finger tips and clogged and dulled his playing.

WHY ONE SPEAKER DRAWS BETTER THAN ANOTHER

Do nothing to dull your energy. It is magnetic. Vitality, aliveness, enthusiasm: they are among the first qualities I have always sought for in employing speakers and instructors of speaking. People cluster around the energetic speaker, the human dynamo of energy, like wild geese around a field of autumn wheat.

I have often seen this illustrated by the open-air speakers in Hyde Park, London. A spot near Marble Arch entrance is a rendezvous for speakers of every creed and opinion. On a Sunday afternoon, one can take his choice and listen to a vegetarian, explaining the dangers of eating meat, to a Socialist, propounding the economic gospel of Karl Marx, to a fanatic, warning that the world is about to come to an end, and so on. Hundreds crowd about one speaker, while another has only a handful. Why? Is the topic always an adequate explanation of the disparity between the drawing powers of different speakers? No. More often the explanation is to be found in the speaker: When that person is more interested in the subject and, consequently more interesting, he or she talks with more life and spirit, and radiates vitality and animation. Such speakers always attract attention.

HOW ARE YOU AFFECTED BY CLOTHES?

An inquiry was sent to a large group of people by a psychologist and university president, asking them the impression clothes made on them. All but unanimously, they testified that when they were well groomed and faultlessly and immaculately attired, the knowledge of it, the feeling of it, had an effect that, while it was difficult to explain, was still very definite, very real. It gave them more confidence; brought them increased faith in themselves; heightened their self-respect. They declared that when they had the look of success they found it easier to think success, to achieve success. Such is the effect of clothes on the wearers themselves.

What effect do they have on an audience? I have noticed time and again that if a speaker is sloppily dressed and has made little effort to be properly groomed that an audience has little respect for that person. Aren't they very likely to assume that his or her mind is as sloppy as the unkempt hair and slipshod attire?

ONE OF THE REGRETS OF GRANT'S LIFE

When General Lee came to Appomattox Court House to surrender his army, he was immaculately attired in a new uniform and, at his side, hung a sword of extraordinary value. Grant was coatless, swordless and was wearing the shirt and trousers of a private. "I must have contrasted very strangely," he wrote in his Memoirs, "with a man so handsomely dressed, six feet high and of faultless form." The fact that he had not been appropriately attired for this historic occasion came to be one of the real regrets of Grant's life.

The Department of Agriculture in Washington has several hundred stands of bees on its experimental farm. Each hive has a large magnifying glass built into it and the interior can be flooded with electric light by pressing a button; so, any moment, night or day, these bees are liable to be subject to the minutest scrutiny. Speakers are like that: They are under the magnifying glass. They are in the spotlight, all eyes are upon them. The smallest disharmony in personal appearance now looms up like Pike's Peak from the plains.

"EVEN BEFORE WE SPEAK, WE ARE
CONDEMNED OR APPROVED"

A number of years ago, I was writing for the *American Magazine* the life story of a certain New York banker. I asked one of his friends to explain the reason for his success. No small amount of it, he said, was due to the man's winning smile. At first thought, that may sound like exaggeration but I believe it is really true. Other people, scores of them, hundreds of them, may have had more experience and as good financial judgment, but he had an additional asset they didn't possess; he had a most agreeable personality; and a warm, welcoming smile was one of the striking features of it. It gained one's confidence immediately. It secured one's good will instantly. We all want to see someone like that succeed; and it is a real pleasure to give him or her, our patronage.

"He who cannot smile," says a Chinese proverb, "ought not to keep a shop." And isn't a smile just as welcome before an audience as behind a counter? I am thinking now of a particular student who attended a course in public speaking in Brooklyn, New York. She always came out before the audience with an air that said she liked to be there, that she loved the job that was before her. She always smiled and acted as if she were glad to see us; and so immediately and inevitably her hearers warmed towards her and welcomed her.

But I have seen speakers, I regret to admit, who walked out before an audience in a cold, perfunctory manner as if they had a disagreeable task to perform, and that, when it was over, they would thank God. We in the audience were soon feeling the same way. These attitudes are contagious.

"Like begets like," observes Harry Overstreet in *Influencing Human Behavior*. "If we are interested in our audience, there is a likelihood that our audience will be interested in us. If we scowl at our audience, there is every likelihood that inwardly or outwardly, they will scowl at us. If we are timid and rather flustered, they likewise will lack confidence in us. If we are brazen and boastful, they will react with their own self-protective egotism. Even before we speak, very often, we are condemned or approved. There is every reason, therefore, that we should make certain that our attitude is such as to elicit warm response."

CROWD YOUR AUDIENCE TOGETHER

As a public lecturer, I have frequently spoken to a small audience scattered through a large hall in the afternoon, and to a large audience

NO TRUMPERY ON THE PLATFORM

And do not hide behind a table or the lectern. People want to look at the whole person. They will even lean out in the aisles to see all of you.

Some well meaning soul is pretty sure to give you a table and a water pitcher and a glass; but if your throat becomes dry, a pinch of salt or a taste of lemon will start the saliva again better than Niagara.

You do not want the water nor the pitcher. Neither do you want all the other useless and ugly impedimenta that clutter up the average platform.

The Broadway sales rooms of the various automobile makers are beautiful, orderly, pleasing to the eye. The Paris offices of the large perfumers and jewelers are artistically and luxuriously appointed. Why? It is good business. One has more respect, more confidence, more admiration for a concern, housed like that.

For the same reason, a speaker ought to have a pleasing background. The ideal arrangement, to my way of thinking, would be no furniture at all. Nothing behind the speaker to attract attention or at either side of him, nothing but a curtain of dark blue velvet.

But what does he usually have behind him? Maps and signs and tables, perhaps a lot of dusty chairs, some piled on top of the others. And what is the result? A cheap, slovenly, disorderly atmosphere. So clear all the trumpery away.

"The most important thing in public speaking," said Henry Ward Beecher, "is the speaker."

So let the speaker stand out like the snow clad top of the Alps, towering against the blue skies of Switzerland.

NO GUESTS ON THE PLATFORM

I was once in London, Ontario, when the Prime Minister of Canada was speaking. Presently the janitor, armed with a long pole, started to ventilate the room, moving about from window to window. What happened? The audience, almost to a man, ignored the speaker for a little while and stared at the janitor, as intently, as if he had been performing some miracle.

163

An audience cannot resist; or, what comes to the same thing, it *will not* resist the temptation to look at moving objects. If you will only remember that truth, you can avoid trouble and needless annoyance.

First, you can refrain from twiddling your thumbs, playing with your clothes or jewelry and making little nervous movements that detract from your talk. I remember seeing a New York audience, watch a well-known speaker's hands, for half an hour, while he spoke and played with the covering of a pulpit at the same time.

Second, the speaker should arrange, if possible, to have the audience seated so they won't have their attention distracted by seeing the latecomers enter.

Third, no guests should be on the platform. Guests have a tendency to shift about and put one leg over the other and back again and so on. Such movements distract the audience. They tend to look away from the speaker to the guest.

THE ART OF SITTING DOWN

Isn't it well for the speaker not to sit facing the audience before being introduced? Isn't it better to arrive as a fresh exhibit than an old one? Unfortunately, we do not usually have this luxury. We are seated on a dais or in front of the group while other speakers speak or just waiting for the formal introduction to be made.

So you must be careful of how you sit. You Don't be one of those people, who look around to find a chair with the modified movements of a foxhound lying down for the night. They turned around and when they did locate a chair, they doubled up and flopped down into it, with all the self-control of a sack of sand.

The right way to sit is to feel the chair strike the back of your legs, and, with your body erect from head to hips, just sinks into the chair.

POISE

We just said, a few pages previously, not to play with your clothes because it attracted attention. There is another reason also. It gives an impression of weakness, a lack of self-control. Every movement that does not add to your presence, detracts from it. There are no neutral movements. None. So stand still and control yourself physically and that will give you an impression of mental control of poise.

After you have risen to address your audience do not be in a hurry to begin. That is the hallmark of the amateur. Take a deep breath. Look over your audience for a moment; and, if there is a noise or disturbance, pause until it quiets down.

Hold your chest high. But why wait until you get before an audience to do this? Why not do it daily in private? Then you will do it unconsciously in public.

Luther H. Gulick in his book, *The Efficient Life,* recommends this daily exercise: "Inhale slowly and as strongly as possible. At the same time, press the neck back firmly against the collar. Now hold it there, hard. There is no harm in doing this in an exaggerated way. The object is to straighten out that part of the back that is directly between the shoulders. This deepens the chest."

And what shall you do with your hands? Forget them. If they fall naturally to your sides, that is ideal. If they feel like a bunch of bananas to you, do not be deluded into imagining that anyone else is paying the slightest attention to them or has the slightest interest in them.

They will look best hanging relaxed at your sides. They will attract the minimum of attention there. Not even the hypercritical can criticize that position. Besides, they will be unhampered and free to flow naturally into gestures when the urge makes itself felt.

But suppose that you are very nervous and that you find putting them behind your back or shoving them into your pockets helps to relieve your self-consciousness; what should you do? Use your common sense. Many, if not most, popular speakers put their hands into their pockets, occasionally, while speaking. If you have something to say worth while, and say it with contagious conviction, surely it will matter little, what you do with your hands and feet. If your head is full and heart stirred, these secondary details will very largely take care of themselves. After all, the stupendously important thing in making a talk is the psychological aspect of it, not the position of the hands and feet.

ABSURD ANTICS TAUGHT IN THE NAME OF GESTURE

And this brings us, very naturally, to the much abused question of gesture. My first lesson in public speaking was given by the president of a college in the Middle West. This lesson, as I

165

remember it, was chiefly concerned with gesturing; it was not only useless but misleading and positively harmful. I was taught to let my arm hang loosely at my side palm facing the rear, fingers half closed and thumb touching my leg. I was drilled to bring the arm up in a graceful curve, to make a classical swing with the wrist and then to unfold the forefinger first, the second finger next and the little finger last. When the whole aesthetic and ornamental movement has been executed, the arm was then to retrace the same graceful and unnatural curve and rest again by the side of the leg. The whole performance was wooden and affected. There was nothing sensible or honest about it. I was drilled to act, as no sane person ever acted anywhere.

There was no attempt, whatever, to get me to put my own individuality into my movements; no attempt to spur me on to feeling like gesturing; no endeavor to get the flow and blood of life in the process, and make it natural and unconscious and inevitable; no urging me to let go, to be spontaneous, to break through my shell of reserve, to talk and act like a human being. No, the whole regrettable performance was as mechanical as a typewriter, as lifeless as a last year's bird nest, as ridiculous as a puppet show.

Nine-tenths of the stuff that has been written on gestures, has been a waste and worse than a waste, of good white paper and good black ink. Any gesture that is gotten out of a book is very likely to look like it. The place to get it is out of yourself, out of your heart, out of your mind, out of your own interest in the subject, out of your own desire to make some one else see as you see, out of your own impulses. The only gestures that are worth one, two, three, are those that are born on the spur of the instant. An ounce of spontaneity is worth a ton of rules.

Gesture is not a thing to be put on at will like a dinner jacket. It is merely an outward expression of inward condition just as are kisses and colic and laughter and seasickness.

Your gestures, like your toothbrush, should be very personal things. And, as all people are different, their gestures will be individual if they will only act natural.

No two people should be drilled to gesture in precisely the same fashion. In the last chapter, I discussed the difference between Lincoln and Douglas as speakers. Imagine trying to make the long, awkward, slow-thinking Lincoln gesture in the same fashion as did the rapidly talking, impetuous and polished Douglas. It would be ridiculous.

"Lincoln," according to his biographer and law partner, Herndon, "did not gesticulate as much with his hands as with his head. He used the latter frequently, throwing it with vim this way and that. This movement was a significant one when he sought to enforce his statement. It sometimes came with a quick jerk, as if throwing off electric sparks into combustible material. He never sawed the air or rent space into tatters and rags as some orators do. He never acted for stage effect. As he moved along in his speech, he became freer and less uneasy in his movements; to that extent, he was graceful. He had a perfect naturalness, a strong individuality; and to that extent, he was dignified. He despised glitter, show, set forms and shams. There was a world of meaning and emphasis in the long, bony finger of his right hand as he dotted the ideas on the minds of his hearers. Sometimes, to express joy or pleasure, he would raise both hands at an angle of about fifty degrees, the palms upward, as if desirous of embracing the spirit of that which he loved. If the sentiment was one of detestation; denunciation of slavery, for example-both arms, thrown upward and fists clenched, swept through the air, and he expressed an execration that was truly sublime. This was one of his most effective gestures, and signified most vividly, a fixed determination to drag down the object of his hatred and trample it in the dust. He always stood squarely on his feet, toe even with toe; that is, he never put one foot before the other. He neither touched nor leaned on anything for support. He made but few changes in his positions and attitudes. He never ranted, never walked backward and forward on the platform. To ease his arms, he frequently caught hold, with his left hand, of the lapel of his coat, keeping his thumb upright and leaving his right hand free to gesticulate." You can see him, in just that attitude, in the statue which stands in Lincoln Park, Chicago.

Such was Lincoln's method. Teddy Roosevelt was more vigorous, more fiery, more active, his whole face alive with feeling, his fist clenched, his entire body, an instrument of expression. Bryan often used the outstretched hand with open palm. Gladstone often struck a table or his open palm with his fist or stamped his foot with a resounding thud on the floor. When Lord Rosebery addressed the House of Lords, he used to raise his right arm and bring it down with a bold sweep that had tremendous force. Ah, but there was force first in the speaker's thoughts and convictions; that was what made the gesture, strong and spontaneous.

Great speakers may use gestures, even lots of them, but they are no more conscious of them than of the air they breathed. Such is the ideal way. And such is the way you, will find yourself making gestures if you will but practice and apply the principles already discussed in this book, I can't give you any rules for gesturing, for everything depends upon your temperament, your preparation, your enthusiasm, your personality, the subject, the audience and the occasion.

SUGGESTIONS THAT MAY PROVE HELPFUL

Here are, however, a few limited suggestions that may prove useful. Do not repeat one gesture until it becomes monotonous. Do not make short, jerky movements from the elbow. The movements from the shoulder look better on the platform. Do not end your gestures too quickly. If you are using the index finger to drive home your thought, do not be afraid to hold that gesture through an entire sentence. The failure to do this is a very common error and a serious one. It distorts your emphasis, making small things unimportant; and truly important points seem trivial by comparison.

When you are doing real speaking before a real audience, make only the gestures that come natural. But while you are practicing before the members of a public speaking course, or with your friends or family, or at a Toastmasters' club meeting, force yourself, if necessary, to use gestures. Force yourself to do it and, as I pointed out in Chapter V, the doing of it will so awaken and stimulate you that your gestures will soon be coming unsought.

Shut your book. You can't learn gestures from a printed page. Your own impulses, as you are speaking, are more to be trusted, more valuable than anything any instructor can possibly tell you.

If you can videotape your rehearsals, and then review the tape over and over again, you will see for yourself how your gestures come across and determine what changes you want to make. Then make them and include them in your next go-around. You may want to have a friend or, if possible, a more experienced speaker view the tape with you and learn from his or her evaluation.

If you forget all else we have said about gesture and delivery, remember this: if you are so wrapped up in what you have to say, if you are so eager to get your message across that you forget yourself and talk and act spontaneously, then your gestures and your delivery, unstudied though they may be, are very likely to be almost above criticism.

IN A NUTSHELL

Personality has more to do with success in life than has superior knowledge. Personality, however, is such an intangible, elusive, mysterious thing that it is almost impossible to give directions for developing it, but some of the suggestions given in this chapter will help you become a more effective speaker.

1.   Don't speak when you are tired. Rest, recuperate, store up a reserve of energy.

2.   Eat sparingly before you speak.

3.   Do nothing to dull your energy. It is magnetic. People cluster around the energetic speaker like wild geese around a field of autumn wheat.

4.   Dress neatly, attractively. The consciousness of being well dressed heightens one's self-respect; and increases self-confidence.

5.   Smile. Come before your hearers with an attitude that seems to say you are glad to he there. If we are interested in our audience, there is every likelihood that our audience will be interested in us. Even before we speak, very often, we are condemned or approved. There is every reason, therefore, that we should make certain that our attitude is such, as to elicit warm response.

6.   Crowd your audience together. No group is easily influenced when it is scattered. An individual, as a member of a compact audience, will laugh at, applaud and approve things that might be questioned and opposed if he or she were addressed singly or were one of a group scattered through a large room.

7.   If you are speaking to a small group, pack them in a small room. Don't stand on a platform. Get down on the same level with them. Make your talk intimate, informal, conversational.

8.   Keep the air fresh.

169

9. Flood the place with light. Stand so that the light will fall directly in your face, so all your features can be seen.

10. Don't stand behind furniture. Push the tables and chairs to one side. Clear away all the unsightly signs and trumpery that often clutter up a platform.

11. If you have guests on the platform, they are sure to move occasionally; and, each time they make the slightest movement, they are certain to seize the attention of your hearers. An audience cannot resist the temptation to look at any moving object or animal or person; so why store up trouble and create competition for yourself?

12. Do not flop down in your chair. Feel it strike the back of your legs and with your body easily erect, sink into it.

13. Stand still. Do not make a lot of nervous movements. They give an impression of weakness. Every movement that does not add to your presence detracts from it.

14. Let your hands fall easily at your sides. That is the ideal position. However, if it makes you feel more comfortable to hold them behind your back, or even to put them in your pockets, it won't matter much. If your head and your heart are full of what you are saying, these secondary details will largely take care of themselves.

15. Don't try to get your gestures out of a book. Get them out of your impulses. Let yourself go. Spontaneity and life and abandon are the indispensable requisites of gesture, not studied grace and an obedience to rules.

16. In gesturing, do not repeat one movement until it becomes monotonous, do not make short jerky movements from the elbow. Above all else, hold your gestures, continue them until the climax of your movements coincides with the climax of your thought.

SPEECH BUILDING
WORDS OFTEN MISPRONOUNCED

"Pronounce not imperfectly, nor bring out your words too hastily, but orderly and distinctly."

-George Washington

Accent the final *s* sound in the following words:

ships	nests	mists
casks	guests	fists

tasks	masts	posts
masks	casts	roads

How do you pronounce *gasoline* and *Jerusalem*?

Utter the following words in pairs. Make the distinction very plain between the *s* and *z* sounds.

bows-booze	hiss-his
bust-buzz	lace-glaze
cost-because	mace-maize
cease-seize	mess-mezzanine
face-phase	most-mosey
fest-fez	muscle-muzzle
gasoline-gaze	post-pose
gust-guzzle	puss-puzzle
haste-hazed	race-raise

Can you pronounce correctly all the italicized words in the following paragraph? If in doubt, consult the exercises in pronunciation given in the previous lessons.

A seed house in *Honolulu* sent its *catalog* to the *address* of a certain *adult* whose *domicile* was on the banks of a *creek* near the *Zoological* gardens in *Toledo*. This poor fellow was a drug *addict*. When he was under the influence of opium, he *marveled* at the *surprisingly* beautiful *pictures* of *tomatoes* and *parsnips* and melons in the sales *literature*. He dreamed dreams. . . . In spite of the fact that he was a *poor* man, and, at times, found it difficult to keep a *roof* over his head, nevertheless, he now ordered *surprisingly* large quantities of seeds, far larger quantities than were *justifiable*, considering his *finances*. For some *inexplicable* reason, the *credulous* chap felt that he could make a *fortune* raising *produce*; so, in order to collect cash, he *voluntarily* sold his *piano*, his *spoons*, his *coupons*, the *carburetor* of his Ford, the *broom* that *swept* his *rooms* and even the very *food* in his *domicile*. He wrote the *Honolulu* concern, saying: "*Gentlemen*, I am very much *interested* in your *admirable catalog* showing the *exquisite* profits to be made in the food growing *industry*. I have a *diploma*. At times, I also have a pain in the *abdomen* due to *indigestion*, but as *soon* as I put a flower on my coat, the *mischievous* hurt becomes *impotent*. I can sell to a *cafeteria* here all the *produce* I raise, so please send me at once a *barrel* of *tomato* and *turnip* and *parsnip* seeds, and the *roots* of a *cranberry* bush." ...Thus ends the *rocking* and *shocking* *romance. Finis.*

ERRORS IN ENGLISH

As this chapter marks the completion of the first half of the book, it is felt that you should be given an opportunity to show how completely you have made the past seven parts of the chapters dealing with English a part of your regular equipment.

Some of the following sentences are correct and others are incorrect. Read them over and instantly decide what changes need to be made in any of them. It may be a good thing for you to write them out.

1. Nobody shall help me. I will drown. (Futurity.)
2. I shall fight it to the bitter end.
3. He was laying down when I came.
4. He laid down to rest every half hour.
5. Set down and take it easy.
6. I set down facing the clock and sat my watch.
7. I shall be setting right here when you want me.
8. The water raised three inches in no time.
9. He begun to complain just like he always did.
10. He drunk heavily but not as much as he used to.
11. He rang the bell and ran home.
12. You was there when he sung.
13. One had ought to pay as he goes along.
14. I seen him, and he swims just like she does.
15. It looks as if he were not going to come.
16. Neither of the men were so honest as she.
17. Either of the horses is all right.
18. I see him, and he said he don't want to come.
19. Everybody ought to mind their own business.
20. Everybody wants his own way.

21. He bid me go, but can I if my superior officer will not leave me depart on such a mission?

22. The shells break around me as I came down the road. The air seemed swelled with the concussions.

23. Each and every person in the audience should have their physical examination once a year. One does not know when their system will succumb to disease. It may have some weakness which could be righted in time.

24. "If you want to invent anything, do not try to find it in the wheels in your head or in the wheels in your machine, but first find out what the people need."

-R. H. Conwell

25. "The world will little note, nor long remember what we say here, but it can never forget what they did here."

-A. Lincoln

CORRECT USAGE OF WORDS

"The habit of thorough investigation into the meaning of words, and of exact discrimination in the use of them, is indispensable to precision and accuracy of thought, and it is surprising how soon the process becomes spontaneous, and almost mechanical and unconscious, so that one finds himself making nice and yet sound distinctions between particular words which he is not aware that he has ever made the subject of critical analysis."

-G.P. March, Lectures On the English Language

DECEIVING. "You are deceiving me." This use is wrong. He may be trying to *deceive* you, but your statement shows that he has failed.

DECISIVE - DECIDED. *Decided* means unmistakable, certain. *Decisive* means putting an end to the question, final, conclusive. A *decided* victory is not always a *decisive* victory.

DECRY - UNDERESTIMATE - UNDERVALUE. To *decry* is to talk down in a conspicuous or public manner. One may, in one's own mind, *underestimate* the achievements of friends; *underrate* and *undervalue* their achievements when conversing with others.

DELIGHTFUL - DELICIOUS. The candy bars are advertised to be "really *delightful.*" They may be *delicious*, but *delightful* refers to the gratification of our mental and spiritual desires, as a *delightful* book. Those things are *delicious* which please the sense of taste and smell; as a *delicious* perfume, a *delicious* pudding.

DIFFER FROM or WITH. You differ *from* people if you are unlike them; you differ *with* them if you disagree with them.

DIFFICULT - HARD - ARDUOUS. A thing that requires skill and dexterity is *difficult*; driving an airplane is *difficult*. That which requires much physical exertion is *hard*; carrying bricks is *hard* work. An *arduous* task demands continuous exertion; *arduous* is usually applied to higher endeavors. Acquiring skill in writing is an *arduous* task. Pitching hay is *laborious* and *toilsome*.

VOICE EXERCISE - REVIEW

1. Here is an exercise that a famous Italian voice teacher, insisted that his students practice daily. It is the foundation exercise of breath technique. Relax the jaw, let it fall open. Feel an incipient yawn in the throat. Now begin by taking in and letting out very short breaths through the mouth. Increase their rapidity until they sound like the panting of a dog that has been running. This panting sound should be the result of the expelled breath striking against the hard palate of the mouth. It should not come from a narrow, constricted throat. Where should the motive power for this pant come from? From the diaphragm. It is acting like a bellows to force the air out in quick spurts. It is fairly pumping it out. You cannot help but feel its action in the middle of your body. Put your hand directly underneath your breast bone and feel its motion there.

2. Relax; feel in the throat the cool, delightful sensation of an oncoming yawn; drink in a deep breath of air; feel your lungs pushing out the lower ribs at your sides, pushing and flattening the arched diaphragm. Now let us try controlling, by means of the diaphragm, the release of this air. Hold a lighted candle close to your mouth. See if you can empty your lungs now so slowly, so evenly that the flame of the candle will not flicker in the slightest even though it is held quite close to the mouth. You should practice this until you can exhale steadily for thirty or forty seconds without disturbing the flame of the candle. But this exercise will be worse

174

than useless if you constrict your throat. The release of the air must be controlled from the center of body. Never forget that. It must be controlled down there where you felt that pumping exercise when you were panting. Try this exercise three or four times. Then blow out the candle by one gust of air forced up by a violent contraction of the diaphragm.

3. We have set down here at the end of this paragraph, Hamlet's immortal advice to the players. It is excellent advice also to students of public speaking. Read it aloud, putting into practice all we have learned so far about diaphragmatic breathing and breath control. Think of the tone as coming in and up as in a yawning, crying feeling. Keep the throat open. Keep always an ample reserve of breath in the lungs. Strike off the emphatic ideas with the tip of your tongue. Feel it hitting neatly, quickly against the back of your front teeth and the front part of the roof of the mouth. Do these things; and you will undoubtedly be highly gratified with the tones you produce. How round and clear they will be. How they will carry.

"Speak the speech, I pray you, as I pronounced it to you, trippingly on the tongue; but if you mouth it, as many of our players do, I had as lief the town-crier spoke my lines. Nor do not saw the air too much with your hand, thus; but use all gently: for in the very torrent, tempest and as I may say, whirlwind of your passion, you must acquire and beget a temperance that may give it smoothness. Oh, it offends me to the soul to hear a robustious periwig-pated fellow tear a passion to tatters, to very rags, to split the car of the groundlings, who, for the most part, are capable of nothing but inexplicable dumb-shows and noise; I would have such a fellow whipped for o'erdoing Termagant; it out-herods Herod: pray you, avoid it."

"Be not too tame neither, but let your own discretion be your tutor: suit the action to the word, the word to the action; with this special observance, that you o'erstep not the modesty of nature; for anything so overdone is from the purpose of playing, whose end, both at the first and now, was and is, to hold, as 'twere, the mirror up to nature; to show virtue her own feature, scorn her own image, and the very age and body of the time his form and pressure. Now this overdone or come tardy off, though it makes the unskillful laugh, cannot but make the judicious grieve; the censure of the which one must in your allowance o'erweigh a whole theater of others. Oh, there be players that I have seen play, and heard others praise, and that highly, not to speak it profanely, that neither having the accent of Christians nor the gait of Christian, pagan, nor man, have so strutted and bellowed, that I thought some of nature's journeymen had made men, and not made them well, they imitated humanity so abominably."

Chapter 9

HOW TO OPEN A TALK

"If you happen to be one of a circle of public speakers who are relating their experiences, you will often hear some one remark apropos of the proper construction of an address. Get a good beginning and a good ending; stuff it with whatever you please."

-Victor Murdock

"In public address, it is all important to make a good start. In the whole hard process of speech-making, there is nothing quite so hard as to make easy and skilful contact with an audience. . . . Much depends upon first impressions and opening words. Often an audience is either won or lost by the first half dozen sentences of a speech."

-Public Speaking For Success Today, by Lockwood-Thorpe

"The golden rule is clearly: Drive into the heart of your subject as soon as may be. Obey this rule to the Point of austerity. Resist the temptation to say ornamental and pretty things. Never, never, never apologize for anything at all. In simple, clear spoken words, get to the point. In writing a speech, as in writing an article, we can usually go back and delete the first paragraph. Begin where you thought your introduction would end."

-Public Speaking For Success for Business Men,
by Sidney F. Wicks

"Tell them what you are going to say; say it; then tell them what you said. That's the art of a good speech."

-Anonymous

Chapter 9

HOW TO OPEN A TALK

A sk any professional speaker what their experience has taught them, Most will respond "To get an arresting opening, something that will seize the attention immediately." To do this, plan in advance almost the precise words of both his opening and closing. Practically, every successful speaker does it.

But does the beginner? Seldom. Planning takes time, requires thought, demands willpower. Cerebration is a painful process. Thomas Edison had this quotation from Sir Joshua Reynolds nailed on the walls of his plants:

"There is no expedient to which a man will not resort to avoid the real labor of thinking."

Lord Northcliffe, who fought his way up from a meager weekly salary to being the richest and most influential newspaper owner in the British Empire in his time, said that these five words from Blasé Pascal had done more to help him succeed than anything else he had ever read:

"To foresee is to rule."

That is also a most excellent motto to have in front of you when you are planning your talk. Foresee how you are going to begin when the mind is fresh to grasp every word you utter. Foresee what impression you are going to leave last, when nothing else follows to obliterate it.

Ever since the days of Aristotle, books on this subject have divided the speech into three sections; the introduction, the body, and the conclusion. Until comparatively recently, the introduction often was, and could really afford to be, as leisurely as a buggy ride. The speaker then was both a bringer of news and an entertainer. For centuries, speech makers often filled the niche in the community that is usurped today by the newspaper, the radio, television and the Internet. But conditions have altered amazingly. The world has been made over. Inventions have speeded up life more in the last hundred years than they had in all the ages since the world began. And the speaker must fall in line with the impatient tempo of the times. If you are going to use an introduction, believe me, it ought to be short as a billboard advertisement. This is about the temper of the average modern audience. You have to grab their attention rapidly and then you can proceed with your talk.

One of the great speakers of the twentieth century was Dr. Martin Luther King. He had a talent of reaching his audiences instantly. Let's reread how he started his famous "I have a dream" speech.

"Five score years ago, a great American, in whose symbolic shadow we stand today, signed the Emancipation Proclamation. This momentous decree came as a great beacon light of hope to millions of Negro slaves, who had been seared in the flames of withering injustice. It came as a joyous daybreak to end the long night of their captivity."

"But one hundred years later, the Negro still is not free. One hundred years later, the life of the Negro is still sadly crippled by the manacles of segregation and the chains of discrimination. One hundred years later, the Negro lives on a lonely island of poverty in the midst of a vast ocean of material prosperity. One hundred years later, the Negro still languishes in the corners of American society and finds himself an exile in his own land."

Mary Fisher was not an experienced speaker, but when she addressed the Republican National Convention in 1992, her talk touched the hearts of all those who heard her at the convention and all over the world on television. Her opening statement captured her audience instantly:

"Less than three months ago, at the platform hearings in Salt Lake City, I asked the Republican party to lift the shroud of silence which has been draped over the issue of HIV/AIDS. I have come tonight to bring our silence to an end."

"I bear a message of challenge, not self-congratulation. I want your attention, not your applause. I would never have asked to be HIV positive. But I believe that in all things there is a good purpose and so I stand before you, and before the nation, gladly."

But most inexperienced speakers usually do not achieve such commendable swiftness and succinctness in their openings. The majority of untrained and unskilled speakers will begin in one of two ways, both of which are bad.

BEWARE OF OPENING WITH A SO-CALLED
HUMOROUS STORY

For some lamentable reason, novices often feel that they ought to be funny as a speaker. They may, by nature, mind you, be as solemn as the encyclopedia, utterly devoid of the lighter touch; yet the moment they stand up to talk they imagine that they feel, or ought to feel, the spirit of Mark Twain or Bob Hope descending upon them. So they inclined to open with a humorous story, especially if the occasion is an after dinner affair. What happens? The chances are twenty to one that the narration is as heavy as the dictionary. The chances are the stories don't "click." In the immortal language of the immortal Hamlet, they prove "weary, state, flat and unprofitable."

If an entertainer were to misfire a few times like that before an audience that had paid for their seats, he or she would be booed off the stage. But the average group listening to a speaker is very sympathetic; so, out of sheer charity, they will do their best to manufacture a few chuckles; while, deep in their hearts, they pity the would be humorous speaker! They themselves feel uncomfortable. Haven't we all witnessed this kind of a fiasco time after time? In all the difficult realm of speech making, what is more difficult, more rare, than the ability to make an audience laugh? Humor is a hair trigger affair; it is so much a matter of individuality, of personality. You are either born with the predilection for being humorous or you are not much as you are born with or without brown eyes.

Remember, it is seldom the story that is funny by and in itself. It is the way it is told that makes it a success. Ninety-nine out of a hundred people will fail woefully with the identical stories that made Mark Twain famous. Read the stories that Lincoln repeated in the taverns of the Eighth Judicial District of Illinois, stories that people drove miles to hear, stories that people sat up all night to hear, stories that, according to an eye witness, sometimes caused the natives to "whoop and roll off their chairs." Read those stories aloud to your family and see if you conjure up a smile. Here is one Lincoln used to tell with roaring success. Why not try it? Privately, please not before an audience.

"A late traveler, trying to reach home over the muddy roads of the Illinois prairies, was overtaken by a storm. The night was black as ink; the rain descended as if some dam in the heavens had broken; thunder rent the angry clouds like the explosion of dynamite. Chain lightning showed trees falling around. The roar of it was very nearly deafening. Finally, a crash more terrific, more terrible, than any the helpless man had ever heard in his life, brought him to his knees. He was not given to praying, usually, but "Oh, Lord," he gasped, "if it is all the same to you, please give us a little more light and a little less noise."

You may be one of those fortunately endowed individuals who has the rare gift of humor. If so, by all means, cultivate it. You will be thrice welcome wherever you speak. But if your talent lies in other directions, it is folly; and it ought to be high treason; for you to attempt to be a comedian.

Good speakers never tell a funny story for the mere sake of humor. It has to be relevant, has to illustrate a point. Humor ought to be merely the frosting on the cake, merely the chocolate between the layers, not the cake itself. Must the opening, then be, heavy-footed, elephantine and excessively solemn? Not at all. Tickle our funny bones, if you can, by some local reference, something about the occasion or the remarks of some other speaker. Observe some incongruity. Exaggerate it. That brand of humor is forty times more likely to succeed than stale jokes that most people probably have heard before.

Perhaps the easiest way to create merriment is to tell a joke on yourself. Depict yourself in some ridiculous and embarrassing situation. That gets down to the very essence of much humor. Most any one can make an audience laugh by grouping incongruous ideas or qualities as, for example, the statement of a newspaper writer that he "hated children, dogs and Democrats."

DO NOT BEGIN WITH AN APOLOGY

The second egregious blunder that the beginner is wont to make in his opening is this: He apologizes. "I am no speaker. . . . I am not prepared to talk. . . . I have nothing to say. . . . Unaccustomed as I am to public speaking. . . ."

Don't! Don't! The opening words of a poem by Kipling are: "There's no use in going further." That is precisely the way an audience feels when a speaker opens in that fashion.

Anyway, if you are not prepared, some of us will discover it without your assistance. Others will not. Why call their attention to it? Why insult your audience by suggesting that you did not think them worth preparing for, that just any old thing you happened to have on the fire would be good enough to serve them? No. No. We don't want to hear your apologies. We are there to be informed and interested, to be *interested*, remember that.

The moment you come before the audience, you have our attention naturally, inevitably. It is not difficult to get it for the first five seconds, but it is difficult to hold it for the next five minutes. If you once lose it, it will be doubly difficult to win it back. So begin with something interesting in your very first sentence. Not the second. Not the third. The first! F-I-R-S-T. First!

"How?" You ask. Rather a large order, I admit. And in attempting to harvest the material to fill it, we must tread our way down devious and dubious paths, for so much depends upon you, upon your audience, your subject, your material, the occasion and so on. However, we hope that the tentative suggestions discussed and illustrated in the remainder of this chapter will yield something usable and of value.

AROUSE CURIOSITY

Here is an opening used by one of the students in my course. Does it get your interest immediately?

"Eighty-two years ago, and just about this time of year, there was published in London a little volume, a story, which was destined to become immortal. Many people have called it 'the greatest little book in the world.' When it first appeared, friends meeting one another on the Strand or Pall Mall, asked the question, 'Have you read it?' The answer invariably was: 'Yes, God bless him, I have.'

"The day it was published a thousand copies were sold. Within a fortnight, the demand had consumed fifteen thousand. Since then it has run into countless editions and has been translated into every language under heaven. A few years ago, J.P. Morgan purchased the original manuscript for a fabulous sum; it now reposes among his other priceless treasures in that magnificent art gallery in New York City that he calls his library."

"What is this world famous book? Dickens 'Christmas Carol.' . . ."

Do you consider that a successful opening? Did it hold your attention, heighten your interest as it progressed? Why? Was it not because it aroused your curiosity, held you in suspense?

183

Curiosity! Who is not susceptible to it? I have seen birds in the woods fly about by the hour watching me out of sheer curiosity. I know a hunter in the high Alps who lures chamois by throwing a bed sheet around him and crawling about and arousing their curiosity. Dogs have curiosity, and so have kittens, and all manner of animals including the well-known *genus homo*.

So arouse your audience's curiosity with your first sentence, and you have their interested attention. Today "Lawrence of Arabia" is world famous. Books have been written about him and a major movie told his story. But this was not always the case. His story was brought to the attention of the public in those pre-radio, pre-TV, pre-movie days by a series of lectures which my colleague, Lowell Thomas and I gave, first in London and then all over England and the United States. I began in this fashion:

"Lloyd George says that he regards Colonel Lawrence as one of the most romantic and picturesque characters of modern times."

That opening had two advantages. In the first place, a quotation from an eminent man always has a lot of attention value. Second, it aroused curiosity, "Why romantic?" was the natural question, and "why picturesque?" "I never heard about him before. . . . What did he do?"

My colleague, Lowell Thomas began his lecture with this statement.

"I was going down Christian Street in Jerusalem one day when I met a man clad in the gorgeous robes of an oriental potentate; and, at his side, hung the curved gold sword worn only by the descendants of the prophet Mohammed. But this man had none of the appearances of an Arab. He had blue eyes; and the Arabs' eyes are always black or brown."

That piques your curiosity, doesn't it? You want to hear more. Who was he? Why was he posing as an Arab? What did he do? What became of him?

The student who opened his talk with this question:

"Do you know that slavery exists in seventeen nations of the world today?" not only aroused curiosity, but in addition, he shocked his auditors. "Slavery? Today? Seventeen countries? Seems incredible. What nations? Where are they?

One can often arouse curiosity by beginning with an effect and making people anxious to hear the cause. For example, one student began with this striking statement:

"A member of one of our legislatures recently stood up in his legislative assembly and proposed the passage of a law prohibiting tadpoles from becoming frogs within two miles of any school house."

You smile. Is the speaker joking? How absurd. Was that actually done? . . . Yes. The speaker went on to explain.

Anne Fisher, who writes a column on jobs and careers for FORTUNE MAGAZINE, aroused the curiosity of her readers with a question: "Do people in your office seem less enthusiastic than they used to?" With twelve words, she announces the subject of her article and arouses your curiosity about why workers have lost their enthusiasm.

Every person who aspires to speak in public ought to study the technique that magazine writers employ to hook the reader's interest immediately. You can learn far more from them about how to open a speech than you can by studying collections of printed speeches.

WHY NOT BEGIN WITH A STORY?

People like to hear stories. From ancient times, story tellers entertained, educated and enlightened listeners from primitive people squatting around a campfire, to villagers assembled in the town square, to audiences in auditoriums and theaters. Troubadours sang ballads or recited poems and sagas telling stories of heroes and heroines, of tribal history and customs, of wars and adventures. We still all want to hear stories. We buy books and magazines, go to theater and the movies, listen to radio and watch TV.

We especially like narratives about a person's own experience. Russell E. Conwell delivered his lecture, "Acres of Diamonds," over six thousand times to vast audiences. Many came back, over and over again, to hear this inspiring message.

And how does this marvelously popular lecture begin ? Read it yourself. It is printed in the Appendix of this book. Here is the way it opens:

"In 1870 we went down the Tigris River. We hired a guide at Baghdad to show us Persepolis, Nineveh, and Babylon ...."

And he is off-with *a story*. That is what hooks the attention. That kind of an opening is almost foolproof. It can hardly fail. It moves.

It marches. We follow. We want to know what is going to happen.

Here are opening sentences from two stories.

1. "The sharp crack of a revolver punctuated the silence."

2. "When men and women work together, there will likely be flirtations, romances and even marriages. What special problems does this present to the company?"

Note that those openings have action. They start something. They arouse your curiosity. You want to read on; you want to know more; you want to find out what it is all about.

Even the unpracticed beginner can usually manage a successful opening by using the story technique to arouse our curiosity.

BEGIN WITH A SPECIFIC ILLUSTRATION

It is difficult, it is arduous for the average audience to follow abstract statements very long. Illustrations are easier to listen to, far easier. Then, why not start with one? It is hard to get speakers to do that. I know. I have tried. They feel somehow that they must first make a few general statements. Not at all. Open with your illustration, arouse the interest; and then follow with your general remarks. If you wish an example of this technique, please turn to the opening of Chapter V of this book, or Chapter VII.

What technique was employed to open this chapter you are now reading?

USE AN EXHIBIT

Perhaps the easiest way in the world to gain attention is to hold up something for people to look at. It can be used sometimes with effectiveness before the most dignified audience. For example, one of my students opened one of her talks by holding up a coupon and waving it above her head. Naturally every one looked. Then she inquired: "Has any one here ever received a coupon like this in the mail? It announces that the recipient will be given a free boat ride and dinner and a tour a beautiful new real estate development on the Hudson River. All he or she has to do is to call and present this coupon." That got their attention. She then proceeded to reveal how this trick was used to entice people to the development so they could be exposed to a high pressure sales pitch.

ASK A QUESTION

Mrs. Ellis' opening has another commendable feature. It begins by asking a question, by getting the audience thinking with the speaker, cooperating with him. Note that the opening of the article on sex and romance on the job asks a question, "What special problems does this present to the company?". . . "How?" The use of this question-key is really one of the simplest, surest ways to unlock the minds of your audience and let yourself in. When other tools prove useless, you can always fall back on it.

WHY NOT OPEN WITH A QUESTION FROM SOME FAMOUS PERSON?

The words of prominent people always have attention power; so a suitable quotation is one of the very best ways of launching a harangue. Do you like the following opening of a discussion on having faith in humanity ?

"You must not lose faith in humanity. Humanity is an ocean; if a few drops of the ocean are dirty, the ocean does not become dirty."

As a starter, that has several commendable features. The initial sentence arouses curiosity; Why should we have faith in humanity? Mahatma Gandhi made this statement. It carries us forward, we want to hear more. If the speaker pauses skillfully after the name, "Mahatma Gandhi," it arouses suspense. "With all the turmoil, poverty and suffering his people in India have experienced, how can he have such faith?" we ask. Quick. Tell us. We may not agree with you, but give us your opinion anyway. The second sentence leads us right into the heart of the subject. He then warms up to his subject, sure there are terrible things in this world, but they are like drops of dirt in the vast ocean of good. . . .

TIE YOUR TOPIC UP TO THE VITAL INTERESTS OF YOUR HEARERS

Begin on some note that goes straight to the selfish interests of the audience. That is one of the best of all possible ways to start. It is sure to get attention. We are mightily interested in the things that touch us significantly, momentously.

That is only common sense, isn't it?

Yet the use of it is very uncommon. For example, I heard a speaker begin a talk on the necessity of periodic health examinations. How did he open? By telling the history of the medical organization with which he is affiliated, how it was organized and the service it was rendering. Absurd! Our hearers have not the foggiest, not the remotest, interest in how some organization was formed; but they are stupendously and eternally interested in themselves.

Why not recognize that fundamental fact? Why not show how that organization is of vital concern to them? Why not begin something like this? "Do you know how long you are expected to live according to the actuarial tables of the Social Security Administration? They have figured it all out. For example, a man at age 30 will probably live 44 more years, a woman of the same age 50. If the man survives to be 60, he will probably have 18 more years, a woman, 23. . . . Is that enough? No, no, we are all passionately eager for more. Yet those tables are based upon millions of records. May you and I, then, hope to beat them? Yes, with proper precaution, we may; but the very first step is to have a thorough physical examination. . . ."

Then, if we explain in detail why the periodic health examination is necessary, the hearer might he interested in some organization formed to render that service. But to begin talking about the organization in an impersonal way. It is disastrous! Deadly!

Take another example. One of my students began a talk on the prime urgency of conserving our forests. He opened like this: "We, as Americans, ought to be proud of our national resources. . . ." From that sentence, he went on to show that we were wasting our timber at a shameless and indefensible pace. But the opening was bad, too general, too vague. He did not make his subject seem vital to us. There was a printer in that audience. The destruction of our forests will mean something very real to his business. There was a mother; it is going to affect her for it will affect the life of her children... and so on. Why not begin, then, by saying: "The subject I am going to speak about affects your business, Mr. Appleby; Mrs. Saulit will, in some measure, affect the price of the food we eat and the rent that we pay. It touches the welfare and prosperity of us all not only in this generation, but far into the future."

Is that exaggerating the importance of conserving our forests? No, I think not. It is only obeying a key factor of good speeches:

"Paint the picture large and put the matter in a way that compels attention."

THE ATTENTION POWER OF SHOCKING FACTS

Shock your audience. Make them sit up and take notice. Say something that will jar them out of their day dreams; to be effective, you must demand attention. A speaker whose subject was, "The Marvels of Radio," began with this statement:

"Do you realize that the sound of a fly walking across a pane of glass in New York can be broadcasted by radio and made to roar away off in Central Africa like the falls of Niagara?"

Here's the way a student began a talk on the *Criminal Situation*:

"The administration of our criminal law," declared William Howard Taft, the chief justice of the supreme court of the United States, "is a disgrace to civilization."

That has the double advantage of being not only a shocking opening, but the shocking statement is quoted from an authority on jurisprudence.

Another speaker on the subject of crime began his address with these arresting statements:

"The American people are the worst criminals in the world. Astounding as that assertion is, it is true. Cleveland, Ohio, has six times as many murders as all London. It has one hundred and seventy times as many robberies, according to its population, as has London. More people are robbed every year, or assaulted with intent to rob, in Cleveland than in all England, Scotland and Wales combined. More people are murdered every year in St. Louis than in all England and Wales. There are more murders in New York City than in all France or Germany or Italy or the British Isles. The sad truth of the matter is that the criminal is not punished. If you commit a murder, there is less than one chance in a hundred that you will ever be executed for it. You, as a peaceful citizen, are ten times as liable to die from cancer as you would be to be hanged if you shot a man."

That opening was successful because the speaker put the requisite power and earnestness behind his words. They lived. They breathed. However, I have heard other students begin their talks on the crime situation with somewhat similar illustrations; yet their openings were mediocre. Why? Words. Words. Words. Their technique of construction was flawless, but their spirit was nil. Their manner vitiated and emaciated all they said.

THE VALUE OF THE SEEMINGLY CASUAL OPENING

How do you like the following opening, and why? Mary E. Richmond, a pioneer in Social Work, addressed the annual meeting of the New York League of Women Voters. Her subject was *Child Marriages in New York State*.

"Yesterday, as the train passed through a city not far away from here, I was reminded of a marriage that took place there a few years ago. Because many other marriages in this state have been just as hasty and disastrous as this one, I am going to begin what I have to say today with some of the details of this individual instance."

"It was on December 12th that a high school girl of fifteen in that city, met for the first time a junior in a nearby college who had just attained his majority. On December 15th, only three days later, they procured a marriage license by swearing that the girl was eighteen and was therefore free from the necessity of procuring parental consent. Leaving the city clerk's office with their license, they applied at once to a clergyman, but very properly, he refused to marry them. In some way, perhaps through this clergyman, the child's mother received news of the attempted marriage. Before she could find her daughter, however, a justice of the peace had united the pair. The bridegroom then took his bride to a hotel where they spent two days and two nights, at the end of which time he abandoned her and never lived with her again."

Personally, I like that opening very much. The very first sentence is good. It forecasts an interesting reminiscence. We want to hear the details. We settle down to listen to a human interest story. In addition to that, it seems very natural. It does not smack of the study, it is not formal. . . . "Yesterday, as the train passed through a city not far from here, I was reminded of a marriage that took place there a few years ago." Sounds natural, spontaneous, human. Sounds like one person relating an interesting story to another. An audience likes that. But it is very liable to shy at something too elaborate, too formal, something that appears to be an artificial device to gain attention. We want the art that conceals art.

IN A NUTSHELL

1.   The opening of a talk is difficult. It is also highly important, for the minds of our hearers are fresh then and comparatively easy to impress. It is of too much consequence to be left to chance; it ought to be carefully worked out in advance.

2.   The introduction ought to be short, only a sentence or two. Often, it can be dispensed with altogether. Wade right into the heart of your subject with the smallest possible number of words. No one objects to that.

3.   Novices are prone to begin either with attempting to tell a humorous story or by making an apology. Both of these are usually bad. Very few people very, very, very few can relate a humorous anecdote successfully. The attempt usually embarrasses the audience instead of entertaining them, Stories should be relevant, not dragged in just for the sake of the story. Humor should be the icing on the cake, not the cake itself. Never apologize. It is usually an insult to your audience; it bores them. Drive right into what you have to say, say it quickly and sit down.

4.   A speaker may be able to win the immediate attention of his audience by:

a.   Arousing curiosity. (Illustration- Story of Dicken's "Christmas Carol.")

b.   Relating a human interest story. (Illustration- "Acres of Diamonds" lecture.)

c.   Beginning with a specific illustration. (See the openings of Chapters V and VII of this book.)

d.   Using an exhibit. (Illustration- The coupon that entitled the recipient to a free boatride and meal.)

e.   Asking a question. (Illustration- "Has any one here ever received a coupon like this in the mail?")

f.   Opening with a striking quotation. (Illustration- Mahatma Gandhi's comments on humanity.)

g.   Showing how the topic affects the vital interest of the audience. (Illustration- "Here's how long the actuaries expect you to live. You may be able to increase that by having periodic health examinations," etc.)

h.   Starting with shocking facts. (Illustration- "The American people are the worst criminals in the civilized world.")

5.   Don't make your opening too formal. Don't let the bones show. Make it appear free, casual, inevitable. This can be done by referring to something that has just happened, or something that has just been said. (Illustration- "Yesterday, as the train passed through a city not far from here, I was reminded. . . .")

SPEECH BUILDING
WORDS OFTEN MISPRONOUNCED

The *A's* which are capitalized in the following should be sounded as "a" in *day*:

Apex	lusitAnia	tornAdo
Aviation	quAsi	ultimAtum
Aviator	rAdiator	utilitArian
blAtant	sAlient	verbAtim
dAta	stAtus	

Can you pronounce correctly all the italicized words in the following story?

Once upon a time, a *stolid* and *senile* Prince in the *Orient* read a *poem* about love. With the *advent* of spring, a hunger for *romance* stole over him, and he was unable to *combat* it. It was so *exquisite*, so *formidable*, so *inexplicable*, so delicious, so *dolorous*, so *shaking* and *quaking*, that he did not even desire to *combat* it. He felt that no one in the wide *domains* of his native land could understand the *marvelous melody* that *swept* through his heart. Consequently, he began to *frequent* the harbor, watching the stately *ships* sail in with high *masts* through the *mists*. His *finances* hardly permitted travel; so he went about *incognito*, using an *alias*, while he sold *alternately brooms* and *coupons* until he was able to stand the *financial* strain of a trip to *Seattle*. There he met a *fragile widow*, who had recently *divorced* a drug *addict*. Although he was not *conversant* with her language, he was an *expert* flatterer. However, she was *tepid* to his advances. She counted the cost *because* she did not want to marry in *haste* when her own mind was *hazy*. She *hissed* in his *face* that she was not *interested* in his proposal, that marriage with him would be *horrid*, *despicable*, *contrary* to her ideals. He received his *chastisement* in silence, tore up the *trousseau* that he had depleted his *finances* to purchase, and, *moaning* and *groaning*, he sailed back to *Honolulu*.

ERRORS IN ENGLISH

In this chapter there will be no specific review. Chapter VIII and the reviews in the preceding chapters, examined the use of every word to which attention had been called. We shall now start on the study of various other ordinary mistakes which are made in the English language.

RULE: Every pronoun which is the subject of a verb, must be in the nominative case, regardless of whether the verb is expressed or understood. In other words, when a pronoun is the subject of a verb, its *form* used should be:

I not *me*	*we* not *us*
he not *him*	*they* not *them*
she not *her*	*who* not *whom*

Right: He can do it as well as *I*.

Wrong: He can do it as well as *me*.

(The last word in this sentence is the subject of the understood verb can; so this is equivalent to saying, "He can do it as well as me can do it.")

Right: *He* and *I* were the first ones here.

Wrong: *Him* and *me* were the first ones here.

Right: *We* Americans will have to take a more active part in world affairs.

Wrong: *Us* Americans will have to take a more active part in world affairs. (Leave out the word *Americans* and the mistake shocks the cars of even the most undiscerning.)

Right: She was only about twelve years older than *I*.

Wrong: "She was only about twelve years older than *me*." (*Than* is a conjunction and takes the same case after it as before. The me in the sentence just quoted is really the subject of an understood verb. If the entire sentence were written, it would read, "She was only about twelve years older than *me* am old." This lamentable error is very common.)

RULE: Do not use a noun and its pronoun when the pronoun immediately follows the noun. Examples are:

Right: Thy rod and Thy staff comfort me.

Wrong: "Thy rod and Thy staff *they* comfort me."

RULE: Such compound pronouns, as *myself, itself, ourselves,* etc. are never to be used as subjects or objects. This usage often happens because the speaker or writer is not sure whether to use a nominative or objective pronoun.

Right: Mr. Jones and *you* will handle the work.

Wrong: Mr. Jones and *yourself* will handle the work.

Right: She handed the money to Nancy and *me*.

Wrong: She handed the money to Nancy and *myself*.

Right: It was *they* who concealed their assets.

Wrong: It was *themselves* who concealed their assets.

RULE: They may be used, however, to refer back to the subject or to express emphasis.

Right: The man hurt *himself*.

Right: The girl *herself* told me so.

RULE: Never use *hisself, theirself, ourself,* and *theirselves*. These are not correct English words.

CORRECT USAGE OF WORDS

The *fair* person attempts to be honest and just and impartial. The open person speaks freely and exactly what is in his or her mind. The *frank* person does it from a natural dislike of restraint. The *ingenuous* person has a natural simplicity and regard for truth that prompts confession of faults and willingness to speak without any reserve. (*Ingenuous* must not be confused with *ingenious*, meaning cleverly contrived.) The *sincere* person never pretends to be anything false; he or she is genuine, real. A person who speaks openly on occasions may not naturally be *frank* and *fair*. A *frank* person may not go so far in outspokenness and confessions as the *ingenuous* person. The *sincere* person may not speak freely, but will never falsely assume to be, what he or she is not.

Candid, candle and *chandelier* all come from the same Latin word *candere*, "to be of glowing white." A candid opinion is a glowing white, shining opinion-giving light on both sides without any attempt at concealment. The *unsophisticated* person is sound and genuine, artless, innocent. He or she does not deal in *sophistry. Unreserved* implies freedom and frankness in words and action. The *undesigning* individual has no schemes or plots or selfish ends to serve. The *unvarnished* statement has no gloss; it does not attempt to smooth over anything with fair words. Other words related in meaning to these are: *artless, free-spoken, guileless, honest, impartial, open, plain-spoken, equitable, unaffected, undisguised, unfeigned, straightforward.*

VOICE EXERCISE - RELAXING THE JAW

In the voice exercises for Chapters III and IV, we pointed out the necessity for relaxation, especially of the throat. The jaw also should be relaxed. Most of us are inclined to hold it rigidly. And what is the result? The tone is forced to squeeze itself out; so it becomes thin and hard. Such a tone, made under such conditions, does not carry well. Our breath is molded into words in our mouth very largely by means of our lips and tongue, the tongue playing the principal part. The set jaw distorts this mouth-mold, and interferes with the beauty and precision of the sounds that should flow from it.

Besides, stiff jaws are very liable to result in clumsy tongues; but it is tongue speed and firmness and elasticity that we prize.

Try these exercises for surrendering the jaw.

1. Drop the head on the breast, until your chin is touching your skin. Raise all of the head now except the lower jaw. If you relax it thoroughly, gravity will hold it down just as gravity pulls your hands down to your sides when you relax them.

2. Sit with your jaw relaxed in the mouth-open, dull-eyed attitude of an idiot until the jaw feels like a dead weight hanging from the rest of the head.

3. Put your fingers about half an inch in front of your ears where the lower jawbone hinges. Open the jaw deliberately. Chew as if you were masticating your food. Note the action underneath your fingertips. Now close the mouth, surrender the jaw this time and let it fall of its own dead weight. If you have done it correctly, if you have not used force, you will not feel the action under your fingertips this time that you felt before.

4. When you are trying to overhear a conversation in the distance, and you can hardly understand it, what do you do? You unconsciously take a deep breath; let your mouth fall open and listen intently, don't you? Imagine you are now listening under such circumstances. Imagine that you have suddenly heard in that distant conversation, something that has surprised you exceedingly. What do you do? You expand and lift your body, take a deeper breath and your throat

opens unconsciously. Now, say "Oh, do you know what he said?" Doesn't the tone flow out easily and freely?

Remember that the only way you can obtain command of the jaw is by relaxing it, so practice these exercises until your jaw is your docile servant, not a stiff, set and obstreperous one.

Review Exercise:

1. Read the following Salutation to the Dawn. It is a beautiful passage from the Sanskrit. Read it aloud in a falsetto voice to develop brightness. (See Voice Exercise, Chapter VII.)

"Look to this day, for it is life, the very life of life. In its brief course lie all the verities and realities of your existence, the bliss of growth, the glory of action, the splendor of beauty. Yesterday is already a dream, and tomorrow is only a vision; but today, well lived, makes every yesterday a dream of happiness and every tomorrow a vision of hope. Look, well, therefore to this day. Such is the salutation of the dawn."

2. Read this aloud now in your natural voice, using the tip of the tongue to strike off the emphatic ideas with a light elastic touch. (See Voice Exercise, Chapter VI.)

3. Take a deep breath from the diaphragm and with an open and relaxed throat, say "ah." Say it without any effort. Say it with perfect ease.

4. Turn to the Voice Exercise, Chapter VII, and read aloud with bright and happy tones, the four verses beginning:

"It isn't raining rain to, me,

It's raining daffodils."

Chapter 10

CAPTURING YOUR AUDIENCE
AT ONCE

"Talking is like playing on the harp. There is as much is laying the hands on the strings to stop the vibrations as in twanging them to bring out their music."

-Oliver Wendell Holmes

"Be Sincere. Be simple in words, manners and gestures. Amuse as well as instruct. If you can make people laugh, you can make them think and make them like and believe you."

-Alfred E. Smith

"The way we generally strive for rights is by getting our fighting blood up; and I venture to say that, that is the long way and not the short way. If you come at me with your fists doubled, I think I can promise you that mine will double as fast as yours; but if you come to me and say, 'Let us sit down and take counsel together, and, if we differ from one another, understand why it is that we differ from one another, just what the points at issue are,' we will presently find that we are not so far apart after all, that the points on which we differ are few and the points on which we agree are many, and that if we only have the patience and the candor and the desire to get together, we "will get together."

-Woodrow Wilson

Chapter 10

CAPTURING YOUR AUDIENCE AT ONCE

S everal years ago the Colorado Fuel and Iron Company, a company owned by the Rockefeller organization, was suffering from labor troubles. Shooting had taken place; there had been bloodshed. The air was electric with bitter hatreds. The very name of Rockefeller was anathema. Yet John D. Rockefeller Jr. wanted to talk to the employees of that concern. He wanted to explain, to persuade them to his way of thinking, to get them to accept his beliefs. He realized that, in the very opening of his speech, he must eradicate all ill feeling, all antagonism. At the very outset, he did it beautifully and sincerely. Most public speakers can study his method with profit:

"This is a red-letter day in my life. It is the first time I have had the good fortune to meet the representatives of the employees of this great company, its officers and superintendents, together, and I can assure you that I am proud to be here, and that I shall remember this gathering as long as I live. Had this meeting been held two weeks ago, I should have stood here a stranger to most of you, recognizing few faces. Having had the opportunity last week of visiting all the camps in the southern coal fields and of talking individually with practically all of the representatives, except those who were away; having visited in your homes, met many of your wives and children, we meet here not as strangers but as friends, and it is in that spirit of mutual friendship that I am glad to have this opportunity to discuss with you our common interests."

"Since this is a meeting of the officers of the company and the representatives of the employees, it is only by your courtesy that I am here, for I am not so fortunate as to be either one or the other; and yet I feel that I am intimately associated with you men, for, in a sense, I represent both the stockholders and the directors."

That is tact, supreme tact. And the speech, in spite of the bitter hatred that had existed, was successful. The men who had been

199

striking and fighting for higher wages never said anything more about it after Rockefeller had explained all the facts in the situation.

A DROP OF HONEY AND TWO-GUN MEN

It is an old and true maxim that a drop of honey catches more flies than a gallon of gall. So it is with people. If you would win people to your cause, first convince them that you are their sincere friend. Therein is a drop of honey that catches their hearts; which is the great high road to reason, and when once gained, you will find but little trouble in convincing their judgment of the justice of your cause, if, indeed, that cause really be a just one.

That was Lincoln's plan. In 1858, during his campaign for the United States Senate, he was announced to speak in what was, at that time, the semi-barbarous part of Southern Illinois called "Egypt." They were a rough lot, the men in that section, and they carried ugly looking knives and pistols strapped to their belts, even on public occasions. Their hatred of all anti-slavery men was equaled only by their love of fighting and corn whiskey. Southern men, some of them slave owners from Kentucky and Missouri, had crossed over the Mississippi and the Ohio to be on hand for the excitement and trouble. Plenty of it was in prospect, for the rougher elements had sworn that, if Lincoln tried to talk, they would "run the damned Abolitionist out of town," and "shoot him to fiddle strings."

Lincoln had heard these threats, and he knew the intense feeling that existed, the positive danger. "But if only they will give me a fair chance to say a few opening words," he declared, "I'll fix them all right." So, before beginning to talk, he had himself introduced to the ringleaders and shook their hands cordially. He made one of the most tactful openings I have ever read:

"Fellow citizens of Southern Illinois, fellow citizens of the State of Kentucky, fellow citizens of Missouri. I am told there are some of you here present who would like to make trouble for me. I don't understand why they should. I am a plain, common man, like the rest of you; and why should I not have as good a right to speak my sentiments as the rest of you? Why, good friends, I am one of you. I am not an interloper here. I was born in Kentucky, and raised in Illinois, just like the most of you, and worked my way along by hard scratching. I know the people of Kentucky, and I know the people of Southern Illinois, and I think I know the Missourians. I am one of them and therefore ought to know them; and they ought to know me better, and if they did know me better, they would know that I am not disposed to make them trouble. Then, why should they, or any one of them, want to make trouble for me? Don't do any such foolish thing, fellow citizens. Let us be friends, and treat each other like friends. I am one of the humblest and most peaceful men in the world, would wrong no man, would interfere with no man's rights. And all I ask is that, having something to say, you give me a decent hearing. And, being Illinoisans, Kentuckians, and Missourians, brave and gallant people, I feel sure that you will do that. And now let us reason together, like the honest fellows we are."

As he spoke these words, his face was the very picture of good nature, and his voice vibrated with sympathetic earnestness. That tactful opening calmed the oncoming storm and silenced his enemies. In fact, it transformed many of them into friends. They cheered his speech, and, later, those rough and rude "Egyptians" were among his most ardent supporters for the Presidency.

"Interesting," you remark, "but what has all this got to do with me? I am no Rockefeller; I am not going to address hungry strikers longing to strangle and batter the life out of me. I am no Lincoln; I am not going to talk to two-gun desperadoes full of corn whiskey and hatred."

True, true, but aren't you, almost every day of your life, talking to people who differ from you on some subject under discussion? Aren't you constantly trying to win people to your way of thinking at home, in the office, in the market place? Is there room for improvement in your methods? How do you begin? By showing Lincoln's tact? And Rockefeller's? If so, you are a person of rare finesse and extraordinary discretion. Most people begin, not by thinking about the other person's views and desires, not by trying to find a common ground of agreement, but by unloading their own opinions.

For example, I have heard hundreds of speeches on the hotly contested subject of gun control. In almost every instance, the speakers, with all the tact of a bull in a china shop, opened with some positive and perhaps belligerent statement. They showed once and for all which direction they faced and under which flag they fought. They showed that their minds were made up so firmly that there was not the slightest chance of it being changed; yet they were expecting others to abandon their cherished beliefs and to accept theirs. The effect? About the same that results from all arguments, no one was convinced. Instantly, they lost by their blunt, aggressive opening the sympathetic attention of all who differed with then; instantly, their audiences discounted all that was said; instantly, they challenged the speakers' statements; instantly, they held their opinions in contempt. The talk served but to entrench them more strongly behind the bulwark of their own beliefs.

You see, they made, at the very outset, the fatal mistake of prodding their listeners, of getting them bending backwards and saying through their shut teeth: "No! No! No!"

Is not that a very serious situation if one wishes to win converts to his way of thinking? A most illuminating statement on this point is the following quotation from Harry Overstreet's lectures before the New School for Social Research in New York City.

"A 'No' response is a most difficult handicap to overcome, When a person has said 'No,' all his pride of personality demands that he remain consistent with himself. He may later feel that the 'No' was ill advised; nevertheless, there is his precious pride to consider! Once having said a thing, he must stick to it. Hence it is of the very greatest importance that we start a person in the affirmative direction." Skillful speakers get "at the outset a number of 'yes-responses.' They have thereby set the psychological processes of their listeners moving in the affirmative direction. It is like the movement of a billiard ball. Propel it in one direction, and it takes some force to deflect it; far more force to send it back in the opposite direction."

Overstreet added, "The psychological patterns here are quite clear. When a person says 'No' and really means it, he is doing far more than saying a word of two letters. His entire organism; glandular, nervous, muscular; gathers itself together into a condition of rejection. There is, usually in minute but sometimes in observable degree, a physical withdrawal or readiness for withdrawal. The whole neuromuscular system, in short, sets itself on guard against acceptance. Where, on the contrary, a person says 'Yes,' none of the withdrawing activities take place. The organism is in a forward moving, accepting and open attitude. Hence the more 'Yesses' we can, at the very outset, induce, the more likely we are to succeed in capturing the attention for our ultimate proposal.

"It is a very simple technique this, yes-response. And yet how much neglected! It often seems as if people get a sense of their own importance by antagonizing at the outset. The radical comes into a conference with his conservative brethren; and immediately he must make them furious! What, as a matter of fact, is the good of it? If he simply does it in order to get some pleasure out of it for himself, he may be pardoned. But if he expects to achieve something, he is only psychologically stupid.

"Get a student to say 'No' at the beginning, or a customer, child, husband, or wife; and it takes the wisdom and the patience of angels to transform that bristling negative into an affirmative."

How is one going to get these desirable "yes-responses" at the very outset? Fairly simple. "My way of opening and winning an argument," confided Lincoln, "is to first find a common ground of agreement." Lincoln found it even when he was discussing the highly inflammable subject of slavery. "For the first half hour," declared a neutral newspaper reporting one of his talks, "his opponents would agree with every word he uttered. From that point he began to lead them off, little by little, until it seemed as if he had got them all into his fold."

SENATOR LODGE'S WAY OF DOING IT

Shortly after the close of the first World War, a major issue before the congress was the ratification of the treaty that created the League of Nations. One of the leading opponents of ratification was Senator Henry Cabot Lodge of Massachusetts. He debated this issue with President Abbbot Lawrence Lowell of Harvard before a Boston audience. Senator Lodge felt that most of the audience was hostile to his view; yet he must win them to his way of thinking. How? By a direct, frontal, aggressive attack on their convictions? Ah, no. The Senator was far too shrewd a psychologist to bungle his plea with such crude tactics. He began with supreme tact, with admirable finesse. The opening of his speech is quoted in a following paragraph. Note that even his most bitter opponents could not have differed with the sentiments expressed in his first dozen sentences. Note how he appeals to their emotion of patriotism in his salutation: "My Fellow Americans." Observe how he minimizes the differences in the views they are to defend, how he deftly stresses the things they cherish in common.

See how he praises his opponent, how he insists upon the fact that they differ only on minor details of method, and not at all upon the vital question of the welfare of America and the peace of the world. He even goes further and admits that he is in favor of a League of Nations of some kind. So, in the last analysis, he differed from his opponent only in this: he felt that we ought to have a more ideal and efficacious League.

"Your Excellency, Ladies and Gentlemen, My Fellow Americans:

"I am largely indebted to President Lowell for this opportunity to address this great audience. He and I are friends of many years, both Republicans. He is the president of our great university, one of the most important and influential places in the United States. He is also an eminent student and historian of politics and government. He and I may differ as to methods in this great question now before the people, but I am sure that in regard to the security of the peace of the world and the welfare of the United States we do not differ in purposes."

"I am going to say a single word, if you will permit me, as to my own position. I have tried to state it over and over again. I thought I had stated it in plain English. But there are those who find in misrepresentation, a convenient weapon for controversy, and there are others, most excellent people, who perhaps have not seen what I have said and who possibly have misunderstood me. It has been said that I am against any League of Nations. I am not; far from it. I am anxious to have the nations, the free nations of the world, united in a league, as we call it, a society, as the French call it, but united, to do all that can be done to secure the future peace of the world and to bring about a general disarmament."

No matter how determined you were beforehand to differ with a speaker, an opening like that would make you soften and relent a bit, wouldn't it? Wouldn't it make you willing to listen to more? Wouldn't it tend to convince you of the speaker's fair mindedness?

What would have been the result had Senator Lodge set out immediately to show those who believed in the League of Nations that they were hopelessly in error, cherishing a delusion? The result would have been futile; the following quotation from James Harvey Robinson's enlightening and popular book, *The Mind in the Making*, shows the psychological reason why such an attack would have been futile:

"We sometimes find ourselves changing our minds without any resistance or heavy emotion, but if we are told we are wrong, we resent the imputation and harden our hearts. We are incredibly heedless in the formation of our beliefs, but find ourselves filled with an illicit passion for them when anyone proposes to rob us of their companionship. It is obviously not the ideas themselves that are dear to us, but our self-esteem which is threatened. . . . The little word "my" is the most important one in human affairs and properly to reckon with, it is the beginning of wisdom. It has the same force whether it is my dinner, my dog and my house, or my faith, my country and my God. We not only resent the imputation that our watch is wrong, or our car shabby, but that our conception of the canals of Mars, of the pronunciation of 'Epictetus,' of the medicinal value of salicine, or of the date of Sargon 1, are subject to revision. . . . We like to continue to believe what we have been accustomed to accept as true, and the resentment aroused when doubt is cast upon any of our assumptions leads us to seek every manner of excuse for clinging to it. The result is that most of our so-called reasoning consists in finding arguments for going on believing as we already do."

THE BEST ARGUMENT IS AN EXPLANATION

Is it not quite evident that the speaker who argues with an audience is merely arousing their stubbornness, putting them on the defensive, making it well nigh impossible for them to change their minds? Is it wise to start by saying, "I am going to prove so and so?" Aren't your hearers liable to accept that as a challenge and remark silently? "Let's see you do it."

Is it not much more advantageous to begin by stressing something that you and all of your hearers believe, and then to raise some pertinent question that everyone would like to have answered? Then take your audience with you in an earnest search for the answer. While on that search, present the facts as you see them so clearly that they will unconsciously be led to accept your conclusions as their own. They will have much more faith in some truth that they believe they have discovered for themselves.

"The best argument is that which seems merely an explanation."

In every controversy, no matter how wide and bitter the differences, there is always some common ground of agreement on which the speaker can invite everyone to assemble for the search after facts that is going to be presented. To illustrate: even if the President of the AFL-CIO. were addressing a convention of the American Bankers' Association, some mutual beliefs, some analogous desires could be found to share with the audience. Here's an example:

"Poverty has always been one of the cruel problems of human society. As Americans, we have always felt it our duty to alleviate, whenever and wherever possible, the sufferings of the poor. We are a generous nation. No other people in all history have poured out their wealth so prodigally, so unselfishly to help the unfortunate. Now, with this same mental generosity and spiritual unselfishness that has characterized our givings in the past, let us examine together the facts of our industrial life and see if we can find some means, fair and just and acceptable to all, that will tend to prevent as well as to mitigate, the evils of poverty."

Who could object to that?

Do we seem to be contradicting here the gospel of force and energy and enthusiasm so fervently praised in Chapter V? Hardly. There is a time for everything. But the time for force is seldom in the beginning of a talk. Tact is more likely to be needed then.

HOW PATRICK HENRY LAUNCHED HIS
STORMY ADDRESS

One of the classic speeches of all time, one most children learn in their first studies of American history is the fiery close of Patrick Henry's famous speech before the Virginia Convention of 1775, "Give me liberty or give me death." But few of them realize the comparative calm, the tactful manner in which Henry launched that stormy and emotional and history making address. Should the American colonies separate from and go to war with England? The question was being debated with intense passion. Feelings flamed at white heat; yet Patrick Henry began by complimenting the abilities and praising the patriotism of those who opposed him. Note, in the second paragraph, how he gets his audience thinking with him by asking questions, by letting them draw their own conclusions:

"Mr. President, no man thinks more highly than I do of the patriotism, as well as abilities, of the very worthy gentlemen who have just addressed the house. But different men often see the same

206

subject in different lights; and, therefore, I hope it will not be thought disrespectful to those gentlemen, if, entertaining as I do opinions of a character very opposite to theirs, I shall speak forth my sentiments freely, and without reserve. This is no time for ceremony. The question before the house is one of awful moment to the country. For my own part, I consider it as nothing less than a question of freedom or slavery. And in proportion to the magnitude of the subject ought to be the freedom of the debate. It is only in this way that we can hope to arrive at truth, and fulfill the great responsibility, which we hold to God and our country. Should I keep back my opinions at such a time, through fear of giving offense, I should consider myself as guilty of treason towards my country, and of an act of disloyalty toward the Majesty of Heaven, which I revere above all earthly things.

"Mr. President, it is natural to man to indulge in the illusions of hope. We are apt to shut our eyes against a painful truth and listen to the song of that Siren till she transforms us into beasts. Is this the part of wise men, engaged in a great and arduous struggle for liberty? Are we disposed to be of the number of those who, having eyes see not, and having ears hear not, the things, which so nearly concern their temporal salvation? For my part, whatever anguish of spirit it may cost, I am willing to know the whole truth; to know the worst and to provide for it."

THE BEST SPEECH SHAKESPEARE WROTE

The most famous speech that Shakespeare put into the mouth of any of his characters, Mark Antony's funeral oration over the body of Julius Caesar, is a classic example of supreme tact.

This was the situation. Caesar had become dictator. Naturally, inevitably, a score of his political enemies were envious, were eager to tear him down, to destroy him, to make his power their own. Twenty-three of them banded together under the leadership of Brutus and Cassius and thrust their daggers into his body. . . . Mark Antony had been Caesar's Secretary of State. He was a handsome chap, this Antony, a ready writer, a powerful speaker. He could represent the government well at public affairs. Small wonder Caesar had chosen him as his right hand man. Now, with Caesar out of the way, what should the conspirators do with Antony? Remove him? Kill him? There had been enough blood shed already;

there was enough to justify as it was. Why not win this Antony to their side, why not use his undeniable influence, his moving eloquence, to shield them and further their own ends? Sounded safe and reasonable; so they tried it. They saw him and went so far as to permit him to "say a few words" over the corpse of the man who had all but ruled the world.

Antony mounts the rostrum in the Roman Forum. Before him lies the murdered Caesar. A mob surges noisily and threateningly about Antony, a rabble friendly to Brutus, Cassius and the other assassins. Antony's purpose is to turn this popular enthusiasm into intense hatred, to stir the plebeians to rise in mutiny and stay those that had struck Caesar down. He raises his hands, the tumult ceases. He starts to speak. Note how ingeniously, how adroitly he begins, praising Brutus and the other conspirators:

"For Brutus is an honorable man;

So are they all, all honorable men."

Observe that he does not argue. Gradually, unobtrusively, he presents certain facts about Caesar; tells how the ransom from his captives filled the general coffers, how he wept when the poor cried, how he refused a crown, how he willed his estates to the public. He presents the facts; asks the mob questions; lets them draw their own conclusions. The evidence is presented, not as something new, but as something they had for the moment forgotten:

"I tell you that which you yourselves do know."

And with a magic tongue through it all, he whipped up their feelings, stirred their emotions, aroused their pity, heated their anger. Antony's masterpiece of tact and eloquence is given here in its entirety. Search where you will, range through all the broad fields of literature and oratory, and I doubt if you will find half a dozen speeches to equal this. It merits the serious study of every man who aspires to excel in the fine art of influencing human nature. But there is another reason, entirely aside from the one we are considering now, why Shakespeare ought to be read and reread by every literate person; he possessed a larger vocabulary than did any other writer who ever lived; he used words more magically, more beautifully. No one can study Macbeth and Hamlet and Julius Caesar without unconsciously brightening and widening and refining his or her own diction.

It is a long selection from a great play. Take the time to read it all.

It is an example of rhetoric that has never been surpassed. Note how Antony gets and keeps his audience's attention. Note how he changes a hostile group, first to one sympathetic to his views and then to action to take revenge for Caesar's murder.

Ant. Friends, Romans, countrymen, lend me your ears:

I come to bury Caesar, not to praise him.

The evil that men do lives after them;

The good is oft interred with their bones.

So let it be with Caesar. The noble Brutus

Hath told you Caesar was ambitious.

If it were so, it was a grievous fault;

And grievously hath Caesar answer'd it.

Here, under leave of Brutus and the rest,

For Brutus is an honorable man;

So are they all, all honorable men,

Come I to speak in Caesar's funeral.

He was my friend, faithful and just to me.

But Brutus says he was ambitious;

And Brutus is an honorable man.

He hath brought many captives home to Rome,

Whose ransoms did the general coffers fill.

Did this in Caesar seem ambitious?

When that the poor have cried, Caesar hath wept.

Ambition should be made of sterner stuff.

Yet Brutus says he was ambitious;

And Brutus is an honorable man.

You all did see that on the Lupercal

I thrice presented him a kingly crown,

Which he did thrice refuse.

Was this ambition?

Yet Brutus says he was ambitious;

And, sure, he is an honorable man.

I speak not to disprove what Brutus spoke,

But here I am, to speak what I do know.
You all did love him once, not without cause;
What cause withholds you, then, to mourn for him?
O judgment, thou art fled to brutish beasts,
And men have lost their reason! Bear with me;
My heart is in the coffin there with Caesar,
And I must pause till it come back to me.

1 *Cit*. Methinks there is much reason in his sayings.

2 *Cit*. If thou consider rightly of the matter, Caesar has had great wrong.

3 *Cit*. Has he not, masters? I fear there will a worse come in his place.

4 *Cit*. Mark'd ye his words? He would not take the crown;
Therefore 'tis certain he was not ambitious.

1 *Cit*. If it be found so, some will dear abide it.

2 *Cit*. Poor soul! his eyes are red as fire with weeping.

3 *Cit*. There's not a nobler man in Rome than Antony.

4 *Cit*. Now mark him; he begins again to speak.

Ant. But yesterday the word of Caesar might
Have stood against the world: now lies he there,
And none so poor to do him reverence.
O masters, if I were dispos'd to stir
Your hearts and minds to mutiny and rage,
I should do Brutus wrong, and Cassius wrong,
Who, you all know, are honorable men.
I will not do them wrong. I rather choose
To wrong the dead, to wrong myself, and you,
Than I will wrong such honorable men.
But here's a parchment with the seal of Caesar,
I found it in his closet, 'tis his will:
Let but the commons hear this testament
(Which, pardon me, I do not mean to read),
And they would go and kiss dead Caesar's wounds,

And dip their napkins in his sacred blood;
Yea, beg a hair of him for memory,
And, dying, mention it within their wills,
Bequeathing it as a rich legacy
Unto their Issue.

4 Cit. We'll hear the will; read it, Mark Antony.

Citizens. The will, the will! We will hear Caesar's will.

Ant. Have patience, gentle friends; I must not read it:
It is not meet you know how Caesar lov'd you.
You are not wood, you are not stones, but men;
And, being men, hearing the will of Caesar,
it will inflame you, it will make you mad.
'Tis good you know not that you are his heirs;
For, if you should, o what would come of it!

4 Cit. Read the will! we'll hear it, Antony;
You shall read us the will-Caesar's will!

Ant. Will you be patient? will you stay awhile?
I have o'ershot myself, to tell you of it.
I fear I wrong the honorable men
Whose daggers have stabb'd Caesar; I do fear it.

4 Cit. They were traitors: honorable men!

Citizens. The will! the testament

2 Cit. They were villains, murderers. The will! read the will!

Ant. You will compel me, then, to read the will?
Then make a ring about the corpse of Caesar,
And let me show you him that made the will.
Shall I descend? and will you give me leave?

Citizens. Come down.

2 Cit. Descend.   [He comes down.

3 Cit. You shall have leave.

4 Cit. A ring! stand round.

1 Cit. Stand from the hearse; stand from the body.

211

2 *Cit.* Room for Antony! most noble Antony!
Ant. Nay, press not so upon me; stand far off.
Citizens. Stand back; room! bear back.
Ant. If you have tears, prepare to shed them now.
You all do know this mantle: I remember
The first time ever Caesar put it on;
'Twas on a summer's evening, in his tent,
That day he overcame the Nervii.
Look, in this place ran Cassius' dagger through:
See what a rent the envious Casea made:
Through this the well-beloved Brutus stabb'd;
And, as he pluck'd his cursed steel away,
Mark how the blood of Caesar follow'd it,
As rushing out of doors, to be resolv'd
If Brutus so unkindly knock'd, or no;
For Brutus, as you know, was Caesar's angel:
Judge, o you gods, how dearly Caesar lov'd him,!
This was the most unkindest cut of all;
For, when the noble Caesar saw him stab,
Ingratitude, more strong than traitors' arms,
Quite vanquish'd him: then burst his mighty heart;
And, in his mantle muffling up his face,
Even at the base of Pompey's statua,
Which all the while ran blood, great Caesar fell.
O, what a fall was there, my countrymen!
Then I, and you, and all of us fell down,
Whilst bloody treason flourish'd over us.
O, now you weep; and, I perceive, you feel
The dint of pity: these are gracious drops.
Kind souls, what, weep you, when you but behold
Our Caesar's vesture wounded? Look you here,
Here is himself, marr'd, as you see, with traitors.

1 *Cit.* O piteous spectacle!

2 *Cit.* O noble Caesar!

3 *Cit.* O woeful day !

4 *Cit.* O traitors, villains!

1 *Cit.* O most bloody sight!

2 *Cit.* We will be reveng'd.

Citizens. Revenge, about, seek, burn, fire, kill, slay, let
not a traitor live!

Ant. Stay, countrymen.

1 *Cit.* Peace there! hear the noble Antony.

2 *Cit.* We'll hear him, we'll follow him, we'll die with him.

Ant. Good friends, sweet friends, let me not stir you up
To such a sudden flood of mutiny.
They that have done this deed are honorable:
What private griefs they have, alas, I know not,
That made them do't; they're wise and honorable,
And will, no doubt, with reasons answer you.
I come not, friends, to steal away your hearts:
I am no orator, as Brutus is;
But, as you know me all, a plain blunt man,
That love my friend; and that they know full well
That gave me public leave to speak of him.
For I have neither wit, nor words, nor worth,
Action, nor utterance, nor the power of speech,
To stir men's blood: I only speak right on;
I tell you that which you yourselves do know;
Show you sweet Caesar's wounds, poor, poor dumb mouths,
And bid them speak for me: but were I Brutus,
And Brutus Antony, there were an Antony
Would ruffle up your spirit, and put a tongue
In every wound of Caesar, that should move
The stones of Rome to rise and mutiny.

213

Citizens. We'll mutiny.

1 *Cit.* We'll burn the house of Brutus.

3 *Cit.* Away, then! come, seek the conspirators.

Ant. Yet hear me, countrymen; yet hear me speak.

Citizens. Peace, ho! hear Antony; most noble Antony.

Ant. Why, friends, you go to do you know not what.

Wherein hath Caesar thus deserv'd your loves?

Alas, you know not; I must tell you, then:

You have forgot the will I told you of.

Citizens. Most true; the will!-let's stay, and hear the will.

Ant. Here is the will, and under Caesar's seal.

To every Roman citizen he gives.

To every several man, seventy-five drachmas.

2 *Cit.* Most noble Caesar! -we'll revenge his death.

3 *Cit.* O, royal Caesar!

Ant. Hear me with patience.

Citizens. Peace, ho!

Ant. Moreover, he hath left you all his walks,

His private arbors, and new-planted orchards,

On this side Tiber; he hath left them you,

And to your heirs for ever; common pleasures,

To walk abroad, and recreate yourselves.

Here was a Caesar! when comes such another?

1 *Cit.* Never, never.-Come, away, away!

We'll burn his body in the holy place,

And with the brands fire the traitors' houses.

Take up the body.

2 *Cit.* Go, fetch fire.

3 *Cit.* Pluck down benches.

4 *Cit.* Pluck down forms, windows, any thing.

[Exeunt Citizens with, the body]

Ant. Now let it work:- Mischief, thou art afoot,

Take thou what course thou wilt!

214

IN A NUTSHELL

1.   Begin on common ground. Get everyone agreeing at the outset.

2.   Don't state your case so that people will be saying "no, no" at the start. When a person once says "no" his pride demands that he stick to it. "The more 'yesses' we can, at the very outset, induce, the more likely we are to succeed in capturing the attention for the ultimate proposal."

3.   Do not begin by saying that you are going to prove so and so. That is liable to arouse opposition. Your hearers may say, "let's see you do it." Raise some pertinent question, and let them go with you in a hunt for the answer.

4.   The most famous speech that Shakespeare ever wrote is Mark Antony's funeral oration over Caesar. It is a classic example of supreme tact. The Roman populace is friendly to the conspirators. Note how adroitly Antony turns this friendliness into a fury of hate. Note that he does it without arguing. He presents the facts, and lets them form their own opinions.

SPEECH BUILDING
WORDS OFTEN MISPRONOUNCED

The *A's* capitalized in the following words should sound like the *a* in *ask*? This first shade-vowel sound of a is difficult to describe on paper. It is not the a in hat; neither is it the *a* in *arm*. It is between them. However, if one must err, it had better be in underdoing rather than in over-doing it. At all hazards, avoid anything that smacks of affectation. Isn't it far better, at least in the United States, to mispronounce the *a* in *bath* and *half*, giving it the sound of *a* in *cat*, rather than to go to the other extreme and use the sound of *a* as in *arm*?

advAnce	Afternoon	Ask
advAntage	Answer	basket
bAss (fish)	demAnd	lAss
bAth	drAft	lAst
behAlf	fAst	lAugh
blAst	flAsk	mAster
brAnch	gAsp	pAss
brAss	ghAstly	pAst
cAlf	girAffe	pAstor

cAn't	glAnce	pAth
cAsh	glAss	plAnt
cAsket	grAft	repAst
cAst	grAnt	shAft
clAsp	grAsp	shA'n't (slang)
contrAst	grAss	slAnt
dAnce	hAlf	tAsk

ERRORS IN ENGLISH

Review. There are four mistakes in the following paragraph. Can you find them?

The president and myself, as officers, sign all checks. He and me were the ones who organized it and know all about the company. As the president often said, "It is our company and no one understands its affairs as well as us. We should reap the benefits of it."

New Study Material.

RULE: The various forms of the verb *to be; am, is, are, was, were, has been, can be, could be, will be, shall be, would be, should be, may be*, are followed by the nominative case. For example:

Right: If you were *I*, what would you say?

Wrong: If you were *me*, what would you say?

Right: It was *I* that telephoned.

Wrong: It was *me* that telephoned.

Right: If I was (or were) *he*, I would study at night.

Wrong: If I was *him*, I would study at night.

Right: I thought it was *she*.

Wrong: I thought it was *her*.

Right: It is *we* who are to blame.

Wrong: It is *us* who are to blame.

RULE: There are seemingly two exceptions to the first rule given above. When *it* precedes *to be* or *to have been*, the verb form is followed by the objective. case of the pronoun. Other subjects may be used like the word *it* in such construction. Examples:

216

Right: I know it to be *her*.

Wrong: I know it to be *she*.

Right: I know Mary to be *her*.

Wrong: I know Mary to be *she*.

Right: She supposed it to have been *them*.

Wrong: She supposed it to have been *they*.

Right: She supposed the robbers to have been *them*.

Wrong: She supposed the robbers to have been *they*.

RULE: If *to be* or *to have been* do not have *it* immediately in front of them, the verb form is followed by the nominative case of the pronoun just the same as in the first rule in this lesson.

Right: It was believed to be *she*.

Wrong: It was believed to be *her*.

Right: It was supposed to have been *they*.

Wrong: It was supposed to have been *them*.

RULE: Sometimes the subject of the principal verb of the sentence is the same as the one used with to be or to have been. In this instance, the infinitive form is followed by the nominative case. Examples are:

Right: Mary was believed to be she.

Wrong: Mary was believed to be her.

Right: Mary was supposed to have been she.

Wrong: Mary was supposed to have been her.

RULE: *Who* is used to refer to persons only. *Which* is used to refer to animals and objects. *That* may be used to refer to persons, animals, or objects. For example:

Right: The only three *who* discussed the matter with me were very angry.

Wrong: The only three *which* discussed the matter with me were very angry.

Right: Every customer with *whom* I talked.

Wrong: Every customer with *which* I talked.

Right: The dog *which* (or *that*) won first prize was sold.

Wrong: The dog *who* won first prize was sold.

CORRECT USAGE OF WORDS

AFFECTED - EFFECTED. *Affect* mean to influence; as, "The market was *affected* by the news." *Effect* means to accomplish or bring to pass; as, "He *effected* a satisfactory settlement of the dispute."

EMIGRANT - IMMIGRANT. When my grandfather left Dublin to settle in the USA, he was an *emigrant* from Ireland and an *immigrant* to the United States.

EMPTY - VACANT. That which contains nothing is *empty*; that which is without its regular occupant is *vacant*. An *empty* pew may not be *vacant*, and a *vacant* pew may not be *empty*.

EAGER - EARNEST - ANXIOUS. *Eager* is more superficial and impatient and less permanent than *earnest*. *Anxious* suggests mental distress and possibility of disappointment. One may be *eager* to send his mother a bouquet of flowers, *earnestly* hope that the investments she has made will provide for her comfort and be *anxious* about her health.

DISINTERESTED - UNINTERESTED. When you are willing to listen to all sides of a case and not take sides you are *disinterested*; if the matter is of no concern to you, you are *uninterested*.

PRESCRIBE - PROSCRIBE. *Prescribe* is to dictate or to give medical directions; *proscribe* means to outlaw or forbid.

VOICE EXERCISE - FLEXIBILITY OF THE LIPS

Nervous tension, and the beginning speaker is almost always troubled with it, especially at the outset of his talk, is very liable to manifest itself by tightening the muscles of the throat, and stiffening the jaws and lips. We have dealt in previous chapters with directions for the relaxation of the throat and jaw. Let us turn our attention now to stiff, inflexible lips. They are a handicap, a liability. The lips ought to be free and flexible to aid in the molding of clear and beautiful tones. You can possess this additional attractiveness and carrying power in your tones, if you are willing to pay for it with attention and practice. All we can do is to write the prescription here; you must take the medicine.

Take the phrase "no man." As you say no, round and protrude your lips. As you say *man*, draw them back as far as possible. Exaggerate the action. Draw them into something like a broad grin.

Imagine that you are posing for one of those smiles you see in the advertisements for tooth paste. Now say it rapidly over and over: *No man, no man, no man, no man.*

Add another phrase and try it again: *No man, no mind, no man, no mind, no man, no mind, no man, no mind, no man, no mind. . . .*

Repeat the following sentences many times, exaggerating the motion of your lips, using them as much as you can:

So-we-do-see-across-the-lea.

I say turn loose the nice cats and let them eat the fat and saucy rats.

Ah, get nice ice and bathe this boot in boiling oil.

The open sea lures the gulls and calls to me.

Review Exercise.

1. Surrender your jaw, let it fall like a dead weight from your head. Take in a deep breath, feel as if you were sucking the air down into your stomach, and chant "ah" with ease, without one tiny trace of effort.

2. Take a deep breath again and say with a sweeping gesture of the hand, "I am at ease. My jaw is relaxed. My throat is open and there is no strain anywhere."

3. Take in a deep breath and using all the principles we have learned so far about diaphragmatic breathing, relaxation, breath control, count as far as you can on one breath. Be sure to control the flow of the breath at the only place where it can be controlled without interfering with the voice, at the diaphragm.

Chapter 11

HOW TO CLOSE A TALK

"The conclusion, too, has definite work to perform. It rounds out the talk; it holds the audience's earnest attention for a brief moment on the speech as a whole. It draws the thread of thought together; it binds and finishes the fabric of the speech. Definitely plan and word your conclusion. Never break off your speech awkwardly and hurriedly with a mumbled: 'I guess that's all I have to say.' Complete your task and let the audience know it is complete."

-Platform Speaking by George Rowland Collins

"The clock has nothing to do with the length of a sermon. Nothing whatever! A long sermon is a sermon that seems long. And the short sermon is the one that ends while people are still wishing for more. It may have lasted only twenty minutes or it may have lasted for an hour and a half. If it leaves the people wishing for more, they do not know nor care what the clock said about the length of it. You cannot tell, therefore, how long a sermon is by watching the hands of a clock, watch the people. See where their hands are. If the hands of the men are for the most part in their vest pockets, pulling out their watches to note again how long you have been at it, this is ominous. See where their eyes are! See where their minds are, then you will know exactly what time of day it is for that particular sermon. It may be high time for it to come to an end."

-The Art of Preaching, by Charles R. Brown
Dean of the Divinity School, Yale University

Chapter 11

HOW TO CLOSE A TALK

Would you like to know in what parts of your speech you are most likely to reveal your inexperience or your expertness, your inaptitude or your finesse? I'll tell you; in the opening and the closing. There is an old saying in the theater, referring, of course, to actors, that goes like this: "By their entrances and their exits shall you know them."

The beginning and the ending! They are the hardest things in almost any activity to manage adroitly. For example, at a social function aren't the most trying feats, the graceful entrance and the graceful leave-taking? In a business interview, aren't the most difficult tasks, the winning approach and the successful close?

The close is really the most strategic point in a speech; what one says last, the final words left ringing in the ears when one ceases; these are likely to be remembered longest. Beginners, however, seldom appreciate the importance of this. Their endings often leave much to be desired.

What are their most common errors? Let us discuss a few and search for remedies.

First, there is the speaker who finishes with: "That is about all I have to say on the matter; so I guess I shall stop." That is not an ending. That is a mistake. That reeks of the amateur. That is almost unpardonable. If that is all you have to say, why not round off your talk, and promptly take your seat and stop without talking about stopping. Do that, and the inference that that is all you have to say may, with safety and good taste, be left to the discernment of the audience.

Then there are speakers who says all they have to say, but they don't know how to stop. They thrash about in a circle, covering the same ground, continually repeating the same ideas, leaving a bad impression.

223

The remedy? An ending has to be planned some time, doesn't it? Is it the part of wisdom to try to do it after you are facing an audience, while you are under the strain and stress of talking, while your mind must be intent on what you are saying? Or does common sense suggest the advisability of doing it quietly, calmly, beforehand?

Such accomplished speakers as Winston Churchill, Franklin Roosevelt, Billy Graham and Martin Luther King, with their admirable command of the English language, felt it necessary to write down and all but memorize the exact words of their closings.

Beginners, if they follow in their footsteps, will seldom have cause to regret it. They ought to know very definitely with what ideas they are going to close. They should rehearse the ending several times, using not necessarily the same phraseology during each repetition, but putting the thoughts definitely into words.

An extemporaneous talk, during the process of delivery, sometimes has to be altered very materially, has to be cut and slashed to meet unforeseen developments, to harmonize with the reactions of one's hearers; so it is really wise to have two or three closings planned. If one does not fit, another may.

Some speakers never get to the end at all. Along in the middle of their journey, they begin to sputter and misfire like an engine when the gasoline supply is about exhausted; after a few desperate lunges, they come to a complete standstill, a breakdown. They need, of course, better preparation, more practice, more gasoline in the tank.

Many novices stop too abruptly. Their method of closing lacks smoothness, lacks finish. Properly speaking, they have no close; they merely cease suddenly, jerkily. The effect is unpleasant, amateurish. It is as if a friend in a social conversation were to break off brusquely and dart out of the room without a graceful leave-taking.

No less a speaker than Lincoln made that mistake in the original draft of his First Inaugural. That speech was delivered at a tense time. The black storm, clouds of dissension and hatred were already milling overhead. A few weeks later, the cyclone of blood and destruction burst upon the nation. Lincoln, addressing his closing words to the people of the South, had intended to end in this fashion:

"In your hands, my dissatisfied fellow countrymen, and not in mine, is the momentous issue of the civil war. The government will not assail you. You can have no conflict without being yourselves, the aggressors. You have no oath registered in heaven to destroy the government, while I have a most solemn one to preserve, protect and defend it. You can forbear the assault upon it. I cannot shrink from the defense of it. With you and not with me is the solemn question of- Shall it be peace or a sword?"

He submitted his speech to Secretary Seward. Seward quite appropriately pointed out that the ending was too blunt, too abrupt, too provocative. So Seward himself tried his hand at a closing; in fact, he wrote two. Lincoln accepted one of them and used it, with slight modifications, in place of the last three sentences of the close he had originally prepared. The result was that his First Inaugural Address now lost its provocative abruptness and rose to a climax of friendliness of sheer beauty and poetical eloquence.

"I am loath to close. We are not enemies but friends. We must not be enemies. Though passion may have strained, it must not break our bonds of affection. The mystic chords of memory, stretching from every battlefield and patriot's grave to every living heart and hearthstone all over this broad land, will swell the chorus of the Union when again touched, as surely they will be, by the better angel of our nature."

How can a beginner develop the proper feeling for the close of an address? Not by mechanical rules; it is too delicate for that. It must be a matter of sensing, almost of intuition. You must feel when it is done harmoniously and adroitly.

However, this *feeling* can be cultivated; this expertness can be developed somewhat, by studying the ways in which accomplished speakers have achieved it. Here is an illustration, President Bill Clinton in a speech commemorating the death of Martin Luther King ended his talk about renewing national unity with these words:

"We have to make a partnership, all the government agencies, all the business folks. But where there are no families, where there is no order, where we have lost jobs because we had to reduce the size of the armed forces after the end of the Cold War, who will be there to give structure, role-modeling, discipline, love, and hope to these children? You must do that, and we will help you. Scripture says, 'You are the salt of the earth and the light of the world, that if your light shines before men, they will give glory to the Father in Heaven.' That is what we must do. That is what we must do. And I will work with you."

This is how a talk should end. Everybody listening to that talk would feel that it was ended. It isn't left dangling in the air like a loose rope. It isn't left ragged and jagged. It is rounded off, it is finished.

"With malice toward none; with charity for all; with firmness in the right, as God gives us to see the right, let us strive on to finish the work we are in; to bind up the nation's wounds; to care for him who shall have borne the battle, and for his widow and his orphan to do all which may achieve and cherish a just and lasting peace among ourselves, and with all nations."

You have just read, my dear reader, what is, in my opinion the most beautiful speech ending ever delivered. Do you agree with my estimate? Where, in all the range of speech literature, will you find more humanity, more sheer loveliness, more sympathy?

"Noble as was the Gettysburg Address," says William E. Barton in *Life of Abraham Lincoln*, "this rises to a still higher level of nobility... It is the greatest of the addresses of Abraham Lincoln and registers his intellectual and spiritual power at their highest altitude."

"This was like a sacred poem," wrote Carl Schurz. "No American President had ever spoken words like these to the American people. America had never had a president who had found such words in the depths of his heart."

But you are not going to deliver immortal pronouncements as the leaders of our nation. Your problem, perhaps, will be how to close a simple talk before a group of men and women like yourself. How shall you set about it? Let us search a bit. Let us see if we cannot uncover some fertile suggestions.

SUMMARIZE YOUR POINTS

Even in a short talk of three to five minutes, a speaker is very apt to cover so much ground that at the close, the listeners are a little hazy about all the main points. However, few speakers realize that. They are misled into assuming that because these points are crystal clear in their own minds, they must be equally lucid to their hearers. Not at all. The speaker has been pondering over these ideas for some time. But the points are all new to the audience; they are flung at the audience like a handful of shot. Some may stick, but most are liable to roll off in confusion. The hearers are liable to remember a mass of things, but nothing distinctly.

Some anonymous Irish politician is reported to have given this recipe for making a speech: "First, tell them that you are going to tell them; then tell them; then tell them that you have told them." Not bad, you know. In fact, it is often highly advisable to "tell them that you have told them." Briefly, of course, speedily a mere outline, a summary.

Here is a good example. The speaker is a woman who is enlisting support for a fund raising "walkathon" for breast cancer research.

"In short, ladies and gentlemen, the statistics I have presented to you prove that the number of women being diagnosed with breast cancer is increasing every year. Much has been learned already to alleviate their pain and suffering, but there is so much more we must learn. Our research is making significant breakthroughs, but we have much more to do. Your help by joining our Walkathon next week will help increase the funds needed for this important endeavor."

You see what she has done? You can see it and feel it without having heard the rest of the talk. She has summed up in a few sentences, in seventy-eight words, practically all the points she had made in the entire talk.

Don't you feel that a summary like that helps? If so, make that technique your own.

APPEAL FOR ACTION

The closing just quoted is an excellent illustration of the appeal for action ending. The speaker wanted something done, raising funds for breast cancer research. She based her appeal for it on the money it would raise, on the pain and suffering it would prevent. The speaker wanted action and got it. This was not a mere practice talk. It was delivered before a group of 50 or so woman gathered in a community center and resulted in more than 30 women signing up and most of the others pledging financial support.

Chapter XV will discuss, in detail, the problems that confront the speaker when he attempts to get action and how to solve them.

A TERSE, SINCERE COMPLIMENT

"The members of this group represent the cultural leaders of this city. It is your hard work that has enabled us to bring top level opera productions to Wichita. It is your devotion to the arts that has led to the development of an opera workshop at the university and the introductory courses in classical music to the school system. We on the opera board are proud of you. We thank you, Wichita thanks you and music lovers from all over appreciate your dedication."

With these words, Burton Pell, president of the Wichita, Kansas Opera Guild, left his hearers pleased, happy, optimistic. That is an admirable way to finish; but, in order to be effective, it must be sincere. No gross flattery. No extravagances. This kind of a closing, if it does not ring true, will ring false, very false. And like a false coin, people will have none of it.

CLOSING WITH A POETICAL QUOTATION

Of all methods of ending, none are more acceptable, when well done, than using poetry or a famous quotation.

When the president of a Fortune-500 company spoke to the employees of his organization on the subject of Loyalty and Cooperation. He closed his address with this ringing verse from Kipling's Second jungle Book:

"Now this is the Law of the jungle; as old and as true as the sky;

And the Wolf that shall keep it may prosper, but the

Wolf that shall break it must die.

As the creeper that girdles the tree-trunk, the Law
runneth forward and back-

For the strength of the Pack is the Wolf, and the strength of the
Wolf is the Pack."

Dr. Sara Hill has devoted her life to developing programs to make the education we give our children, more effective and meaningful. In a talk she gave to a meeting of teachers in Long Island, New York, she challenged the superficiality that permeates so many school subjects. After presenting cogent arguments to support her point, she concluded with these famous lines from Alexander Pope

"A little learning is a dangerous thing.

Drink deep or taste not the Pierian spring;

There shallow draughts intoxicate the brain

And drinking largely sobers us again."

If you will go to the public library in your town and tell the librarian that you are preparing a talk on a certain subject and that you wish a poetical quotation to express this idea or that, she may be able to help you find something suitable in some reference volume such as Bartlett's book of quotations.

THE CLIMAX

The climax is a popular way of ending. It is often difficult to manage and is not an ending for all speakers nor for all subjects. But, when well done, it is excellent. It works up to a crest, a peak, getting stronger sentence by sentence. A good illustration of the climax will be found in the close of the prize winning speech on Philadelphia in Chapter III.

Lincoln used the climax in preparing his notes for a lecture on Niagara Falls. Note how each comparison is stronger than the preceding, how he gets a cumulative effect by comparing its age to Columbus, Christ, Moses, Adam, and so on.

"It calls up the indefinite past. When Columbus first sought this continent, when Christ suffered on the cross, when Moses led Israel through the Red Sea-nay, even when Adam first came from the hands of his Maker; then, as now, Niagara was roaring here. The eyes of that species of extinct giants whose bones fill the mounds of America have gazed on Niagara, as ours do now. Contemporary with the first race of men, and older than the first man, Niagara is as strong and fresh today as ten thousand years ago. The Mammoth and Mastodon, so long dead that fragments of their monstrous bones alone testify that they ever lived, have gazed on Niagara in that long, long time never still for a moment, never dried, never frozen, never slept, never rested."

Wendell Phillips, one of the principal anti-slavery orators in pre Civil War America, employed this selfsame technique in his address on Toussaint L'Ouverture, the leader of the slave revolt in Haiti against France in the early 1800s and who was later lured to France by Napoleon and there imprisoned and killed. Toussant is almost forgotten today in most of the world, but in the nineteenth century, he was looked upon as a hero not only in Haiti, but particularly among the abolitionists in the United States.

The close of it is quoted below. This selection is often cited in books on public speaking. It has vigor, vitality. It is interesting even though it is a bit too ornate for this practical age. This speech was written more than a century ago. Amusing, isn't it, to note how woefully wrong were Wendell Phillips' prognostications concerning the historical significance of John Brown and Toussaint L'Ouverture "fifty years hence when truth gets a hearing"? It is as hard evidently to guess history as it is to foretell next year's stock market.

"I would call him Napoleon, but Napoleon made his way to empire over broken oaths and through a sea of blood. This man never broke his word. 'No Retaliation' was his great motto and the rule of his life; and the last words uttered to his son in France were these: 'My boy, you will one day go back to Haiti; forget that France murdered your father.' I would call him Cromwell, but Cromwell was only a soldier, and the state he founded went down with him into his grave. I would call him Washington, but the great Virginian held slaves. This man risked his empire rather than permit the slave trade in the humblest village of his dominions.

"You think me a fanatic tonight, for you read history, not with your eyes, but with your prejudices. But fifty years hence, when Truth gets a hearing, the Muse of History will put Phocion for the Greek, and Brutus for the Roman, Hampden for England, Lafayette for France, choose Washington as the bright, consummate flower of our earlier civilization, and John Brown the ripe fruit of our noonday, then, dipping her pen in the sunlight, will write in the clear blue, above them all, the name of the soldier, the statesman, the martyr, Toussaint L'Ouverture."

WHEN THE TOE TOUCHES

Hunt, search, experiment until you get a good ending and a good beginning. Then get them close together.

Speakers who do not cut their talks to fit in with the prevailing mood of this hurried, rapid age will be unwelcome and sometimes positively disliked.

No less a saint than Saul of Tarsus sinned in this respect. He preached until a chap in the audience, "a young man named Eutychus," went to sleep and fell out of a window and all but broke his neck. Even then he may not have stopped talking. Who knows? I remember a speaker, a doctor, standing up one night at the University Club in Brooklyn. It had been a long banquet. Many speakers had already talked. It was two o'clock in the morning when his turn came. Had he been endowed with tact and fine feeling and discretion, he would have said half a dozen sentences and let us go home. But did he? No. Not he. He launched into a forty-five minute tirade against vivisection. Long before he was half way through his audience were wishing that he, like Eutychus, would fall out of a window and break something, anything, to silence him.

Horace Lorimer, the editor of the Saturday Evening Post, told me that he always stopped a series of articles in the Post when they were at the height of their popularity, and people were clamoring for more. Why stop then? Why then of all times? "Because," said Mr. Lorimer, and he ought to know, "the point of satiation is reached very soon after that peak of popularity."

The same wisdom will apply, and ought to be applied to speaking. Stop while the audience is still eager to have you go on.

The greatest speech Christ ever delivered, the Sermon on the Mount, can be repeated in five minutes. Lincoln's Gettysburg address has only ten sentences. One can read the whole story of creation in Genesis in less time than it takes to peruse a murder story in the morning paper. . . . Be brief ! Be brief !

Doctor Johnson, Archdeacon of Nyasa, wrote a book about the primitive peoples of Africa. He had lived among them, observed them, for forty-nine years. He related that when a speaker talks too long at a village gathering, the audience silences him with shouts of "Imetosha!" "Imetosha!" "Enough!" "Enough!"

Another tribe is said to permit a speaker to hold forth only so long as he can stand on one foot. When the toe of the lifted member touches the ground, he has come to an end.

And audiences everywhere, even though they may be more polite, more restrained, dislike long speeches as much as do those African tribesmen.

So be warned by their lot,

Which I know you will not,

And learn about speaking from them.

ANSWERING QUESTIONS FROM AUDIENCE

Quite often, during or after your talk, the audience will ask you questions. As most speakers prefer not to have their talks interrupted, they request that questions be deferred until after the formal presentation. If you have depth knowledge of your subject, you probably can anticipate the questions that might be asked. They usually pertain to matters touched upon in your talk that may not have been fully covered. However, you can never anticipate those off-base questions that may reflect the personal agenda of the questioner. By knowing ten times more about your subject than you have time to include in your formal talk, you will be prepared to answer most questions.

There are two ways questions may be presented. If you are conducting a workshop or seminar, answering questions is an integral part of the program. To facilitate this, provide 3 x 5 cards so that members of the group can write their questions on the card. Collect the cards after your closing remarks. The advantage of this is that you can scan the cards rapidly and select the most pertinent questions to address first. This also gives you a chance to think about what you will say before responding. Read the question aloud to the audience and then make your comments. Make them brief ! You do not have the time to give another long speech. If the answer requires considerable time, explain that to the audience and if possible refer them to sources where the information can be obtained. Another advantage is that you can screen the questions and ignore those that are trivial or perhaps too controversial.

However getting written questions is not always feasible. At many meetings, the audience asks the questions directly. In such cases, follow these guidelines:

1. Repeat the question. This is important because many people in the audience may not have heard the question. The questioner may have not spoken clearly or loudly enough.

2. Give your response clearly and concisely. Do not repeat what you said in your talk, but refer to it and if the questions indicate that your original comments need clarification, do this by giving examples based on your experience.

3. Don't get into arguments with the questioner. If he or she presents a conflicting point of view, comment that you respect that

person's opinion. Then state the key points you feel validate your viewpoint.

4. Don't let any one questioner dominate the meeting. Once you have responded, you may allow one follow up question, but if he or she persists in debating you, say in a friendly way. "Thank you for your comments, but let's hear from some others who may have comments or questions."

Occasionally, a member of the audience may become belligerent or heckle a speaker. Do NOT try to "put him or her down" with sarcasm. It usually only reinforces the audience's support of the heckler. Smile. Stay silent for minute. Then turn to the audience and ask "Who has the next question?" At most meetings, the chairperson will determine when the time is up and will usually stand and say that there is time for one more question. Take that question, and once it is answered, ignore the waving hands of those who want to continue, thank the audience and sit down.

IN A NUTSHELL

1.   The close of a speech, is really, its most strategic element. What is said last, is likely to be remembered longest.

2.   Do not end with: "That is about all I have to say on the matter; so I guess I shall stop." Stop, but don't talk about stopping.

3.   Plan your ending carefully in. Rehearse. Know almost word for word how you are going to close. Round off your talk. Don't leave it rough and broken like a jagged rock.

4.   Some suggested ways of closing:

- Summarizing, restating, outlining briefly the main points you have covered.

- Appealing for action.

- Paying the audience a sincere compliment.

- Quoting a fitting verse of poetry.

- Building up a climax.

5.   Get a good ending and a good beginning; and get them close together. Always stop before your audience wants you to. "The point of satiation is reached

very soon after the peak of popularity."

6.   Be prepared to answer questions from the audience. If possible, have participants write the questions on a card, screen them and answer as many as you can in the allotted time. If questions are asked from the floor, repeat the question before answering it. Follow the suggestions presented in this chapter.

SPEECH BUILDING
WORDS OFTEN MISPRONOUNCED

The *o* in *comely*, and the capitalized *U's* in *sUpple*, *sUburban* and *lUscious* are sounded as *u* in *up*.

The letters capitalized in the following should be sounded, not as the *oo* in *ooze*, but as the *u* in *futility* and *music*. This, the long *U* sound, consists of a close union of the sound of *i* in *it*, and the *oo* in *ooze*. The precise sounding of the long *u* is rare and is an infallible sign of cultured pronunciation. In a few words, it is always enunciated correctly. For example, we never say *moosic* for *music*, *foo* for *few*, *food* for *feud*, *footure* for *future*, *boogle* for *bugle*, or *coopid* for *cupid*; but how many of us say *noo* for *new*, *dooty* for *duty*, and *Toosday* for *Tuesday*!

AbsolUte	gratitUde	opportUnity
assUme	illUsion	pictUre
attitUde	institUte	prodUce
avenUe	institUtion	renEW
carbUretor	lUbricate	resolUtion
constitUtion	LUcy	seclUde
consUme	lUre	solUtion
credUlity	lUte	stUdent
cUlinary	measUre	stUpid
delUde	multitUde	subdUe
delUsion	neUtral	sUit
deW	nEW	sUpine
dilUte	nEWs	tUbe
dUbious	nEWspaper	tUberculosis
dUe	nUcleus	TUesday
dUet	nUde	tUmor

dUke	nUisance	tUmult
dUly	nUmerous	tUne
dUty	nUtrition	tUtor
furnitUre	obtUse	

ERRORS IN ENGLISH

Review. There are *four* mistakes in the following paragraph. See if you can discover them.

Which was the man who did the deed? The evidence all pointed to Mr. Watson. I thought it to be he but it was supposed by the others to have been them who escaped in the night. In the long run, it was us who were wrong in both cases.

New Study Material.

RULE: When a pronoun is the direct object of a verb, it is always in the objective case. In other words, if the verb in the sentence denotes an action that passes over to or affects the pronoun, then the pronoun must be in the objective case. For example:

Right: He asked you and *me* to lunch.

Wrong: He asked you and *I* to lunch.

Right: The manager asked *her* and *me* to do it.

Wrong: The manager asked *she* and *I* to do it.

Right: I cannot say *whom* we will hire.

(In the above sentence, *whom* is the object of the transitive verb *will hire*, and consequently the pronoun must be in the objective case.)

Wrong: I cannot say *who* we will hire.

Right: A landslide hit their home, demolishing their house and killing both *him* and his wife instantly.

Wrong: "A landslide hit their home, demolishing their house and killing both *he* and his wife instantly." (From an advertisement issued by the Illinois Commercial Men's Association.) (There should be another change in this sentence, making it read, in part, "both his wife and him." This is, perhaps, a rather fine point, but careful speakers usually mention the lady first.)

Right: The school graduated *us* and our classmates.

Wrong: The school graduated *we* and our classmates.

Here, again, attention should be called to the improper use of the compounds. We are prone to use *myself, yourself, herself,* when we do not intend to express reflected action or emphasis. You recall that this was discussed in Chapter IX. As stated before, this generally happens because we are not sure whether to use the nominative or objective form of the pronoun.

Right: The wrecking car brought the automobile and *them* back home.

Wrong: The wrecking car brought the automobile and *themselves* back home.

CORRECT USAGE OF WORDS

"We think by words, and therefore thought and words cannot but set and reset on each other. As a man speaks, so he thinks, and, 'as a man thinketh in his heart, so he is.'"

-G. P. Marsh, Lectures On The English Language

FRIENDLY - AMICABLE. *Friendly* is stronger and less formal than *amicable*. A man who is *companionable* and *sociable* may not be *cordial* and *genial*. The first two words denote manner and behavior and may be applied where no genuine feeling exists; the last two qualities imply a sincere and warm friendliness.

GENEROUS - LIBERAL - MAGNANIMOUS. *Generous* means giving freely and at a sacrifice. *Liberal* refers to the amount of the gift. If a minimum wage laborer gave twenty dollars to a charity, it would be *generous*. If the United States Steel Corporation contributed ten millions it would be *liberal*. *Magnanimous* means lofty, noble, raised above what is low and mean. It is *magnanimous* of you to forgive those who have wronged you.

HEALTHFUL - HEALTHY. *Healthful* means promoting or preserving health; as, a *healthful* climate. *Healthy* means enjoying health; as, a *healthy* man. Do not speak of *"healthy food"* or *"healthy exercise."*

HONEST - HONORABLE. The *honest* person does not lie, or steal, or defraud; the *honorable* person takes no unfair advantage, and may even willingly sacrifice for the cause of right.

236

VOICE EXERCISE - DEVELOPING RESONANCE

The three fundamental principles of good tone production are correct breath control, relaxation and resonance. We have already dealt with the first two principles; now for the third: resonance. Your body acts as a sounding board for your voice much in the same way that the body of a violin or piano amplifies and beautifies the tones produced by the musician. The initial tone is made by the vocal chords, but this rises and reverberates against the hard bony structures of the chest, the teeth, the roof of the mouth, the nasal cavities and other parts of the face. This reverberation gives to the voice its most important quality. Think of the voice as a skyrocket rising from the diaphragm up through the darkness of your relaxed throat and breaking into a shower of sound against the nostrils and other bony parts of the head.

Our problem is not to speak with resonance. You have been speaking with it all your life. You could not be heard ten feet without it. Our task is to speak with increased resonance. How shall we set about it? Let me quote an interesting paragraph from a volume by Fucito and Beyer, entitled *Caruso and the Art of Singing*.

"A great deal has been said about the value of humming as a vocal exercise. . . . Humming, if correctly practiced, will develop the resonance of the voice. The humming of most people sounds like a caterwaul because the jaw, the lips, the tongue and the vocal membranes are all painfully rigid. Of course, the vocal organs should be in the same position for humming, as for good tone production: there should be complete relaxation of the facial muscles, the jaw, and the tongue, just as they are kept when in a state of repose or while sleeping; the lips are to be lightly united, Thus the tone vibrations will neither be deadened by obstructing muscles nor forced through the nose by the strain; instead they will resonate within the nasal cavities and make the notes round and beautiful."

Now with relaxed tongue, throat, lips and jaw, let us hum the music of *My Old Kentucky Home*:

The sun shines bright in my old Kentucky home,

'Tis summer, the people are gay;

The corntop's ripe, and the meadow's all in bloom,

While the birds make music all the day.

The young folks roll on the little cabin floor,

237

All merry, all happy and bright;
By'n'by hard times comes a-knocking at the door,
Then my old Kentucky home, good-night!

CHORUS
Weep no more, my lady,
Oh! Weep no more today!
We will sing one song for the old Kentucky home,
For the old Kentucky home, far away.

The first time you hum this, put the palm of your hand on top of your head and feel the vibration there. This is most important; in practicing all these exercises for resonance, let your first step be the taking of a deep breath at the diaphragm and relaxing the chest and feeling it riding on the breath. Note the open feeling that you have in your face and nose and head as you drink the air in. As you begin to hum and exhale, do not think of exhaling at all. Imagine that you are still inhaling, still feeling that open sensation in the head. That means open cavities to reinforce and amplify your resonance. Cultivate this inhaling sensation in all your speaking.

Now hum this song once more. Place your hand this time on the back of your head and feel the vibration there.

A third time, think the tone in your nose. Feet as if it were flowing up and into the nose, the same sensation as in inhaling. Hold the bony part of your nose, just a little below the eyes, with a thumb and a forefinger. Feel the vibration there this time as you hum.

For the sake of variety, let us hum now the tune of *The Old Folks at Home*:

Way down upon the Swanee River,
Far, far away,
There's where my heart is turning ever
There's where the old folks stay.
All up and down the whole creation,
Sadly I roam,
Still longing for the old plantation,
And for the old folks at home.

CHORUS

All the world is sad and dreary,

Everywhere I roam

Oh, dear ones, how my heart grows weary

Far from the old folks at home.

As you hum it this time, think it forward on the lips. Place your forefinger on your lips and feel them vibrate. They ought to vibrate until they tickle.

Now hum it again in as low a tone as possible; and, placing your open palm on your chest, feel the vibration there.

Hum it once more, keeping the palm of your right hand on your chest and moving the palm of the left over various parts of the head and face. Feel your whole body vibrating, causing resonance. I have known singers who, when they hummed, felt the vibrations even in their fingers and toes.

Singing is a splendid voice exercise in itself; so, using all the principles of voice production discussed in these lessons, let us sing now these two old familiar songs that we have been humming.

HOW TO MAKE YOUR MEANING CLEAR

"Nine readers out of ten take a lucid statement for a true one."

-Encyclopedia Britannica

"Study carefully what you have to say and put it into words by writing or by speaking aloud to an imaginary person. Arrange your points in order. Stick to your order. Divide your time among your points according to their importance. Stop when you are through."

-Dr. Edward Everett Hale

"If speaking on Solomon to a group of business men, refer to him as the J.P. Morgan of his day. If talking to baseball fans about Samson call him the Babe Ruth of his time. When Frank Simonds undertook to describe Foch's strategy in battering down the Hindenburg line he used the figure of pounding at the two hinges of a gate. In a similar manner Hugo used the letter I to illustrate the battlefield of Waterloo, and Elson the horseshoe in describing the battle of Gettysburg. Everyone is acquainted with gates, horseshoes and the alphabet, although not everyone has seen battles."

-Glenn Clark, Self-Cultivation in Extemporaneous Speaking

"One picture is worth ten thousand words."

-Chinese Proverb

"My father was a man of great intellectual energy. My best training came from him. He was intolerant of vagueness, and from the time I began to write until his death when he was eighty-one years old, I carried everything I wrote to him. He would make me read it aloud, which was always painful to me. Every now and then he would stop me. 'What do you mean by that?' I would tell him, and, of course, in doing so would express myself more simply than I had on paper. 'Why didn't you say so?' He would go on. 'Don't shoot at your meaning with birdshot and hit the whole countryside; shoot with a rifle at the thing you have to say."

-Woodrow Wilson

241

Chapter 12

HOW TO MAKE YOUR
MEANING CLEAR

E ven the most skilled orators will fail to communicate effectively
if the audience can't understand them. Good communication
starts with understanding your audience. Choose words that your
listeners will easily comprehend. If the people you address come
from a technical or specialized background, you can use the jargon
or terminology commonly used in their fields. Your listeners will
clearly and readily understand your message. However, if you use
the same language to an audience unfamiliar with those terms, you
lose your listeners.

For example, at a meeting of the Rotary Club in White Plains,
New York, a prominent lawyer was addressing an audience of men
and women, most of whom owned or managed small businesses in
the community. They were eager to hear his explanation of some
new laws that had been passed that affected their businesses. After
some introductory remarks, he launched an erudite discussion of
the laws, laced with legal jargon. You can guess how the audience
reacted. As he droned on and on, the loss of interest was physically
perceptible. People shifted in their seats, men and women with pens
ready to take notes began doodling on their pads; some even got up,
moved around the room or just left.

These were intelligent men and women, with a desire to learn
about a matter of which they had some concern, but they could no
more understand legalese than they could if the speaker were talking
in a foreign language.

An effective speaker would have taken into consideration, the
level of knowledge of his audience and recognized that the legal
jargon that was second nature to members of the bar were
gobbledegook to the members of the audience being addressed and
would have approached the subject quite differently.

It is your responsibility, not your audience's to ensure that your message gets across. If you can explain technical matters in layperson's terms, do so. If it is necessary to use a technical, legal or other unfamiliar term, take the time to explain it the first time you use it, and at least once again, if you feel, it needs reinforcement.

KNOW THE PURPOSE OF YOUR TALK

1. When you are asked to address a group, there is usually a reason for it. You have not been invited to just chat. Be sure that what you say satisfied that purpose. Every talk, regardless of whether the speaker realizes it or not, has one of four major goals - to make something clear.

2. To impress and convince.

3. To get action.

4. To entertain.

Let us illustrate these by a series of concrete examples.

Lincoln, who was always more or less interested in mechanics, once invented and patented a device for lifting stranded boats off sand bars and other obstructions. He worked in a mechanic's shop near his law office, making a model of his apparatus. Although the device finally came to naught, he was decidedly enthusiastic over its possibilities. When friends came to his office to view the model, he took no end of pains to explain it. The main purpose of those explanations was clearness.

When he delivered his immortal oration at Gettysburg, when he gave his first and second inaugural addresses, when Henry Clay died and Lincoln delivered an eulogy on his life; on all these occasions, Lincoln's main purpose was impressiveness and conviction. He had to be clear, of course, before he could be convincing; but, in these instances, clearness was not his major consideration.

In his talks to juries, he tried to win favorable decisions. In his political talks, he tried to win votes. His purpose, then, was action.

Two years before he was elected President, Lincoln prepared a lecture on inventions. His purpose was entertainment. At least, that should have been his goal; but he was evidently not very successful in attaining it. His career as a popular lecturer was, in fact, a distinct disappointment. In one town, not a person came to hear him.

But he did succeed and he succeeded famously in the other speeches of his that I have referred to. And why? Because, in those instances, he knew his goal, and he knew how to achieve it. He knew where he wanted to go and how to get there. And because so many speakers don't know just that, they often flounder and come to grief.

For example: I once saw a United States Congressman hooted and hissed and forced to leave the stage, because he had unconsciously, no doubt, but nevertheless, unwisely chosen clearness as his goal. He chose to lecture them about the importance of a bill he was sponsoring in Congress. The crowd did not want to be instructed. They wanted to be entertained. They listened to him patiently, politely, for ten minutes, a quarter of an hour, hoping the performance would come to a rapid end. But it didn't. He rambled on and on; patience snapped; the audience would not stand for more. Someone began to cheer ironically. Others took it up. In a moment, a thousand people were whistling and shouting. The speaker, obtuse and incapable as he was of sensing the temper of his audience, had the bad taste to continue. That aroused them. A battle was on. Their impatience mounted to ire. They determined to silence him. Louder and louder grew their storm of protest. Finally, the roar of it, the anger of it, drowned his words, he could not have been heard twenty feet away. So he was forced to give up, acknowledge defeat and retire in humiliation.

Profit by his example. Know your goal. Choose it wisely before you set out to prepare your talk. Know how to reach it. Then set about it, doing it skillfully and with science.

All this requires knowledge, special and technical instruction. And so important is this phase of speech construction that four chapters of this course will be devoted to it. The remainder of this chapter will show you how to make your talks clear. Chapter XIII will indicate how to make them impressive and convincing. Chapter XIV will show how to make them interesting. Chapter XV will demonstrate a scientific method for getting action.

USE COMPARISONS TO PROMOTE CLEARNESS

Experienced public speakers agree that the most important is knowledge of the subject, preparation and making the talk clear to the audience being addressed.

The great General Von Moltke, at the outbreak of the Franco-Prussian War, said to his officers: "Remember, gentlemen, that any order that *can* be misunderstood, *will* be misunderstood."

Napoleon recognized the same danger. His most emphatic and oft-reiterated instruction to his secretaries was: "Be clear! Be clear!"

When the disciples asked Christ why He taught the public by parables, He answered: "Because they seeing, see not; and hearing, hear not; neither do they understand."

And when you talk on a subject strange to your hearer or hearers, can you hope that they will understand you any more readily than people understood the Master?

Hardly. So what can we do about it? What did He do when confronted by a similar situation? Solved it in the most simple and natural manner imaginable: described the things people did not know by likening them to things they did know. The kingdom of Heaven. . . what would it be like? How could those untutored peasants of Palestine know? So Christ described it in terms of objects and actions with which they were already familiar:

"The kingdom of Heaven is like unto leaven, which a woman took, and hid in three measures of meal, till the whole was leavened."

"Again, the kingdom of Heaven is like unto a merchant-man seeking goodly pearls. . . . "

"Again, the kingdom of Heaven is like unto a net that was cast into the sea. . . ."

That was lucid; they could understand that. The housewives in the audience were using leaven every week; the fishermen were casting their nets into the sea daily; the merchants were dealing in pearls.

And how did David make clear the watchfulness and loving kindness of Jehovah?

"The Lord is my shepherd, I shall not want. He makes me to lie down in green pastures, He leads me beside the still waters."

Green grazing grounds in that almost barren country ; still waters, where the sheep could drink, those pastoral people could understand that.

Here is a rather striking and half amusing example of the use of this principle: some missionaries were translating the Bible into the dialect of a tribe living near equatorial Africa. They progressed to the verse: "Though your sins be as scarlet, they shall be white as snow." How were they to translate that? Literally? Meaningless. Absurd. The natives had never shoveled off the sidewalk on a February morning. They did not even have a word for snow. They could not have told the difference between snow and coaltar; but they had climbed coconut trees many times and shaken down a few nuts for lunch; so the missionaries likened the unknown to the known, and changed the verse to read, "Though your sins be as scarlet, they shall be as white as the meat of a coconut."

Under the circumstances, it would be hard to improve on that, wouldn't it?

At the State Teachers' College at Warrensburg, Missouri, I once heard a lecturer on Alaska who failed, in many places, to be either clear or interesting because, unlike those African missionaries, he neglected to talk in terms of what his audience knew. He told us, for example, that Alaska had a gross area of 590,804 square miles, and a population of 64,356.

Half a million square miles, what does that mean to the average person? Precious little. Most of us are not used to thinking in terms of square miles. They conjure up no mental picture. We don't have any idea whether half a million square miles are approximately the size of Maine or Texas. Suppose the speaker had said that the coast line of Alaska and its islands is longer than the distance around the globe, and that its area more than equals the combined areas of Vermont, New Hampshire, Maine, Massachusetts, Rhode Island, Connecticut, New York, New Jersey, Pennsylvania, Delaware, Maryland, West Virginia, North Carolina, South Carolina, Georgia, Florida, Mississippi and Tennessee. Would not that give everyone a fairly clear conception of the area of Alaska?

He said the population was 64,356. The chances are that not one person in ten remembered the census figures for five minutes or even one minute. Why? Because the rapid saying of "sixty-four thousand, three hundred and fifty-six" does not make a very clear impression. It leaves only a loose, insecure impression, like words written on the sand of the seashore. The next wave of attention quite obliterates them. Would it not have been better to have stated the census in terms of something with which they were very familiar? For example: St. Joseph was not very far away from that little Missouri town where the audience lived. Many of them had been to St. Joseph;

and, Alaska had, at that time, ten thousand less people than St. Joseph. Better still, why not talk about Alaska in terms of the very town where you are speaking? Wouldn't the speaker have been far clearer had he said: "Alaska is eight times as large as the state of Missouri; yet it has only thirteen times as many people as living right here in Warrensburg"?

In the following illustrations, which are the clearer, the *a* statement or the *a* or *b* ?

(a) Our nearest star is thirty-five trillion miles away.

(b) A train going at the rate of a mile a minute would reach our nearest star in forty-eight million years; if a song were sung there and the sound could travel here; it would be three million, eight hundred thousand years; before we could bear it. A spider's thread reaching to it would weigh five hundred tons.

(a) St. Peter's, the biggest church in the world, is 232 yards long, and 364 feet wide.

(b) It is about the size of two buildings, each as large as the capitol at Washington piled on top of one another.

The world renowned physicist, Sir Oliver Lodge happily used this method when explaining the size and nature of atoms to a popular audience. I heard him tell a European audience that there were as many atoms in a drop of water as there were drops of water in the Mediterranean Sea; and many of his hearers had spent over a week sailing from Gibraltar to the Suez Canal. To bring the matter still closer home, he said there were as many atoms in one drop of water as there were blades of grass on all the earth.

"The novelist, Richard Harding Davis, told a New York audience that the Mosque of St. Sophia was "about as big as the auditorium of the Fifth Avenue theater." He said that the Italian port of Brindisi "looks like Long Island City when you come into it from the rear."

Use this principle, henceforth, in your talks. If you are describing the great pyramid, first tell your hearers it is 451 feet, then tell them how high that is in terms of some building they see every day. Tell how many city blocks the base would cover. Don't speak about so many thousand gallons of this or so many hundred thousand barrels of that without also telling how many rooms the size of the one you are speaking in could be filled with that much liquid. Instead of saying twenty feet high, why not say one and a half times as high as this ceiling? Instead of talking about distance in terms of rods or miles, is it not clearer to say as far as from here to the union station, or to such and such a street ?

AVOID TECHNICAL TERMS

If you belong to a profession, the work of which is technical; if you are a lawyer, a physician, an engineer, or are in a highly specialized line of business; be doubly careful when you talk to outsiders to express yourself in plain terms and to give necessary details.

I say be doubly careful, for, as a part of my professional duties, I have listened to hundreds of speeches that failed right at this point and failed woefully. The speakers appeared totally unconscious of the general public's widespread and profound ignorance regarding their particular specialties. So what happened? As did the lawyer in the example, presented at the beginning of this chapter, they rambled on and on, uttering thoughts, using phrases that fitted into their experience and were instantly and continuously meaningful to them; but to the uninitiated, they were about as clear as the Missouri River, after the June rains have fallen on the newly plowed corn fields of Iowa and Kansas.

What should such a speaker do? He ought to read and heed the following advice from the facile pen of Ex-Senator Alfred Beveridge of Indiana:

"It is a good practice to pick out the least intelligent looking person in the audience and strive to make that person interested in your argument. This can be done only by lucid statement of fact and clear reasoning. An even better method is to center your talk on some small boy or girl present with parents."

"Say to yourself that you will try to be so plain that the child will understand and remember your explanation of the question discussed, and after the meeting, be able to tell what you have said."

I remember hearing a physician, a student in my course, remark in the course of his talk that "diaphragmatic breathing is a distinct aid to the peristaltic action of the intestines and a boon to health." He was about to dismiss that phase of his talk with that one sentence and to rush on to something else, I stopped him; and asked for a show of hands of those who had a clear conception of how diaphragmatic breathing differs from other kinds of breathing, why

249

it is especially beneficial to physical well- being and what peristaltic action is. The result of the vote surprised the doctor; so he went back, explained, enlarged in this fashion:

"The diaphragm is a thin muscle forming the floor of the chest at the base of the lungs and the roof of the abdominal cavity. When inactive and during chest breathing, it is arched like an inverted washbowl."

"In abdominal breathing, every breath forces this muscular arch down until it becomes nearly flat and you can feel your stomach muscles pressing against your belt. This downward pressure of the diaphragm, massages and stimulates the organs of the upper part of the abdominal cavity-the stomach, the liver, the pancreas, the spleen, the solar plexus."

"When you breathe out again, your stomach and your intestines will be forced up against the diaphragm and will be given another massage. This massaging helps the process of elimination."

"A vast amount of ill health originates in the intestines. Most indigestion, constipation, and auto-intoxication would disappear if our stomachs and intestines were properly exercised through deep diaphragmatic breathing."

Did the audience get the message? You bet they did.

THE SECRET OF LINCOLN'S CLEARNESS

Lincoln had a deep and abiding affection for putting a proposition so that it would be instantly clear to everyone. In his first message to Congress, he used the phrase "sugar-coated." Mr. Defrees, the public printer, being Lincoln's personal friend, suggested to him that although the phrase might be all right for a stump speech in Illinois, it was not dignified enough for a historical state paper. "Well, Defrees," Lincoln replied, "if you think the time will ever come when the people will not understand what 'sugar-coated' means, I'll alter it; otherwise, I think I'll let it go."

He once explained to Dr. Gulliver, the President of Knox College, how he developed his "passion" for plain language, as he phrased it:

"Among my earliest recollections, I remember how, when a mere child, I used to get irritated when anybody talked to me in a way I could not understand. I don't think I ever got angry at anything

250

else in my life. But that always disturbed my temper, and has ever since. I can remember going to my little bedroom, after hearing the neighbors talk of an evening with my father, and spending no small part of the night walking up and down and trying to make out the exact meaning of some of their, to me, dark sayings. I could not sleep, though I often tried to, when I got on such a hunt after an idea, until I had caught it and when I thought I had got it I was not satisfied until I had repeated it over and over, until I had put it in language plain enough, as I thought for any boy I knew to comprehend. This was a kind of passion with me, and it has since stuck by me."

A passion? Yes, it must have amounted to that, for Mentor Graham, the schoolmaster of New Salem, testified: "I have known Lincoln to study for hours, the best way of three to express an idea."

An all too common reason, why people fail to be intelligible is this: the thing they wish to express is not clear even to themselves. Hazy impressions! Indistinct, vague ideas! The result? Their minds work no better in a mental fog than a camera does in a physical fog. They need to be as disturbed over obscurity and ambiguity as Lincoln was. They need to use his methods.

APPEAL TO THE SENSE OF SIGHT

The nerves that lead from the eye to the brain are, as we observed in Chapter IV, many times larger than those leading from the ear; and science tells us that we give twenty-five times as much attention to eye suggestions as we do to ear suggestions.

"One seeing," says an old Japanese proverb, "is better than a hundred times telling about."

So, if you wish to be clear, picture your points, visualize your ideas. That was the plan of John H. Patterson, president of the National Cash Register Company. He wrote an article for System Magazine, outlining the methods he used in speaking to his employees and his sales forces:

"I hold that one cannot rely on speech alone to make oneself understood or to gain and hold attention. A dramatic supplement is needed. It is better to supplement, whenever possible, with pictures which show the right and the wrong way; diagrams are more convincing than mere words and pictures are, more convincing than

251

diagrams. The ideal presentation of a subject is one in which every subdivision is pictured and in which the words are used only to connect them. I early found that showing a picture was worth more than anything I could say."

"Little grotesque drawings are wonderfully effective. I have a whole system of cartooning or 'chart talks.' A circle with a dollar mark means one piece of money, a bag marked with a dollar is a lot of money. Many good effects can be had with moon faces. Draw a circle, put in a few dashes for the eyes, nose, mouth, and ears. Twisting these lines gives the expressions. The out-of-date person has the corner of the mouth down; the chipper, up-to-date person has the curves up. The drawings are homely, but the most effective cartoonists are not the people who make the prettiest pictures; the thing is to express the idea and the contrast."

"The big bag and the little bag of money, side by side, are the natural heads for the right way as opposed to the wrong way; the one brings much money, the other little money. If you sketch these rapidly as you talk, there is no danger of people's letting their minds wander; they are bound to look at what you are doing and thus, to go with you, through the successive stages, to the point you want to make. And again, the funny figures put people in good humor."

"I used to employ an artist to hang around in the shops with me and quietly make sketches of things that were not being done right. Then the sketches were made into drawings and I called the workers together and showed them exactly what they were doing. When I heard of the slide projector, I immediately bought one and projected the drawings on the screen, which, of course, made them even more effective than on paper. Then came the moving picture. I think that I had one of the first machines ever made and now we have a big department with many motion picture films and more than 60,000 colored slides."

In the computer age, more and more speakers use power point presentations to illustrate the key points they present.

Not every subject or occasion, of course, lends itself to exhibits and drawings; but let us use them when we can. They attract attention, stimulate interest and often make our meaning doubly clear.

ROCKEFELLER RAKING OFF THE COINS

You will remember how John D. Rockefeller, Jr. appealed to the workers of the Colorado Fuel and Iron Company (see Chapter X). Let's see how he appealed to the sense of sight to make clear the company's financial situation "I found that they (the employees of the Colorado Fuel and Iron Co.) imagined the Rockefellers had been drawing immense profits from their interests in Colorado; no end of people had told them so. I explained the exact situation to them. I showed them that during the fourteen years in which we had been connected with the Colorado Fuel and Iron Co., it had never paid one cent in dividends upon the common stock."

"At one of our meetings, I gave a practical illustration of the finances of the company. I put a number of coins on the table. I swept off a portion that represented their wages; for the first claim upon the company is the pay roll. Then I took away more coins to represent the salaries of the officers, and then the remaining coins to represent the fees of the directors. There were no coins left for the stockholders. And when I asked, is it fair, in this corporation where we are all partners, that three of the partners should get all the earnings, be they large or small; all of them; and the fourth nothing?"

"After the illustration, one of the workers made a speech for higher wages. I asked him, 'Is it fair for you to want more wages when one of the partners gets nothing?' He admitted that it did not look like a square deal; I heard no more about increasing the wages."

Make your eye appeals, definite and specific. Paint mental pictures that stand out as sharp and clear as a stag's horn, silhouetted against the setting sun. For example, the word "dog" calls up a more or less definite picture of such an animal, perhaps a cocker spaniel, a Scotch terrier, a St. Bernard, or a Pomeranian. Notice how much more distinct an image springs into your mind when I say "bulldog," the term is less inclusive. Doesn't "a Boston bulldog" call up a still more explicit picture? Is it not more vivid to say "a black Shetland pony" than to talk of "a horse"? Doesn't "a white bantam rooster with a broken leg" give a much more definite and sharp picture than merely the word "fowl"?

RESTATE YOUR IMPORTANT IDEAS IN
DIFFERENT WORDS

Napoleon declared repetition to be the only serious principle of rhetoric. He knew that because an idea was clear to him, was not always proof, that it was instantly grasped by others. He knew that it takes time to comprehend new ideas, that the mind must be kept focused on them. In short, he knew, they must be repeated, not in exactly the same language. People will rebel at that, and rightly so. But if the repetition is couched in fresh phraseology, if it is varied, your hearers will never regard it as repetition at all.

Let us take a specific example. William Jennings Bryan said:

"You cannot make people understand a subject, unless you understand that subject yourself. The more clearly you have a subject in mind, the more clearly can you present that subject to the minds of others."

The last sentence here, is merely, a restatement of the idea contained in the first; but when these sentences are spoken, the mind does not have time to see that it is repetition. It only feels that the subject has been made clearer.

I seldom teach a single session of my course without hearing one or perhaps half a dozen talks that would have been more clear, more impressive, had the speaker but employed this principle of restatement. It is almost entirely ignored by the beginner. And what a pity!

USE GENERAL ILLUSTRATIONS AND
SPECIFIC INSTANCES

One of the surest and easiest ways to make your points clear is to follow them with general illustrations and concrete cases. What is the difference between the two? One, as the term implies, is general; the other, specific.

Let us illustrate the difference between them and the uses of each with a concrete example. Suppose we take the statement: "There are professional men and women who earn astonishingly large incomes."

Is that statement very clear? Have you a clear-cut idea of what the speaker really means? No, and the speaker cannot be sure of what such an assertion will call up in the minds of others. It may cause the country doctor in the Ozark Mountains to think of a family doctor in a small city with an income of twenty-five thousand. It may cause a successful business executive to think in terms of managers who make several hundred thousand a year. The statement, as it stands, is entirely too vague and loose. It needs to be tightened. A few illuminating details ought to be given to indicate what professions the speaker refers to and what is meant by "astonishingly large."

"There are lawyers, prize fighters, song writers, novelists, playwrights, painters, actors and singers who make more than the President of the United States."

Now, hasn't one a much clearer idea of what the speaker meant? However, the message was not individualized.

General illustrations, not specific people were cited. It would have been far more powerful if the speaker specified by name, famous actors or singers, who earn high incomes, as is done in the following paragraph.

"Samuel Unterrnyer and Max D. Steuer, two of the great trial lawyers of their time, are said to earn a million dollars a year. Benny Leonard, the lightweight boxing champion in the 1920s it is estimated, has had his income up to a third of a million in a year. Jack Dempsey, the heavyweight champion is reputed to have achieved the half million mark. Irving Berlin's ragtime music is reported to have brought him in as much as a quarter of a million in twelve months." As this was in an era when five dollars a day was considered good pay, you can guess how those audiences would react.

Now, has not one an extremely plain and vivid idea of exactly and precisely, what the speaker wanted to convey?

Be concrete. Be definite. Be specific. This quality of definiteness not only makes for clearness but for impressiveness and conviction and interest also.

DO NOT EMULATE THE MOUNTAIN GOAT

William James, in one of his talks to teachers, paused to remark that one can make only one point in a lecture, and the lecture he referred to lasted an hour. Yet I recently heard a speaker, who was limited by a stopwatch to three minutes, begin by saying that he wanted to call our attention to eleven points. Sixteen and a half seconds to each phase of his subject! Seems incredible, doesn't it, that an intelligent man should attempt anything so manifestly absurd. True, I am quoting an extreme case; but the tendency to err in that fashion, if not to that degree, handicaps almost every novice. It is like a Cook's guide who shows Paris to the tourist in one day. It can be done, just as one can walk through the American Museum of Natural History in thirty minutes. But neither clearness nor enjoyment results. Many a talk fails to be clear because the speaker seems intent upon establishing a world's record for ground covered in the allotted time. That speaker leaps from one point to another with the swiftness and agility of a mountain goat.

The talks that students give in my course must, owing to the pressure of time, be short. I caution students to cut their cloth accordingly. If, for example, they are to speak on Labor Unions, do not attempt to tell us in three or six minutes, why they came into existence, the methods they employ, the good they have accomplished, the evil they have wrought, and how to solve industrial disputes. No, no; if you strive to do that, no one will have a very clear conception of what has been said. It will be all confused, a blur, too sketchy, too much of a mere outline.

Wouldn't it be the part of wisdom to take one phase and one phase only of labor unions, and cover that adequately and illustrate it? It would. That kind of a speech leaves a single impression. It is lucid, easy to listen to, easy to remember.

However, if several phases of your topic must be covered, it is often advisable to summarize briefly at the end. Let us see how that suggestion operates. Here is a summary of this lesson. Does the reading of it, help to make the message we have been presenting, more lucid, more comprehensible?

IN A NUTSHELL

1.   To be clear is highly important and often very difficult. Christ declared that He had to teach by parables,

"Because they (His hearers) seeing, see not; and hearing, hear not; neither do they understand."

2.   Christ made the unknown clear by talking of it in terms of the known. He likened the Kingdom of Heaven to leaven, to nets cast into the sea, to merchants buying pearls. "Go thou, and do likewise." If you wish to give a clear conception of the size of Alaska, do not quote its area in square miles; name the states that could be put into it; enumerate its population in terms of the town where you are speaking.

3.   Avoid technical terms when addressing a lay audience. Follow Lincoln's plan of putting your ideas into language plain enough for any boy to comprehend.

4.   Be sure that the thing you wish to speak about, is first, as clear as noonday sunshine in your own mind.

5.   Appeal to the sense of sight. Use exhibits, pictures, illustrations when possible. Be definite. Don't just say "dog" if you mean "a fox terrier with a black splotch over his right eye."

6.   Restate your big ideas; but don't repeat, don't use the same phrases twice. Vary the sentences, but reiterate the idea without letting your hearers detect it.

7.   Make your abstract statement clear by following it with general illustrations, and what is often better still, by specific instances and concrete cases.

8.   Do not strive to cover too many points. In a short speech, one cannot hope to treat adequately more than one or two phases of a big topic.

9.   Close with a brief summary of your points.

SPEECH BUILDING
WORDS OFTEN MISPRONOUNCED

"A well educated gentleman may not know many languages, may not be able to speak any but his own. But whatever languages he knows, he knows precisely; whatever word he pronounces, he pronounces rightly."

-Ruskin

These words have four, not three, syllables. Read them aloud correctly.

ac-cu-ra-cy	in-er-ti-a
a-e-ri-al	mem-o-ra-ble
a-mi-a-ble	mis-er-a-ble
a-wak-en-ing	Na-po-le-on
cer-e-mon-y	pneu-mo-ni-a

de-lir-i-ous	pre-pos-ter-ous
de-lir-i-um	ri-dic-u-lous
de-liv-er-y	tem-per-a-ment
dis-cov-er-y	tem-pes-tu-ous
ex-pe-di-ent	u-su-al-ly
gen-er-al-ly	val-u-a-ble
ge-og-ra-phy	ven-er-a-ble
hy-gi-en-ic	

These words have five, not four, syllables.

ac-com-pa-ni-ment
con-si-der-a-ble
lab-o-ra-to-ry

ERRORS IN ENGLISH

Review. As this chapter completes three-fourths of the book you will find that the following sentences review many of the points which have already been taken up in the study of your language. Some of them are incorrect and some are not. Look them over and give your reason for the decision, which you make in each case.

Us men will have to settle the matter.

If you were him, I know what you would do.

It is us who are to blame.

I interviewed three people, none of which were satisfactory.

The horse who won the Derby sold for two hundred thousand dollars.

Nobody knows who she will take.

I seen him. Wasn't you there?

It looks as if there was going to be trouble sure.

Don't lay down now.

He bored three oil wells and sunk a lot of money, but neither of them paid.

She is not so prosperous as she once was.

Either of the cars are all right, but he don't intend to buy nothing.

He has always drunk heavily.

She had ought to have known better.

Everybody ought to take their own bait and tackle.

New Study Material.

RULE: So many people use *who* when they should say *whom* in short questions ending or beginning with a preposition. Look at the sentences given below and you will find that if you turn them around so that the preposition stands first, you will probably not make the mistake. Some authorities claim that you should never close a sentence with a preposition. This is the better rule.

Right: *Whom* did you ask for? Or For *whom* did you ask?

Wrong: *Who* did you ask for?

Right: *Whom* are you going to the dinner with? Or With *whom* are you going to the dinner?

Wrong: *Who* are you going to the dinner with?

RULE: Whenever you have any form of the verb *to be*, the nominative case is used after it instead of the objective case.

Right: *Who* did you say the girl was?

Wrong: *Whom* did you say the girl was?

Right: Do you know *who* it is that is doing this?

Wrong: Do you know *whom* it is that is doing this?

RULE: We are in the habit of putting certain expressions, like "I am certain," etc., into sentences. This makes it more difficult to decide whether *who* or *whom* should be used.

Right: I am giving you an assistant *who*, I am sure, will render satisfactory service. (*Who* is the right word because it is the subject of *will* render.)

Wrong: I am giving you an assistant *whom*, I am sure, will render satisfactory service.

Right: He is a person *whom*, I am certain, you can place in any position. (Here, *whom* is the object of *can place*, therefore it is the correct form.)

Wrong: He is a person *who*, I am sure, you can place in any position.

Right: The president *who*, as you know, was to blame, has been impeached. (The key to this is to drop as *you know*. *Who* is the

subject of *was* in the clause, *who was to blame*.)

Wrong: The president *whom*, as you know, was to blame, has been impeached.

RULE: *Whoever* and *whomever* are used just the same as *who* and *whom*.

Right: I will fight with *whoever* gives me the best offer.

Wrong: I will fight with *whomever* gives me the best offer.

Right: *Whoever* wins will take the gate money.

Wrong: *Whomever* wins will take the gate money.

Right: You may fight *whomever* you desire.

Wrong: You may fight *whoever* you desire.

Right: When a money order is endorsed to someone other than the payee, the post office must pay the amount to *whoever* brings it to the window if he can identify himself. (*Whoever* is correct here because it is the subject of *brings*. The preposition *to* has an object but it is the whole clause, *whoever* brings it to the *window*, etc., that is so considered.)

CORRECT USAGE OF WORDS

INDIFFERENCE - APATHY. *Indifference* expresses absence of feeling toward certain things. *Apathy* is an entire lack of feeling. You may be *indifferent* about an election in your city. You are *apathetic* about the elections in Johnson County, Missouri.

LIKELY - APT - LIABLE. (Wrong) "His obstinacy is *likely* to get him into trouble."

Better say: "His obstinacy is *liable* (or *apt*) to get him into trouble." *Apt* suggests a natural tendency; as, people are *apt* to blame their misfortunes on Fate. *Likely* refers to a probable and not unpleasant contingency; as, Our horse is *likely* to win the Bellair *Handicap* Race. *Liable* suggests something unpleasant; as, We are *liable* to have trouble.

PERMIT - ALLOW. You *permit* people to cross a field if you approve, sanction, or authorize the crossing, but if you do not attempt to prevent it, you *allow* it.

RECOLLECT - REMEMBER. *Remember* does not necessarily suggest an effort; *recollect* does.

Try this exercise for developing. Do you remember, when you were a child, how, when you stuck your head into the half-empty rain barrel, and uttered a sound, the wonderful effect produced fairly made your ears ring? That effect was due to resonance or sympathetic vibration. The sound you produced was magnified many times by being communicated to the air partially enclosed in the upper part of the barrel. All musical instruments, the drum with its barrel, the born with its tube and bell, the piano with its sounding board, the violin with its body of seasoned wood, all these are constructed on the principle that a comparatively weak initial sound can be reinforced and multiplied in power by communicating itself to a suitable elastic medium whether it be air, wood, or metal. The human voice is such a musical instrument. The feeble buzzing of the vocal cords is the initial sound which sets in vibration the chest and the partially open air cavities of the pharynx, mouth, and nose where it is wonderfully re-enforced and gains greatly in power and grandeur. If we heard only the initial buzz of the vocal cords, a voice would be heard only a few feet away and would have none of the characteristics, we associate with human speech. The resonance of the chest is largely automatic while that of the cavities of the head is under the control of the will and by skillful use can be made to produce both beautiful and powerful effects. A speaker of my acquaintance, who used to have a singularly toneless and empty voice, has by careful study and faithful practice, gained full use of his head resonance and now for some years, has been noted for the ringing quality of his voice and for his ability to fill large auditoriums with ease. Instruction in the proper use of your resonators, especially the mouth and the nose, must be an important part of your education as a public speaker.

Taking the vibrating air as it leaves the larynx or voice- box, we follow it up through the open throat until it reaches the veil of the soft palate which you can see hanging at the back of the mouth. Under its arch, a part of the breath stream enters the mouth and another part rises through the passageway, back of this veil or curtain into the nose.

Of these two cavities, the nose is the larger and has as irregular and varied a surface as the interior of a rocky cavern. Have you ever talked loudly or hallooed in a cave? Reverberations, such as you never heard before, greeted your astonished ears. In a similar way, brilliant and rich qualities are added to your voice in the queer-shaped cavernous spaces of your nose and head. This is called "head resonance." At the same time the other stream, which entered the mouth under the arch of the palate, is undergoing an entirely different change. Besides being re-enforced in volume just as was the stream that entered the nasal cavity by the rear door, this second breath stream is modified by the shape given to the interior of the mouth by the plastic tongue and mobile lips. These mouth modifications of the feeble initial tone are called vowels. Thus we learn that vowels are merely mouth resonances, not made at all by the vocal cords. At the larynx, all vowels are the same. The mold temporarily given to the inside of the mouth, largely by the tongue, determines what vowel shall come out. Thus the mouth is the vowel chamber, where also the interferences called consonants are made. We will now show you how to use the three resonating cavities, most effectively.

The chest cavity resounds *automatically* when you support your tone firmly on your controlled breath as you learned in Chapter V. You can feel it when you place your hand upon, your upper chest. It is stronger on the deeper tones of low pitch; but can be felt throughout the speaking range of the adult male voice. Support your voice with your deep breath on every word uttered and you will get full aid from your chest resonance.

As for your nasal resonance, this valuable aid can only be obtained by special training. At the very outset we must know the difference between nasal resonance and nasal "twang." The "twang" is produced when the tone does not go through the nose freely. Close both your nostrils with thumb and forefinger. Now try to say, "The moon is beaming." Notice the disagreeable nasality. Remove the obstruction and you can imitate the effect by voluntarily preventing the tone from going through the nose. Now say the sentence by allowing the tone to flow freely through the nose. The disagreeable quality has disappeared. You must talk with the word pronounced "forward" in the mouth but the tone must pass freely through the nose at the same time. Here are some exercises which will help to give you good head resonance and carrying power.

Exercise 1. Inhale deeply. Gradually expel the breath with a soft hissing sound forming the consonants. Repeat, and while hissing, suddenly close the lips without stopping the steady flow of breath, which will now pass through the nose, making the humming consonant m.

Exercise 2. Inhale deeply. Hum *m*. Then without stopping the hum change it to n by opening the lips and lifting the tip of the tongue to the hard palate. Alternate *m* and *n* repeatedly, keeping up a continuous stream of resonance, sounding like "minim," repeated continuously. Notice where the sensation of vibrating air is felt.

Exercise 3. Vary Exercise 2 by introducing the vowel sound *ee* between the hums and *m* and *n*; thus, *meeneemeenee*, etc. Notice the clear resonance of the vowel in the front of the mouth chamber while the hum still continues in the nose without interruption. This humming sound during the utterance of the vowel is important. Feel it as well as hear it.

Exercise 4. Repeat Exercise 3, then without stopping the stream of resonance, change ee into *ah*, forming *mene ah*, which will give a clear ringing ah sound heard in the front of the mouth just back of the upper front teeth while the hum must be heard simultaneously in the head cavities.

Exercise 5. Repeat slowly *"mean, mine"* several times without stopping the stream of resonance in the nasal cavities.

Chapter 13

HOW TO BE IMPRESSIVE AND CONVINCING

"The secret of success in tile consists in knowing how to, change men's minds. It is this power that makes the successful lawyer, grocer, politician or Preacher."

-Dr. Frank Crane

"The recipe for perpetual ignorance is be satisfied with your opinions and content with your knowledge."

-Elbert Hubbard

"The public speaker must set forth with power and attractiveness the very same topic which others discuss in such tame and bloodless phraseology."

-Cicero

"The practice of public speaking, the effort to marshal all one's forces in a logical and forceful manner, to bring to a focus all the power one possesses, is a great awakener of all the faculties. The sense of power that comes from holding the attention, stirring the emotions, or convincing the reason of an audience, gives self-confidence, assurance, self-reliance, arouses ambition and tends to make one more effective in every way."

-Dr. Orison Swett Marden

Chapter 13

HOW TO BE IMPRESSIVE AND CONVINCING

H ere is a psychological discovery of tremendous import. "Every idea, concept or conclusion which enters the mind," said Walter Dill Scott, President of Northwestern University, "is held as true unless hindered by some contradictory idea. If we can give a man any sort of an idea, it is not necessary to convince him of the truth of the idea, if we can keep conflicting ideas from arising in his mind. If I can get you to read the sentence, 'United States tires are good tires,' you will believe that they are good tires and that too without any further proof if any contradictory ideas do not surge up into your mind."

Dr. Scott is here speaking about suggestion, one of the most powerful influences the public speaker or private one, too, for that matter, can employ.

Three centuries before the Wise Men of the East followed the star of Bethlehem on the first Christmas, Aristotle taught that man was a reasoning animal, that he acted according to the dictates of logic. He flattered us. Acts of pure reasoning are as rare as romantic thoughts before breakfast. Most of our actions are the result of suggestion.

Suggestion is getting the mind to accept an idea without offering any proof or demonstration. If I say to you, "Pillsbury Flour is absolutely pure," and do not attempt to prove it, I am using suggestion. If I present an analysis of the product and the testimony of well-known chefs regarding it, I am trying to prove my assertion.

Those who are most successful in handling others, rely more upon suggestion, than upon argument. Salesmanship and modern advertising are based chiefly on suggestion.

It is easy to believe; doubting is more difficult. Experience and knowledge and thinking are necessary before we can doubt and question intelligently. Tell a child that Santa Claus comes down the chimney or a savage that thunder is the anger of the gods and the child and the savage will accept your statements until they acquire sufficient knowledge to cause them to demur. Millions in India passionately believe that the waters of the Ganges are holy, and that it is as wrong to kill a cow as it is to kill a person. They accept these concepts not because they have been proved but because the suggestion has been deeply imbedded in their minds.

Such beliefs are not limited to people in different cultures than ours. If we examine the facts closely, we will discover that the majority of our opinions, our most cherished beliefs, our creeds, the principles of conduct on which many of us base our very lives, are the result of suggestion, rather than reasoning. To take a concrete illustration from business. We have come to regard Arrow shirts, Cadillac cars, Heinz pickles, Pillsbury flour, Ivory soap as among the leading, if not the best, products of their kind. Why? Have we adequate reason for these judgments? Reason? Most of us have none at all. Have we made a careful comparison of the value of these brands and the output of competing firms? No! We have come to believe things for which no proof has been given. Prejudiced, biased, and reiterated assertions, not logic, have formulated our beliefs.

We are creatures of suggestion. Let us take a homely illustration that shows how most of us are being influenced by suggestion every day:

You have read many times that coffee is harmful. Let us suppose you intend to abstain from drinking it. You go into your favorite restaurant for dinner. If the waitress is not skilled in the niceties of salesmanship, she may inquire, "Do you wish coffee?" If she does, the arguments for and against it may battle momentarily in your mind, and your self-control perhaps wins. You want good health more than you wish the immediate gratification of your palate. However, if she phrases it negatively, "You don't want any coffee, do you?" You find it still simpler to say "no." The idea of refusing what she has put into your mind passes into action. (Haven't you heard many an unschooled and undiscerning salesperson, greet a prospective customer with just such a negative proposal?) But suppose she asks, "Will you have your coffee now or later?" What happens? She has subtly assumed that there is no question about your wanting it; she concentrates your entire attention on when you wish it served; and so she excludes other considerations from your mind, rendering it difficult for contradictory ideas to arise,

HOW TO BE IMPRESSIVE AND CONVINCING

making it easy for the thought of ordering coffee to pass into action. The result? You say "bring it now," when you really didn't intend to order it at all. This has happened to the writer. It has happened to most of the people who read these lines. It, and a thousand things like it, are happening every day. Department stores train their sales people to inquire, "Will you take it with you?" Because they have learned that "Do you wish to have it sent?", increases delivery costs immediately.

Not only does every idea that enters the mind tend to be accepted as true; but it is a well-known psychological fact that it also tends to pass into action. For example, you cannot even think of a letter of the alphabet, without moving ever so slightly, the muscles used in pronouncing it. You cannot think of swallowing, without moving ever so slightly, the muscles used in that act. The movement may be imperceptible to you; but there are machines delicate enough to register that muscular reaction. The only reason that you do not do everything you think of is because another idea; the uselessness of it, the expense, the trouble, the absurdity, the danger or some such thought; arises to slay the impulse.

OUR MAIN PROBLEM

So in the last analysis, our problem of getting people to accept our beliefs or to act upon our suggestions, is just this: to plant the idea in their minds and to keep contradictory and opposing ideas from arising. One who is skilled in doing that will have power in speaking and profit in business.

HELPS PSYCHOLOGY HAS TO OFFER

Has psychology any suggestions that will prove helpful to you in this connection? Emphatically, yes. Let us see what they are. First, haven't you noticed that contradictory ideas are much less likely to arise in your mind when the main idea is presented with feeling and contagious enthusiasm? I say "contagious," for enthusiasm is just that. It lulls the critical faculties. It is an insurmountable barrier to all dissenting, to all negative and opposing ideas. When your aim is impressiveness, remember, it is more productive to stir emotions, than to arouse thoughts. Feelings are more powerful than cold ideas. To arouse feelings one must be intensely in earnest. Insincerity rips

269

the vitals out of delivery. Regardless of the pretty phrases you may concoct; regardless of the illustrations you may assemble; regardless of the harmony of your voice, and the grace of your gestures. If you do not speak sincerely, these are hollow and glittering trappings. If you would impress an audience, be impressed yourself. Your spirit, shining through your eyes, radiating through your voice and proclaiming itself through your manner, will communicate itself to your auditors.

LIKEN WHAT YOU WISH PEOPLE TO ACCEPT TO SOMETHING THEY ALREADY BELIEVE

An atheist once declared to a devout clergyman that there was no God, and he challenged him to disprove his contention. The clergyman, very quietly took out his watch, opened the case and showed the works to the unbeliever, saying, "If I were to tell you that those levers and wheels and springs made themselves and fitted themselves together and started running on their own account, wouldn't you question my intelligence? Of course, you would. But look up at the stars. Every one of them has its perfect appointed course and motion; the earth and planets around the sun and the whole group pitching along at more than a million miles a day. Each star is another sun with its own group of worlds, rushing on through space like our own solar system. Yet there are no collisions, no disturbance, no confusion. All quiet, efficient and controlled. Is it easier to believe that they just happened or that someone made them so?"

Rather impressive, isn't it? What technique did the speaker use? Let us see. He began on common ground, got his opponent saying "yes" and agreeing with him at the outset, as we advised in Chapter X. Then he went on to show that belief in a deity is as simple, as inevitable, as belief in a watchmaker.

Suppose he had retorted to his antagonist at the outset, "No God? Don't be a silly ass. You don't know what you are talking about." What would have happened? Doubtlessly a verbal joust, a wordy war would have ensued, as futile as it was fiery. The atheist would have risen with an unholy zeal upon him to fight with all the fury of a fanatic for his opinions. Why? Because they were his opinions, and his precious, indispensable self-esteem would have been threatened; his pride would have been at stake.

Since pride is such a fundamentally explosive characteristic of human nature, wouldn't it be the part of wisdom to get a person's pride working for us, instead of against us? How? By showing, as the clergyman did, that the thing we propose is very similar to something that our opponent already believes. That renders it easier for the opponent to accept than to reject your proposal. That prevents contradictory and opposing ideas from arising in the mind, to vitiate, what we have said.

The clergyman showed delicate appreciation of how the human mind functions. Most people, however, lack this subtle ability to enter the citadel of a person's beliefs, arm in arm, with the owner. They erroneously imagine that in order to take the citadel, they must storm it, batter it down by a frontal attack. What happens? The moment hostilities commence, the drawbridge is lifted, the great gates are slammed and bolted, the mailed archers draw their long bows; the battle of words and wounds is on. Such frays always end in a draw; neither has convinced the other of anything.

SAINT PAUL'S SAGACITY

This more sensible method we are advocating, is not new. It was used long ago by Saint Paul. He employed it in that famous address of his to the Athenians on Mars Hill, employed it with an adroitness and finesse that compels our admiration across twenty centuries. He was a man of finished education; and, after his conversion to Christianity, his eloquence made him its leading advocate. One day he arrived at Athens, an Athens that had passed the summit of its glory and was now on the decline. The Bible says of it at this period:

"All the Athenians and strangers which were there, spent their time in nothing else, but either to tell or to hear some new thing."

No radios, no cables, no news-flashes; those Athenians must have been hard put, in those days, to scratch up something fresh every afternoon. Then Paul came. Here was something new. They crowded about him, amused, curious, interested. And asked:

"May we know what this new doctrine, whereof thou speakest, is?"

"For thou bringest certain strange things to our ears, we would know therefore what these things mean."

271

In other words, they invited a speech; and, of course, Paul agreed. In fact, that was what he had come for. He probably stood up on a block or stone and being a bit nervous, as all good speakers are at the very outset, he may have given his hands a dry wash and have cleared his throat, before he began.

However, he did not altogether approve of the way they had worded their invitation; "New doctrines . . . strange things." That was poison. He must eradicate those ideas. They were fertile ground for the propagating of contradictory and clashing opinions. He did not wish to present his faith as something strange and alien. He wanted to tie it up to, liken it to, something they already believed. That would smother dissenting suggestions. But how? He thought a moment; hit upon a brilliant plan; he began his immortal address:

"Ye men of Athens, I perceive that in all things Ye are very superstitious."

Some translations read, "ye are very religious." I think that is better, more accurate. They worshipped many gods; they were very religious. They were proud of it. He complimented them, pleased them. They began to warm toward him. One of the rules of the art of public speaking is to support a statement by an illustration. He does just that:

"For, as I passed by, and beheld your devotions I found an altar with this inscription, TO THE UNKNOWN GOD."

That proves, you see, that they were very religious. They were so afraid of slighting one of the deities that they had put up an altar to the unknown God, a sort of blanket insurance policy to provide against all unconscious slights and unintentional oversights. Paul, by mentioning this specific altar, indicated that he was not dealing in flattery; he showed that his remark was a genuine appreciation born of observation.

Now, here comes the consummate rightness of this opening:

"Whom therefore ye ignorantly worship,

Him declare I unto you."

"New doctrine. . . strange things"? Not a bit of it. He was there merely to explain a few truths about a God they were already worshipping without being conscious of it. Likening the things they did not believe, you see, to something they already passionately accepted, such was his superb technique.

He propounded his doctrine of salvation and resurrection, quoted a few words from one of their own Greek poets; and he was done. The whole speech had consumed less than two minutes. Some of his hearers mocked, but others said:

"We will hear thee again on this matter."

Just in passing, let us note that, that is one of the advantages of a two minute talk, you may be asked to speak again, as Paul was. A Philadelphia politician once remarked to me that the main rules to remember in making a speech were: make it short and make it snappy. Saint Paul, on this occasion, did both.

This technique that Saint Paul used at Athens is employed by the more discriminating companies of today in their selling talks and advertising. For example, here is a paragraph lifted from a sales letter that recently arrived at my desk:

"Old Hampshire Bond costs less than one half cent more per letter than the cheapest paper available. If you write a customer or a prospect ten letters a year, the influence of Old Hampshire will cost you less than a car fare, less than giving your customer a good cigar once every five years."

Who could possibly object to paying a carfare for a customer once a year or offering him a Havana twice in a decade? Surely, no one. And using Old Hampshire Bond would cost no more than that in additional expense? Doesn't that tend to forestall contradictory ideas regarding prohibitive cost?

MAKING SMALL SUMS APPEAR LARGE AND LARGE SUMS APPEAR SMALL

In much the same way, a large sum can be made to appear small by distributing it over a long period of time and comparing the daily outlay with something that seems trivial.

For example, In their ads, car dealers point out in big print, how small the monthly payment is, but list in small print the number of months, it will take to pay it off.

Small sums, on the other hand, can be made to appear huge by reversing this process, by massing them. A telephone company official

273

heaped insignificant minutes together to impress his audience with the vast amount of time lost by New Yorkers neglecting to answer telephones promptly:

"Out of each one hundred telephone connections made, seven show a delay of more than a minute before the person called answers. Every day 280,000 minutes are lost in this way. In the course of six months, this minute's delay in New York is about equal to all the business days that have elapsed since Columbus discovered America."

NOW TO MAKE FIGURES IMPRESSIVE

Mere numbers and amounts, taken by themselves, are never very impressive. They have to be illustrated; they ought, if possible, to be put in terms of our experiences, our recent experiences and our feeling experiences. For example, A British alderman used this technique when he was addressing the Borough Council of London about labor conditions. He stopped abruptly in the middle of his speech, took out his watch, and stood staring in blank silence at the audience for one minute and twelve seconds. The other members of the Borough Council twisted in their seats uneasily, looked questioningly at the speaker, at each other. What was wrong? Had the alderman suddenly lost his mind? Resuming his speech, he declared, "You have just sat through and fidgeted through the seventy-second eternity of time which it takes the average workman to lay one brick."

Was this method of doing it effective? It was so effective that it was cabled to all parts of the world, printed in newspapers across the seas. It was so effective that the Amalgamated Union of Building Trades at once called a strike "in protest against this insult to our dignity."

Which of the two following statements drives the point home with the greater force?

1. The Vatican has 15,000 rooms.

2. The Vatican has so many rooms that one might occupy a different one every day for forty years without having lived in them all.

Which of the following methods gives you a more impressive

conception of the incredible amount of the deficit faced by the United States in 2004?

1. According to the General Accounting Office, the U.S. deficit for the fiscal year will be over $450 billion. To most people this figure is unfathomable. It is impossible to really comprehend.

2. But if you would say that there have been approximately a billion minutes since the beginning of the A.D. era, the deficit is equivalent to spending four hundred dollars for every minute that has passed night and day since Christ was born.

WHAT RESTATEMENT WILL DO

Restatement is another club that we can use to prevent contradictory and dissenting ideas from arising to challenge our assertions. "It is not by advancing a political truth once or twice, or even ten times, that the public will take it up and adopt it," declared Daniel O'Connell, the famous Irish orator. O'Connell had had a lot of experience with audiences and the public. His testimony ought to merit consideration. "Incessant repetition," he continued, "is required to impress political truths upon the mind. By always hearing the same thing, people insensibly associate them with truisms. They find the facts at last quietly reposing in a corner of their minds, and no more think of doubting them than if they formed a part of their religious beliefs."

John Wesley's mother knew the truth O'Connell expressed. That is why, when her husband asked her why she repeated the same truths to her sons twenty times, she replied: "Because they have not learned the lesson when I have repeated it nineteen times."

Woodrow Wilson knew the truth O'Connell expressed. That is why he used it in his addresses.

Note that he merely reiterates and rephrases in the last two sentences, the idea he had stated in the first.

"You know that the pupils in the colleges in the last several decades, have not been educated. You know that, with all of our teaching, we train nobody. You know that with all of our instructing, we educate nobody."

However, in spite of all that we have said in praise of the principle of restatement, we ought to be warned that in the hands of an inexpert speaker, it may prove to be a dangerous tool. Unless you have a fairly rich phraseology, your restatement may deteriorate into an unadorned and all too evident repetition. That is deadly. If the audience catches you at that, they will begin twisting in their seats, looking at their watches.

GENERAL ILLUSTRATIONS AND SPECIFIC INSTANCES

There is little danger, however, of boring people when you employ general illustrations and specific instances. Interesting, easy to pay attention to, they are extremely valuable when the purpose of your talk is to impress and convince. They help to keep contradictory ideas from rising.

People like to have a speaker give names and dates, something they can examine for themselves if they wish. That kind of procedure is frank, honest. It wins confidence. It impresses.

For example, suppose I say, "Many wealthy people lead very simple lives." I have not been impressive. The statement is too vague, isn't it? It does not leap off the page and strike you between the eyes. It will soon drop out of your mind. It is neither clear nor interesting nor convincing. Memories of newspaper reports, to the contrary, will probably arise, to cast doubt upon the assertion.

If I believe that many rich people lead simple lives, how did I reach that conclusion? Through observing several concrete cases; so the best way to make you believe as I do, is to exhibit those specific instances to you. If I can show you what I have seen, you may arrive at the same conclusion that I have arrived at; and you will probably do it without any urging on my part.

A conclusion that I let you discover for yourself from concrete cases and evidence that I supply, will have twice, three, five times the force of a ready made conclusion that I might hand you on a platter. To illustrate:

John D. Rockefeller, Sr., had a leather couch in his office at 26 Broadway, and took a midday nap each day.

John H. Patterson, founder of the National Cash Register Company, neither smoked nor drank.

Frank Vanderlip, at one time the president of the largest bank in America, ate only two meals a day.

Andrew Carnegie's favorite dish was oatmeal and cream.

Cyrus H. Curtis, owner of the *Saturday Evening Post and the Ladies Home Journal*, loved no food better than baked beans.

Warren Buffet, one of the wealthiest men in the world, continues to live in the house he bought for $32,000 forty years ago, and lunches on hamburgers and cokes.

What is the effect of these specific instances on your mind? Do they dramatize the statement that rich men often lead simple lives? Do they impress you with the truth of it? As you listen to them, isn't it very unlikely that contradictory ideas will arise in your mind?

THE PRINCIPLE OF CUMULATION

Do not expect a hurried reference to one or possibly two specific instances to have the desired effect.

There must be a succession of impressions, all emphasizing the first. Over and over again, must the mind have its attention riveted upon the thought; experience upon experience must be piled up until the very weight imbeds the thought deep in the tissues of the brain. Then it becomes a part of that person and neither time nor events can rub it out. And the working principle that does this is called "cumulation."

Note, how this principle of cumulation was used in marshalling an array of specific instances in the preceding section of this chapter to prove that rich people often lead simple lives. Note, how it was employed on earlier in this book to prove that Philadelphia is "the greatest workshop of the world." Note, how one politician employed it in the following paragraph to prove that humanity has been able to right the wrongs of injustice and oppression only by force. What would have been the result, had two-thirds of these specific references been omitted?

"When has a battle for humanity and liberty ever been won except by force? What barricade of wrong, injustice and oppression has ever been carried, except by force?"

"Force compelled the signature of unwilling royalty to the great Magna Charta; force put life into the Declaration of Independence and made effective the Emancipation Proclamation; force beat with naked hands upon the iron gateway of the Bastile and made reprisal in one awful hour for centuries of kingly crime; force waved the flag of revolution over Bunker Hill and marked the snows of Valley Forge with bloodstained feet; force held the broken line of Shiloh, climbed the flame swept hill at Chattanooga and stormed the clouds on Lookout Heights; force marched with Sherman to the sea, rode with Sheridan in the valley of the Shenandoah and gave Grant victory at Appomattox; force saved the Union and kept the stars in the flag."

GRAPHIC COMPARISONS

Many years ago, a student in one of my courses told in a speech the number of houses that had been destroyed by fire during the previous year. He further said that, if these burned buildings had been placed side by side, the line would have reached from New York to Chicago, and that if the people who had been killed in those fires had been placed half a mile apart, that gruesome line would reach back again from Chicago to Brooklyn.

The figures he gave I forgot almost immediately; but ten years have passed and without any effort on my part, I can still see that line of burning buildings stretching from Manhattan Island to Cook County, Illinois.

Why is that so? Because ear impressions are hard to retain. They roll away like sleet striking the smooth bark of a beech tree. But eye impressions? I saw, a few years ago, a cannon ball imbedded in an old house standing on the banks of Danube, a cannon ball that Napoleon's artillery had fired at the battle of Ulm. Visual impressions are like that cannon ball; they come with a terrific impact. They imbed themselves. They stick. They tend to drive out all opposing suggestions as Bonaparte drove away the Austrians.

The power of the clergyman's reply to the atheist was due in no small degree to the fact that it was visual. Edmund Burke used this technique when, in denouncing the taxation of the American colonies, he declared with prophetic vision "We are shearing, not a sheep, but a wolf."

CALL IN AUTHORITY TO BACK YOU UP

As a boy in Missouri, I used to amuse myself by holding a stick across a gateway that the sheep had to pass through. After the first few sheep had jumped over the stick, I took it away; but all the other sheep leaped through the gateway over an imaginary barrier. The only reason for their jumping was that those in front had jumped. The sheep is not the only animal with that tendency. Almost all of us are prone to do what others are doing, to believe what others believe, to accept, without question, the testimony of prominent men.

The student in the New York Chapter of the American Institute of Banking, who began his talk on thrift in this manner, had a distinct advantage:

"Benjamin Franklin said, 'If you want to know whether you are going to succeed, the test is easy. Are you able to save money? If not, drop out. You will surely lose. You may not think it, but you will lose as sure as you live.' "

That was the next best thing to having Ben Franklin himself there. His words impressed. Their influence tended to prevent opposing ideas from arising.

However, in quoting authorities, bear these four points in mind.

1. *Be Definite*.

Which of these statements is the more impressive and convincing?

(a) Statistics show that Seattle is the healthiest city in the world.

(b) "According to the official federal mortality statistics, Seattle's annual death rate for the last fifteen years has been 9.78 per thousand; Chicago's, 14.65; New York's, 15.83; New Orleans', 21.02."

Beware of beginning "statistics show. . ." What statistics? Who gathered them and why? Be careful "Figures won't lie, but liars will figure."

The usual phrase, "many authorities declare," is ridiculously vague. Who are the authorities? Name one or two. If you do not know who they are, how can you be sure of what they said?

Be definite. It wins confidence. It demonstrates to the audience that you know, whereof, you speak. Even Theodore Roosevelt thought he could not afford to be vague. In an address at Louisville, Kentucky, during the administration of Woodrow Wilson, he said:

"Mr. Wilson's promises before election, both those made in his own speeches and those made in the platform, have been so well nigh invariably broken that the breaking of them has become a subject for jest even among his own friends. One of Mr. Wilson's prominent Democratic supporters in Congress stated with refreshing frankness, the exact truth about Mr. Wilson's pre-election promises and those made on his behalf when, in answer to some charge of inconsistency, he responded by saying that 'our platform was made to get into office on and we have won.' You *will find this remark* on page 4618 of the Congressional Record, the third session of the Sixty-second Congress."

2. *Quote a Popular Man.*

Our likes and dislikes have more to do with our beliefs than most of us would care to admit. I once saw the political reformer, Samuel Untermyer hissed while he was engaged in a socialistic debate at Carnegie Hall, New York. What he said was polite enough, and it seemed to me, in all truth, harmless enough, quiet enough. But most of the audience were socialists. They despised him. They would almost have been inclined to question the veracity of the multiplication table, had he but quoted it.

3. *Quote Local Authorities.*

If you are speaking in Detroit, quote a Detroit man. Your hearers can look him up, can investigate the matter. They will be more impressed with his testimony than with the words of some unknown individual, away off in Spokane or San Antonio.

4. *Quote Someone Qualified to Speak.*

Ask yourself such questions as these: Is this person generally recognized as an authority on this subject? Why? Is he or she a prejudiced witness? Has he or she any selfish ends to serve?

The student at the Brooklyn Chamber of Commerce who opened his talk on Specialization with the following quotation from Andrew Carnegie chose wisely. Why? Because his audience had an abiding respect for the great steel magnate. Besides, Mr. Carnegie was being quoted on business success, a subject on which a lifetime of experience and observation had qualified him to speak.

"I believe the true road to preeminent success in any line, is to make yourself master in that line. I have no faith in the policy of scattering one's resources, and in my experience, I have rarely if ever, met a man who achieved preeminence in moneymaking, certainly never one in manufacturing, who was interested in many concerns. Those who have succeeded are those who have chosen one line and stuck to it."

IN A NUTSHELL

"Every idea, concept or conclusion which enters the mind is held as true unless hindered by some contradictory idea." Our problem then, when the purpose of our talk is impressiveness and conviction, is twofold: first, to set forth our own ideas; second, to prevent opposing ideas from arising to render them null and void. Here are eight suggestions that will aid in achieving that consummation:

1.   Convince yourself before you attempt to convince others. Speak with contagious enthusiasm.

2.   Show how the thing you want people to accept is very similar to something they already believe.

3.   Restate your ideas. When restating figures, illustrate them.

4.   Use general illustrations.

5.   Use specific instances, cite concrete cases.

6.   Use the principle of cumulation. "Experience upon experience must be piled up until the very weight imbeds the thought deep in the tissues of the brain."

7.   Use graphic comparisons. Ear impressions are easily obliterated. Visual impressions stick like an imbedded cannon ball.

8.   Back up your statements with unpre-judiced authority. Quote a well-known person. Quote a local person. Quote someone qualified to speak on that subject.

SPEECH BUILDING
WORDS OFTEN MISPRONOUNCED

The words *ath-lete* and *al-ien* have two, not three, syllables.

These words have three, not two syllables:

ac-cu-rate	fed-er-al
bar-ri-er	fo-li-age
bev-er-age	gal-ler-y
bois-ter-ous	gen-er-al
boun-da-ry	gen-tle-men
bur-i-al	gro-cer-y

281

cas-u-al	his-tor-y
Cath-o-lic	i-vo-ry
cel-er-y	jo-vi-al
ce-re-al	la-bor-er
Ches-a-peake	Laz-a-rus
choc-o-late	li-bra-ry
dexterous	lit-er-al
di-a-mond	me-di-um
em-per-or	mem-o-ry
fam-i-ly	

ERRORS IN ENGLISH

As Chapter XII contained a thorough review, this chapter will start right off with some new examples of English as it should be spoken.

RULE: When two or more pronouns are united by "and" and governed by the same preposition or verb, they must both be in the same case. Many a speaker blunders here. You will note that the same matter is discussed as was taken up in Chapter XI, where the rule stated that, when a pronoun is a direct object of a verb, it is always in the objective case. Here we have added examples where pronouns are objects of prepositions. Examples:

Right: Between you and *me*.

Wrong: Between you and *I*.

(It is the I coming after the "and" that causes the trouble. Few would be guilty of *between I and you*, or *between I and he*.)

Right: There was not much said about you and *me*.

Wrong: There was not much said about you and *I*.

Right: Let you and *me*. . .

Wrong: Let you and *I*. . .

Right: Every member was present except you and *me*.

Wrong: Every member was present except you and *I*.

Right: He said he would wait for you and *me*.

Wrong: He said he would wait for you and *I*.

Right: The letters were mailed by the secretary and *me*.

Wrong: The letters were mailed by the secretary and *I*.

Right: The bank was started by *him* and his wife.

Wrong: The bank was started by *he* and his wife.

Right: The civil service jobs were won by *her* and her sister.

Wrong: The civil service jobs were won by *she* and her sister.

Right: It was too late for him and *me* to be out.

Wrong: It was too late for him and *I* to be out.

Right: The loan was made by *her* and *him*.

Wrong: The loan was made by *she* and *he*.

Right: The house was built for them and *me*.

Wrong: The house was built for them and *I*.

Right: The sales were put on by him and *them*.

Wrong: The sales were put on by him and *they*.

Right: The statements were made to *her* and *them*.

Wrong: The statements were made to *she* and *they*.

Right: Life has been happy for them, *him* and *me*.

Wrong: Life has been happy for them, *he* and *I*.

Right: Business between *her* and *me* was done through them.

Wrong: Business between *she* and *I* was done through them.

Right: The manufacturing was done by them and *us*.

Wrong: The manufacturing was done by them and *we*.

Right: The dividends were issued to them, *him* and *us*.

Wrong: The dividends were issued to them, *he* and *we*.

You and *me* must never be used as the subject of a sentence.

For example:

Right: You and *I* ought to go right now.

Wrong: You and *me* ought to go right now.

Right: Were you and *I* invited?

Wrong: Were you and *me* invited?

CORRECT USAGE OF WORDS

RETICENT - RESERVED - TACITURN. The *reticent* man keeps his own counsel; the *reserved* woman usually is cold and restrained in addition to being *reticent*; the *taciturn* person is habitually uncommunicative.

SELECT - CHOOSE - PREFER. (Wrong) "She has no preference, so she *selected* the first one she put her hands on." *Select* suggests a careful choice. *Preference* implies a desire. Out of regard for his wife, a man may *choose* (not *select*) the seashore for his vacation, when he himself *prefers* a fortnight in the Canadian woods.

SOCIAL - SOCIABLE. (Wrong) "He is a *social* man." *Social* refers to society; as, *social* intercourse, *social* questions. *Sociable* means companionable; as, she is a *sociable* woman.

UNIQUE - RARE. *Unique* means the only one of its kind. *Rare* signifies infrequent. Enduring speeches are *rare*. Lincoln's Gettysburg address is *unique*.

VOICE EXERCISE - NASAL RESONANCE

Theodore Roosevelt, during his first political campaign, found his voice giving out on him very soon after he started on a strenuous speaking tour. He secured a vocal instructor to travel with him on the train; and between stations Roosevelt was practicing "ding-dong, sing-song, hong-kong," accentuating the *ng* sound, making it ring through his nose to develop nasal resonance. Nasal resonance gives both brightness and carrying power; and is highly desirable when one is speaking at a distance.

Practice the exercise that Roosevelt used. Then read aloud, not once, but once a day, the following verse from Poe's *The Bells*. I am asking you to read these for the following reasons.

1. Practice it for nasal resonance. Let the sound of *bells, bells, bells* ring through the cavern of your nose, and, in fact, through all the irregular cavities of your head. As we have pointed out in previous chapters, breathe in deeply and then try to feel while you are reading and using breath, that same open feeling in the head, that you experienced when inhaling.

2. Read this also as an exercise for developing strength and agility in the tip of your tongue. The *l* sounds, so frequent in these verses,

are almost ideal for that purpose. To refresh your mind on this exercise, turn to the voice exercise in Chapter VI.

3. Read these verses as a means of developing the bright, happy overtones of your voice. (See Voice Exercise, Chapter VII.)

4. Read the first verse aloud in a falsetto pitch. (See Chapter VII.)

"Hear the sledges with the bells,
Silver bells
What a world of merriment their melody foretells!
How they tinkle, tinkle, tinkle,
In the icy air of night!
While the stars that oversprinkle
All the heavens seem to twinkle
With a crystalline delight;
Keeping time, time,
In a sort of Runic rhyme
To the tintinnabulation that so musically wells
From the bells, bells, bells, bells,
Bells, bells, bells,-
From the jingling and the tinkling of the bells.
Hear the mellow wedding-bells,
Golden bells!
What a world of happiness their harmony foretells!
Through the balmy air of night
How they ring out their delight!
From the molten-golden notes,
And all in tune,
What a liquid ditty floats
To the turtle-dove that listens while she gloats
On the moon!
Oh, from out the sounding cells,
What a world of happiness their harmony foretells!
How it swells!

How it dwells.
On the Future! How it tells
Of the rapture that impels
To the swinging and the ringing
Of the bells, bells, bells,
Of the bells, bells, bells, bells,
Bells, bells, bells
To the rhyming and the chiming of the bells!"

Chapter 14

HOW TO INTEREST YOUR AUDIENCE

"There is in all communication, written or spoken, a certain dead line of interest. If we can cross that dead line, we have the world with us, temporarily at least. If we cannot cross it, we may as well retire. The world will have none of us."

-H.A. Overstreet, in Influencing Human Behavior

"Always have something to say. The man who has something to say, and who is known never to speak unless he has, is sure to be listened to. Always know before what you mean to say. If your own mind is muddled, much more will the minds of your bearers be confused. Always arrange your thoughts in some sort of order. No matter how brief they are to be, they will be better for having a beginning, a middle and an end. At all hazards, be clear. Make your meaning, whatever it is plain to your audience. In controversial speaking, aim to anticipate your adversary's argument. Reply to his jests seriously and to his earnestness by jest. Always reflect before hand upon the kind of audience you are likely to have. . . . Never, if you can help it, be dull."

-Lord Bryce

Chapter 14

HOW TO INTEREST YOUR AUDIENCE

I f you had been invited to dine at the home of a rich man in certain sections of the old Chinese Empire, it would be proper to toss chicken bones and olive seeds over your shoulder onto the floor. You pay your host a compliment when you do that. You show that you realize that he is wealthy, that he has plenty of servants to tidy up after the meal. And he likes it.

You can be reckless with the remains of your sumptuous meal in a rich man's home; but in some parts of China, the poorer people must save even the water they bathe in. To heat water costs so much that they must buy it at a hot water shop. After they have bathed in it, they can take it back and sell it, second hand, to the shopkeeper from whom they purchased it. When the second customer has soiled it, the water still retains a market value, although the price has softened a bit.

Have you found these facts about Chinese life interesting? If so, do you know why? Because those are very unusual aspects of very usual things. They are strange truths about such commonplace events as dining out and bathing.

That is what interests us, something new about the old.

Let us take another illustration. This page you are reading now, this sheet of paper you are looking at, it is very ordinary, isn't it? You have seen countless thousands of such pages. It seems dull and insipid now; but if I tell you a strange fact about it, you are almost sure to be interested. Let us see! This page seems like solid matter as you look at it now. But, in reality, it is more like a cobweb than solid matter. The physicist knows it is composed of atoms. And how small is an atom? There are as many atoms in one drop of water as there are drops of water in the Mediterranean sea; there are as many atoms in one drop of water as there are blades of grass in all the world. And the atoms that make this paper are composed of what? Still smaller things called electrons and protons. These electrons are all rotating around the central proton of the atom, as far from it, relatively speaking, as the moon is from the earth. And they are swinging through their orbits, these electrons of this tiny universe, at the inconceivable speed, of approximately, ten thousand miles a second. So the electrons that compose this sheet of paper you are holding, have moved, since you began reading this very sentence, a distance equal to that which stretches between New York and Tokyo.

And only two minutes ago you may have thought this piece of paper was still and dull and dead; but, in reality, it is one of God's mysteries. It is a veritable cyclone of energy.

If you are interested in it now, it is because you have learned a new and strange fact about it. There lies one of the secrets of interesting people. That is a significant truth, one that we ought to profit by in our every day intercourse. The entirely new is not interesting; the entirely old has no attractiveness for us. We want to be told something new about the old. You cannot, for example, interest an Illinois farmer with a description of the Cathedral at Bourges or the Mona Lisa. They are too new to him. There is no tieup to his old interests. But you can interest him by relating the fact that farmers in Holland till land below the level of the sea and dig ditches to act as fences and build bridges to serve as gates. Your Illinois farmer will listen open mouthed while you tell him that Dutch farmers keep the cows, during the winter, under the same roof that houses the family and sometimes the cows look out through face curtains at driving snows. He knows about cows and fences; new slants, you see, on old things. "Lace curtains! For a cow!" He'll exclaim. "I'll be doggoned!" And he will retell that story to his friends.

Here is a talk delivered by a New York City student of my course. As you read it, see if it interests you. If it does, do you know why?

HOW SULPHURIC ACID AFFECTS YOU

"Most liquids are measured by the pint, quart, gallon or barrel. We ordinarily speak of quarts of wine, gallons of milk and barrels of molasses. When a new oil gusher is discovered, we speak of its output as so many barrels per day. There is one liquid, however, that is manufactured and consumed in such large quantities that the unit of measurement employed is the ton. This liquid is sulphuric acid."

"It touches you in your daily life in a score of ways. If it were not for sulphuric acid, your car would stop, and you would go back to "old Dobbin" and the buggy, for it is used extensively in the refining of kerosene and gasoline. The electric lights that illuminate your office, that shine upon your dinner table, that show you the way to bed at night, would not be possible without it."

"When you get up in the morning and turn on the water for your bath, you use a nickle-plated faucet, which requires sulphuric acid in its manufacture. It was required also in the finishing of your enameled tub. The soap you use has possibly been made from greases or oils that have been treated with the acid. Your towel has made its acquaintance before you made the acquaintance of your towel. The bristles in your hairbrush have required it, and your plastic comb could not have been produced without it. Your razor, no doubt, has been pickled in it after annealing."

"You put on your underwear; you button up your outer garments. The bleacher, the manufacturer of dyes and the dyer himself used it. The button-maker possibly found the acid necessary to complete your buttons. The tanner used sulphuric acid in making the leather for your shoes, and it serves us again when we wish to polish them."

"You come down to breakfast. The cup and saucer, if they were other than plain white, could not have come into being without it. It is used to produce the gilt and other ornamental colorings. Your spoon, knife and fork have seen a bath of sulphuric acid, if they are silverplated."

"The wheat of which your bread or rolls are made, has possibly been grown by the use of a phosphate fertilizer, whose manufacture rests upon this acid. If you have buckwheat cakes and syrup, your syrup needed it."

"And so on through the whole day, its work affects you at every turn. Go where you will, you cannot escape its influence. We can neither go to war without it nor live in peace without it. So it hardly seems possible that this acid, so essential to mankind, should be totally unfamiliar to the average person. . . . But such is the case."

THE THREE MOST INTERESTING THINGS
IN THE WORLD

What would you say they are, the three most interesting subjects in the world? Sex, property and religion. By the first we can create life, by the second we maintain it, by the third we hope to continue it in the world to come.

But it is *our* sex, *our* property, *our* religion that interests us. Our interests swarm about our own egos.

We are not interested in a talk on How to Make Wills in Peru; but we may be interested in a talk entitled: How to Make Our Wills. We are not interested except, perhaps, out of curiosity; in the religions of the people in India; but we are vitally interested in a religion that insures *us* unending happiness in the world to come.

When the Lord Northcliffe was asked what interests people, he answered with one word and that word was "themselves." Northcliffe ought to have known for he was the wealthiest newspaper owner in Great Britain.

Do you want to know what kind of a person you are? Ah, now, we are on an interesting topic. We are talking about *you*. Here is a way for *you* to hold the mirror up to your real self, and see *you* as *you* really are. Watch your reveries. What do we mean by reveries? James Harvey Robinson answered this in his book *The Mind in the Making*:

"We all appear to ourselves to be thinking all the time during our waking hours, and most of us are aware that we go on thinking while we are asleep, even more foolishly than when awake. When uninterrupted by some practical issue we are engaged in, what is now known as a reverie. This is our spontaneous and favorite kind of thinking. We allow our ideas to take their own course and this course is determined by our hopes and fears, our spontaneous desires, their fulfillment or frustration; by our likes and dislikes, our loves and hates and resentments. There is nothing else anything like so interesting to ourselves as ourselves. All thought that is not more or less laboriously controlled and directed will inevitably circle about the beloved ego. It is amusing and pathetic to observe this tendency in ourselves and in others. We learn politely and generously to overlook this truth, but if we dare to think of it, it blazes forth like the noontide sun. Our reveries form the chief index of our fundamental character. They are a reflection of our nature as modified by often hidden and forgotten experiences. The reverie doubtless influences all our speculations in its persistent tendency to self-magnification and self-justification, which are its chief preoccupations."

So remember that the people you are to talk to, spend most of their time when they are not concerned with the problems of business, in thinking about and justifying and glorifying themselves. Remember that most of us are more concerned about the cook leaving than about Italy paying her debts to the United States. We are more wrought up over a dull razor blade than over a revolution in South America. Our own toothache will distress us more than an earthquake in Asia destroying half a million lives. Most of us would rather listen to someone say some nice thing about us than hear that person discuss the ten greatest people in history.

HOW TO BE A GOOD CONVERSATIONALIST

The reason so many people are poor conversationalists is because they talk about only the things that interest them. That may be deadly boring to others. Reverse the process. Lead the other person into talking about *her* interests, *his* business, *her* hobbies, *his* golf score or *her* children. Do that and listen intently and you will give pleasure; consequently, you will be considered a good conversationalist, even though you have done very little of the talking.

One of my students made an extraordinarily successful speech at a banquet that marked the final session of my public speaking course. He talked about each person in turn around the entire table, commented on how that person had talked when the course started, how he or she had improved; recalled the talks various members had made, the subjects they had discussed; he mimicked some of them, exaggerated their peculiarities, had everyone laughing, had everyone pleased. With such material, he could not possibly have failed. It was absolutely ideal. No other topic under the blue dome of Heaven would have so interested that group.

AN IDEA THAT WON TWO MILLION READERS

Some years ago, the *American Magazine* enjoyed an amazing growth. Its sudden leap in circulation became one of the sensations of the publishing world. The secret? The secret was its editor, John M.

293

Siddall and his ideas. When I first met Siddall he had charge of the Interesting People Department of that periodical. I had written a few articles for him; and one day he sat down and talked to me for a long time:

"People are selfish," he said. "They are interested chiefly in themselves. They are not very much concerned about whether the government should own the railroads; but they do want to know how to get ahead, how to draw more salary, how to keep healthy. If I were editor of this magazine," he went on, "I would tell them how to take care of their teeth, how to take baths, how to keep cool in summer, how to get a position, how to handle employees, how to buy homes, how to remember, how to avoid grammatical errors, and so on. People are always interested in human stories, so I would have some rich man tell how he made a million in real estate. I would get prominent bankers and presidents of various corporations to tell the stories of how they battled their ways up from the ranks to power and wealth."

Shortly after that, Siddall was made editor. The magazine then had a small circulation, was comparatively a failure. Siddall did just what he said he would do. The response? It was overwhelming. The circulation figures climbed up to two hundred thousand, three, four, half a million. . . . Here was something the public wanted. Soon a million people a month were buying it, then a million and a half, finally two millions. Siddall appealed to the selfish interests of his readers.

HOW DR. CONWELL INTERESTED MILLIONS OF HEARERS

What was the secret of the most popular lecture of its time, "Acres of Diamonds"? Just the thing we have been talking about. John M. Siddall discussed this lecture in the conversation I have just referred to; and I think that its enormous success had something to do with determining the policy of his magazine.

Turn to it again, please, in the Appendix. It tells people how they can get ahead, how they can make more out of themselves in their present environment.

It was never a static lecture. Dr. Conwell made it personal to each town where he spoke. That was of immense importance. The local references made it appear fresh and new. They made that town, that audience, seem important. Here is his own story of how he did it:

"I visit a town or city, and try to arrive there early enough to see the postmaster, the barber, the keeper of the hotel, the principal of the schools, and the ministers of some of the churches, and then go into some of the factories and stores, and talk with the people, and get into sympathy with the local conditions of that town or city and see what has been their history, what opportunities they had and what they had failed to do; and every town fails to do something; and then go to the lecture and talk to those people about the subjects which apply to their locality. Acres of Diamonds, the idea, has continuously been precisely the same."

"The idea is that in this country of ours, all of us have the opportunity to make more of ourselves than we do in our own environment, with our own skill, with our own energy and with our own friends."

THE KIND OF SPEECH MATERIAL THAT ALWAYS HOLDS ATTENTION

You may possibly bore people if you talk about things and ideas, but you can hardly fail to hold their attention when you talk about people. Tomorrow there will be millions of conversations floating over fences in the backyards of America, over tea tables and dinner tables and what will be the predominating note in most of them? Personalities. He said this. Mrs. So and so did that. I saw her doing this, that and the other. He is making a "killing," and so on.

I have addressed many gatherings of school children in the United States and Canada; and I soon learned by experience that in order to keep them interested, I had to tell them stories about people. As soon as I became general and dealt with abstract ideas, Susie became restless and wiggled in her seat, Tommy made a face at someone, Billy threw something across the aisle.

True, these were audiences of children; but the adults are just as likely to get restless when a talk become boring. So one can hardly go wrong in making a generous use of human interest stories. Our magazines that are read by millions and the most popular radio and television programs are filled with them.

I once asked a group of American business executives in Paris to

295

talk on *How to Succeed*. Most of them praised the homely virtues, preached at, lectured to, and bored their hearers. So I halted this class and said something like this: "We don't want to be lectured to. No one enjoys that. Remember you must be entertaining or we will pay no attention whatever to what you are saying. Also remember that one of the most interesting things in the world is sublimated, glorified gossip. So tell us the stories of two people you have known. Tell why one succeeded and why the other failed. We will gladly listen to that, remember it and possibly profit by it. It will also, by the way, be far easier for you to deliver than are these wordy, abstract preachments."

There was a certain member of that course who invariably found it difficult to interest either himself or his audience. This night, however, he seized the human story suggestion; and told us of two of his classmates in college. One of them had been so conservative that he had bought shirts at the different stores in town, and made charts showing which ones laundered best, wore longest and gave the most service per dollar invested. His mind was always on pennies; yet, when he graduated, it was an engineering college, he had such a high opinion of his own importance that he was not willing to begin at the bottom and work his way up, as the other graduates were doing. Even when the third annual reunion of the class came, he was still making laundry charts of his shirts, while waiting for some extraordinarily good thing to come his way. It never came. A quarter of a century has passed since then, and this man, dissatisfied and soured on life, still holds a minor position.

The speaker then contrasted with this failure, the story of one of his classmates who had surpassed all expectations. This particular chap was a good mixer. Everyone liked him. Although he was ambitious to do big things later, he started as a draughtsman. But he was always on the lookout for opportunity. Plans were then being made for the Pan-American exposition in Buffalo. He knew engineering talent would be needed there; so he resigned from his position in Philadelphia and moved to Buffalo. Through his agreeable personality, he soon won the friendship of a Buffalo man with considerable political influence. The two formed a partnership, and engaged immediately in the contracting business. They did considerable work for the telephone company, and this man was finally taken over by that concern at a large salary. Today, he is a multimillionaire, one of the principal owners of his company.

We have recorded here only the bare outline of what the speaker told. He made his talk interesting and illuminating with a score of amusing and human details. He talked on and on; this man who could not ordinarily find material for a three-minute speech; and he was surprised beyond words to learn when he stopped that he had held the floor on this occasion for half an hour. The speech had been so interesting that it seemed short to everyone. It was this student's first real triumph.

Almost every student can profit by this incident. The average speech would be far more appealing if it were rich and replete with human interest stories. The speaker ought to attempt to make only a few points and to illustrate them with concrete cases. Such a method of speech building can hardly fail to get and hold attention.

If possible, these stories ought to tell of struggles, of things fought for and victories won. All of us are tremendously interested in fights and combats. There is an old saying that all the world loves a lover. It doesn't. What all the world loves is a scrap. It wants to see two lovers struggling for the hand of one woman. As an illustration of this fact, read almost any novel, magazine story or go to see almost any film drama. When all the obstacles are removed and the reputed hero takes the so-called heroine in his arms, the audience begins reaching for their hats and coats. Almost all romance fiction is based on this formula. Make the reader like the hero or heroine. Make him or her long for something intensely. Make that something seem impossible to get. Show how the hero or heroine fights and gets it.

The story of how a person battled in business or profession or for a just but unpopular political cause against discouraging odds, and won, is always inspiring, always interesting. A magazine editor once told me that the real, inside story of any person's life is entertaining. If one has struggled and fought, and who hasn't? That story, if correctly told, will appeal. There can be no doubt of that.

BE CONCRETE

The writer once had, in the same course in public speaking, a Doctor of Philosophy and a rough and ready fellow, who had spent his youth thirty years ago in the British Navy. The polished scholar was a university professor; his classmate from the seven seas was the proprietor of a small side street moving van establishment. Strange to say, the moving van man's talks during the course would have held a popular audience far better than the talks of the college professor. Why? The college man spoke in beautiful English, with a demeanor of culture and refinement, and with logic and clearness; but his talks lacked one essential ingredient, concreteness. They were too vague, too general. On the other hand, the van owner possessed hardly enough brainpower to generalize. When he talked, he got right down to business immediately. He was definite; he was concrete. That quality, coupled with his virility and his fresh phraseology, made his talks very entertaining.

I have cited this instance, not because it is typical either of university professors or moving van proprietors, but because it illustrates the interest getting power that accrues to the individual, regardless of education, who has the happy habit of being concrete and definite in speaking.

This principle is so important that we are going to use several illustrations to try to lodge it firmly in your mind. We hope you will never forget it, never neglect it.

Is it, for example, more interesting to state that Martin Luther, as a boy, was "stubborn and intractable," or is it better to say that he confessed that his teachers had flogged him as often as "fifteen times in a forenoon?"

Words like "stubborn and intractable" have very little attention value. But isn't it easy to listen to the flogging count?

The old method of writing a biography was to deal in a lot of generalities, which Aristotle called, and rightly called, "The refuge of weak minds." The new method is to deal with concrete facts that speak for themselves. The old fashioned biographer said that John Doe was born of "poor but honest parents." The new method would say that John Doe's father couldn't afford a pair of overshoes, so when the snow came, he had to tie gunny sacking around his shoes to keep his feet dry and warm; but, in spite of his poverty, he never watered the milk and he always gave full value when selling his crops. That shows that his parents were "poor but honest," doesn't it? And doesn't it do it in a way that is far more interesting than the "poor but honest" method?

If this method works for modern biographers, it will work also for modern speakers.

Let us take one more illustration. Suppose you wished to state that the potential horsepower wasted at Niagara every day was appalling. Suppose you said just that, and then added, that if it were utilized and the resulting profits turned to purchasing the necessities of life, crowds could be clothed and fed. Would that be the way to make it interesting and entertaining? No-No. Isn't this far better? We are quoting from an article in the *Daily Science News Bulletin*.

"We are told that there are some millions of people in poverty and poorly nourished in this country, yet here at Niagara is wasted the equivalent of 250,000 loaves of bread an hour. We may see with our mind's eye 600,000 nice fresh eggs dropping over the precipice every hour and making a gigantic omelet in the whirlpool. If cloth were continuously pouring from the looms in a stream 4,000 feet wide like Niagara River, it would represent the same destruction of property. If a Carnegie Library were held under the spout it would be filled with good books in an hour or two. Or we can imagine a big department store floating down from Lake Eric every day and smashing its varied contents on the rocks 160 feet below. That would be an exceedingly interesting and diverting spectacle, quite as attractive to the crowd as the present, and no more expensive to maintain. Yet some people might object to that on the ground of extravagance who now object to the utilization of the power of the failing water."

PICTURE-BUILDING WORDS

In this process of interest getting, there is one aid, one technique that is of the highest importance; yet it is all but ignored. The average speaker does not seem to be aware of its existence. He or she has probably never consciously thought about it at all. I refer to the process of using words that create pictures. The speaker who is easy to listen to is the one who sets images floating before your eyes. The one who employs foggy, common place, colorless symbols sets the audience to nodding.

Pictures. Pictures. Pictures. They are as free as the air you breathe. Sprinkle them through your talks, your conversation; and you will be more entertaining, more influential.

To illustrate: let us take the excerpt just quoted from the *Daily Science News Bulletin* regarding Niagara. Look at the picture words. They leap up and go scampering away in every sentence, as thick as rabbits in Australia: "25,000 loaves of bread, 600,000 eggs dropping over the precipice, gigantic omelette in the whirlpool, cloths pouring from the looms in a stream 4,000 feet wide, Carnegie library held under the spout, books, a big department store floating, smashing, rocks below, falling water."

It would be almost as difficult to ignore such a talk or article as it would be to pay not the slightest attention to the scenes from a film unwinding on the silver screen of the motion picture theater.

Herbert Spencer, in his famous little essay on the *Philosophy of Style*, pointed out long ago the superiority of terms that call forth bright pictures:

"We do not think," says he, "in generals but in particulars. . ." We should avoid such a sentence as:

"In proportion as the manners, customs and amusements of a nation are cruel and barbarous, the regulations of their penal code will be severe."

And in place of it, we should write:

"In proportion as people delight in battles, bull fights and combats of gladiators, will they punish by hanging, burning and the rack."

Picture-building phrases swarm through the pages of the Bible and through Shakespeare like bees around a cider mill. For example, a commonplace writer would have said that a certain thing would be superfluous, like trying to improve the perfect. How did Shakespeare express the same thought? With a picture phrase that is immortal: "To gild refined gold, to paint the lily, to throw perfume on the violet."

Did you ever pause to observe that the proverbs that are passed on from generation to generation are almost all visual sayings? "A bird in the hand is worth two in the bush." "It never rains but it pours." "You can lead a horse to water but you can't make him drink." And you will find the same picture element in almost all the similes that have lived for centuries and grown hoary with too much use: "Sly as a fox." "Dead as a door nail." "Flat as a pancake." "Hard as a rock."

Lincoln continually talked in visual terminology. When he became annoyed with the long, complicated, redtape reports that came to his desk in the White House, he objected to them, not with a colorless phraseology, but with a picture phrase that it is almost impossible to forget. "When I send a man to buy a horse," said he, "I don't want to be told how many hairs the horse has in his tail. I wish only to know his points."

Successful people use word pictures. Audrey L. sells computers. In discussing problems faced by one of her prospects, she learned that he was primarily concerned with the messy office he supervised. "Papers and files are all over the place," he complained, "and I can never find the files I need they're always out, probably in one of those piles."

After describing the technical aspects of her company's product, she said, "Let's look ahead to six months from now. You walk into your office. There are no piles of papers on desks or chairs. Your people are working at their computers. You need a file. You sit down a terminal and key in the file name. Instantly, the information desired appears on your screen. No waiting. No frustration."

Audrey has drawn a word picture of the future. The manager does not require much imagination to visualize this and recognize the value of making the purchase. It works for sales people and it will work for you when making a speech.

THE INTEREST GETTING VALUE OF CONTRASTS

Listen to the following condemnation of King Charles I by the British historian, Thomas Babington Macaulay. Note that Macaulay not only uses pictures, but he also employs balanced sentences. Violent contrasts almost always hold our interests; violent contrasts are the very brick and mortar of this paragraph:

"We charge him with having broken his coronation oath; and we are told that he kept his marriage vow! We accuse him of having given up his people to the merciless inflections of the most hotheaded of prelates; and the defense is that he took his little son on his knee and kissed him! We censure him for having violated the articles of the Petition of Right, after having, for good and valuable consideration, promised to observe them; and we are informed that he was accustomed to hear prayers at six o'clock in the morning! It is to such considerations as these, together with his Vandyke dress, his handsome face and his peaked beard, that he owes, we verily believe, most of his popularity with the present generation."

INTEREST IS CONTAGIOUS

We have been discussing so far the kind of material that interests an audience. However, one might mechanically follow all the suggestions made here and yet be vapid and dull. Catching and holding the interest of people is a delicate thing, a matter of feeling and spirit. It is not like operating a steam engine. No book of precise rules can be given for it.

Interest, be it remembered, is contagious. Your hearers are almost sure to catch it if you have a bad case of it yourself. A short time ago, a gentleman rose during a session of my course in Baltimore and warned his audience that if the present methods of catching rockfish in Chesapeake Bay were continued, the species would become extinct. And in a very few years! He felt his subject. It was important. He was in real earnest about it. Everything about his matter and manner showed that. When he arose to speak, I did not know that there was such an animal as a rockfish in Chesapeake Bay. I imagine that most of the audience shared my lack of knowledge and lack of interest. But before the speaker finished, all of us had caught something of his concern. All of us would probably have been willing to sign a petition to the legislature to protect the rockfish by law.

I once asked Richard Washburn Child, the American Ambassador to Italy, the secret of his success as an interesting writer. He replied, "I am so excited about life that I cannot keep still. I just have to tell people about it." One cannot keep from being enthralled with a speaker or writer like that.

I recently went to hear a speaker in London, after he was through, one of our party remarked that he enjoyed the last part of the talk far more than the first. When I asked him why, he replied, "The speaker himself seemed more interested in the last part, and I always rely on the speaker to supply the enthusiasm and interest."

Everyone does. Remember that.

IN A NUTSHELL

1. We are interested in extraordinary facts about ordinary things.
2. Our chief interest is ourselves.
3. The person who leads others to talk about themselves and their interests

and listens intently will generally be considered a good conversationalist, even though he does very little talking.

4.   Glorified gossip, stories of people, will almost always win and hold attention. The speaker ought to make only a few points and to illustrate them with human interest stories.

5.   Be concrete and definite. Do not belong to the "poor-but-honest" school of speakers. Do not merely say that Martin Luther was "stubborn and intractable" as a boy. Announce that fact. Then follow it with the assertion that his teachers flogged him as often as "fifteen times in a forenoon." That makes the general assertion clear, impressive and interesting.

6.   Sprinkle your talks with phrases that create pictures, with words that set images floating before your eyes.

7.   If possible use balanced sentences and contrasting ideas.

8.   Interest is contagious. The audience is sure to catch it if the speaker has a bad case of it. But it cannot be won by the mechanical adherence to mere rules.

SPEECH BUILDING
WORDS OFTEN MISPRONOUNCED

Do not drop the *H* sound in words like the following. In these the *W* is pronounced as if it were after the *H*; as *hwy* for *why*. Say:

whack	not	wack
wharf	not	warf
wheat	not	weat
wheel	not	weel
when	not	wen
whether	not	wether
which	not	wich
whip	not	wip
whiskey	not	wiskey
white	not	wite
whittle	not	wittle
whoa	not	wo

303

ERRORS IN ENGLISH

Review. There are *three* errors in the following paragraph. Can you locate them?

"Was this done by you, or who?" Was the shout exploded at us as we came through the door. It was a question of whether he or myself should take the blame. He don't feel that the fault was his, and I feel that it was not mine.

New Study Material.

RULE: Words joined to the subject by such expressions as with, *together with, as well as, in addition to*, do not pluralize the subject and do not cause the subject to require a plural verb. For example:

Right: The task of getting proper machinery, with that of raising capital and of employing experienced workers, *was* enormous.

Wrong: The task of getting proper machinery, with that of raising capital and of employing experienced workers, *were* enormous.

Right: The invoice mailed yesterday, in addition to the bills due last month, *has* been paid.

Wrong: The invoice mailed yesterday, in addition to the bills due last month, *have* been paid.

Right: Major Harvey, as well as Colonel Mills, *has* appraised the property.

Wrong: Major Harvey, as well as Colonel Mills, *have* appraised the property.

Right: Our entire factory with all of its contents, together with three adjoining storerooms, *was* burned yesterday.

Wrong: Our entire factory with all of its contents, together with three adjoining storerooms, *were* burned yesterday.

RULE: Do not use the double negative. Note the examples that follow:

Right: I can hardly see.

Wrong: I *can't* hardly see.

Right: I never cause any harm to anyone.

Wrong: I *never* cause *no* harm to *nobody*.

RULE: Do not use *never* to take the place of *not*. Examples of this are as follows:

Right: I did *not* bring my notebook to take dictation.

Wrong: I *never* brought my notebook to take dictation.

RULE: In certain sections of the country especially, it is customary to misuse *yet, already, once,* and *however.*

Right: The letter is still here.

Wrong: The letter is here *yet.*

Right: He has gone already.

Wrong: He has gone already *yet.*

RULE: At the beginning of a sentence do not use such introductory words as *why, well, then, now, see* and *again,* unless they are needed. They are very often used because the speaker has gotten into such a habit. Effective speaking, both in public and in conversation, is often marred by this habit.

Some contracted forms cause trouble in speaking. The most important of these are *don't, doesn't, hain't, ain't. Don't* is a contraction of *do not,* and therefore should be used with plural subjects and with *I.* You may say I don't, we don't, you don't, they don't, and don't with any other plural subject, but you should never say he don't, she don't, it don't.

Examples:

Right: He *does not* care for the theater.

Wrong: He *don't* care for the theater.

Hain't is a provincialism and is used very extensively in certain sections of the United States. If possible, it is more erroneous than *ain't.* Both of these expressions are improper contractions for *are not, aren't, have not, haven't, has not, hasn't, is not, isn't.*

Right: *Isn't* he here?

Wrong: *Ain't* he here?

Right: *Haven't* you got it?

Wrong: *Hain't* (or *ain't*) you got it?

CORRECT USAGE OF WORDS

"BENT - BIAS - INCLINATION - PREPOSSESSION. These words agree in describing a permanent influence upon the mind that tends to decide its actions. *Bent* denotes a fixed tendency of the mind in a given direction. It is the widest of these terms and applies to the will, the intellect and the affections taken conjointly; as, the whole bent of his character was toward evil practices. *Bias* is literally a weight fixed on one side of a ball used in bowling and causing it to swerve from a straight course. Used figuratively, *bias* applies particularly to the judgment, and denotes something that acts with a permanent force on the character through that faculty; as, the *bias* of early education, early habits, etc. *Inclination* is an excited state of desire or appetency; as, a strong *inclination* to the study of law. *Prepossession* is a mingled state of feeling and opinion in respect to some person or subject that has taken hold of and occupied the mind previous to inquiry. The word is commonly used in a good sense, an unfavorable impression of this kind being denominated a *prejudice*. 'Strong minds will be strongly *bent*, and usually labor under a strong *bias*; but there is no mind so weak and powerless as not to have its *inclinations*, and none so guarded to be without its *prepossessions*.'- Crabb. " -*Webster's International Dictionary.*

ENORMOUS - IMMENSE - EXCESSIVE. *Enormous* means out of due proportion, beyond the normal. A prize fighter has *enormous* strength. *Immense* denotes a very large quantity, a vast extent. *Excessive* means beyond what is just, and always denotes something evil. The Queen Elizabeth II is an *enormous* ship sailing across an *immense* expanse of sea. If a person of moderate means were obliged to pay for one of its *deluxe* suites he or she would undoubtedly consider the price *enormous, excessive.*

VOICE EXERCISE - HOW TO BE HEARD AT A DISTANCE

It is not necessary to shout and yell in order to make yourself heard in a large hall or out of doors. It is necessary only to use your voice correctly. A whisper, if reinforced by the right tone conditions, will carry to the farthest corner of the largest theater. Usually, a public address system will be available in large rooms or auditoriums. How to use such systems effectively was discussed in Chapter V. If there is no public address system or you choose not to use it, here are some suggestions that will aid you in being heard:

1. Do not gaze at the floor. That is amateurish. It is annoying to an audience. It destroys a sense of communication, a feeling of give and take, between the listeners and talker. It also directs the tone

toward the floor and interferes with its floating out over the audience.

2. "The breath," said Madame Schumann-Heink," is the motive power of voice. Without it under intelligent control, nothing can be accomplished. One might as well try to run an automobile without gasoline as to sing without breath." Yes, or to speak without it. It is the powder behind the bullets of your words. There should be, at all times, a reserve of breath in your lungs to act as a spring board, a catapult, to launch your words. You have doubtlessly seen, in store windows or in shooting galleries, little balls dancing up and down, on jets of water. Your words should be buoyed up by breath like that. They should ride like a kite on a cushion of air. So breathe deeply, feeling the lower part of the lungs expanding at the lower ribs and pushing down and flattening out the arched diaphragm. When you start to speak, do not use up all your breath at once. Use as little as possible. Control it according to the directions given in Chapter V.

3. Relax the throat, the lips, the jaw. (See Chapters IV, IX and X.) Constricted tones will not carry because they have little vibration.

4. Pounding with a hammer on a piece of iron will make a disagreeable noise which is all but deafening close at hand; but it will not carry. But the music of an orchestra or a band can be heard playing for a long distance through a racket and uproar. Why the difference? That is easy to explain- the instruments of the band make pure, harmonious sounds, sounds with resonance; but the hammer striking the iron makes only a dull, ugly clangor without resonance. Only a few days ago, the author stood beside a bugler sounding a call. Had the bugler used the same amount of breath in a harsh shout, it would not have carried very far; but this breath sent into the bugle, vibrating in its resonance chambers, created sound waves which carried a long, long distance.

Now we can understand why some voices that seem very loud to those in the front rows, do not carry far. They lack resonance and it is resonance that makes a sound carry resonance and openness and breath reserve.

So practice often the voice exercises given for this purpose in Chapters IV, IX and X.

As you are listening to the radio, hum the tunes that are played, feeling with your open palm the vibrations in the top and back of your head, in the nose, on the lips, in the cheeks, in the chest. To make the most of your natural resonance, speak with the same open sensation in your head that you have when you are drinking in the air. This is most important.

5. Sound your vowels distinctly. They are the very heart of your words. It is the vibration of the vowel sounds that carries. Consequently; they must not be neglected or slighted. They must be spoken with freedom and openness and accuracy. Here are the most commonly used vowel sounds. Practice them aloud now: *mate, mote, mute, moot, rack, reck, rick, rock, ruck, rook; bah, boil.* As you say them, relax and drop the jaw.

Say them again, using them this time as an exercise for flexibility of the lips.

The correct use of the lips is all important in the sounding of the vowels. The following are sometimes called small vowels. They express delicacy. The lips should be stuck out almost into a pout as they are pronounced. Try them now. We have connected these vowel sounds with n to give them a singing quality.

en as in *men*
ain as in *drain*
een as in *seen*
in as in *sin*

Here are the bright vowels, expressing joy, sunshine and gladness. Say them with the lips drawn back into something like a smiling position:

an as in *can*
ein as in *line*
ahn as in *ah*

These are the heavy vowels, expressing strength, sonority, richness, fullness, depth. Say them with the lips a little more open than in the whistling position, chin relaxed, dropped and very loose.

on as in *on*
ohn as in *oh*
oon as in *boon*
own as in *own*

6. The pitch of your voice ought to vary, ought to flow up and down the scale, naturally and spontaneously as you speak. This principle of delivery was discussed in Chapter VII. This change of pitch will help to individualize your words, to make them more distinctive.

7. In order to be heard at a distance, we need volume. Do not confuse this with mere loudness. One who does not mean what one says and has slight interest in it, will not, other things being equal, be heard as far as the one who puts his or her heart and soul and sincerity into the talk. It is not emptiness that carries. It is richness.

One of the first things that the physician notices on entering the sick room is the voice. It reflects one's vitality. A robust voice with carrying power does not come from a sick or even tired body. So rest before you speak. Obey the laws of sensible living.

"A beautiful voice, beautifully used can only continue to come from a healthy body. . . . Robust health is essential to any large measure of success. . . . Plenty of fresh air, simple nourishing food and eight or nine hours of sleep are all necessary to the singer or speaker whose larynx invariably reflects his or her bodily conditions."

HOW TO GET ACTION

"The truly effective speakers never have enthroned blind impulse as their god. They have controlled and directed it with the judgment born of a careful study of the laws governing action and belief."

-Effective Speaking, by Arthur Edward Phillips

"What then, in brief, does a cultivated modern audience demand of a speaker? It insists, first, that the speaker himself be genuine; second, that he know something worthwhile and know it well; third, that his own feelings and convictions be fully enlisted in the theme that he presents; and, fourth, that he talk straight to the point in simple, natural, forceful language."

-Public Speaking For Success Today, by Lockwood Thorpe

"The great end of life is not knowledge but action."

-Thomas H. Huxley

"Action is the distinguishing characteristic of greatness."

-E. St. Elmo Lewis

"We are more easily persuaded, in general, by the reasons we ourselves discover, than by those which have been suggested to us by others."

-Pascal

"We are made for action, and for the right action-for thought and for true thought. Let us live while we live; let us be alive and doing; let us act on what we have, since we have not what we wish."

-John Henry Cardinal Newman

Chapter 15

HOW TO GET ACTION

I f you could have the power of any talent that you now possess doubled and trebled for the mere asking, which one would you select to have this mighty boon conferred upon? Wouldn't you very likely designate your ability to influence others to get action? That would mean additional power, additional profit and additional pleasure.

Must this art, so essential to our success in life, remain forever a hit and miss affair with most of us? Must we blunder along depending upon our instinct, upon rule of thumb methods only? Or is there a more intelligent way to set about achieving it?

There is, and we shall discuss it at once, a method based on the rules of common sense, on the rules of human nature, your nature and mine, a method that the writer has frequently employed himself, a method that he has trained others to use successfully.

The first step in this method is to gain interested attention. Unless you do that, people will not listen closely to what you say.

How to do this was dealt with at length in Chapters IX and XIV. Would it not be well to reread and review them in this connection?

The second step is to gain the confidence of your hearers. Unless you do that, they will have no faith in what you say. And here is where many a speaker falls down. Here is where many an advertisement fails, many a business letter, many an employee, many a business enterprise. Here is where many an individual fails to make himself effective within his or her own human environment.

WIN CONFIDENCE BY DESERVING IT

The prime way to win confidence is to deserve it. The elder J. Pierpont Morgan said that character was the biggest element in obtaining credit. It is also one of the biggest elements in obtaining the confidence of an audience. I have noticed time without number that facile and witty speakers, if those are their chief qualities, are not nearly as effective as those who are less brilliant but more sincere.

A certain member of a course that the author was recently conducting had been blessed with a striking appearance; and when he stood up to speak, he possessed an admirable fluency of thought and language. When he had finished, however, people said, "clever chap." He made a ready, surface impression; but it was only on the surface, it never amounted to much. In that same group, there was an insurance representative, a woman small of stature, a woman who groped sometimes for a word, a woman lacking grace of diction; but her deep sincerity shone through her eyes and vibrated in her voice. Her hearers listened intently to what she said, had faith in her, warmed to her without being conscious of why they did it.

Sincerity, a great deep genuine sincerity, is the first characteristic of all credible people. Not the sincerity that calls itself sincere; ah, no, that is a very poor matter indeed, a shallow braggart, conscious sincerity, most often self-conceit mainly. Real sincerity is of the kind a person cannot speak of, indeed, is not conscious of.

There is no use trying to pretend a sympathy or sincerity that one does not feel. It won't work. It must be genuine. It must have the right ring.

The profoundest feeling among the masses, the most influential element in their character, is the religious element. It is as instinctive and elemental as the law of self-preservation. It informs the whole intellect and personality of the people. And one who would greatly influence the people by uttering their unformed thoughts, must have this great and unanalyzable bond of sympathy with them.

Lincoln had this sympathy with the people. He was seldom dazzling. I do not think anyone called him "an orator." In his debates with Stephen Douglas, he lacked the grace and smoothness and rhetoric of his opponent. People christened Douglas "The Little Giant." And what did they call Lincoln? "Honest Abe."

Douglas had a charming personality, and he was a man of extraordinary spirit and vitality; but he was a man who tried to carry water on both shoulders, he put policy above principle, expediency above justice. That was his final undoing.

And Lincoln? Well, when he spoke, there was a certain rugged flavor that emanated from the man and doubled the power of his words. People felt his honesty and sincerity and his unimpeachable character. As far as knowledge of law is concerned, scores of other men outstripped him; but few of them had more influence with a jury. He was not much concerned about serving Abe Lincoln. He was a thousand times more concerned about serving justice and eternal truth. And people felt it when he spoke.

SPEAK OUT OF YOUR OWN EXPERIENCE

The second way to gain the confidence of the audience is to speak discreetly out of your own experience. That helps immensely. If you give opinions, people may question them. If you relate hearsay or repeat what you have read, the thing may have a secondhand flavor. But what you yourself have gone through and lived through, that has a genuine ring, a tang of truth and veracity; and people like it. They believe it. They recognize you as the world's leading authority on that particular topic.

Read in the appendix to this book, *A Message to Garcia.* The world had amazing confidence in what Elbert Hubbard said on that occasion. He was speaking out of his own experiences. You know that. You feel it. The whole article breathes it: "I have carried a dinner pail, and I have worked for day's wages, and I have also been an employer of labor and I know there is something to be said on both sides."

BE PROPERLY INTRODUCED

Many a speaker fails to gain the attention of his audience immediately because he is not introduced properly.

An introduction; that term was fashioned from two Latin words, intro, to the inside, and ducere, to lead; so an introduction ought to lead us to the inside of the topic sufficiently to make us want to hear it discussed. It ought to lead us to the inside facts regarding the speaker, facts that demonstrate his or her fitness for discussing this particular topic. In other words, an introduction ought to "sell" the topic to the audience and it ought to "sell" the speaker. And it ought to do these things in the briefest amount of time possible.

That is what it ought to do. But does it? Nine times out of ten, no, emphatically NO. Most introductions are poor affairs, feeble and inexcusably inadequate.

For example, I heard a well-known speaker, a man who ought to have known better, introduce the Irish poet, W. B. Yeats. Yeats was to read his own poetry. Three years prior to that, he had been awarded the Nobel Prize in literature, the highest distinction that can be bestowed upon a man of letters. I am confident that not ten percent of that particular audience knew of either the award or its significance. Both ought, by all means, to have been mentioned. They ought to have been announced even if nothing else were said. But what did the chairman do? He utterly ignored these facts, and wandered off into talking about mythology and Greek poetry. He was doubtlessly entirely unconscious of the fact that his own ego was prompting him to impress the audience with his own knowledge, his own importance.

That chairman, in spite of the fact that he is known internationally as a speaker and had been introduced a thousand times himself, was a total failure in introducing another. If a man of his caliber makes such a *faux pas*, what can we expect of the average chairman?

And what are we going to do about it? With all due humility of soul and meekness of spirit, go to the person who will introduce you beforehand and provide a few facts to use in the introduction. Your suggestions will be greatly appreciated. Indicate the things you would like to have mentioned, the things that show why you are in a position to talk about this particular subject, the simple facts that the audience ought to know, the facts that will win you a hearing. Write them on an index card, so the introducer can refer to them when making the introduction.

BLUE GRASS AND HICKORY WOOD ASHES

One autumn the author was conducting courses in public speaking at various Y.M.C.A.'s in greater New York. The star salesman of one of the best-known selling organizations in the city was a member of one of those courses, and one evening, he made the preposterous statement that he had been able to make blue grass grow without the aid of seed or roots. He had, according to his story, scattered hickory wood ashes over newly plowed ground. Presto! Blue grass had appeared. He firmly believed that the hickory wood ashes and the hickory wood ashes alone were responsible for the blue grass.

In criticizing his talk, I smilingly pointed out to him that his phenomenal discovery would, if true, make him a millionaire, for blue grass seed was worth several dollars a bushel. I also told him that it would make him immortal, that it would make him the outstanding scientist of all history. I informed him that no person, living or dead, had ever been able to perform the miracle he claimed to have performed, nobody had ever been able to produce life from an inanimate substance.

I told him that very quietly, for I felt that his mistake was so palpable, so absurd, as to require no emphasis in the refutation. When I had finished, every other member of the course saw the folly of his assertion; but he did not see it, not for a second. He was in earnest about his contention, deadly in earnest. He leaped to his feet and informed me that he was not wrong. He had not been relating theory, he protested, but personal experience. He knew whereof he spoke. He continued to talk, enlarging on his first remarks, giving additional information, piling up additional evidence, a rugged sincerity and honesty shining through his voice.

Again I informed him that there was not the remotest hope in the world of his being right or even approximately right or within a thousand miles of the truth. In a second, he was on his feet once more, offering to bet me five dollars and to let the U.S. Department of Agriculture settle the matter.

I noticed that he had soon won over several members of the course to his way of thinking. Marveling at their credulity, I inquired why they had now come to believe in his contention. His earnestness, that was the only explanation they could give, earnestness.

Earnestness. The power of it is incredible, especially with a popular audience.

Very few people have the capacity for independent thought. But all of us have feelings and emotions, and all of us are influenced by the speaker's feeling. If he or she believes a thing *earnestly* enough, and says it *earnestly* enough, even though the claim is preposterous, the speaker will gain some adherents and win some disciples, even among a supposedly sophisticated and unquestionably intelligent audience.

After you have won the audience's interested attention and their confidence, the real work begins. The third step then is to state the facts, to-

317

EDUCATE PEOPLE REGARDING THE MERITS OF YOUR PROPOSITION

This is the very heart of your talk, the meat. This is where you will need to devote most of your time. Now you will need to apply all you have learned in Chapter XII about Clearness, all you have learned in Chapter XIII about Impressiveness and Conviction.

Here is where your preparation will count. Here is where the lack of it will rise up like Banquo's ghost and mock you.

Here you are on the firing line. And "a battle field," says Marshal Foch, "does not give an opportunity for study. One does what one can to apply what one already knows, therefore it is necessary that one should know thoroughly and be able to use this knowledge quickly."

Here is where you need to know a score of times more about your topic than you can possibly use. When the White Knight in *Alice Through the Looking Glass* started out on his journey, he prepared for every possible contingency, he took a mouse trap lest he should be troubled with mice at night and he carried a bee hive in case he should find a stray swarm of bees. If the White Knight had prepared public talks like that, he would have been a winner. He would have been able to overwhelm with a torrent of information every objection that could be brought forth. He would have known his subject so well and he would have planned it so thoroughly that he could hardly have failed.

HOW PATTERSON ANSWERED OBJECTIONS

If you are addressing a business group on some proposal that affects them, you should not only educate them; but you should let them educate you. You should ascertain what is in their minds, otherwise you may be dealing with something entirely beside the point. Let them express their minds; answer their objections; then they will be in a more placid state to listen to you. Here is the way John H. Patterson, the first president of the National Cash Register Company, handled a situation of that kind. We are quoting from his article in *System Magazine:*

"It became necessary to raise the prices of our cash registers. The agents and sales managers protested; they said that our business would go, that prices had to be kept where they were. I called them all in to Dayton and we had a meeting. I staged the affair. Back of me on the platform I had a great sheet of paper and a sign painter."

"I asked the people to state their objections to the increasing of prices. The objections came ripping out from the audience like shots from a machine gun. As fast as they came, I had the sign man post them on the big sheet. We spent all of the first day gathering objections. I did nothing but exhort. When the meeting closed, we had a list of at least a hundred different reasons why the prices should not be raised. Every possible reason was up there before the men, and it seemed conclusively settled in the minds of the audience that no change should be made. Then the meeting adjourned."

"On the next morning, I took up the objections one by one and explained by diagrams and words exactly why each was unsound. The people were convinced. Why? Everything that could be said contra war, up in black and white and the discussion centered. No loose ends were left. We settled everything on the spot."

"But in a case such as this one, it would not have been enough, in my mind, merely to have settled the point in dispute. A meeting of agents should break up with all of the audience filled with a new lot of enthusiasm; perhaps the points of the register itself might have been a little blurred in the discussion. That would never do. We had to have a dramatic climax. I had arranged for that and just before the close of the conference, I had a hundred men march, one by one, across the stage; each bore a banner and on that banner was a picture of a part of the latest register and just what it did. Then when the last man passed across, they all came back into a kind of grand finale the complete machine. The meeting ended with the agents on their feet and cheering wildly!"

SETTING ONE DESIRE TO FIGHTING ANOTHER

The fourth step in this method is to appeal to the motives that make people act.

This earth and all things in it and on it and in the waters underneath it are run, not haphazardly, but according to the immutable law of cause and effect.

"For the world was made in order,

And the atoms march in tune."

Everything that ever has happened or ever will happen has been, or will be, the logical and inevitable effect of something that preceded it, the logical and inevitable cause of something that follows. It is as true of earthquakes and Joseph's coat of many colors, and the honking of wild geese and jealousy and the price of baked beans, and the Kohinoor diamond, and the beautiful harbor in Sydney; it is as true of those things as it is of putting a coin in a slot and getting a package of gum. . . . When one recognizes this, one understands, once and for all, why superstition is unspeakably silly for how can the unchangeable laws of nature be stopped or altered or affected in the slightest by thirteen people sitting at a table or because one breaks a mirror?

What causes every conscious and deliberate act we perform? By some desire. The things that actuate us are not many. We are ruled hour by hour, dominated day and night by a surprisingly small number of longings.

All that means just this: if one knows what these motives are and can appeal to them with sufficient force, one will have extraordinary power. The wise speaker attempts to do precisely that. But the blunderer gropes his or her way blindly and to no purpose.

For example, a father finds that his young son has been smoking cigarettes surreptitiously. He grows irate, fumes, scolds, commands the boy to have done with the pernicious habit, warns him that it will ruin his health.

But suppose that the boy is not concerned about his health, that he loves the flavor and adventure of smoking a cigarette more than he fears physical consequences. What will happen? The father's appeal will prove futile. Why? Because the parent was not shrewd enough to play upon a motive that touched his son. The parent played only on the motives that actuated himself. He did not get over on the boy's side of the fence at all.

However, it is quite probable that that boy longs with all his heart to make the track team at school to compete for the hundred yard dash, to excel at athletics. So if the father will only cease unloading his own feelings, and show his son that smoking is going to impede and interfere with his cherished athletic ambitions, the father will probably get the desired action, get it smoothly and completely, and get it by the eminently sensible process of putting a stronger desire against a weaker one. This is precisely what does happen in one of the biggest sporting events in the world, the Oxford-Cambridge boat race. The oarsmen deny themselves the use of tobacco all during their training. Compared to the winning of the race, every other desire is secondary.

One of the most serious problems that faces the world today is the battle with insects. Some years ago, the Oriental fruit moth was imported into this country on some cherry trees which were a gift from the Japanese government and were used to ornament the borders of a lake at our national capital. This moth spread and threatened the fruit crop of some of the eastern states. Spraying seemed to have no effect, so finally, the government was obliged to import another insect from Japan and turn it loose here to prey upon this moth. So our agricultural experts are fighting one pest with another.

People skilled in getting action employ similar tactics. They set one motive to war against another. This method is so sensible, so simple, so utterly apparent that one might imagine that the use of it was all but universal. Far from it. We often see exhibitions that make us inclined to suspect that the use of it is very rare.

To cite a concrete case: the writer recently attended a noonday luncheon club in a certain city. A golf party was being organized to play over the country club course of a neighboring city. Only a few members had put down their names. The president of the club was displeased; something he was behind was about to fall; his prestige was at stake. So he made what he imagined was an appeal for more members to go. His talk was woefully inadequate; he based his urge very largely on the fact that *he wanted them to go*. That was no appeal at all. He was not handling human nature skillfully; he was merely unloading his own feelings. Like the irate father with the cigarette smoking son, he neglected entirely to talk in terms of the desires of his hearers.

What should he have done? He should have used a generous supply of common sense; he should have had a little quiet talk with himself before he spoke to the others; and he should have addressed himself somewhat in this fashion: "Why aren't more of these people going on this golfing party? Some probably imagine they cannot spare the time; others may be thinking of the railway fare and various expenses. How can I overcome these objections? I will show them that recreation is not lost time, that grinds are not the most successful people, that one can do more in five days when fresh than can be accomplished in six when the batteries need recharging. Of course, they know this already; but they need to be reminded of it. I will play up things that they ought to want more than they want to save the small expense connected with this party. I will show them that it is an investment in health and pleasure. I will stir their imaginations, make them see themselves out on the course, the west wind in their faces, the green sward under their feet, feeling sorry for those back in the hot city who live for nothing but money."

Would such a procedure, in your opinion, have been more likely to succeed than the mere "I want you to go" appeal that the speaker used?

THE DESIRES THAT DETERMINE OUR ACTIONS

What, then, are these basic and human longings that should mold our conduct and make us behave like human beings? If an understanding of them and a playing upon them is so essential to our success, then out with them. Let us have the light upon them, let us examine and dissect and analyze them.

We shall devote the rest of this chapter to discussing and telling a few stories about them. That, you will agree, is the way to make them clear, the way to make them convincing, the way to engrave them deep upon the walls of your memory.

One of the very strongest of these motives is the desire for gain. That will be largely responsible for a few hundred million people getting out of bed tomorrow morning, two or three hours earlier, than they would otherwise arise without this spur. Is it necessary to discourse further upon the potency of this well-known urge?

And even stronger than the money motive is the desire for self-protection. All health appeals are based on that. For example, when a city advertises its healthful climate, when a food manufacturer features the purity and strength giving qualities of its product, when a patent medicine vendor enumerates all the ills that its nostrums will alleviate, when a dairy producer's association tells us that milk is rich in vitamins, a product indispensable to the maintenance of life, when a speaker for an anticigarette society tells us that about 3% of all tobacco is nicotine and that one drop of nicotine will kill a dog and eight drops will destroy a horse; all of these people are appealing to our innate desire to preserve life.

To make the appeal to this motive strong, make it personal. Don't, for example, quote statistics to show that cancer is on the increase. No. Tie it right down to the people who are listening to you, e.g. "There are thirty people in this room. If all of you live to be forty-five, three of you, according to the law of medical averages, will die of cancer. I wonder if it will be you, or you, or you over there."

As strong as the desire for money; in fact, in many people it is far stronger; is the wish to be thought well of, to be admired. In other words, pride. Pride with a capital P. *Pride* in italics. PRIDE in capital letters.

Pride, what crimes have been committed in your name! For many years thousands and thousands of young girls suffered excruciating pains in China, screamed with it and did it willingly because the dictates of pride said that their feet must be bound and not allowed to grow. At this very moment, thousands of native women in certain parts of Central Africa are wearing wooden discs in their lips. Incredible as it may seem, these discs are as large as the plate on which you ate breakfast this morning. When the little girls in these tribes reach eight years of age, a slit is made in the outer portion of their lips and a disc is inserted. As the seasons pass, one disc is replaced by another progressively larger. Finally the teeth have to be removed to make room for this much prized ornament. These cumbersome appendages render it impossible for these unfortunate girls to utter an intelligible sound. The rest of the tribe can seldom understand their attempts at talking. But all this is endured, even silence is endured by these women, in order that they may appear beautiful, in order that they may be admired, in order that they may stand high in their own estimation, in order that their pride may be appeased.

Although we don't go quite that far in Melbourne, or Montreal, or Cleveland, nevertheless,

"The colonel's lady and Judy O'Grady,

Are sisters under the skin."

So the appeal to pride, if done skillfully, has a force only a trifle less potent than T.N.T.

Ask yourself why you are taking this course. Were you influenced, to some extent, by the wish to make a better impression? Did you covet the glow of inward satisfaction that comes from making a creditable talk? Won't you feel a very pardonable pride in the power, leadership and distinction that naturally pertain to the public speaker?

The editor of a mail order journal recently stated in a public address that of all the appeals that one could put in a sales letter, none were so effective as the appeals to pride and profit.

Lincoln won a lawsuit once by a clever appeal to this pride motive. It was in the Tazewell County Court in 1847. Two brothers by the name of Snow had purchased two yokes of oxen and a prairie plow from a Mr. Case. In spite of the fact that they were minors, he accepted their joint note for two hundred dollars. When it fell due, and he tried to collect it, he got laughter, not cash. It wasn't promising laughter, either; so he employed Lincoln and had them into court. The Snow brothers pleaded that they were minors and that Case knew they were minors when he accepted the note. Lincoln admitted everything they claimed and the validity of the minor act. "Yes, gentlemen, I reckon that is so," he said to point after point. It seemed as if he had given his entire case away. However, when his turn came, he addressed the twelve good men and true, in this fashion: "Gentlemen of the jury, are you willing to allow these boys to begin life with this shame and disgrace attached to their character? As Shakespeare wrote in "Othello:"

"Good name in man or woman, dear my Lord,
 Is the immediate jewel of their souls:
Who steals my purse, steals trash; 'tis something, nothing;
'Twas mine, 'tis his, and has been slave to thousands;
But he that filches from me my good name
Robs me of that which not enriches him
And makes me poor indeed!"

Then, he pointed out that these boys might never have stooped to this villainy, had it not been for the unwise counsel of their attorney. Showing how the noble profession of law was sometimes prostituted to prevent rather than to promote justice, he turned and scathingly rebuked the opposing attorney. "And now, gentlemen of the jury," he continued, "you have it in your power to set these boys right before the world." Surely these men would not lend their names nor their influence to shielding patent dishonesty? They could not be true to their ideals and do it; such was his plea. He appealed to their pride, you see; and, without leaving their seats, the jury voted that the debt must be paid.

Lincoln in this instance appealed also to the jury's innate love of justice. It is native to almost all of us. We will stop on the street to take the part of a small boy who is being mistreated by a larger one.

We are creatures of feeling, who long for comforts and pleasures. We drink coffee and wear comfortable clothes, and go to the theater and sleep on the bed instead of the floor, not because we have reasoned out that these things are good for us, but because they are pleasant. So show that the thing you propose will add to our comforts and increase our pleasures, and you have touched a powerful spring of action.

When Seattle advertised that its death rate was the lowest of any large city in the United States and that a child born there had the best chances of surviving and living long, to what motive was the city appealing? A very strong one, one that is responsible for much of the conduct of the world affection. Patriotism is also based on the motives of affection and sentiment.

Sometimes an appeal to the sentiments will produce action when all others fail. That was the experience of the well-known real estate auctioneer of New York City, Joseph P. Day. He closed the largest sale of his life by such an appeal. Here is his own story of how he did it.

"Expert knowledge is not the all of selling. In my largest single sale I used no technical knowledge whatsoever. I had been negotiating with Judge Gary for the sale to the United States Steel Corporation of the building at 71 Broadway, which has always contained its offices. I thought I had closed the sale when, calling upon Judge Gary, he said very quietly but very decisively:

" 'Mr. Day, we have had the offer of a much more modern building near here and it would seem to answer our purpose better. It is,' pointing to the woodwork, 'a better finished building. This building is too old-fashioned; you know it is a very old structure. Some of my associates here think that, all in all, the other building will answer our purposes more adequately than this one.' "

"There was a $5,000,000 sale drifting out of the window! I did not answer for a moment, and Judge Gary did not go on. He had given his decision. If a pin had dropped to the floor, it would have sounded like a bomb. I did not attempt to answer. Instead, I asked:

" 'Judge Gary, where was, your first office when you came to New York?' "

325

" 'Right here,' he said, 'or rather in the room on the other side.' "

" 'Where was the Steel Corporation organized?' "

" 'Why, right here in these offices,' he mused rather than answered. And then, of his own accord: 'some of the younger executives have from time to time, had more elaborate offices than this. They have not been quite satisfied with the older furniture. But,' he added, 'none of those men are with us now.' "

"The sale was over. The next week we formally closed."

"Of course, I knew what building had been offered to him, and I might have compared the structural merits of the two. Then I should have Judge Gary arguing, with himself if not with me, over material points of construction. Instead I appealed to sentiment."

RELIGIOUS MOTIVES

There is another powerful group of motives that influence us mightily. Shall we call them religious motives? I mean religious, not in the sense of orthodox worship or the tenets of any particular creed or sect. I mean rather that broad group of beautiful and eternal truths, justice and forgiveness and mercy, serving others and loving our neighbors as ourselves.

No one likes to admit, even to oneself, that he or she is not good and kind and magnanimous. So we love to be appealed to on these grounds. It implies a certain nobleness of soul. We take pride in that.

For a great many years, C.S. Ward was a secretary of the International Committee of the Y.M.C.A., devoting all of his time to conducting campaigns to raise funds for Association buildings. It does not mean self-preservation or an increase of property or power for a person to write a check for a thousand dollars to the local Y.M.C.A.; but many people will do it out of a desire to be noble and just and helpful.

Setting up a campaign in a northwestern city, Mr. Ward approached a well-known business executive who had never been identified with the church or with social movements. What? Was he expected to neglect his business for a week to raise funds for a Y.M.C.A. building? The idea was preposterous. He finally consented to come to the opening meeting of the campaign, and was so moved there by Mr. Ward's appeal to his nobleness and altruism that he devoted an entire week to an enthusiastic money raising campaign. Before the week was over, this man who had been noted for his constant use of profanity, was praying for the success of the undertaking.

A group of men once called upon the railroad magnate, James J. Hill to persuade him to establish Y.M.C.A.'s along his railroad lines in the Northwest. Money was required, a considerable outlay of it; and, knowing Hill to be a shrewd businessman they unwisely based their principal arguments upon his desire for gain. These Associations, they pointed out, would make for happy, contented workmen and would enhance the value of his property.

"You have not yet mentioned," Mr. Hill replied, "the thing that will really lead me to establish these Y.M.C.A.'s, that is the desire to be a force for righteousness and to build character."

A long standing dispute over some frontier territory had, in 1900, brought Argentine and Chile to the brink of war. Battleships had been built, armaments amassed, taxes increased, and costly preparations made to settle the issue by blood. On Easter day, 1900, an Argentine bishop made a passionate appeal for peace in the name of Christ. Across the Andes, the Chilean bishop re-echoed the message. The bishops went from village to village appealing for peace and brotherly love. At first, their audiences were only women; but finally this appeal stirred the entire nations. Popular petitions and public opinion forced the governments to arbitrate and to reduce their armies and navies. The frontier fortresses were dismantled and the guns melted and cast into a huge bronze figure of Christ. Today high in the lofty Andes, guarding the disputed frontiers, towers this statue of the Prince of Peace holding the cross. On the pedestal is written: "These mountains themselves shall fall and crumble to dust before the peoples of Chile and the Argentine Republic shall forget their solemn covenant sworn at the feet of Christ."

Such is the power of the appeal to the religious emotions and convictions.

HAS THE AUTHOR USED SUCCESSFULLY THE METHOD HE HAS BEEN DESCRIBING?

First step: Did the writer gain your interested attention by emphasizing the importance of this matter of influencing human nature and by declaring that there was a scientific method of going about it and that we would discuss it forthwith?

Second step: Did the writer gain your confidence by telling you that this system was based upon the rules of common sense, that he himself had employed it and had taught thousands of others to do it?

Third step: Did the writer state the facts clearly, did he educate you regarding the working and the merits of the method?

Fourth step: Did the writer convince you that the use of this method will bring you additional influence and profit? Will you, as a result of reading this chapter, endeavor to use this method? In other words, has the writer gotten action?

IN A NUTSHELL

1.   Get interested attention of the audience.

2.   Win their confidence by deserving it, by your sincerity, by being properly introduced, by being qualified to speak on your subject, by telling the things that your experience has taught you.

3.   State your facts, educate your audience regarding the merits of your proposal and answer their objections.

4.   Appeal to the motives that make people act: the desire for gain, self-protection, pride, pleasures, sentiments, affections, and religious ideals, such as justice, mercy, forgiveness, love.

This method, if used wisely, will not only help the speakers in public; it will help them also in private. It will help them in the writing of sales letters, in constructing advertisements, in managing their households, it will help them in their interpersonal relationships with their families, their friends and members of their community.

SPEECH BUILDING
WORDS OFTEN MISPRONOUNCED
Watch your first syllables, do not substitute *uh* for *a*. Do not say:

uhbate	for	abate	uhlert	for	alert
uhbout	"	about	uhlow	"	allow

uhcount	for	account	uhmonia	for	ammonia
uhdorn	"	adorn	uhnoy	"	annoy
uhdress	"	address	uhpear	"	appear
uhfect	"	affect	uhrest	"	arrest
uhgree	"	agree	uhsume	"	assume
uhgrieve	"	aggrieve	uhtach	"	attach

Do not shorten or change the sound of be and de in the following words. Do not say:

buh-cause	or	b'cuz	for	because
buh-lieve	"	b'lieve	"	believe
buh-come	"	b'come	"	become
buh-fore	"	b'fore	"	before
buh-gin	"	b'gin	"	begin
duh-bate	"	d'bate	"	debate
duh-cide	"	d'cide	"	decide
duh-test	"	d'test	"	detest
duh-fer	"	d'fer	"	defer
duh-gree	"	d'gree	"	degree

ERRORS IN ENGLISH

Review. Read over the following paragraph and note the errors contained in it:

Mr. Jones, as well as two other friends of mine, have endorsed the note. He, with the others, have learned of the increased demand for my patented article and feel that money in addition to talent are necessary for the marketing of the machine.

New Study Material.

RULE: Always place your adjectives and adverbs so that it is very easy to tell which words they modify. There are daily errors in the use of *only, nearly, almost, etc.*

Right: I had *only one* minute to catch the train.

Wrong: I *only had* one minute to catch the train.

RULE: Do not use the superlative degree for the comparative. If you are comparing but two objects, use the comparative degree.

Examples:

Right: This day is the *worse* of the two.

Wrong: This day is the *worst* of the two.

RULE: Do not use *these* or *those* before such words as *type, kind, sort.* Examples:

Right: *That kind* of houses seldom lasts long.

Wrong: *Those kind* of houses seldom last long.

Right: We can never get *this sort* of prices.

Wrong: We can never get *these sort* of prices.

RULE: Do not say *kind of a, sort of a, type of a,* Note the following examples:

Right: That *kind of* job is simply a blind alley.

Wrong: That *kind of* a job is simply a blind alley.

Right: That *sort of* employer deserves labor troubles.

Wrong: That *sort of* an employer deserves labor troubles.

Right: That *type of* engine is very expensive.

Wrong: That *type of* an engine is very expensive.

RULE: We are in the habit of using certain superfluous words in some of our expressions. You will be able to see for yourself, in the following examples the reasons why the right hand column is not correct:

Right	**Wrong**
back of (or behind)	in back of
is but one left	is not but one left
more than you think	more than you think for
inside	inside of
a beginner	a new beginner
an infant	a little infant
anywhere, everywhere, nowhere	anywheres, everywheres, nowheres

RULE: There are certain words which are always plural in form but which take the singular verb. Among these are: *physics, ethics, mathematics, news, etc.*

RULE: When such words as *dozen, score, yoke,* have a numeral in front of them, no "s" is needed, as "He bought two *dozen* eggs." Another use is "*Dozens* of men were killed in the charge."

RULE: There are certain foreign words, which have retained their own plurals. Among these are: *addendum, alumnus, alumna* (fem.), *analysis, crisis, datum, erratum, parenthesis, phenomenon, synopsis.*

These plurals are *addenda, alumni, alumnae* (fem.), *analyses, crises, data, errata, parentheses, phenomena, synopses.* The modern tendency seems to take *memorandum* out of this class and to make memorandums the new plural. You will find, however, that many persons are accustomed to use *memoranda*, which is perfectly correct as most dictionaries still hold.

RULE: When you talk about several *pairs*, it should be so written, as "Five *pairs* of shoes were sold." It comes under the same ruling as "five *years* ago." Both these expressions are correct and the singular form of these nouns should never be used when there is a plural numeral in front of them.

RULE: In compound nouns, the important part of the compound receives the mark of the plural, as *mothers-in-law*. The mark of possessive will come on the last part of the compound, as "my mother- in-*law's* husband."

CORRECT USAGE OF WORDS

A *skillful* person has profited both from knowledge and practice, as a *skillful* physician. *Dexter* means pertaining to the right hand. *Dexterous* implies habitual ease and sureness, such as we have in our right hands. *Adroit* is very close to *dexterous* in meaning, but it also implies the ability to make quick, sure movements, either mental or physical. *Apt* means especially qualified, but it is not so strong a term as *expert*. *Sharp* denotes a keen intelligence and a quick, nice discrimination. The *proficient* person has gone forward and made considerable progress. *Competent* is often used to indicate the general, natural ability that fits one to perform a task. *Qualified* commonly refers to specific training. A *competent* musician might, with study and practice, *qualify* for a position with the Philharmonic Orchestra. *Initiated* refers to instructions in the beginnings and rudiments. It is derived from the same source as the word *initial*. A man who is *initiated* in the problems of finance may not be *qualified* to handle the financial affairs of a large corporation.

PUBLIC SPEAKING FOR SUCCESS

VOICE EXERCISE - SPEAKING MORE DISTINCTLY

According to a special article in the *New York Times*, one man out of every seven who sought to become officers in our army during the war was refused a commission because of "poor articulation, lack of voice and imperfect enunciation."

These handicaps are just as prevalent, and almost as serious, in civil life. Aren't you sometimes forced to ask people to repeat in conversation, especially strangers? Haven't you been annoyed by listening to some speaker whom you found it difficult, at times, to understand?

How often even those whom we can understand lack that clearcut articulation which, according to the author of *Acres of Diamonds,* is the charm of speaking. How delightful it is to listen to. It is generally felt to be an infallible sign of refinement and culture.

All of us can improve our enunciation and articulation by practice. Deaf mutes are trained to use accurately the muscles of their lips and cheeks and tongues. As a result, they are taught to speak almost as distinctly as many who possess the faculty of hearing. Imagine, then, what such training can do for the average man.

The easiest sounds to begin with are the consonants, which are made by closing the lips. There are five of them: *p, b, m, w* and *wh*. Here are some rules:

Press the lips *tightly together* for these sounds *always*. Tighter than you are accustomed to do, and for a *longer time*. Many people hardly *touch* the lips together in making *p*, or *b*, or *m*; are you one of them? Exaggerate the sound, as if it were doubled.

Sound	*Almost like*
copy	cop-py
big	bbig
moving	mmoving
weather	wweather
white	whwhite

The last sound, *wh*, used to be spelled, long ago, *hw*. Think of it like that; make the sound of *h*, and then bring the lips together for the *w*, and you will have no trouble in making it distinct. Many people sound *white, why, what* almost like *wite, wy, wat*. Do you?

Localize the *sensation,* feel the *pressure* of the *m* of *moving,* the *b* of *big,* etc., at the very *center* of your lips, in front of the middle teeth. Use *both lips,* upper as well as lower. Do you use your upper lip now? Stand in front of a mirror and *see.*

And don't be afraid to push the lips slightly *outward* on these sounds, like a little megaphone. You cannot make them plainly otherwise.

Some Exercises for Daily Use: Repeat single lip- sounds: *me-me-me-me; pep-pep-pep-pep; wo-wo-wo.*

Try these nonsense sentences:

Mobile millions of amiable men.

Prohibitive problems prepare to appear.

Breezes are blowing big billows about the bay.

Why whisper, when warbling will win everywhere?

The following consonants are made by touching the tongue to some part of the roof of the mouth: *t, d, th, n, l, sh, z, ch, j, r, k, g* (hard), *ng*. Tongue consonants enter into nearly all words. For convenience we may group these 14 sounds as follows:

1.   *t, d, th, n, ch, j, z.*
2.   *k, g (hard), ng.*
3.   *l, s, sh, r.*

We shall here consider the first group.

To make the sounds of *t, d, th, n, ch, j* and *z* accurately, easily and quickly, take pains to press the tongue tightly against the roof of the mouth. Most people use their tongues lazily. They say "cer'nly" when they think they are saying "certainly"; "moun'n" when they think they are saying "mountain." That is downright carelessness. Make yourself squeeze the tongue tight; this alone will go far toward making your speech distinct.

To make these sounds quickly and easily, *narrow* the tongue to a point like a pencil, and use only the *tip,* the first quarter-inch or so; don't slap the whole broad surface upward as you say *t, d,* etc. And touch the roof of the mouth *just behind the front teeth,* not further back.

Hold a mirror before your mouth and repeat these nonsense phrases, using your muscles actively, as directed; or make up other phrases of your own:

333

Tip-toeing daintily down to dine.

Lolita laughing neatly taught the tune.

Cherish jealously the jolly ginger jar.

"Caruso's faultless articulation," according to Fucito and Beyer in their book *Caruso and the Art of Singing*, "was due to the flexibility of his lips and tongue. . . . An excellent exercise for the flexibility of the tongue and lips (and also for the distinct enunciation of the *R*) is: *tra, tre, tro, tru*; and *bra, bre, bri, bro, bru*."

The Italian voice teachers train their singers a great deal on l. With the tip of the tongue on the roof of the mouth, lips out, chin loose, say *lul, lul, lul, lul, tul, lul, lul*.

L, n and *m* are called the singing consonants. They should naturally sing, but most speakers do not make them sing. *n* is very good for practise because it gives one the most head tone. We used it in connection with the vowel sounds in the last chapter: *ain, een*, etc.

◻◻◻

Chapter 16

IMPROVING YOUR DICTION

"The ear of the world must he tickled in order to be made attentive clearness, force and beauty of style are absolutely necessary to one who would draw men to his way of thinking; nay, to anyone who would induce the great mass of mankind to give so much as passing heed to what he has to say."

-Woodrow Wilson

"Whatever is in the sermon must be in the preacher first; clearness, logicalness, vivacity, earnestness must be personal qualities in him before they are qualities of thought and language in what he utters."

-Phillips Brooks

"Men who talk well read more, as a rule, than the average. Without conscious effort, they absorb many ideas and the words that express them. Something of the style and taste of superior writers gets into their thought and speech. Reading is usually considered the most potent single factor in the enlargement of vocabulary."

-Public Speaking For Success for Business Men, Hoffman

"You don't want a diction gathered from newspapers, caught from the air, common and unsuggestive; but you want one whose every word is full freighted with suggestion and association, with beauty and power."

-Rufus Choate

"Soak yourself full of the world's best literature so that you will have words, strong words, clear words, for your speaking."

-Dr. Lynn Harold Hough

Chapter 16

IMPROVING YOUR DICTION

When Janice D. got up to speak at a meeting of the school board, few people in the room bothered to listen. A few of the Board members took a quick look at this average appearing middle aged woman, assumed she was just another parent with some personal gripe about a teacher or some minor school problem, and began to shuffle the papers on their table. And indeed, Janice did bring up a matter that had been discussed at length previously, but after a few minutes, the attitudes of the Board members and others in the room changed. They stopped looking at the papers; they looked up and paid close attention to her words. It wasn't so much what she was saying; they had heard much of those arguments from previous speakers; it was the way she said it. Her diction was flawless, her voice well modulated, her major points clearly modulated. It was a pleasure to listen to her.

This woman's story is not really extraordinary; It illustrates a broad and fundamental truth, namely, that we are judged each day by our speech. Our words reveal our refinements; they tell discerning listeners that we have a background of education and culture.

We have only four contacts with the world, you and I. We are evaluated and classified by four things: by what we do, by how we look, by what we say and by how we say it. Yet many people blunder through a long life time, after leaving school, without any conscious effort to enrich their stock of words, to master their shades of meaning, to speak with precision and distinction. They habitually use the overworked and exhausted phrases of the office and street. Small wonder that their talk lacks distinction and individuality. Small wonder that they often violate the accepted traditions of pronunciation, and that they sometimes transgress the very canons of English grammar itself. I have heard even college graduates say "ain't," and "he don't," and "between you and I." And if people with academic degrees gracing their names commit such errors, what can we expect of those whose education has been cut short by the pressure of economic necessity?

Years ago, I stood one afternoon daydreaming in the Coliseum at Rome. A stranger approached me, an English colonial. He introduced himself, and began talking of his experiences in the Eternal City. He had not spoken three minutes until he had said "you was," and "I done." That morning, when he arose, he had polished his shoes and put on spotless linen in order to maintain his own self-respect and to win the respect of those with whom he came in contact; but he had made no attempt whatever to polish his phrases and to speak spotless sentences. He would have been ashamed, for example, of wearing an unpressed suit; but he was not ashamed, no, he was not even conscious of violating the usages of grammar, of offending the ears of discriminating auditors. By his own words, he stood revealed and placed and classified. His woeful use of the English language proclaimed to the world continually and unmistakably that he was not a person of culture.

Dr. Charles W. Eliot, after he had been president of Harvard for a third of a century, declared: "I recognize but one mental acquisition, as a necessary part of the education of a lady or gentleman, namely, an accurate and refined use of the mother tongue." This is a significant pronouncement. Ponder over it.

But how, you ask, are we to become intimate with words to speak them with beauty and accuracy? Fortunately, there is no mystery about the means to be employed, no legerdemain. The method is an open secret. Lincoln used it with amazing success. No other American ever wove words into such comely patterns, or produced with prose such matchless music: "with malice towards none, with charity for all." Was Lincoln, whose father was a shiftless, illiterate carpenter and whose mother was a woman of no extraordinary attainments, was he endowed by nature with this gift for words? There is no evidence to support such an assumption. When he was elected to Congress, he described his education in the official records at Washington, with one adjective: "defective." He had attended school less than twelve months in his entire life. Lincoln had meager assistance in obtaining an education, and little inspiration from his daily environment.

The farmers and merchants, the lawyers and litigants with whom he associated in the Eighth Judicial District of Illinois, possessed no magic with words. But Lincoln did not; and this is the significant fact to remember; Lincoln did not squander all his time with his mental equals and inferiors. He made boon companions out of the elite minds, the singers and the poets of the ages. He could repeat from memory, whole pages of Burns and Byron and Browning. He wrote a lecture on Burns. He had one copy of Byron's poems for his office and another for his home. The office copy had been used so much that it fell open, whenever it was lifted, to *Don Juan*. Even when he was in the White House and the tragic burdens of the Civil War were sapping his strength and etching deep furrows in his face, he often found time to take a copy of Thomas Hood's poems to bed. Sometimes he awoke in the middle of the night and, opening the book, he chanced upon verses that especially stirred or pleased. Getting up, clad only in his nightshirt and slippers, he stole through the halls until he found his secretary and read to him poem after poem. In the White House, he found time to repeat long, memorized passages from Shakespeare, to criticize the actor's reading of them, to give his own individual interpretation. "I have gone over some of Shakespeare's plays," he wrote, "perhaps as frequently as any unprofessional reader. *Lear, Richard III, Henry VIII, Hamlet,* and especially *Macbeth.* I think nothing equals *Macbeth.* It is wonderful!"

Lincoln was devoted to verse. Not only did he memorize and repeat it, both in private and public, but he even essayed to write it. He read one of his long poems at his sister's wedding. Later, in middle life, he filled a notebook with his original compositions, but he was so shy about these creations that he never permitted even his closest friends to read them.

"This self-educated man," writes Luther E. Robinson in his book, *Lincoln as a Man of Letters,* "clothed his mind with the materials of genuine culture. Call it genius or talent, the process of his attainment, he was simply educating himself by the only pedagogical method which ever yet produced any results anywhere, namely, by the method of his own tireless energy in continuous study and practice."

This awkward pioneer, who used to shuck corn and butcher hogs for 31 cents a day on the Pigeon Creek farms of Indiana, delivered, at Gettysburg, one of the most beautiful addresses ever spoken by mortal man. One hundred and seventy thousand men fought there. Seven thousand were killed. Yet Charles Sumner said, shortly after Lincoln's death, that Lincoln's address would live when the memory of the battle was lost, and that the battle would one day be remembered largely because of the speech. Who will doubt the correctness of this prophecy? Isn't it, even in this generation, beginning to be fulfilled? Do you not, even now, think of the speech as much as of the fighting when you hear the name, "Gettysburg"?

Edward Everett spoke for two hours at Gettysburg; all that he said has long since been forgotten. Lincoln spoke for less than two minutes, a photographer attempted to take his picture while delivering the speech, but Lincoln had finished before the primitive camera could be set up and focused.

Lincoln's address has been cast in imperishable bronze and placed in a library at Oxford as an example of what can be done with the English language. It ought to be memorized by every student of public speaking.

Four score and seven years ago, our fathers brought forth on this continent a new nation, conceived in liberty and dedicated to the proposition that all men are created equal. Now we are engaged in a great civil war, testing whether that nation, or any nation so conceived and so dedicated, can long endure. We are met on a great battlefield of that war. We have come to dedicate a portion of that field as a final resting place for those who here gave their lives that that nation might live. It is altogether fitting and proper that we should do this. But in a larger sense, we cannot dedicate, we cannot consecrate, we cannot hallow this ground. The brave men, living and dead, who struggled here, have consecrated it, far above our poor power to add or detract. The world will little note, nor long remember, what we say here, but it can never forget what they did here. It is for us, the living, rather to be dedicated here to the unfinished work, which they who fought here, have thus far, so nobly advanced. It is, rather for us, to be here dedicated to the great task remaining before us, that from these honored dead, we take increased devotion to that cause for which they gave the last full measure of devotion; that we here highly resolve that these dead shall not have died in vain; that this nation, under God, shall have a new birth of freedom; and that government of the people, by the people, for the people, shall not perish from the earth.

It is commonly supposed that Lincoln originated the immortal phrase, which closed this address; but did he? Herndon, his law partner, had given Lincoln, several years previously, a copy of Theodore Parker's addresses. Lincoln read and underscored in this book the words "Democracy is direct self-government, over all the people, by all the people, and for all the people." Theodore Parker may have borrowed his phraseology from Daniel Webster who had said, four years earlier, in his famous reply to Robert Hayne: "The people's government, made for the people, made by the people, and answerable to the people." Webster may have borrowed his phraseology from President James Monroe who had given voice to the same idea a third of a century earlier. And to whom was James Monroe indebted? Five hundred years before Monroe was born, John Wyclif had said, in the preface to the translation of the Scriptures that "this Bible is for the government of the people, by the people, and for the people." And long before Wyclif lived, more than 400 years before the birth of Christ, Cleon, in an address to the men of Athens, spoke of a ruler "of the people, by the people, and for the people." And from what ancient source Cleon drew his inspiration, is a matter lost in the fog and night of antiquity.

How little there is that is new! How much even the great speakers owe to their reading and to their association with books!

Books! There is the secret! To enrich and enlarge your stock of words you must soak your mind constantly in the vats of literature. "The only lamentation that I always feel in the presence of a library," said John Bright, "is that life is too short and I have no hope of a full enjoyment of the ample repast spread before me." Bright left school at fifteen, and went to work in a cotton mill, and he never had the chance of schooling again. Yet he became one of the most brilliant speakers of the generation, famous for his superb command of the English language. He read and studied and copied in notebooks and committed to memory long passages from the poetry of Byron and Milton, Wadsworth and Whittier, and Shakespeare and Shelley. He went through Paradise Lost each year to enrich his stock of words.

The younger William Pitt's practice was to look over a page or two of Greek or Latin and then to translate the passage into his own language. He did this daily for ten years, and "he acquired an almost unrivalled power of putting his thoughts, without pre-meditation, into words well selected and well arranged."

Demosthenes copied Thucydides' history eight times in his own handwriting in order that he might acquire the majestic and impressive phraseology of that famous historian. The result? Two thousand years later, in order to improve his style, Woodrow Wilson studied the works of Demosthenes. British Prime Minister Herbert

Asquith found his best training in reading the works of Bishop Berkeley.

Tennyson studied the Bible daily. Tolstoy read and reread the Gospels until he knew long passages by memory. John Ruskin's mother forced him by steady, daily toil to memorize long chapters of the Bible and to read the entire Book through aloud each year, "every syllable, hard names and all, from Genesis to the Apocalypse." To that discipline and study, Ruskin attributed his taste and style in literature.

R.L.S. are said to be the best-loved initials in the English language. Robert Louis Stevenson was essentially a writer's writer. How did he develop the charming style that made him famous? Fortunately, he has told us the story himself.

"Whenever I read a book or a passage that particularly pleased me, in which a thing was said or an effect rendered with propriety, in which there was either some conspicuous force or some happy distinction in the style, I must sit down at once and set myself to ape that quality. I was unsuccessful, and I knew it; and tried again, and was again unsuccessful, and always unsuccessful; but at least in these vain bouts I got some practice in rhythm, in harmony, in construction and coordination of parts."

"I have thus played the sedulous ape to Hazlitt, to Lamb, to Wordsworth, to Sir Thomas Browne, to Defoe, to Hawthorne, to Montaigne."

"That, like it or not, is the way to learn to write; whether I have profited or not, that is the way. It was the way Keats learned, and there never was a finer temperament for literature than Keats'."

"It is the great point of these imitations that there still shines beyond the student's reach, his inimitable model. Let him try as he pleases, be it still sure of failure; and it is an old and very true saying that failure is the only high road to success."

Enough of names and specific stories. The secret is out. Lincoln wrote it to a young man eager to become a successful lawyer: "It is only to get the books and to read and study them carefully. Work, work, work is the main thing."

"I have given up newspapers in exchange for Tacitus and Thucydides, for Newton and Euclid," wrote Thomas Jefferson, "and I find myself much the happier." Don't you believe that you, by following Jefferson's example at least to the extent of cutting your newspaper reading in half, would find yourself happier and wiser as the weeks go by? How many hours do you waste watching television programs? Studies show that most of us spend two to three hours a day in front of the tube. By just using only a third of that time reading good books, you would increase your knowledge, enlarge your vocabulary and be on the road to an improved self.

Aren't you, at any rate, willing to try it for a month? Carry a paperback book with you. It will fit easily into your pocket or purse. Read a few pages while waiting for elevators, on the checkout line in the supermarket and those interminable waits in doctors' offices? Visit your public library regularly. Get to know the librarian. He or she will be happy to recommend books that will improve your mind as well as those that entertain and inspire you.

Ralph Waldo Emerson expressed this best in his famous essay on *Self-Reliance*. Let him whisper into your ear marching sentences like these:

"Speak your latent conviction, and it shall be the universal sense; for always the inmost becomes the outmost; and our first thought is rendered back to us by the trumpets of the Last judgment. Familiar as the voice of the mind is to each, the highest merit we ascribe to Moses, Plato and Milton, is that they set at naught, books and traditions, and spoke not what men said but what they thought. A man should learn to detect and watch that gleam of light, which flashes across his mind from within, more than the luster of the firmament of bards and sages. Yet he dismisses without notice his thought, because it is his. In every work of genius, we recognize our own rejected thoughts: they come back to us with a certain alienated majesty. Great works of art have no more affecting lesson for us than this. They teach us to abide by our spontaneous impression with good-humored inflexibility, then most, when the whole cry of voices is on the other side. Else, tomorrow a stranger will say with masterly good sense, precisely, what we have thought and felt till the time, and we shall be forced to take with shame our own opinion from another."

"There is a time in every man's education when he arrives at the conviction that envy is ignorance; that imitation is suicide; that he must take himself for better, for worse, as his portion; that though the wide universe is full of good, no kernel of nourishing corn can come to him but through his toil bestowed on that plot of ground which is given to him to till. The power which resides in him is new in nature, and none but he knows what that is which he can do, nor does he know until he has tried."

When Sir Henry Irving was asked to furnish a list of what he regarded as the hundred best books, he replied: "Before a hundred books, commend me to the study of two: the Bible and Shakespeare." Sir Henry was right. Drink from these two great fountain sources of English literature. Drink long and often. Toss your evening newspaper aside, turn off that TV, and say, "Shakespeare, come here and talk to me tonight of Romeo and his Juliet, of Macbeth and his ambition."

If you do these things, what will be your reward? Gradually, unconsciously but inevitably, your diction will begin to take on added beauty and refinement. Gradually, you will begin to reflect somewhat the glory and beauty and majesty of your companions. "Tell me what you read," observed Goethe, "and I will tell you what you are."

This reading program that I have suggested will require little but will power, little but a more careful husbanding of time. . . . Pocket copies of Emerson's essays and Shakespeare's plays are available in every bookstore and are reasonably priced.

THE SECRET OF MARK TWAIN'S WAY WITH WORDS

How did Mark Twain develop his delightful facility with words? As a young man, he traveled all the way from Missouri to Nevada by the ponderously slow and really painful stagecoach. Food, and sometimes even water, had to be carried for both passengers and horses. Extra weight might have meant the difference between safety and disaster; baggage was charged for by the ounce; and yet Mark Twain carried with him a Webster's Unabridged Dictionary over mountain passes, across scorched deserts, and through a land infested with bandits and Indians. He wanted to make himself master of words, and with his characteristic courage and common sense, he set about doing the things necessary to bring that mastery about.

Both Pitt and Lord Chatham studied the dictionary twice, every page, every word of it. Browning pored over it daily, finding in it entertainment as well as instruction. Lincoln "would sit in the twilight," records his biographers, Nicolay and Hay, "and read a dictionary as long as he could see." These are not exceptional instances. Every writer and speaker of distinction has done the same.

Woodrow Wilson was superbly skillful with the English language. Some of his writings will undoubtedly take a place in literature. Here is his own story of how he learned to marshal words:

"My father never allowed any member of his household to use an incorrect expression. Any slip on the part of one of the children was at once corrected; any unfamiliar word was immediately explained; each of us was encouraged to find a use for it in our conversation so as to fix it in our memories."

A well-known speaker, who is often complimented upon the firm texture of his sentences and the simple beauty of his language, during the course of a conversation recently, lifted the embargo on the secret of his power to choose true and incisive words. Each time he discovers an unfamiliar word in conversation or reading matter, he notes it in his memorandum book. Then, just prior to retiring at night, he consults his dictionary and makes the word his own. If he has gathered no material in this fashion during the day, he studies a page or two of Roget's Thesaurus noting the exact meaning of the words, which he would ordinarily interchange as perfect synonyms. A new word a day-that is his motto. This means in the course of a year, three hundred and sixty-five additional tools for expression. These new words are stored away in a small pocket notebook, and their meanings reviewed at odd moments during the day. He has found that a word becomes a permanent acquisition to his vocabulary when he has used it three times.

ROMANTIC STORIES BEHIND THE WORDS YOU USE

Use a dictionary not only to ascertain the meaning of the word, but also to find its derivation. Its history, its origin is usually set down in brackets after the definition. Do not imagine for a moment that the words you speak each day are only dull, listless sounds. They are reeking with color; they are alive with romance. You cannot, for example, say so prosaic a thing as "Telephone the grocer for sugar," without using words that we have borrowed from many different languages and civilizations. *Telephone* is made from two Greek words, *tele*, meaning far and *phone*, meaning sound. *Grocer* comes from an old French word, *grossier*, and the French came from the Latin, *grossarius*; it literally means one who sells by the wholesale or gross. We got our word *sugar* from the French; the French borrowed it from the Spanish; the Spanish lifted it from the Arabic; the Arabic took it from the Persian; and the Persian word *shaker* was derived from the Sanskrit *carkara*, meaning candy.

You may work for or own a *company*. *Company* is derived from an old French word meaning *companion*; and *companion* is literally *com*, with; and *panis*, bread. Your *companion* is one with whom you have bread. A *company* is really an association of people who are trying to make their bread together. Your *salary* literally means your *salt* money. The Roman soldiers drew a certain allowance for *salt*, and one day some wag spoke of his entire income as his *salarium*, and created a bit of slang which has long since become respectable English. You are holding in your hand a *book*. It literally means *beech*, for a long time ago the Anglo-Saxons scratched their words on *beech* trees and on tablets of *beech* wood. The *dollar* that you have in your pocket literally means *valley*. *Dollars* were first coined in St. Joachim's *Thaler* or *dale* or valley in the sixteenth century.

The words *janitor* and *January* have both come down from the name of an Etruscan blacksmith who lived in Rome and made a specialty of locks and bolts for doors. When he died, he was deified as a pagan god, and was represented as having two faces, so that he could look both ways at the same time, and was associated with the opening and closing of doors. So the month that stood at the close of one year and the opening of another was called *January*, or the month of *Janus*. So when we talk of *January* or a *janitor*, a keeper of doors, we are honoring the name of a blacksmith who lived a thousand years before the birth of Christ and who had a wife by the name of Jane.

The seventh month, *July*, was named after *Julius Caesar*; so the Emperor Augustus, not to be out done, called the next month *August*. But the eighth month had only thirty days at that time, and Augustus did not propose to have the month named after him any shorter than a month named after Julius; so he took one day away from February and added it to August, and the marks of this vainglorious theft are evident on the calendar hanging in your home today. Truly, you will find the history of words fascinating.

Please look up in a large dictionary the derivation of these words: atlas, boycott, cereal, colossal, concord, curfew, education, finance, lunatic, panic, palace, pecuniary, sandwich, tantalize. Get the stories behind them. It will make them doubly colorful, doubly interesting. You will use them, then, with added zest and pleasure.

One of the most fascinating dictionaries is the Oxford English Dictionary (OED), a multivolume tome which not only gives the definitions of virtually every word in the English language, but the history of the words and phrases delving deep into their past usages. The editors keep it current by adding words that have been coined or changes in meanings of older words and phrases in each new edition. If you want to spend a most interesting and productive afternoon, go to the public library and just browse through the OED, You'll be amazed at how meanings of words have changed over the years.

RE-WRITING ONE SENTENCE A HUNDRED AND FOUR TIMES

Strive to say precisely what you mean, to express the most delicate nuances of thought. That is not always easy, not even for experienced writers. Fanny Hurst told me that she sometimes rewrote her sentences from fifty to a hundred times. Only a few days prior to the conversation, she said she had rewritten one sentence one hundred and four times by actual count. Yet she was so accomplished a writer, that the *Cosmopolitan Magazine* was paying her two thousand dollars a story. Another author confided to me that she sometimes spent an entire afternoon eliminating only one or two sentences from a short story that was to be syndicated through the newspapers.

Gouverneur Morris wrote how Richard Harding Davis labored incessantly for just the right word:

"Every phrase in his fiction was, of all the myriad phrases he could think of, the fittest in his relentless judgment to survive. Phrases, paragraphs, pages, whole stories even, were written over and over again. He worked upon a principle of elimination. If he wished to describe an automobile turning in at a gate, he made first a long and elaborate description from which there was omitted no detail, which the most observant pair of eyes has ever noted with reference to just such a turning. Thereupon, he would begin a process of omitting one by one, those details which he had been at such pains to recall; and after each omission be would ask himself, 'Does the picture remain?' If it did not, he restored the detail which he had just omitted, and experimented with the sacrifice of some other, and so on, and so on, until after Herculean labor there remained for the reader one of those swiftly flashed iceclear pictures (complete in

347

every detail) with which his tales and romances are so delightfully and continuously adorned."

Most readers of this book have neither time nor disposition to search as diligently for words as the authors just described. These instances are cited to show you the importance successful writers attach to proper diction and expression, in the hope that it may encourage you to take an increased interest in the use of English. It is, of course, not practical for a speakers to hesitate in a sentence and uh-uh about, hunting for the word which will exactly express the shade of meaning they desires to convey, but preciseness of expression should be practiced in all conversations until it comes unconsciously. Milton is reported to have employed eight thousand words and Shakespeare fifteen thousand. A Standard Dictionary contains fifty thousand less than half a million; but the average person, according to popular estimates, gets along with approximately two thousand. We use some verbs, enough connectives to stick them together, a handful of nouns, and a few overworked adjectives. We are too lazy mentally or too absorbed in business, household chores or other activities to train our minds for precision and exactness. The result? Let me give you an illustration. I once spent a few unforgettable days on the rim of the Grand Canyon of the Colorado. In the course of an afternoon, I heard a lady apply the same adjective to a Chow dog, an orchestral selection, a man's disposition, and the Grand Canyon itself. They were all "beautiful."

What should she have said? Here are the synonyms that Roget lists for *beautiful*. Which adjectives do you think she should have employed?

Adjective: *beautiful*, beauteous, handsome, pretty, lovely, graceful, elegant, exquisite, delicate, dainty.

comely, fair, goodly, bonny, good-looking, well- favored, well-formed, well-proportioned, shapely, symmetrical, harmonious.

bright, bright-eyed, rosy-cheeked, rosy, ruddy, blooming, in full bloom.

trim, trig, tidy, neat, spruce, smart, jaunty, dapper.

brilliant, shining, sparkling, radiant, splendid, resplendent, dazzling, glowing, glossy, sleek, rich, gorgeous, superb, magnificent, grand, fine.

artistic, aesthetic, picturesque, pictorial, enchanting, attractive, becoming, ornamental.

perfect, unspotted, spotless, immaculate, undeformed, undefaced.

passable, presentable, tolerable, not amiss.

The synonyms just quoted have been taken from Roget's *Treasury of Words*. It is an abridged edition of Roget's *Thesaurus*. What a help this book is. Personally, I never write without having it at my elbow. I find occasion to use it ten times as often as I use the dictionary.

It is not a book to be stored away on a library shelf. It is a tool to be used constantly. Use it when writing out and polishing the diction of your talks. Use it in writing your letters and your business reports. Use it daily, and it will double and treble your power with words.

SHUN WORN-OUT PHRASES

Strive not only to be exact, but to be fresh and original. Avoid cliches, those worn out, overused phrases. For example, centuries ago some original mind first used the comparison, "cool as a cucumber." It was extraordinarily good then because it was extraordinarily fresh. But no speaker with any degree of originality would be guilty of repeating it today.

Here are a dozen similes to express coldness. Aren't they just as effective as the hackneyed "cucumber" comparison, and far fresher and more acceptable?

Cold as a frog.

Cold as a hot-water bag in the morning.

Cold as a ramrod.

Cold as a tomb.

Cold as Greenland's icy mountains.

Cold as clay.   *-Coleridge*

Cold as a turtle.   *-Richard Cumberland*

Cold as the drifting snow.   *-Allan Cunningham*

Cold as salt.   *-James Huneker*

Cold as an earthworm.   *-Maurice Maeterlinck*

Cold as dawn.

Cold as rain in autumn.

While the mood is upon you, think now of similes of your own to convey the idea of coldness. Have the courage to be distinctive. Write them here:

Cold as ....

Cold as ....

Cold as ....

Cold as ....

Cold as ....

I once asked Kathleen Norris, who was reputed to be America's highest paid writer of magazine serial fiction of her time, how style could be developed. "By reading classics of prose and poetry," she replied, "and by critically eliminating stock phrases and hackneyed expressions from your work."

A magazine editor once told me that when he found two or three hackneyed expressions in a story submitted for publication, he returned it to the author without wasting time reading it; for, he added, one who has no originality of expression will exhibit little originality of thought.

IT'S NOT ONLY WHAT YOU SAY, BUT HOW YOU SAY IT

Many speakers have excellent vocabularies and a wonderful array of similes, metaphors and cryptic phrases to express their ideas, and when you read their speeches, they are inspiring and enlightening. But, alas, often when listening to them, their beauty is lost because of poor diction or articulation.

No matter how well thought your message is, no one will understand it if you don't express it clearly and distinctly. Following are the six most common problems people have in speaking clearly:

1. *Mumbling*. Do you swallow word endings? Do you speak with your mouth almost closed? Practice in front of a mirror. Open up those lips.

2. *Speaking too fast*. Whoa! Give people a chance to absorb what you are saying. Listen to tape recordings of your speeches. Time your speed. If you talk faster than 150 words per minute, you are talking too fast.

3. *Speaking too slowly*. Speak too slowly and you will lose your

audience. While you are plodding through your speech, the audience's minds wander to other matters. (a guideline is to talk no slower than 120 words per minute, except when emphasizing a point. Slowing down, then, is advantageous.

4. *Mispronouncing words*. Review the exercises included in the Speech Building sections, after each chapter, to help with this.

5. *Avoid "word whiskers."* Those extra sounds, words or phrases peppered throughout many people's speech."er", "uhhh."y'know," are just a few. They distract from your thoughts. Listen to yourself and shave off those "whiskers."

6. *Speaking in a monotone*. Vary the inflection of the tone and pitch of your voice. Otherwise you will put your listeners to sleep.

IN A NUTSHELL

1.   We have only four contacts with people. We are evaluated and classified by four things: by what we do, by how we look, by what we say, and how we say it. How often we are judged by the language we use. Charles W. Eliot, after he had been president of Harvard for a third of a century, declared: "I recognize but one mental acquisition as a necessary part of the education of a lady or gentleman, namely, an accurate and refined use of the mother tongue."

2.   Your diction will be very largely a reflection of the company you keep. So follow Lincoln's example and keep company with the masters of literature. Spend your evenings, as he often did, with Shakespeare and the other great poets and masters of prose. Do that and unconsciously, inevitably, your mind will be enriched and your diction will take on something of the glory of your companions.

3.   "I have given up newspapers in exchange for Tacitus and Thucydides, for Newton and Euclid," wrote Thomas Jefferson, "and I find myself much the happier." Why not follow his example? Don't give up the newspapers completely, but skim through in half the time you now devote to them. Reduce the number of hours you waste watching televison. Give the time, you thus salvage, to the reading of some enduring book. Buy inexpensive paperback editions. Carry one in your pocket or purse, read it at odd moments during the day.

4.   Read with a dictionary by your side. Look up the unfamiliar word. Try to find a use for it so that you may fix it in your memory.

5.   Study the derivation of the words you use. Their histories are not dull

and dry; often they are replete with romance.

6. Don't use cliches, shopworn, threadbare words. Be precise, exact, in your meaning. Keep Roget's Thesaurus on your desk. Refer to it often.

7. Don't use trite comparisons such as "cool as a cucumber." Strive for freshness. Create similes of your own. Have the courage to be distinctive.

8. Articulate clearly. Don't mumble, speak too fast or slow, mispronounce works, use "word whiskers" or speak in a monotone.

SPEECH BUILDING
WORDS OFTEN MISPRONOUNCED

See if you can pronounce all of the italicized words in the following selection:

On his *awakening*, after the *tempestuous* day, the *aviator* rose from his bed before the broken *hearth* and looked over his *radiator* and carburetor *carefully* to see that they were not injured. After all parts were *lubricated*, even before the *dew* was off the *grass*, he flew *due* cast as his *duty* called.

His *aerial* trip was aided by his knowledge of the *geography* of the country. He was an *athlete*; the *boisterous* and *jovial* events of the past evening did not *affect* his *dexterous handling* of the *white* ship. He did not need the *whip* of *whiskey* to *steady* his hand on the *wheel*. Neither did the *memories* of the plaudits of the *gallery* nor the past *history* of his comrades of the squadron *abate* his constant watch over the *boundaries*.

ERRORS IN ENGLISH

Review. You will find in the following examples that an attempt has been made to cover most of the important rules that have been placed before you. If you can avoid all the pitfalls that have been shown in the previous lessons you will speak a quality of English which is far above that usually heard.

- How many of these sentences are incorrect, and why?
- He told you and I a different story.
- Just between you and me, I admit she done the best she could.
- Let's you and I go now.
- Were you and I invited the day he come home?

- John is taller than me.
- Mr. Smith and I work together.
- Everybody cashed their checks in order to enjoy the holiday.
- I am introducing a stenographer who you will like.
- She had bidden $20 for the coat and didn't get it.
- The man was hanged after he had been convicted before a jury.
- Eliza had not swum across the river because of the ice.
- Part of the material have been shipped.
- A thousand dollars were lost in the deal.
- That kind of a house will not stand the climate.
- He, as well as I, have taken the risk.
- These sort of investments are not safe.
- Scarcely had the lamp been lighted when it was shot out.
- She had two son-in-laws who were worthless.
- My two mothers-in-law's husbands were drowned.
- The robbers hunted everywheres for the money.
- Mr. Long don't take chances on margin buying.
- Do you suppose it to be him?
- Us and our friends play bridge together.
- He had lain the mail on the desk, but the president had not saw them.
- Neither Mr. Blank or him were to blame for the mistake.
- The file clerk had went through the files carefully.
- The firm likes these kind of letter heads. They are finer than your's.
- A person can save money by paying your bills on time.
- A man can't drive a car without he has a driver's license.
- We have never had quite as much fun as we did in this class.
- "I didn't do nothing," is the wail that many a child raises.
- It only has been a comparatively few years since the government was founded.
- He has almost exhausted all his resources.
- If your laundry don't give satisfaction, try ours.

CORRECT USAGE OF WORDS

Which of the following sentences are incorrect, and why?

1. There must be a spirit of loyalty between all the states in the Union.
2. I have acquired an antipathy for the man.
3. He is bound to succeed at all costs.
4. He was fortunate in getting a good education.
5. She has the ability to sing well when she wants to.
6. May I call tomorrow?
7. We had a delightful dinner.
8. He was greatly effected by the news of her death.
9. He tried to enthuse me over both plans.
10. Onions are a very healthy food.
11. Swimming is a healthful exercise.
12. We are likely to have difficulties.
13. This is a unique opportunity to get a bargain in real estate.
14. He is a very social person.
15. He has an extraordinary capacity for hard work.
16. I anticipated this advance in prices when I ordered last autumn.
17. The pugilist has immense strength.
18. He has a bias toward the manual trades.
19. The event transpired but it did not become known.
20. Our horse is liable to win.

VOICE EXERCISE - REVIEW

1. Turn to the poem The *Cataract of Lodore*, in Chapter VI. Read this aloud, paying special attention to four things.
a. Be sure that you are breathing from the diaphragm.
b. Be sure that you have a reserve of breath in your lungs to act as a spring board, to launch your words, to give them carrying power.
c. Be sure that your throat is open and utterly free and relaxed.
d. Be sure that you are using nasal resonance.

(See Voice Exercise, Chapter XIII.) Accentuate the *ng* sounds that are found in almost every line of this poem. Let them ring through your nose.

2. Read the following verses aloud using the falsetto voice to develop brightness. (See Voice Exercise, Chapter VII.)

"True worth is in being, not seeming,

In doing each day that goes by

Some little good, not in dreaming

Of great things to do by and by.

"For whatever men say in their blindness,

And in spite of the follies of youth,

There is nothing so kingly as kindness,

And nothing so royal as truth."

3. Read the following verses aloud, paying special attention to the tip of the tongue. Feel it striking the back of the teeth with an elastic touch. This will give vivacity and a sense of speed to your reading. (See Chapter VI.)

THE FIRST OF SEPTEMBER

"The first of September, remember

The day of supremest delight.

Get ready the cartridge, the partridge

Must fall in the stubble ere night.

"The breech-loader's ready, and steady

The dog that we taught in old days;

He's firm to his duty, a beauty

That comes for but one person's praise.

"He is careful in stubble, no trouble,

In turnips he's keen as a man;

But looks on acutely, and mutely

Seems saying 'Shoot well, if you can.'

"They flash from the cover, what lover

Of sport does not thrill as they rise
In feathered apparel? Each barrel
Kills one, as the swift covey flies.
"One pipe, then be doing, pursuing
The sport that no sport can eclipse:
So homeward to dinner, a winner
Of praise from the fairest of lips."

-Savile Clark in Punch.

4. Hum the tune of the *Long, Long Trail*. Following the directions given in the Voice Exercise for Chapter XI, feel the resonance, the vibrations, in the top of your head, the back of your head, the chest, the nasal cavities, the face. As you hum, try to feel in the head, the same cool, open, taking in sensation that you experience when you are inhaling:

LONG, LONG TRAIL

"There's a long, long trail a-winding
Into the land of my dreams,
Where the nightingales are singing
And a white moon beams;
There's a long, long night of waiting
Until my dreams all come true;
Till the day when I'll be going down
That long, long trail with you."

5. Read the following poem, "The Vagabond," by Robert Louis Stevenson, with the same spirit of happiness singing in your voice that must have sung in Stevenson's heart, when he wrote it. As we pointed out in the Voice Exercise for Chapter VII, the reading of joyous poetry is one of the very best means for developing bright, attractive tones.

"Give me the life I love,
Let the lave go by me,
Give the jolly heavens above
And the byway nigh me.

356

Bed in the bush with stars to see.
Bread I dip in the river-
There's the life for a man like me,
There's the life forever.
"Let the blow fall soon or late,
Let what will be o'er me;
Give the face of earth around
And the road before me.
Wealth I seek not, hope nor love,
Nor a friend to know me;
All I seek, the heaven above
And the road below me."

In conclusion, let us warn the student that the mere reading and casual practising now and then of the voice exercises outlined in this course, will not procure the most desirable results. They ought to be practised daily. You will get out of them only what you put into them nothing more, nothing less.

❑❑❑

INTRODUCTION TO APPENDIX

Dale Carnegie included the following essays in the original edition of this book because, although they were not directly related to public speaking, he felt the strong positive messages they presented, would be inspirational to the readers.

These essays were written at the end of the nineteenth century in the style, language and culture of that era. They are reprinted in this edition, exactly as they were originally written.

APPENDIX

ACRES OF DIAMONDS

By RUSSELL H. CONWELL

No other lecture has ever been delivered as often by its author as "Acres of Diamonds." If one were to deliver the same lecture, each night in the year for fifteen years, he would not at the end of that time have equaled Dr. Conwell's record. The noted Philadelphian preached his "Acres of Diamonds" philosophy more than five thousand seven hundred times. If the proceeds from this lecture had been put out at compound interest, the sum would aggregate more than eight million dollars. With the profits from his various lectures, this man who in his youth waged such a bitter struggle to get an education, helped more than three thousand men through college.

ACRES OF DIAMONDS

By RUSSELL H. CONWELL

I n 1870 we went down the Tigris River. We hired a guide at Baghdad to show us Persepolis, Nineveh and Babylon, and the ancient countries of Assyria as far as the Arabian Gulf. He was well acquainted with the land, but he was one of those guides who love to entertain their patrons; he was like a barber that tells you many stories in order to keep your mind off the scratching and the scraping. He told me so many stories that I grew tired of his telling them and I refused to listen; looked away whenever he commenced; that made the guide quite angry. I remembered that toward evening, he took his Turkish cap off his head and swung it around in the air. The gesture I did not understand and I did not look at him for fear, I should become victim of another story. But, I did look and the instant I turned my eyes upon that worthy guide, he was off again. He said, "I will tell you a story now which I reserve for my particular friends!" So then, counting myself a particular friend, I listened, and I have always been glad I did.

He said, there once lived not far from the River Indus, an ancient Persian by the name of Al Hafed. He said that Al Hafed owned a very large farm with orchards, grain fields, and gardens. He was a contented and wealthy man; contented because he was wealthy and wealthy because he was contented. One day, there visited this old farmer, one of those ancient Buddhist priests, and he sat down by Al Hafed's fire and told that old farmer, how this world of ours was made. He said that this world was once a mere bank of fog, which is scientifically true, and he said that the Almighty thrust his finger into the bank of fog and then began slowly to move his finger around and gradually to increase the speed of his finger until at last he whirled that bank of fog into a solid ball of fire, and it went rolling through the universe, burning its way through other cosmic banks of fog, until it condensed the moisture without, and fell in floods of rain upon the heated surface and cooled the outward crust. Then the internal flames burst through the cooling crust and threw up the mountains and made the hills and the valleys of this wonderful world of ours. If this internal melted mass burst out and cooled very quickly it became granite; that which cooled less quickly became silver; and less quickly, gold; and after gold, diamonds were made. Said the old priest, "A diamond is a congealed drop of sunlight."

This is a scientific truth also. You all know that a diamond is pure carbon, actually deposited sunlight; and he said another thing I would not forget; he declared that a diamond is the last and highest of God's mineral creations, as a woman is the last and highest of God's animal creations. I suppose that is the reason why the two have such a liking for each other. And the old priest told Al Hafed that if he had a handful of diamonds, he could purchase a whole country and with a mine of diamonds he could place his children upon thrones through the influence of their great wealth. Al Hafed heard all about diamonds and how much they were worth, and went to his bed that night a poor man, not that he had lost anything, but poor because he was discontented and discontented because he thought he was poor. He said, "I want a mine of diamonds." So he lay awake all night, and early in the morning sought out the priest. Now, I know from experience that a priest when awakened early in the morning, is cross. He awoke that priest out of his dreams and said to him, "Will you tell me where I can find diamonds?" The priest said, "Diamonds? What do you want with diamonds?" "I want to be immensely rich," said Al Hafed, "but I don't know where to go." "Well," said the priest, "if you will find a river that runs over white sand between high mountains, in those sands you will always see diamonds." "Do you really believe that there is such a river?" "Plenty of them, plenty of them; all you have to do is just go and find them, then you have them." Al Hafed said, "I will go." So he sold his farm, collected his money at interest, left his family in charge of a neighbor, and away he went in search of diamonds. He began very properly, to my mind, at the Mountains of the Moon. Afterwards he went around into Palestine, then wandered on into Europe, and at last when his money was all spent, and he was in rags, wretchedness and poverty, he stood on the shore of that bay in Barcelona, Spain, when a tidal wave came rolling through the Pillars of Hercules and the poor, afflicted, suffering man could not resist the awful temptation to cast himself into that incoming tide, and he sank beneath its foaming crest, never to rise in this life again.

When that old guide had told me that very sad story, he stopped the camel I was riding and went back to fix the baggage on one of the other camels, and I remember thinking to myself, "Why did he reserve that for his particular friends?" There seemed to be no beginning, middle or end, nothing to it. That was the first story I had ever heard, told or read in which the hero was killed in the first chapter. I had but one chapter of that story and the hero was dead. When the guide came back and took up the halter of my camel again, he went right on with the same story. He said that Al Hafed's successor led his camel out into the garden to drink, and as the camel put its nose down into the clear water of the garden brook, Al Hafed's successor noticed a curious flash of light from the sands of the shallow stream, and reaching in he pulled out a black stone having an eye of light that reflected all the colors of the rainbow, and he took that curious pebble into the house and left it on the mantel, then went on his way and forgot all about it. A few days after that, this same old priest who told Al Hafed how diamonds were made, came in to visit his successor. When he saw that flash of light from the mantel, he rushed up and said, "Here is a diamond, here is a diamond! Has Al Hafed returned?" "No, no; Al Hafed has not returned and that is not a diamond; that is nothing but a stone; we found it right out here in our garden." "But I know a diamond when I see it," said he; "that is a diamond!"

Then together they rushed to the garden and stirred up the white sands with their fingers and found other more beautiful, more valuable diamonds than the first, and thus, said the guide to me, were discovered the diamond mines of Golconda, the most magnificent diamond mines in all the history of mankind, exceeding the Kimberley in its value. The great Kohinoor diamond in England's crown jewels and the largest crown diamond on earth in Russia's crown jewels, which I had often hoped she would have to sell before they had peace with Japan, came from that mine, and when the old guide had called my attention to that wonderful discovery, he took his Turkish cap off his head again and swung it around in the air to call my attention to the moral. Those Arab guides have a moral to each story, though the stories are not always moral. He said, had Al Hafed remained at home and dug in his own cellar or in his own garden, instead of wretchedness, starvation, poverty and death in a strange land, he would have had "acres of diamonds" for every acre, yes, every shovelful of that old farm afterwards revealed the gems which since have decorated the crowns of monarchs. When he had given the moral to his story, I saw why he had reserved this story for his "particular friends." I didn't tell him I could see it; I was not going to tell that old Arab that I could see it. For it was that mean old Arab's way of going around a thing, like a lawyer, and saying indirectly, what he did not dare say directly, that there was a certain young man that day traveling down the Tigris River that might better be at home in America. I didn't tell him I could see it.

I told him his story reminded me of one, and I told it to him quick. I told him about that man out in California, who, in 1847, owned a ranch out there. He read that gold had been discovered in Southern California, and he sold his ranch to Colonel Sutter and started off to hunt for gold. Colonel Sutter put a mill on the little stream in that farm and one day his little girl brought some wet sand from the raceway of the mill into the house and placed it before the fire to dry, and as that sand was falling through the little girl's fingers, a visitor saw the first shining scales of real gold that were ever discovered in California; and the man who wanted the gold had sold this ranch and gone away, never to return. I delivered this lecture two years ago in California, in the city that stands near that farm, and they told me that the mine is not exhausted yet, and that a one-third owner of that farm has been getting during these recent years twenty dollars of gold every fifteen minutes of his life, sleeping or waking. Why, you and I would enjoy an income like that.

But the best illustration that I have now of this thought was found in Pennsylvania. There was a man living in Pennsylvania who owned a farm there, and he did what I should do if I had a farm in Pennsylvania, he sold it. But before he sold it he concluded to secure employment collecting coal oil for his cousin in Canada. They first discovered coal oil there. So this farmer in Pennsylvania decided that he would apply for a position with his cousin in Canada. Now, you see, this farmer was not altogether a foolish man. He did not leave his farm until he had something else to do. Of all the simpletons the stars shine on there is none more foolish than a man who leaves one job before he has obtained another. And that has a special reference to gentlemen of my profession and has not reference to a man seeking a divorce. So I say this old farmer did not leave one job until he had obtained another. He wrote to Canada, but his cousin replied that he could not engage him because he did not know anything about the oil business. "Well, then," said he, "I will understand it." So he set himself at the study of the whole subject. He began at the second day of the creation, he studied the subject from the primitive vegetation to the coal oil stage, until he knew all about it. Then he wrote to his cousin and said, "Now I understand the oil business." And his cousin replied to him, "All right, then, come on."

That man, by the record of the county, sold his farm for eight hundred and thirty-three dollars, even money, "no cents." He had scarcely gone from that farm before the man who purchased it went out to arrange for watering the cattle and be found that the previous owner had arranged the matter very nicely. There is a stream running down the hillside there, and the previous owner had gone out and put a plank across that stream at an angle, extending across the brook and down edgewise a few inches under the surface of the water. The purpose of the plank across that brook was to throw over to the other bank a dreadful looking scum through which the cattle would not put their noses to drink above the plank, although they would drink the water on one side below it. Thus that man who had gone to Canada had been himself damming back for twenty- three years a flow of coal oil which the State Geologist of Pennsylvania declared officially, as early as 1870, was then worth to our State, a hundred millions of dollars. The city of Titusville now stands on that farm and those Pleasantville wells flow on, and that farmer who had studied all about the formation of oil since the second day of God's creation clear down to the present time, sold that farm for $833, no cents, again I say, "no sense."

But I need another illustration; and I found that in Massachusetts, and I am sorry I did, because that is my old State. This young man, I mention went out of the State to study, went down to Yale College and studied Mines and Mining. They paid him fifteen dollars a week during his last year, for training students who were behind their classes in mineralogy, out of hours; of course, while pursuing his own studies. But when he graduated, they raised his pay from fifteen dollars to forty-five dollars and offered him a professorship. Then he went straight home to his mother and said, "Mother, I won't work for forty-five dollars a week. What is forty-five dollars a week for a man with a brain like mine! Mother, let's go out to

California and stake out gold claims and be immensely rich." "No," said his mother, "it is just as well to be happy as it is to be rich."

But as he was the only son he had his way, they always do; and they sold out in Massachusetts and went to Wisconsin, where he went into the employ of the Superior Copper Mining Company, and he was lost from sight in the employ of that company at fifteen dollars a week again. He was also to have an interest in any mines that he should discover for that company. But I do not believe that he has ever discovered a mine. I do not know anything about it, but I do not believe he has. I know he had scarcely gone from the old homestead before the farmer who had bought the homestead went out to dig potatoes, and as he was bringing them in a large basket through the front gateway, the ends of the stone wall came so near together at the gate that the basket hugged very tight. So he set the basket on the ground and pulled, first at one side and then on the other side. Our farms in Massachusetts are mostly stonewalls and the farmers have to be economical with their gateways in order to have some place to put the stones. That basket hugged so tight there that as he was hauling it through, he noticed in the upper stone next to the gate, a block of native silver, eight inches square; and this professor of mines and mining and mineralogy, who would not work for forty-five dollars a week, when he sold that homestead in Massachusetts, sat right on that stone to make the bargain. He was brought up there; he had gone back and forth by that piece of silver, rubbed it with his sleeve, and it seemed to say, "Come now, now, now, here's a hundred thousand dollars. Why not take me?" But he would not take it. There was no silver in Newburyport; it was all away off; well, I don't know where; he didn't, but somewhere else and he was a professor of mineralogy.

I do not know of anything I would enjoy better than to take the whole time tonight telling of blunders like that I have heard professors make. Yet I wish I knew what that man is doing out there in Wisconsin. I can imagine him out there, as he sits by his fireside, and he is saying to his friends, "Do you know that man Conwell that lives in Philadelphia?" "Oh, yes, I have heard of him." "And do you know that man Jones that lives in that city?" "Yes, I have heard of him." And then he begins to laugh and laugh and says to his friends, "They have done the same thing I did, precisely." And that spoils the whole joke, because you and I have done it.

368

Ninety out of every hundred people here have made that mistake this very day. I say you ought to be rich; you have no right to be poor. To live in Philadelphia and not be rich is a misfortune, and it is doubly a misfortune, because you could have been rich just as well as be poor. Philadelphia furnishes so many opportunities. You ought to be rich. But persons with certain religious prejudice will ask. "How can you spend your time advising the rising generation to give their time to getting money; dollars and cents; the commercial spirit?"

Yet I must say that you ought to spend time getting rich. You and I know there are some things more valuable than money; of course, we do. Ah, yes! By a heart made unspeakably sad by a grave on which the autumn leaves now fall, I know there are some things higher and grander and sublimer than money. Well does the man know, who has suffered, that there are some things sweeter and holier and more sacred than gold. Nevertheless, the man of common sense also knows that there is not any one of these things that is not greatly enhanced by the use of money. Money is power. Love is the grandest thing on God's earth, but fortunate the lover who has plenty of money. Money is power; money has powers; and for a man to say, "I do not want money," is to say, "I do not wish to do any good to my fellowman." It is absurd thus to talk. It is absurd to disconnect them. This is a wonderfully great life, and you ought to spend your time getting money, because of the power there is in money. And yet this religious prejudice is so great that some people think it is a great honor to be one of God's poor. I am looking in the faces of people who think just that way. I heard a man once say in a prayer meeting that he was thankful that he was one of God's poor, and then I silently wondered what his wife would say to that speech, as she took in washing to support the man while he sat and smoked on the veranda. I don't want to see any more of that kind of God's poor. Now, when a man could have been rich just as well and he is now weak because he is poor, he has done some great wrong; he has been untruthful to himself; he has been unkind to his fellowman. We ought to get rich if we can by honorable and Christian methods, and these are the only methods that sweep us quickly toward the goal of riches.

I remember, not many years ago, a young theological student who came into my office and said to me that he thought it was his duty to come in and "labor with me." I asked him what had happened, and he said, "I feel it is my duty to come in and speak to you, sir, and say that the Holy Scriptures declare that money is the root of all evil." I asked him where he found that saying, and he said he found it in the Bible. I asked him whether he had made a new Bible, and he said, no, he had not got a new Bible, that it was in the old Bible. "Well," I said, "If it is in my Bible, I never saw it. Will you please get the textbook and let me see it?" He left the room and soon came stalking in with his Bible open, with all the bigoted pride of the narrow sectarian, who founds his creed on some misinterpretation of Scripture, and he put the Bible down on the table before me and fairly squealed into my ear, "There it is. You can read it for yourself." I said to him, "Young man, you will learn when you get a little older, that you cannot trust another denomination to read the Bible for you." I said, "Now, you belong to another denomination. Please read it to me, and remember that you are taught in a school where emphasis is exegesis." So he took the Bible and read it, "The love of money is the root of all evil." Then he had it right. The Great Book has come back into the esteem and love of the people, and into the respect of the greatest minds of earth, and now you can quote it and rest your life and your death on it without more fear. So, when he quoted right from the Scriptures he quoted the truth. "The love of money is the root of all evil." Oh, that is it. It is the worship of the means instead of the end, though you cannot reach the end without the means. When a man makes an idol of the money instead of the purposes for which it may be used, when he squeezes the dollar until the eagle squeals, then it is made the root of all evil. Think, if you only had the money, what you could do for your wife, your child, and for your home and your city. Think how soon you could endow the Temple College yonder if you only had the money and the disposition to give it; and yet, my friend, people say you and I should not spend the time getting rich. How inconsistent the whole thing is. We ought to be rich, because money has power. I think the best thing for me to do is to illustrate this, for if I say you ought to get rich, I ought, at least, to suggest how it is done. We get a prejudice against rich men because of the lies that are told about them. The lies that are told about Mr. Rockefeller because he has two hundred million dollars, so many believe them; yet how false is the representation of that man to the world. Now little we can tell what is true nowadays when newspapers try to sell their papers entirely on some sensation! The way they lie about the rich men is something terrible, and I do not know that there is anything to illustrate this better than what the newspapers now say about the city of Philadelphia. A young man came to me the other day and said, "If Mr. Rockefeller, as you think, is a good man, why is it that everybody says so much against him?" It is because he has gotten ahead of us; that is the whole of it, just gotten ahead of us. Why is it Mr. Carnegie's criticized so sharply by an envious world? Because he has gotten more than we have. If a man knows more than I know, don't I incline to criticize somewhat his learning? Let a man stand in a pulpit and preach to thousands, and if I have fifteen people in my church, and they're all asleep, don't I criticize him? We always do that to the man who gets ahead of us. Why, the man you are criticizing has one hundred millions, and you have fifty cents, and both of you have just what you are worth. One of the richest men in this country came into my home and sat down in my parlor and said, "Did you see all those lies about my family in the paper?" "Certainly I did; I knew they were lies when I saw them." "Why do they lie about me the way they do?" "Well," I said to him, "if you will give me your cheque for one hundred millions, I will take all the lies along with it." "Well," said he, "I don't see any sense in their thus talking about my family and myself. Conwell, tell me frankly, what do you think the American people think of me?" "Well," said I, "they think you are the blackest-hearted villain that ever trod the soil!" "But what can I do about it?" There is nothing he can do about it, and yet he is one of the sweetest Christian men I ever knew. If you get a hundred millions you will have the lies; you will be lied about, and you can judge your success in any line by the lies that are told about you. I say that you ought to be rich. But there are ever coming to me young men who say, "I would like to go into business, but I cannot." "Why not?" "Because I have no capital to begin on." Capital, capital to begin on! What! young man! Living in Philadelphia and looking at this wealthy generation, all of whom began as poor boys, and you want capital to begin on? It is fortunate for you that you have no capital. I am glad you have no money. I pity a rich man's son. A rich man's son in these days of ours occupies a very difficult position. They are to be pitied. A rich man's son cannot know the very best things in human life. He cannot. The statistics of Massachusetts show use that not one out of seventeen rich men's sons ever die rich. They are raised in luxury, they die in poverty. Even if a rich man's son retains his father's money, even then, he cannot know the best things of life.

A young man in our college yonder asked me to formulate for him what I thought was the happiest hour in a man's history, and I studied it long and came back convinced that the happiest hour that any man ever sees in any earthly matter is when a young man takes his bride over the threshold of the door, for the first time, of the house he himself has earned and built, when he turns to his bride and with an eloquence greater than any language of mine, he says to his wife, "My loved one, I earned this home myself; I earned it all. It is all mine, and I divide it with thee." That is the grandest moment a human heart may ever see. But a rich man's son cannot know that. He goes into a finer mansion, it may be, but he is obliged to go through the house and say, "Mother gave me this, mother gave me that, my mother gave me that, my mother gave me that," until his wife wishes she had married his mother. Oh, I pity a rich man's son. I do, until he gets so far along in his dudeism that he gets his arms up like that and can't get them down. Didn't you ever see any of them astray at Atlantic City? I saw one of these scarecrows once and I never tire thinking about it. I was at Niagara Falls lecturing, and after the lecture I went to the hotel, and when I went up to the desk, there stood there a millionaire's son from New York. He was an indescribable specimen of anthropologic impotency; he carried a gold-headed cane under his arm, more in its head than he had in his. I do not believe, I could describe the young man if I should try. But still, I must say that he wore an eyeglass he could not see through; patent leather shoes he could not walk in and pants he could not sit down in; dressed like a grasshopper! Well, this human cricket came up to the clerk's desk, just as I came in. He adjusted his unseeing eyeglass in this wise and lisped to the clerk, because it's "Hinglish, you know," to lisp, "Thir, thir, will you have the kindness to fuhnish me with thome papah and thome enveloth!" The clerk measured that man quick, and he pulled out a drawer and took some envelopes and paper and cast them across the counter and turned away to his books. You should have seen that specimen of humanity when the paper and envelopes came across the counter; he whose wants had always been anticipated by servants. He adjusted his unseeing eyeglass and he yelled after that clerk, "Come back here, thir, come right back here. Now, thir, will you order a thervant to take that papah

372

and thothe envelopth and carry them to yondah dethk." Oh, the poor miserable, contemptible American monkey. He couldn't carry paper and envelopes twenty feet. I suppose he could not get his arms down. I have no pity for such travesties of human nature. If you have no capital, I am glad of it. You don't need capital; you need common sense, not copper cents.

A.T. Stewart, the great princely merchant of New York, the richest man in America in his time, was a poor boy; he had a dollar and a half and went into the mercantile business. But he lost eighty-seven and a half cents of his first dollar and a half because he bought some needles and thread and buttons to sell, which people didn't want.

Are you poor? It is because you are not wanted and are left on your own hands. There was the great lesson. Apply it whichever way you will it comes to every single person's life, young or old. He did not know what people needed, and consequently bought something they didn't want and had the goods left on his hands a dead loss. A.T. Stewart learned there the great lesson of his mercantile life and said, "I will never buy anything more until I first learn what the people want; then I'll make the purchase." He went around to the doors and asked them what they did want, and when he found out what they wanted he invested his sixty two and a half cents and began to supply "a known demand." I care not what your profession or occupation in life may be; I care not whether you are a lawyer, a doctor, a housekeeper, a teacher, or whatever else, the principle is precisely the same. We must know what the world needs first and then invest ourselves to supply that need, and success is almost certain. A.T. Stewart went on until he was worth forty millions. "Well," you will say, "a man can do that in New York, but cannot do it here in Philadelphia." The statistics very carefully gathered in New York in 1889 showed one hundred and seven millionaires in the city worth over ten millions apiece. It was remarkable and people think they must go there to get rich. Out of that one hundred and seven millionaires only seven of them made their money in New York, and the others moved to New York after their fortunes were made, and sixty-seven out of the remaining hundred made their fortunes in towns of less than six thousand people, and the richest man in the country at that time lived in a town of thirty-five hundred inhabitants, and always lived there and never moved away. It is not so much where you are as what you are. But at the same time, if the largeness of the city comes into the problem, then remember it is the smaller city that furnishes the great opportunity to make the millions of money. The best illustration that I can give, is in reference to John Jacob Astor, who was a poor boy and who made all the money of the Astor family. He made more than his successors have ever earned, and yet he once held a mortgage on a millinery store in New York, and because the people could not make enough money to pay the interest and the rent, he foreclosed the mortgage and took possession of the store and went into partnership with the man who had failed. He kept the same stock, did not give him a dollar capital, and he left him alone and went out and sat down upon a bench in the park. Out there on that bench in the park he had the most important, and to my mind, the pleasantest part of that partnership business. He was watching the ladies as they went by; and where is the man that wouldn't get rich at that business? But when John Jacob Astor saw a lady pass, with her shoulders back and her head up, as if she did not care if the whole world looked on her, he studied her bonnet; and before that bonnet was out of sight he knew the shape of the frame and the color of the trimmings, the curl of the something on a bonnet. Sometimes I try to describe a woman's bonnet, but it is of little use, for it would be out of style tomorrow night. So John Jacob Astor went to the store and said: "Now, put in the show window just such a bonnet as I describe to you because," said he "I have just seen a lady who likes just such a bonnet. Do not make up any more till I come back." And he went out again and sat on that bench in the park, and another lady of a different form and complexion passed him with a bonnet of different shape and color, of course. "Now," said he, "put such a bonnet as that in the show window." He didn't fill his show window with hats and bonnets which drive people away and then sit in the back of the store and bawl because the people go somewhere else to trade. He didn't put a hat or bonnet in that show window, the like of which he had not seen before it was made up.

In our city, especially, there are great opportunities for manufacturing, and the time has come when the line is drawn very sharply between the stockholders of the factory and their employees. Now, friends, there has also come a discouraging gloom upon this country and the laboring men are beginning to feel that they are being held down by a crust over their heads through which they find it impossible to break, and the aristocratic money-owner himself is so far above that he will never descend to their assistance. That is the thought that is in the minds of our people. But, friends, never in the history of our country was there an opportunity so great for the poor man to get rich as there is now in the city of Philadelphia. The very fact that they get discouraged is what prevents them from getting rich. That is all there is to it. The road is open, and let us keep it open between the poor and the rich. I know that the labor unions have two great problems to contend with and there is only one way to solve them. The labor unions are doing as much to prevent its solving as are the capitalists today, and there are positively two sides to it. The labor union has two difficulties, the first one is that it began to make a labor scale for all classes on a par, and they scale down a man that can earn five dollars a day to two and a half a day, in order to level up to him an imbecile that cannot earn fifty cents a day. That is one of the most dangerous and discouraging things for the working man. He cannot get the results of his work if he does better work or higher work or work longer; that is a dangerous thing, and in order to get every laboring man free and every American equal to every other American, let the laboring man ask what he is worth and get it, not let any capitalist say to him: "You shall work for me for half of what you are worth;" nor let any labor organization say "You shall work for the capitalist for half your worth." Be a man, be independent, and then shall the laboring man find the road ever open from poverty to wealth. The other difficulty that the labor union has to consider, and this problem they have to solve themselves, is the kind of orators who come and talk to them about the oppressive rich. I can, in my dreams, recite the oration I have heard again and again under such circumstances. My life has been with the laboring man. I am a laboring man myself. I have often, in their assemblies, heard the speech of the man who has been invited to address the labor union. The man who gets up before the assembled company of honest laboring men and he begins by saying: "Oh, you honest, industrious laboring men, who have furnished all the capital of the world, who have built all the palaces and constructed all the railroads and covered the ocean with her steamships. Oh, you laboring men! You are nothing but slaves; you are ground down in the dust by the capitalist, who is gloating over you, as he enjoys his beautiful estates and as he has his banks filled with gold, and every dollar he owns is coined out of the heart's blood of the honest laboring man." Now, that is a lie, and you know it is a lie; and yet that is the kind of speech that they are all the time hearing, representing the capitalists as wicked and the laboring men so enslaved. Why, how wrong it is! Let the man who loves his flag and believes in American principles endeavor with all his soul to bring the capitalist and the laboring man together until they stand side by side, and arm in arm, and work for the common good of humanity.

He is an enemy to his country who sets capital against labor or labor against capital.

Suppose I were to go down through this audience and ask you to introduce me to the great inventors who live here in Philadelphia. "The inventors of Philadelphia," you would say, "Why we don't have any in Philadelphia. It is too slow to invent anything." But you do have just as great inventors, and they are here in this audience, as ever invented a machine. But the probability is that the greatest inventor to benefit the world with his discovery is some person, perhaps some lady, who thinks she could not invent anything. Did you ever study the history of invention and see how strange it was that the man who made the greatest discovery did it without any previous idea that he was an inventor? Who are the great inventors? They are persons with plain, straightforward common sense, who saw a need in the world and immediately applied themselves to study that need. If you want to invent anything, don't try to find it in the wheels in your head nor in the wheels in your machine, but first find out what the people need, and then apply yourself to that need, and this leads to invention on the part of the people you would not dream of before. The great inventors are simply great men; the greater the man the more simple the man, and the more simple a machine, the more valuable it is. Did you ever know a really great man? His ways are so simple, so common, so plain, that you think any one could do what he is doing. So it is with the great men the world over. If you know a really great man, a neighbor of yours, you can go right up to him and say, "How are you, Jim, good morning, Sam." Of course you can, for they are always so simple.

When I wrote the life of General Garfield, one of his neighbors took me to his back door, and shouted, "Jim, Jim, Jim!" and very soon "Jim" came to the door and General Garfield let me in, one of the grandest men of our century. The great men of the world are ever so. I was down in Virginia and went up to an educational institution and was directed to a man who was setting out a tree. I approached him and said, "Do you think it would be possible for me to see General Robert E. Lee, the President of the University?" He said, "Sir, I am General Lee." Of course, when you meet such a man, so noble a man as that, you will find him a simple, plain man. Greatness is always just so modest and great inventions are simple.

I asked a class in school once who were the great inventors, and a little girl popped up and said, "Columbus." Well, now, she was not so far wrong. Columbus bought a farm and he carried on that farm just as I carried on my father's farm. He took a hoe, and went out and sat down on a rock. But Columbus, as he sat upon that shore and looked out upon the ocean, noticed that the ships, as they sailed away, sank deeper into the sea the farther they went. And since that time some other "Spanish ships" have sunk into the sea. But as Columbus noticed that the tops of the masts dropped down out of sight, he said, "That is the way it is with this hoe handle; if you go around this hoe handle, the farther off you go the farther down you go. I can sail around to the East Indies." How plain it all was. How simple the mind-majestic, like the simplicity of a mountain in its greatness. Who are the great inventors? They are ever the simple, plain, everyday people who see the need and set about to supply it.

I was once lecturing in North Carolina, and the cashier of the bank sat directly behind a lady who wore a very large hat. I said to that audience, "Your wealth is too near to you; you are looking right over it." He whispered to his friend, "Well, then, my wealth is in that hat." A little later, as he wrote me, I said, "Wherever there is a human need there is a greater fortune than a mine can furnish." He caught my thought, and drew up his plan for a better hatpin than was in the hat before him, and the pin is now being manufactured. He was offered fifty-five thousand dollars for his patent. That man made his fortune before he got out of that hall. This is the whole question: Do you see a need?

I remember well a man up in my native hills, a poor man, who for twenty years was helped by the town in his poverty, who owned a wide-spreading maple tree that covered the poor man's cottage like a benediction from on high. I remember that tree, for in the spring; there were some roguish boys around that neighborhood when I was young; in the spring of the year the man would put a bucket there and the spouts to catch the maple sap, and I remember where that bucket was; and when I was young the boys were, oh, so mean, that they went to that tree before that man had gotten out of bed in the morning, and after he had gone to bed at night, and drank up that sweet sap. I could swear they did it. He didn't make a great deal of maple sugar from that tree. But one day he made the sugar so white and crystalline that the visitor did not believe it was maple sugar; thought maple sugar must be red or black. He said to the old man: "Why don't you make it that way and sell it for confection?" The old man caught his thought and invented the "rock maple crystal," and before that patent expired, he had ninety thousand dollars and had built a beautiful palace on the site of that tree. After forty years owning that tree, he awoke to find it had fortunes of money indeed in it. And many of us are right by the tree that has a fortune for us, and we own it, possess it, do what we will with it, but we do not learn its value because we do not see the human need; and in these discoveries and inventions, this is one of the most romantic things of life.

I have received letters from all over the country and from England, where I have lectured, saying that they have discovered this and that, and one man out in Ohio took me through his great factories last spring, and said that they cost him $680,000, and said he, "I was not worth a cent in the world when I heard your lecture, 'Acres of Diamonds'; but I made up my mind to stop right here and make my fortune here, and here it is." He showed me through his unmortgaged possessions. And this is a continual experience now as I travel through the country, after these many years. I mention this incident, not to boast, but to show you that you can do the same if you will.

Who are the great inventors? I remember a good illustration in a man who used to live in East Brookfield, Mass. He was a shoemaker, and he was out of work, and he sat around the house until his wife told him to "go outdoors." And he did what every husband is compelled by law to do; he obeyed his wife. And he went out and sat down on an ash barrel in his back yard. Think of it. Stranded on an ash barrel and the enemy in possession of the house! As he sat on that ash barrel, he looked down into that little brook which ran through the back yard into the meadows, and he saw a little trout go flashing up the stream and hiding under the bank. I do not suppose he thought of Tennyson's beautiful poem:

"I chatter, chatter, as I flow,
To join the brimming river;
For men may come, and men may go,
But I go on forever."

But as this man looked into the brook, he leaped off that ash barrel and managed to catch the trout with his fingers, and sent it to Worcester. They wrote back that they would, give him a five dollar bill for another such trout as that, not that it was worth that much, but they wished to help the poor man. So this shoemaker and his wife, now perfectly united, that five dollar bill in prospect, went out to get another trout. They went up the stream to its source and down to the brimming river, but not another trout could they find in the whole stream; and so they came home disconsolate and went to the minister. The minister didn't know how trout grew, but he pointed the way. Said he, "Get Seth Green's book, and that will give you the information you want." They did so, and found all about the culture of trout. They found that a trout lays thirty-six hundred eggs every year and every trout gains a quarter of a pound every year, so that in four years a little trout will furnish four tons per annum to sell to the market at fifty cents a pound. When they found that, they said they didn't believe any such story as that, but if they could get five dollars apiece they could make something. And right in that same back yard with the coal sifter up stream and window screen down the stream, they began the culture of trout. They afterwards moved to the Hudson, and since then he has become the authority in the United States upon the raising of fish, and he has been next to the highest on the United States Fish Commission in Washington. My lesson is that man's wealth was out there in his back yard for twenty years, but he didn't see it until his wife drove him out with a mop stick.

I remember meeting personally a poor carpenter of Hingham, Massachusetts, who was out of work and in poverty. His wife also drove him out of doors. He sat down on the shore and whittled a soaked shingle into a wooden chain. His children quarreled over it in the evening, and while he was whittling a second one, a neighbor came along and said, "Why don't you whittle toys if you can carve like that?" He said, "I don't know what to make!" There is the whole thing. His neighbor said to him, "Why don't you ask your own children?" Said he, "What is the use of doing that? My children are different from other people's children." I used to see people like that when I taught school. The next morning when his boy came down the stairway, he said, "Sam, what do you want for a toy?" "I want a wheelbarrow." When his little girl came down, he asked her what she wanted, and she said, "I want a little doll's washstand, a little doll's carriage, a little doll's umbrella," and went on with a whole lot of things that would have taken his lifetime to supply. He consulted his own children right there in his own house and began to whittle out toys to please them. He began with his jackknife, and made those unpainted Hingham toys. He is the richest man in the entire New England States, if Mr. Lawson is to be trusted in his statement concerning such things, and yet that man's fortune was made by consulting his own children in his own house. You don't need to go out of your own house to find out what to invent or what to make. I always talk too long on this subject.

I would like to meet the great men who are here tonight. The great men! We don't have any great men in Philadelphia. Great men! You say that they all come from London, or San Francisco, or Rome, or Manayunk, or anywhere else but here; anywhere else but Philadelphia; and yet, in fact, there are just as great men in Philadelphia as in any city of its size. There are great men and women in this audience. Great men, I have said, are very simple men, just as many great men here as are to be found anywhere. The greatest error in judging great men is that we think that they always hold an office. The world knows nothing of its greatest men. Who are the great men of the world? The young man and young woman may well ask the question. It is not necessary that, they should hold an office, and yet that is the popular idea. That is the idea we teach now in our high schools and common schools, that the great men are those who hold some high office, and unless we change that very soon and do away with that prejudice, we are going to change to an empire. There is no question about it. We must teach that men are great only on their intrinsic value and not on the position that they may incidentally happen to occupy. And yet, don't blame the young men saying that they are going to be great when they get into some official position. I ask this audience again, who of you are going to be great? Says a young man, "I am going to be great." "When are you going to be great?" "When I am elected to some political office." Won't you learn the lesson, young man, that it is prima facie evidence of littleness to hold public office under our form of government? Think of it. This is a government of the people, and by the people, and for the people, and not for the office-holder, and if the people in this country rule as they always should rule, an office-holder is only the servant of the people, and the Bible says, "the servant cannot be greater than his master." The Bible says, "He that is sent cannot be greater than him who sent him." In this country, the people are the masters, and the office-holders can never be greater than the people; they should be honest servants of the people, but they are not our greatest men. Young man, remember that you never heard of a great man holding any political office in this country unless he took that office at the expense of himself. It is a loss to every great man to take a public office in our country. Bear this in mind, young man, that you cannot be made great by a political election.

Another young man says, "I am going to be a great man in Philadelphia some time." "Is that so? When are you going to be great?" "When there comes another war! When we get into difficulty with Mexico, or England, or Russia, or Japan, or with Spain again over Cuba, or with New Jersey, I will march up to the cannon's mouth, and amid the glistening bayonets I will tear down their flag from its staff, and I will come home with stars on my shoulders, and hold every office in the gift of the government, and I will be great." "No, you won't! No, you won't; that is no evidence of true greatness, young man." But don't blame that young man for thinking that way; that is the way he is taught in the high school. That is the way history is taught in college. He is taught, that the men who held the office, did all the fighting.

I remember, we had a Peace Jubilee here in Philadelphia soon after the Spanish war. Perhaps some of these visitors think we should not have had it until now in Philadelphia, and as the great procession was going up Broad street, I was told that the tally ho coach stopped right in front of my house, and on the coach was Hobson, and all the people threw up their hats and swung their handkerchiefs, and shouted "Hurrah for Hobson!" I would have yelled too, because he deserves much more of his country than he has ever received. But suppose I go into the High School tomorrow and ask, "Boys, who sunk the Merrimac?" If they answer me "Hobson," they tell me seven-eighths of a lie, seven-eighths of a lie, because there were eight men who sunk the Merrimac. The other seven men, by virtue of their positions, were continually exposed to the Spanish fire, while Hobson, as an officer, might reasonably be behind the smokestack. Why, my friends, in this intelligent audience gathered here tonight I do not believe I could find a single person that can name the other seven men who were with Hobson. Why do we teach history in that way? We ought to teach that however humble the station a man may occupy, if he does his full duty in his place, he is just as much entitled to the American people's honor as is a king upon a throne. We do teach it as a mother did her little boy in New York when he said, "Mamma, what great building is that?" "That is General Grant's tomb." "Who was General Grant?" "He was the man who put down the rebellion." Is that the way to teach history?

Do you think we would have gained a victory if it had depended on General Grant alone? Oh, no. Then why is there a tomb on the Hudson at all? Why, not simply because General Grant was personally a great man himself, but that tomb is there because he was a representative man and represented two hundred thousand men who went down to death for their nation and many of them as great as General Grant. That is why that beautiful tomb stands on the heights over the Hudson.

I remember an incident that will illustrate this, the only one that I can give tonight. I am ashamed of it, but I don't dare leave it out. I close my eyes now; I look back through the years to 1863; I can see my native town in the Berkshire Hills, I can see that cattleshow ground filled with people; I can see that church there and the town hall crowded, and hear bands playing, and see flags flying and handkerchiefs streaming; well, do I recall at this moment that day. The people had turned out to receive a company of soldiers, and that company came marching up on the Common. They had served out one term in the Civil War and had re-enlisted, and they were being received by their native townsmen. I was but a boy, but I was captain of that company, puffed out with pride on that day; why, a cambric needle would have burst me all to pieces. As I marched on the Common at the head of my company, there was not a man more proud than I. We marched into the town hall and then they seated my soldiers down in the center of the house and I took my place down on the front seat, and then the town officers filed through the great throng of people, who stood close and packed in that little hall. They came up on the platform, formed a half circle around it, and the mayor of the town, the "chairman of the Selectmen" in New England, took his seat in the middle of that half circle. He was an old man, his hair was gray; he never held an office before in his life. He thought that an office was all he needed to be a truly great man, and when he came up he adjusted his powerful spectacles and glanced calmly around the audience with amazing dignity. Suddenly his eyes fell upon me, and then the good old man came right forward and invited me to come up on the stand with the town officers. Invited me up on the stand! No town officer ever took notice of me before I went to war. Now, I should not say that. One town officer was there who advised the teacher to "whale" me, but I mean no "honorable mention." So I was invited up on the stand with the town officers. I took my seat and let my sword fall on the floor, and folded my arms across my breast and waited to be received. Napoleon the Fifth! Pride goes before destruction and a fall. When I had gotten my seat and all became silent through the hall, the chairman of the Selectmen arose and came forward with great dignity to the table, and we all supposed he would introduce the Congregational minister, who was the only orator in the town, and who would give the oration to the returning soldiers. But, friends, you should have seen the surprise that ran over that audience when they discovered that this old farmer was going to deliver that oration himself. He had never made a speech in his life before, but he fell into the same error that others have fallen into, he seemed to think that the office would make him an orator. So he had written out a speech and walked up and down the pasture until he had learned it by heart and frightened the cattle, and he brought that manuscript with him, and taking it from his pocket, he spread it carefully upon the table. Then he adjusted his spectacles to be sure that he might see it, and walked far back on the platform and then stepped forward like this. He must have studied the subject much, for he assumed an elocutionary attitude; he rested heavily upon his left heel, slightly advanced the right foot, threw back his shoulders, opened the organs of speech, and advanced his right hand at an angle of forty-five degrees. As he stood in that elocutionary attitude this is just the way that speech went, this is it precisely. Some of my friends have asked me if I do not exaggerate it, but I could not exaggerate it. Impossible I This is the way it went; although I am not here for the story but the lesson that is back of it.

"Fellow citizens." As soon as he heard his voice, his hand began to shake like that, his knees began to tremble, and then he shook all over. He coughed and choked and finally came around to look at his manuscript. Then he began again: "Fellow citizens, We. . are. . we are. . we are. . we are. . . . We are very happy. . we are very happy. . we are very happy. . to welcome back to their native town these soldiers who have fought and bled and come back to their native town. We are especially. . we are especially. . we are especially. . we are especially pleased to see with us today this young hero (that meant me), this young hero who in imagination (friends, remember, he said "imagination," for if he had not said that, I would not be egotistical enough to refer to it), this young hero who, in imagination, we have seen leading. . we have seen leading. . we have seen leading his troops on to the deadly breach. We have seen his shining. . his shining. . we have seen his shining. . we have seen his shining. . his shining sword flashing in the sunlight as he shouted to his troops, Come on!"

Oh, dear, dear, dear, dear! How little that good, old man knew about war. If he had known anything about war, he ought to have known what any soldier in this audience knows is true, that it is next to a crime for an officer of infantry ever in time of danger to go ahead of his men. I, with my shining sword flashing in the sunlight, shouting to my troops, "Come on." I never did it. Do you suppose I would go ahead of my men to be shot in the front by the enemy and in the back by my own men? That is no place for an officer. The place for the officer is behind the private soldier in actual fighting. How often, as a staff officer, I rode down the line when the Rebel cry and yell was coming out of the woods, sweeping along over the fields, and shouted, "Officers to the rear! Officers to the rear!" and then every officer goes behind the line of battle, and the higher the officer's rank, the farther behind he goes. Not because he is any the less brave, but because the laws of war require that to be done. If the general came up on the, front line and were killed you would lose your battle anyhow, because he has the plan of the battle in his brain and must be kept in comparative safety. I, with my "shining sword flashing in the sunlight." Ah! There sat in the hall that day men who had given that boy their last hardtack, who had carried him on their backs through deep rivers. But some were not there; they had gone down to death for their country. The speaker mentioned them, but they were but little noticed, and yet they had gone down to death for their country, gone down for a cause they believed was right and still believe was right, though I grant to the other side the same that I ask for myself. Yet these men who had actually died for their country were little noticed, and the hero of the hour was this boy. Why was he the hero? Simply because that man fell into the same foolishness. This boy was an officer, and those were only private soldiers. I learned a lesson that I will never forget. Greatness consists not in holding some office; greatness really consists in doing some great deed with little means, in the accomplishment of vast purposes from the private ranks of life; that is true greatness. He who can give to this people better streets, better homes, better schools, better churches, more religion, more of happiness, more of God, he that can be a blessing to the community in which he lives tonight will he great anywhere, but he who cannot be a blessing where he now lives will never be great anywhere on the face of God's earth. "We live in deeds, not years; in feeling, not in figures on a dial; in thoughts, not breaths; we should count time by heart throbs, in the cause of right." Bailey says, "He most lives who thinks most."

If you forget everything I have said to you, do not forget this, because it contains more in two lines than all I have said. Bailey says, "He most lives who thinks most, who feels the noblest, and who acts the best."

A MESSAGE TO GARCIA

By ELBERT HUBBARD

This is not a speech. It originally appeared as an article in the March, 1899, Philistine Magazine. It is given here because it is representative of the messages popular in the business world.

About a million and a half copies of this article were distributed by the New York Central Railroad. It has been translated into all written languages.

During the war between Russia and Japan, every Russian soldier who went to the front was given a copy of the Message to Garcia.

The Japanese, finding the booklets in possession of the Russian prisoners, concluded that it must be a good thing, and accordingly translated it into Japanese.

And on an order of the Mikado, a copy was given to every man in the employ of the Japanese Government, soldier or civilian.

Over forty million copies of A Message to Garcia have been printed. This is said to be a larger circulation than any other literary venture has ever attained during the lifetime of the author, in all history.

A MESSAGE TO GARCIA

By ELBERT HUBBARD

I n all this Cuban business there is one man stands out on the horizon of my memory like Mars at Perihelion.

When war broke out between Spain and the United States, it was very necessary to communicate quickly with the leader of the Insurgents. Garcia was somewhere in the mountain fastnesses of Cuba; no one knew where. No mail or telegraph message could reach him. The President must secure his cooperation, and quickly.

What to do!

Someone said to the President, "There is a fellow by the name of Rowan will find Garcia for you, if anybody can."

Rowan was sent for and given a letter to be delivered to Garcia. How the "fellow by the name of Rowan" took the letter, sealed it up in an oilskin pouch, strapped it over his heart, in four days landed by night off the coast of Cuba from an open boat, disappeared into the jungle, and in three weeks came out on the other side of the Island, having traversed a hostile country on foot, and delivered his letter to Garcia, are things I have no special desire now to tell in detail. The point that I wish to make is this: McKinley gave Rowan a letter to be delivered to Garcia; Rowan took the letter and did not ask, "Where is he at?"

By the Eternal! there is a man whose form should be cast in deathless bronze and the statue placed in every college of the land. It is not book learning young men need or instruction about this and that, but a stiffening of the vertebra which will cause them to be loyal to a trust, to act promptly, concentrate their energies; do the thing, "Carry a message to Garcia."

General Garcia is dead now, but there are other Garcias. No man who has endeavored to carry out an enterprise where many hands were needed, but has been well-nigh appalled at times by the imbecility of the average man, the inability or unwillingness to concentrate on a thing and do it.

Slipshod assistance, foolish inattention, dowdy indifference, and half-hearted work seem the rule; and no man succeeds, unless by hook or crook, or threat he forces or bribes other men to assist him; or perhaps, God in His goodness performs a miracle, and sends him an Angel of Light for an assistant.

You, reader, put this matter to a test. You are sitting now in your office; six clerks are within call. Summon any one and make this request: "Please look in the encyclopedia and make a brief memorandum for me concerning the life of Correggio."

Will the clerk quietly say, "Yes, sir," and go to the task? On your life he will not. He will look at you out of a fishy eye and ask one or more of the following questions:

Who was he?

Which encyclopedia?

Where is the encyclopedia?

Was I hired for that?

Don't you mean Bismarck?

What's the matter with Charlie doing it?

Is he dead?

Is there any hurry?

Sha'n't I bring you the book and let you look it up yourself?

What do you want to know for?

And I will lay you ten to one that after you have answered the questions, and explained how to find the information, and why you want it, the clerk will go off and get one of the other clerks to help him try to find Correggio, and then come back and tell you there is no such man. Of course I may lose my bet, but according to the Law of Averages I will not. Now, if you are wise, you will not bother to explain to your "assistant" that Correggio is indexed under the C's, not in the K's, but you will smile very sweetly and say, "Never mind," and go look it up yourself. And this incapacity for independent action, this moral stupidity, this infirmity of the will, this unwillingness to cheerfully catch hold and lift; these are the things that put pure Socialism so far into the future. If men will not act for themselves, what will they do when the benefit of their effort is for all?

A first mate with a knotted club seems necessary; and the dread of getting "the bounce" Saturday night, holds many a worker to his place. Advertise for a stenographer, and nine out of ten who apply, can neither spell nor punctuate and do not think it necessary to. Can such a one write a letter to Garcia?

"You see that bookkeeper," said the foreman to me in a large factory.

"Yes; what about him?"

"Well, he's a fine accountant, but if I'd send him uptown on an errand, he might accomplish the errand all right, and on the other hand, might stop at four saloons on the way, and when he got to Main Street would forget what he had been sent for."

Can such a man be entrusted to carry a message to Garcia?

We have recently been hearing much maudlin sympathy expressed for the "downtrodden denizens of the sweatshop," and the " homeless wanderer searching for honest employment," and with it all often go many hard words for the men in power.

Nothing is said about the employer who grows old before his time in a vain attempt to get frowsy ne'er-do-wells to do intelligent work; and his long, patient striving after "help" that does nothing but loaf when his back is turned. In every store and factory, there is a constant weeding out process going on. The employer is constantly sending away "help" that have shown their incapacity to further the interests of the business and others are being taken on. No matter how good times are, this sorting continues; only, if times are hard and work is scarce, the sorting is done finer; but out, and forever out, the incompetent and unworthy go. It is the survival of the fittest. Self-interest prompts every employer to keep the best, those who can carry a message to Garcia.

I know one man of really brilliant parts who has not the ability to manage a business of his own, and yet who is absolutely worthless to anyone else, because he carries with him constantly the insane suspicion that his employer is oppressing, or intending to oppress, him. He cannot give orders, and he will not receive them. Should a message be given him to take to Garcia, his answer would probably be "Take it yourself!"

Tonight this man walks the streets looking for work, the wind whistling through his threadbare coat. No one who knows him dare employ him, for he is a regular firebrand of discontent. He is

391

impervious to reason, and the only thing that can impress him is the toe of a thick-soled number nine boot.

Of course, I know that one so morally deformed is no less to be pitied than a physical cripple; but in our pitying let us drop a tear, too, for the men who are striving to carry on a great enterprise, whose working hours are not limited by the whistle, and whose hair is fast turning white through the struggle to hold in line dowdy indifference, slipshod imbecility, and heartless ingratitude which, but for their enterprise, would be both hungry and homeless.

Have I put the matter too strongly? Possibly I have; but when all the world has gone a slumming, I wish to speak a word of sympathy for the man who succeeds, the man who, against great odds, has directed the efforts of others, and having succeeded, finds there's nothing in it, nothing but bare board and clothes. I have carried a dinner pail and worked for day's wages, and I have also been an employer of labor, and I know there is something to be said on both sides. There is no excellence, per se, in poverty; rags are no recommendation; and all employers are not rapacious and high-handed, any more than all poor men are virtuous. My heart goes out to the man who does his work when the "boss" is away, as well as when he is at home; and the man who, when given a letter for Garcia, quietly takes the missive, without asking any idiotic questions, and with no lurking intention of chucking it into the nearest sewer, or of doing aught else but deliver it, never gets "laid off," nor has to go on a strike for higher wages. Civilization is one long, anxious search for just such individuals. Anything such a man asks shall be granted. He is wanted in every city, town, and village, in every office, shop, store, and factory. The world cries out for such; he is needed and needed badly; the man who can "Carry a Message to Garcia."

AS A MAN THINKETH

By JAMES ALLEN

This little essay, "As A Man Thinketh," is exercising a commanding, influence in many lives today.

Read it, not hastily, but thoughtfully and often.

You will find in it not a single reference to speaking but you will discover much that has to do with building the prime requisites of a successful speaker: an abiding self-confidence and sincerity and personality.

All effective speaking and real leadership of men issues from effective thinking.

We have known of many cases in which this little message has become a prodigious power in people's lives.

AS A MAN THINKETH

By JAMES ALLEN

THOUGHT AND CHARACTER

T he aphorism, "As a man thinketh in his heart so is he," not only embraces the whole of a man's being, but is so comprehensive as to reach out to every condition and circumstance of his life. A man is literally what he thinks, his character being the complete sum of all his thoughts.

As the plant springs from, and could not be without, the seed, so every act of a man springs from the hidden seeds of thought and could not have appeared without them. This applies equally to those acts called "spontaneous" and "unpremeditated" as to those which are deliberately executed.

Act is the blossom of thought, and joy and suffering are its fruits; thus does a man garner in the sweet and bitter fruitage of his own husbandry.

"Thought in the mind hath made us. What we are
By thought was wrought and built. If a man's mind
Hath evil thoughts, pain comes on him as comes
The wheel the ox behind. . .
. . .If one endure
In purity of thought, joy follows him
As his own shadowy-sure."

Man is a growth by law, and not a creation by artifice, and cause and effect is as absolute and undeviating in the hidden realm of thought as in the world of visible and material things. A noble and Godlike character is not a thing of favor or chance, but is the natural result of continuous effort and right thinking, the effect of long cherished association with Godlike thought. An ignoble and bestial character, by the same process, is the result of the continued harboring of groveling thoughts.

Man is made or unmade by himself; in the armory of thought he forges the weapons by which he destroys himself; he also fashions the tools with which he builds for himself heavenly mansions of joy and strength and peace. By the right choice and true application of thought, man ascends to the Divine Perfection; by the abuse and wrong application of thought, he descends below the level of the beast. Between these two extremes are all the grades of character, and man is their maker and master.

Of all the beautiful truths pertaining to the soul which have been restored and brought to light in this age, none is more gladdening or fruitful of divine promise and confidence than this; that man is the master of thought, the molder of character and the maker and shaper of condition, environment and destiny.

As a being of Power, Intelligence and Love and the lord of his own thoughts, man holds the key to every situation; and contains within himself that transforming and regenerative agency by which he may make himself what he wills.

Man is always the master, even in his weakest and most abandoned state; but in his weakness and degradation, he is the foolish master who misgoverns his "household." When he begins to reflect upon his condition, and to search diligently for the Law upon which his being is established, he then becomes the wise master, directing his energies with intelligence, and fashioning his thoughts to fruitful issues. Such is the conscious master, and man can only thus become by discovering within himself the laws of thought; which discovery is totally a matter of application, self-analysis and experience.

Only by such searching and mining are gold and diamonds obtained, and man can find every truth connected with his being, if he will dig deep into the mine of his soul; and that he is the maker of his character, the molder of his life, and the builder of his destiny, he may unerringly prove, if he will watch, control and alter his thoughts, tracing their effects upon himself, upon others and upon his life and circumstances, linking cause and effect by patient practice and investigation and utilizing his every experience, even to most trivial, everyday occurrence, as a means of obtaining that knowledge of himself which is Understanding, Wisdom, Power. In this direction, as in no other, is the law absolute that "He that seeketh findeth; and to him that knocketh it shall be opened"; for only by patience, practice and ceaseless importunity can a man enter the Door of the Temple of Knowledge.

EFFECT OF THOUGHT ON CIRCUMSTANCES

A man's mind may be likened to a garden, which may he intelligently cultivated or allowed to run wild; but whether cultivated or neglected, it must and will *bring forth*. If no useful seeds are put into it, then an abundance of useless weed seeds will *fall* therein and will continue to produce their kind.

Just as the gardener cultivates his plot, keeping it free from weeds, and growing the flowers and fruits which he requires, so may a man tend the garden of his mind, weeding out all the wrong, useless and impure thoughts, and cultivating toward perfection the flowers and fruits of right, useful and pure thoughts. By pursuing this process, a man sooner or later discovers that he is the master gardener of his soul, the director of his life. He also reveals, within himself, the laws of thought, and understands, with ever increasing accuracy, how the thought forces and mind elements operate in the shaping of his character, circumstances and destiny.

Thought and character are one, and as character can only manifest and discover itself through environment and circumstance, the outer conditions of a person's life will always be found to be harmoniously related to his inner state. This does not mean that a man's circumstances at any given time are an indication of his entire character, but that those circumstances are so intimately connected with some vital thought - element within himself that, for the time being, they are indispensable to his development.

Every man is where he is by law of his being; the thoughts, which he has built into his character, have brought him there, and in the arrangement of his life there is no element of chance, but all is the result of a law, which cannot err. This is just as true of those who feel "out of harmony" with their surroundings as of those who are contented with them.

As a progressive and evolving being, man is where he is, that he may learn, that he may grow; and as he learns the spiritual lesson, which any circumstance contains for him, it passes away and gives place to other circumstances.

Man is buffeted by circumstances so long as he believes himself to be the creature of outside conditions, but when he realizes that he is a creative power, and that he may command the hidden soil and seeds of his being out of which circumstances grow, he then becomes the rightful master of himself.

That circumstances grow out of thought every man knows who has for any length of time practiced self-control and self-purification, for he will have noticed that the alteration in his circumstances has been in exact ratio with his altered mental condition. So true is this that when a man earnestly applies himself to remedy the defects in his character, and makes swift and marked progress, he passes rapidly through a succession of vicissitudes.

The soul attracts that which it secretly harbors; that which it loves, and also that which it fears; it reaches the height of its cherished aspirations; it falls to the level of its unchastened desires, and circumstances are the means by which the soul receives its own.

Every thought seed sown or allowed to fall into the mind, and to take root there, produces its own, blossoming sooner or later into act, and bearing its own fruitage of opportunity and circumstance. Good thoughts bear good fruit, bad thoughts bad fruit.

The outer world of circumstance shapes itself to the inner world of thought, and both pleasant and unpleasant external conditions are factors, which make for the ultimate good of the individual. As the reaper of his own harvest, man learns both by suffering and bliss.

Following the inmost desires, aspirations, thoughts, by which he allows himself to be dominated (pursuing the will-o'-the-wisps of impure imaginings or steadfastly walking the highway of strong and high endeavor), a man at last arrives at their fruition and fulfillment in the outer conditions of his life. The laws of growth and adjustment everywhere obtain.

A man does not come to the pothouse or the jail by the tyranny of fate or circumstance, but by the pathway of groveling thoughts and base desires. Nor does a pure minded man fall suddenly into crime by stress of any mere external force; the criminal thought had long been secretly fostered in the heart, and the hour of opportunity revealed its gathered power. Circumstance does not make the man; it reveals him to himself. No such conditions can exist as descending into vice and its attendant sufferings apart from vicious inclinations, or ascending into virtue and its pure happiness without the continued cultivation of virtuous aspirations; and man, therefore, as the lord and master of thought, is the maker of himself, the shaper and author of environment. Even at birth the soul comes to its own, and through every step of its earthly pilgrimage it attracts those combinations of conditions which reveal itself, which are the reflections, of its own purity and impurity, its strength and weakness.

Men do not attract that which they want, but that which they are. Their whims, fancies, and ambitions are thwarted at every step, but their inmost thoughts and desires are fed with their own food, be it foul or clean. The "divinity that shapes our ends" is in ourselves; it is our very self. Man is manacled only by himself, thought and action are the jailers of Fate; they imprison, being base; they are also the angels of Freedom; they liberate, being noble. Not what he wishes and prays for does a man get, but what he justly earns. His wishes and prayers are only gratified and answered when they harmonize with his thoughts and actions.

In the light of truth, what, then, is the meaning of "fighting against circumstances?" It means that a man is continually revolting against an effect without, while all the time, he is nourishing and preserving its cause in his heart. That cause may take the form of a conscious vice or an unconscious weakness; but whatever it is, it stubbornly retards the efforts of its possessor and thus calls aloud for remedy.

Men are anxious to improve their circumstances, but are unwilling to improve themselves; they therefore remain bound. The man who does not shrink from self-crucifixion can never fail to accomplish the object upon which his heart is set. This is true of earthly as of heavenly things. Even the man, whose sole object is to acquire wealth, must be prepared to make great personal sacrifices before he can accomplish his object; and how much more so he who would realize a strong and well-poised life?

Here is a man who is wretchedly poor. He is extremely anxious that his surroundings and home comforts should be improved, yet all the time he shirks his work, and considers he is justified in trying to deceive his employer on the ground of the insufficiency of his wages. Such a man does not understand the simplest rudiments of these principles which are the basis of true prosperity, and is not only totally unfitted to rise out of his wretchedness, but is actually attracting to himself a still deeper wretchedness by dwelling in and acting out, indolent, deceptive and unmanly thoughts.

Here is a rich man who is the victim of a painful and persistent disease as a result of gluttony. He is willing to give large sums of money to get rid of it, but he will not sacrifice his gluttonous desires. He wants to gratify his taste for rich and unnatural viands and have his health as well. Such a man is totally unfit to have health, because he has not yet learned the first principles of a healthy life.

Here is an employer of labor who adopts crooked measures to avoid paying the regulation wage, and in the hope of making larger profits, reduces the wages of his work people. Such a man is altogether unfitted for prosperity, and when he finds himself bankrupt, both as regards to reputation and riches, he blames circumstances, not knowing that he is the sole author of his condition.

I have introduced these three cases merely as illustrative of the truth that man is the causer (though nearly always unconsciously) of his circumstances, and that, whilst aiming at a good end, be is continually frustrating its accomplishment by encouraging thoughts and desires which cannot possibly harmonize with that end. Such cases could be multiplied and varied almost indefinitely, but this is not necessary, as the reader can, if he so resolves, trace the action of the laws of thought in his own mind and life, and until this is done, mere external facts cannot serve as a ground of reasoning.

Circumstances, however, are so complicated, thought is so deeply rooted, and the conditions of happiness vary so vastly with individuals, that a man's entire soul condition (although it may be known to himself) cannot be judged by another from the external aspects of his life alone. A man may he honest in certain directions, yet suffer privations; a man may be dishonest in certain directions, yet acquire wealth; but the conclusion usually formed that the one man fails *because of his particular honesty,* and that the other prospers *because of his particular dishonesty,* is the result of a superficial judgment, which assumes that the dishonest man is almost totally corrupt, and the honest man almost entirely virtuous. In the light of a deeper knowledge and wider experience, such judgment is found to be erroneous. The dishonest man may have some admirable virtues, which the other does not possess; and the honest man obnoxious vices, which are absent in the other. The honest man reaps the good results of his honest thoughts and acts; he also brings upon himself the sufferings which his vices produce. The dishonest man likewise garners his own suffering and happiness.

It is pleasing to human vanity to believe that one suffers because of one's virtues; but not until a man has extirpated every sickly, bitter, and impure thought from his mind, and washed every sinful stain from his soul, can he be in a position to know and declare that his sufferings are the result of his good, and not of his bad qualities; and on the way to, yet long before he has reached that supreme perfection he will have found, working in his mind and life, the Great Law which is absolutely just, and which cannot, therefore, give good for evil, evil for good. Possessed of such knowledge, he will then know, looking back upon his past ignorance and blindness, what his life is, and always was, justly ordered, and that all his past experiences, good and bad, were the equitable outworking of his evolving, yet unevolved self.

Good thoughts and actions can never produce bad results; bad thoughts and actions can never produce good results. This is but saying that nothing can come from corn but corn, nothing from nettles but nettles. Men understand this law in the natural world, and work with it; but few understand it in the mental and moral world (though its operation there is just as simple and undeviating, and they, therefore, do not cooperate with it).

Suffering is *always* the effect of wrong thought in some direction. It is an indication that the individual is out of harmony with himself, with the Law of his being. The sole and supreme use of suffering is to purify, to burn out all that is useless and impure. Suffering ceases for him who is pure. There could be no object in burning gold after the dross had been removed, and a perfectly pure and enlightened being could not suffer.

The circumstances, which a man encounters with suffering, are the result of his own mental inharmony. The circumstances, which a man encounters with blessedness, are the result of his own mental harmony. Blessedness, not material possessions, is the measure of right thought; wretchedness, not lack of material possessions, is the measure of wrong thought. A man may be cursed and rich; he may be blessed and poor. Blessedness and riches are only joined together, when the riches are rightly and wisely used; and the poor man only descends into wretchedness when he regards his lot as a burden unjustly imposed.

Indigence and indulgence are the two extremes of wretchedness. They are both equally unnatural and the result of mental disorder.

A man is not rightly conditioned until he is a happy, healthy, and prosperous being; and happiness, health and prosperity are the result of a harmonious adjustment of the inner with the outer, of the man with his surroundings.

A man only begins to be a man when he ceases to whine and revile, and commences to search for the hidden justice which regulates his life. And as he adapts his mind to that regulating factor, he ceases to accuse others as the cause of his condition, but builds himself up in strong and noble thoughts; ceases to kick against circumstances, but begins to use them as aids to his more rapid progress, and as a means, of discovering the hidden powers and possibilities within himself.

Law, not confusion, is the dominating principle in the universe; justice, not injustice, is the soul and substance of life; and righteousness, not corruption, is the molding and moving force in the spiritual government of the world. This being so, man has but to right himself to find that the universe is right; and during the process of putting himself right, he will find that as he alters his thoughts towards things and other people, things and other people will alter towards him.

The proof of this truth is in every person, and it therefore admits of easy investigation by systematic introspection and self-analysis. Let a man radically alter his thoughts, and he will be astonished at the rapid transformation it will effect in the material conditions of his life. Men imagine that thought can be kept secret, but it cannot; it rapidly crystallizes into habit, and habit solidifies into circumstance. Bestial thoughts crystallize into habits of drunkenness and sensuality, which solidify into circumstances of destitution and disease; impure thoughts of every kind crystallize into enervating and confusing habits, which solidify into distracting and adverse circumstances; thoughts of fear, doubt, and indecision crystallize into weak, unmanly, and irresolute habits, which solidify into circumstances of failure, indigence, and slavish dependence; lazy thoughts crystallize into habits of uncleanliness and dishonesty, which solidify into circumstances of foulness and beggary; hateful and condemnatory thoughts crystallize into habits of accusation and violence, which solidify into circumstances of injury and persecution; selfish thoughts of all kinds crystallize into habits of self-seeking, which solidify into circumstances more or less distressing.

On the other hand, beautiful thoughts of all kinds crystallize into habits of grace and kindliness, which solidify into genial and sunny circumstances; pure thoughts crystallize into habits of temperance and self-control, which solidify into circumstances of repose and peace; thoughts of courage, self-reliance and decision crystallize into manly habits, which solidify into circumstances of success, plenty, and freedom; energetic thoughts crystallize into habits of cleanliness and industry, which solidify into circumstances of pleasantness; gentle and forgiving thoughts crystallize into habits of gentleness, which solidify into protective and preservative circumstances; loving and unselfish thoughts crystallize into habits of self forgetfulness for others, which solidify into circumstances of sure and abiding prosperity and true riches.

A particular train of thought persisted in, be it good or bad, cannot fail to produce its results on the character and circumstances. A man cannot directly choose his circumstances, but be can choose his thoughts, and so indirectly, yet surely, shape his circumstances.

Nature helps every man to the gratification of the thoughts, which he most encourages, and opportunities are presented which will most speedily bring to the surface, both the good and evil thoughts.

Let a man cease from his sinful thoughts, and all the world will soften towards him, and be ready to help him; let him put away his weakly and sickly thoughts, and lo! opportunities will spring up on every hand to aid his strong resolves; let him encourage good thoughts, and no hard fate shall bind him down to wretchedness and shame. The world is your kaleidoscope, and the varying combinations of colors, which at every succeeding moment it presents to you are the exquisitely adjusted pictures of your evermoving thoughts.

> "You will be what you will to be;
> Let failure find its false content
> In that poor world, 'environment,'
> But spirit scorns it, and is free.

> "It masters time, it conquers space;
> It cows that boastful trickster, Chance,
> And bids the tyrant Circumstance
> Uncrown, and fill a servant's place.

"The human Will, that force unseen,
The offspring of a deathless Soul,
Can hew a way to any goal,
Though walls of granite intervene.

"Be not impatient in delay,
But wait as one who understands;
When spirit rises and commands,
The gods are ready to obey."

EFFECT OF THOUGHT ON HEALTH AND BODY

The body is the servant of the mind. It obeys the operations of the mind, whether they be deliberately chosen or automatically expressed. At the bidding of unlawful thoughts the body sinks rapidly into disease and decay; at the command of glad and beautiful thoughts it becomes clothed with youthfulness and beauty.

Disease and health, like circumstances, are rooted in thought. Sickly thoughts will express themselves through a sickly body. Thoughts of fear have been known to kill a man as speedily as a bullet, and they are continually killing thousands of people just as surely though less rapidly. The people who live in fear of disease are the people who get it. Anxiety quickly demoralizes the whole body, and lays it open to the entrance of disease; while impure thoughts, even if not physically indulged, will soon shatter the nervous system.

Strong, pure and happy thoughts build up the body in vigor and grace. The body is a delicate and plastic instrument, which responds readily to the thoughts by which it is impressed, and habits of thought will produce their own effects, good or bad, upon it.

Men will continue to have impure and poisoned blood, so long as they propagate unclean thoughts. Out of a clean heart comes a clean life and a clean body. Out of a defiled mind proceeds a defiled life and a corrupt body. Thought is the font of action, life, and manifestation; make the fountain pure, and all will be pure.

Change of diet will not help a man who will not change his thoughts. When a man makes is thoughts pure, he no longer desires impure food.

Clean thoughts make clean habits. The so-called saint who does not wash his body is not a saint. He who has strengthened and purified his thoughts does not need to consider the malevolent microbe.

If you would perfect your body, guard your mind. If you would renew your body, beautify your mind. Thoughts of malice, envy, disappointment, despondency, rob the body of its health and grace. A sour face does not come by chance; it is made by sour thoughts. Wrinkles that mar are drawn by folly, passion, pride.

I know a woman of ninety-six who has the bright, innocent face of a girl. I know a man well under middle age whose face is drawn into inharmonious contours. The one is the result of a sweet and sunny disposition; the other is the outcome of passion and discontent.

As you cannot have a sweet and wholesome abode unless you admit the air and sunshine freely into your rooms, so a strong body and a bright, happy or serene countenance can only result from the free admittance into the mind of thoughts of joy and good will and serenity.

On the faces of the aged, there are wrinkles made by sympathy, others by strong and pure thought and others are carved by passion. Who cannot distinguish them? With those who have lived righteously, age is calm, peaceful and softly mellowed, like the setting sun. I have recently seen a philosopher on his deathbed. He was not old except in years. He died as sweetly and peacefully as he had lived.

There is no physician like cheerful thought for dissipagting the ills of the body; there is no comforter to compare with good will for dispersing the shadows of grief and sorrow. To live continually in thoughts of ill will, cynicism, suspicion, and envy, is to be confined in a selfmade prison hole. But to think well of all, to be cheerful with all, to patiently learn to find the good in all, such unselfish thoughts are the very portals of heaven; and to dwell day by day in thoughts of peace toward every creature will bring abounding peace to their possessor.

Until thought is linked with purpose there is no intelligent accomplishment. With the majority the barque of thought is allowed to "drift" upon the ocean of life. Aimlessness is a vice, and such drifting must not continue for him who would steer clear of catastrophe and destruction.

They, who have no central purpose in their life, fall an easy prey to petty worries, fears, troubles, and self pityings, all of which are indications of weakness, which lead, just as surely as deliberately planned sins (though by a different route), to failure, unhappiness, and loss, for weakness cannot persist in a power evolving universe.

A man should conceive of a legitimate purpose in his heart, and set out to accomplish it. He should make this purpose the centralizing point of his thoughts. It may take the form of a spiritual ideal, or it may be a worldly object, according to his nature at the time being; but whichever it is, he should steadily focus his thought forces upon the object, which he has set before him. He should make this purpose his supreme duty, and should devote himself to its attainment, not allowing his thoughts to wander away into ephemeral fancies, longings, and imaginings. This is the royal road to self-control and true concentration of thought. Even if he fails again and again to accomplish his purpose (as he necessarily must until weakness is overcome), the *strength* of *character* gained will be the measure of his *true* success, and this will form a new starting point for future power and triumph.

Those who are not prepared for the apprehension of a *great* purpose, should fix the thoughts upon the faultless performance of their duty, no matter how insignificant their task may appear. Only in this way can the thoughts be gathered and focused, and resolution and energy be developed, which being done, there is nothing which may not be accomplished.

The weakest soul, knowing its own weakness, and believing this truth; *that strength can only be developed by effort and practice,* will, thus believing, at once begin to exert itself, and, adding effort to effort, patience to patience, and strength to strength; will never cease to develop and will at last grow divinely strong.

As the physically weak man can make himself strong by careful and patient training, so the man of weak thoughts can make them strong by exercising himself in right thinking.

To put away aimlessness and weakness, and to begin to think with purpose, is to enter the ranks of those strong ones who only recognize failure as one of the pathways to attainment; who make all conditions serve them, and who think strongly, attempt fearlessly, and accomplish masterfully.

Having conceived of his purpose, a man should mentally make out a *straight* pathway to its achievement, looking neither to the right nor the left. Doubts and fears should be rigorously excluded; they are disintegrating elements, which break up the straight line of effort, rendering it crooked, ineffectual, useless. Thoughts of doubt and fear never accomplish anything and never can. They always lead to failure. Purpose, energy, power to do, and all strong thoughts cease when doubt and fear creep in.

The will to do, springs from the knowledge, that we can do. Doubt and fear are the great enemies of knowledge, and he who encourages them, who does not slay them, thwarts himself at every step.

He who has conquered doubt and fear has conquered failure. His very thought is alive with power, and all difficulties are bravely met and wisely overcome. His purposes are seasonably planted, and they bloom and bring forth fruit which does not fall prematurely to the ground.

Thought allied fearlessly to purpose becomes creative force: he who *knows* this is ready to become something higher and stronger than a mere bundle of wavering thoughts and fluctuating sensations; he who *does* this has become the conscious and intelligent wielder of his mental powers.

THE THOUGHT FACTOR IN ACHIEVEMENT

All that a man achieves and all that he fails to achieve is the direct result of his own thoughts. In a justly ordered universe, where loss of equipoise would mean total destruction, individual responsibility must be absolute. A man's weakness and strength, purity and impurity, are his own, and not another man's; they are brought about by himself, and not by another; and they can only be altered by himself, never by another. His condition is also his own, and not another man's. His suffering and his happiness are evolved from within. As he thinks, so he is; as he continues to think, so he remains. A strong man cannot help a weaker unless that weaker is *willing* to be helped, and even then the weak man must become strong of himself; he must, by his own efforts, develop the strength which he admires in another. None but himself can alter his condition. It has been usual for men to think and, to say, "Many men are slaves because one is an oppressor; let us hate the oppressor." Now, however, there is amongst an increasing few a tendency to reverse this judgment, and to say, "One man is an oppressor because many are slaves; let us despise the slaves." The truth is that oppressor and slave are cooperators in ignorance, and while seeming to afflict each other, are in reality afflicting themselves. A perfect Knowledge perceives the action of law in the weakness of the oppressed and the misapplied power of the oppressor; a perfect love, seeing the suffering, which both states entail, condemns neither; a perfect Compassion embraces both oppressor and oppressed.

He who has conquered weakness, and has put away all selfish thoughts, belongs neither to oppressor nor oppressed. He is free.

A man can only rise, conquer, and achieve by lifting up his thoughts. He can only remain weak, and abject, and miserable by refusing to lift his thoughts.

Before a man can achieve anything, even in worldly things, he must lift his thoughts above slavish animal indulgence. He may not, in order to succeed, give up *all* animality and selfishness, by any means; but a portion of it must, at least, be sacrificed. A man whose first thought is bestial indulgence could neither think clearly nor plan methodically; he could not find and develop his latent resources, and would fail in any undertaking. Not having commenced to manfully control his thoughts, he is not in a position to control affairs and to adopt serious responsibilities. He is not fit to act independently and stand alone. But he is limited only by the thoughts, which he chooses.

There can be no progress, no achievement, without sacrifice, and a man's worldly success will be in the measure that he sacrifices his confused animal thoughts, and fixes his mind on the development of his plans, and the strengthening of his resolution and self-reliance. And the higher he lifts his thoughts, the more manly, upright, and righteous he becomes, the greater will be his success, the more blessed and enduring will be his achievements.

The universe does not favor the greedy, the dishonest, the vicious, although on the mere surface, it may sometimes appear to do so; it helps the honest, the magnanimous, the virtuous. All the great Teachers of the ages have declared this in varying forms, and to prove and know it a man has but to persist in making himself more and more virtuous by lifting up his thoughts.

Intellectual achievements are the result of thought consecrated to the search for knowledge, or for the beautiful and true in life and nature. Such achievements may be sometimes connected with vanity and ambition, but they are not the outcome of those characteristics; they are the natural out growth of long and arduous effort, and of pure and unselfish thoughts.

Spiritual achievements are the consummation of holy aspirations. He who lives constantly in the conception of noble and lofty thoughts, who dwells upon all that is pure and unselfish, will, as surely as the sun reaches its zenith and the moon its full, become wise and noble in character, and rise into a position of influence and blessedness.

Achievement, of whatever kind, is the crown of effort, the diadem of thought. By the aid of self-control, resolution, purity, righteousness, and well-directed thought, a man ascends; by the aid of animality, indolence, impurity, corruption and confusion of thought a man descends.

A man may rise to high success in the world, and even to lofty altitudes in the spiritual realm, and again descend into weakness and wretchedness by allowing arrogant, selfish and corrupt thoughts to take possession of him.

Victories attained by right thought can only be maintained by watchfulness. Many give way when success is assured, and rapidly fall back into failure.

All achievements, whether in the business, intellectual, or spiritual world, are the result of definitely directed thought, are governed by the same law and are of the same method; the only difference lies in the *object of attainment*.

He who would accomplish little must sacrifice little; he who would achieve much must sacrifice much; he who would attain highly must sacrifice greatly.

VISIONS AND IDEALS

The dreamers are the saviors of the world. As the visible world is sustained by the invisible, so men, through all their trials and sins and sordid vocations, are nourished by the beautiful visions of their solitary dreamers. Humanity cannot forget its dreamers; it cannot let their ideals fade and die; it lives in them; it knows them as the realities which it shall one day see and know.

Composer, sculptor, painter, poet, prophet, sage, these are the makers of the afterworld, the architects of heaven. The world is beautiful because they have lived; without them, laboring humanity would perish.

He who cherishes a beautiful vision, a lofty ideal in his heart, will one day realize it. Columbus cherished a vision of another world, and he discovered it; Copernicus fostered the vision of a multiplicity of worlds and a wider universe, and he revealed it; Buddha beheld the vision of a spiritual world of stainless beauty and perfect peace, and he entered into it.

Cherish your visions; cherish your ideals; cherish the music that stirs in your heart, the beauty that forms in your mind, the loveliness that drapes your purest thoughts, for out of them will grow all delightful conditions, all heavenly environment; of these, if you but remain true to them, your world will at last be built.

To desire is to obtain; to aspire is to achieve. Shall man's basest desires receive the fullest measure of gratification, and his purest aspirations starve for lack of sustenance? Such is not the Law, such a condition of things can never obtain, "Ask and receive."

Dream lofty dreams, and as you dream, so shall you become. Your Vision is the promise of what you shall one day be; your Ideal is the prophecy of what you shall at last unveil.

The greatest achievement was at first and for a time a dream. The oak sleeps in the acorn; the bird waits in the egg; and in the highest vision of the soul a waking angel stirs. Dreams are the seedlings of realities.

Your circumstances may be uncongenial, but they shall not long remain so if you but perceive an Ideal and strive to reach it. You cannot travel *within* and stand still *without*. Here is a youth hard pressed by poverty and labor; confined long hours in an unhealthy workshop; unschooled, and lacking all the arts of refinement. But he dreams of better things; he thinks of intelligence, of refinement, of grace and beauty. He conceives of, mentally builds up, an ideal condition of life; the vision of a wider liberty and a larger scope takes possession of him; unrest urges him to action, and he utilizes all his spare time and means, small though they are, to the development of his latent powers and resources. Very soon so altered has his mind become that the workshop can no longer hold him. It has become so out of harmony with his mentality that it falls out of his life as a garment is cast aside, and, with the growth of opportunities, which fit the scope of his expanding powers, he passes out of it, forever. Years later, we see this youth as a full-grown man. We find him a master of certain forces of the mind, which he wields with worldwide influence and almost unequaled power. In his hands, he holds the cords of gigantic responsibilities; he speaks, and lo! lives are changed; men and women hang upon his words and remold their characters, and, sunlike, he becomes the fixed and luminous center round which innumerable destinies revolve. He has realized the Vision of his youth. He has become one with his Ideal.

And you, too, youthful reader, will realize the Vision (not the idle wish) of your heart, be it base or beautiful, or a mixture of both, for you will always gravitate toward that which you, secretly, most love. Into your hands will be placed the exact results of your own thoughts; you will receive that which you earn; no more, no less. Whatever your present environment may be, you will fall, remain or rise with your thoughts, your Vision, your Ideal. You will become as small as your controlling desire; as great as your dominant aspiration; in the beautiful words of Stanton Kirkham Davis, "You may be keeping accounts, and presently you shall walk out of the door that for so long has seemed to you the barrier of your ideals, and shall find yourself before an audience; the pen still behind your ear, the ink stains on your fingers; and then and there shall pour out the torrent of your inspiration. You may be driving sheep, and you shall wander to the city, bucolic and open-mouthed; shall wander under the intrepid guidance of the spirit into the studio of the master, and after a time he shall say, 'I have nothing more to teach you.' And now, you have become the master, who did so recently dream of great things while driving sheep. You shall lay down the saw and the plane to take upon yourself the regeneration of the world."

The thoughtless, the ignorant, and the indolent, seeing only the apparent effects of things and not the things themselves, talk of luck, of fortune, and chance. Seeing a man grow rich, they say, "How lucky he is!" Observing another become intellectual, they exclaim, "How highly favored he is!" And noting the saintly character and wide influence of another, they remark, "How chance aids him at every turn!" They do not see the trials and failures and struggles which these men have voluntarily encountered in order to gain their experience; have no knowledge of the sacrifices they have made, of the undaunted efforts they have put forth, of the faith they have exercised, that they might overcome the apparently insurmountable and realize the Vision of their heart. They do not know the darkness and the heartaches; they only see the light and joy, and call it "luck"; do not see the long and arduous journey, but only behold the pleasant goal, and call it "good fortune"; do not understand the process, but only perceive the result, and call it "chance."

In all human affairs there are efforts, and there are results, and the strength of effort is the measure of the result. Chance is not. "Gifts," powers, material, intellectual, and spiritual possessions are the fruits of effort, they are thoughts completed, objects accomplished, visions realized.

The Vision that you glorify in your mind, the Ideal that you enthrone in your heart, this you will build your life by, this you will become.

SERENITY

Calmness of mind is one of the beautiful jewels of wisdom. It is the result of long and patient effort in self-control. Its presence is an indication of ripened experience, and of a more than ordinary knowledge of the laws and operations of thought.

A man becomes calm in the measure that he understands himself as a thought-evolved being, for such knowledge necessitates the understanding of others as the result of thought, and as he develops a right understanding, and sees more and more clearly, the internal relations of things by the action of cause and effect, he ceases to fuss and fume and worry and grieve, and remains poised, steadfast, serene.

The calm man, having learned how to govern himself, knows how to adapt himself to others; and they, in turn, reverence his spiritual strength, and feel that they can learn of him and rely upon him. The more tranquil a man becomes, the greater is his success, his influence, his power for good. Even the ordinary trader will find his business prosperity increase as he develops a greater self-control and equanimity, for people will always prefer to deal with a man whose demeanor is strongly equable.

The strong, calm man is always loved and revered. He is like a shade-giving tree in a thirsty land, or a sheltering rock in a storm.

"Who does not love a tranquil heart, a sweet tempered, balanced life? It does not matter whether it rains or shines, or what changes come to those possessing these blessings, for they are always sweet serene and calm. That exquisite poise of character, which we call serenity, is the last lesson of culture; it is the flowering of life, the fruitage of the soul. It is precious as wisdom. More to be desired than gold yea, than even fine gold. How insignificant mere money seeking looks in comparison with a serene life, a life that dwells in the ocean of Truth, beneath the waves, beyond the reach of tempests, in the Eternal Calm."

"How many people we know who sour their lives, who ruin all that is sweet and beautiful by explosive tempers, who destroy their poise of character, and make bad blood! It is a question whether the great majorities of people do not ruin their lives and mar their happiness by lack of self-control. How few people we meet in life who are well balanced, who have that exquisite poise which is characteristic of the finished character!"

Yes, humanity surges with uncontrolled passion, is tumultuous with ungoverned grief, is blown about by anxiety and doubt. Only the wise man, only be whose thoughts are controlled and purified, makes the winds and the storms of the soul obey him.

Tempest-tossed souls, wherever you may be, under whatsoever conditions you may live, know this, in the ocean of life the isles of Blessedness are smiling, and the sunny shore of your ideal awaits your coming. Keep your hand firmly upon the helm of thought. In the barque of your soul reclines the commanding Master; He does but sleep: wake Him. Self-control is strength; Right Thought is mastery; Calmness is power. Say unto your heart, "Peace, be still!"